Negotiation of Identities in Multilingual Contexts

BILINGUAL EDUCATION AND BILINGUALISM
Series Editors: Professor Colin Baker, *University of Wales, Bangor, Wales, Great Britain*
and Professor Nancy H. Hornberger, *University of Pennsylvania, Philadelphia, USA*

Other Books in the Series
At War With Diversity: US Language Policy in an Age of Anxiety
James Crawford
Continua of Biliteracy: An Ecological Framework for Educational Policy, Research,
and Practice in Multilingual Settings
Nancy H. Hornberger (ed.)
Cross-linguistic Influence in Third Language Acquisition
J. Cenoz, B. Hufeisen and U. Jessner (eds)
English in Europe: The Acquisition of a Third Language
Jasone Cenoz and Ulrike Jessner (eds)
Identity and the English Language Learner
Elaine Mellen Day
An Introductory Reader to the Writings of Jim Cummins
Colin Baker and Nancy Hornberger (eds)
Language and Literacy Teaching for Indigenous Education: A Bilingual Approach
Norbert Francis and Jon Reyhner
Languages in America: A Pluralist View (2nd Edition)
Susan J. Dicker
Language Rights and the Law in the United States: Finding our Voices
Sandra Del Valle
Language Revitalization Processes and Prospects
Kendall A. King
Language Socialization in Bilingual and Multilingual Societies
Robert Bayley and Sandra R. Schecter (eds)
Language Use in Interlingual Families: A Japanese-English Sociolinguistic Study
Masayo Yamamoto
The Languages of Israel: Policy, Ideology and Practice
Bernard Spolsky and Elana Shohamy
Multilingual Classroom Ecologies
Angela Creese and Peter Martin (eds)
The Native Speaker: Myth and Reality
Ian Davies
Power, Prestige and Bilingualism: International Perspectives on Elite Bilingual
Education
Anne-Marie de Mejía
Reflections on Multiliterate Lives
Diane Belcher and Ulla Connor (eds)
Trilingualism in Family, School and Community
Charlotte Hoffmann and Jehannes Ytsma (eds)
World English: A Study of its Development
Janina Brutt-Griffler

Please contact us for the latest book information:
Multilingual Matters, Frankfurt Lodge, Clevedon Hall,
Victoria Road, Clevedon, BS21 7HH, England
http://www.multilingual-matters.com

BILINGUAL EDUCATION AND BILINGUALISM 45
Series Editors: Nancy H. Hornberger and Colin Baker

Negotiation of Identities in Multilingual Contexts

Edited by
Aneta Pavlenko and Adrian Blackledge

MULTILINGUAL MATTERS LTD
Clevedon • Buffalo • Toronto • Sydney

Library of Congress Cataloging in Publication Data
Negotiation of Identities in Multilingual Contexts/Edited by Aneta Pavlenko and
Adrian Blackledge – 1st edn.
Bilingual Education and Bilingualism: 45
Includes bibliographical references and index.
1. Multilingualism. 2. Identity (Psychology) I. Pavlenko, Aneta II. Blackledge, Adrian.
III. Series.
P115.N44 2003
306.44'6--dc21   2003008658

British Library Cataloguing in Publication Data
A catalogue entry for this book is available from the British Library.

ISBN 1-85359-647-7 (hbk)
ISBN 1-85359-646-9 (pbk)

Multilingual Matters Ltd
UK: Frankfurt Lodge, Clevedon Hall, Victoria Road, Clevedon BS21 7HH.
USA: UTP, 2250 Military Road, Tonawanda, NY 14150, USA.
Canada: UTP, 5201 Dufferin Street, North York, Ontario M3H 5T8, Canada.
Australia: Footprint Books, PO Box 418, Church Point, NSW 2103, Australia.

Typeset by Florence Production Ltd.
Printed and bound in Great Britain by the Cromwell Press Ltd.

Contents

Preface vii

Contributors viii

Introduction: New Theoretical Approaches to the Study of
Negotiation of Identities in Multilingual Contexts
Aneta Pavlenko and Adrian Blackledge 1

1 'The Making of an American': Negotiation of Identities at
the Turn of the Twentieth Century
Aneta Pavlenko 34

2 Constructions of Identity in Political Discourse in
Multilingual Britain
Adrian Blackledge 68

3 Negotiating Between *Bourge* and *Racaille*: Verlan as Youth
Identity Practice in Suburban Paris
Meredith Doran 93

4 Black Deaf or Deaf Black? Being Black and Deaf in Britain
Melissa James and Bencie Woll 125

5 Mothers and Mother Tongue: Perspectives on
Self-construction by Mothers of Pakistani Heritage
Jean Mills 161

6 The Politics of Identity, Representation, and the Discourses of
Self-identification: Negotiating the Periphery and the Center
Frances Giampapa 192

v

7 Alice Doesn't Live Here Anymore: Foreign Language
   Learning and Identity Reconstruction
   Celeste Kinginger 219

 8 Intersections of Literacy and Construction of Social
   Identities
   Benedicta Egbo 243

 9 Multilingual Writers and the Struggle for Voice in Academic
   Discourse
   Suresh Canagarajah 266

10 Identity and Language Use: The Politics of Speaking ESL
   in Schools
   Jennifer Miller 290

11 Sending Mixed Messages: Language Minority Education at
   a Japanese Public Elementary School
   Yasuko Kanno 316

Index 339

Preface

This book originated in our belief that negotiation of identities in multi-lingual settings frequently occurs in encounters where relations of power are unequal. It is also our view that such encounters are profoundly influenced by the social, cultural, political, and historical settings in which they occur. In putting together this collection it was not difficult to identify colleagues throughout the world who were engaging with these issues in their research. Some were established authors in their field, others new talents undertaking original and stimulating work. All were readily responsive to our invitation to participate in the project. We owe them a debt of gratitude for their willingness to contribute, and for their patience with our requests in the editing process.

We are grateful for the easy working relationship provided by Tommi, Marjukka, and Mike Grover at Multilingual Matters. They were supportive throughout the process of writing, editing, and bringing the volume to its conclusion. We also wish to acknowledge the support and enthusiasm of the series editors, Colin Baker and Nancy Hornberger. They welcomed the volume proposal almost immediately, and were encouraging and helpful throughout.

Working on opposite sides of the Atlantic Ocean on a substantial academic project is not straightforward. Almost all of our editing, decision-making, and intellectual endeavour was conducted through the wonders of computer technology. Busy periods of course do not always coincide; however, we got there in the end, and produced what we believe is a highly readable and stimulating text, which in many ways breaks new ground in our field.

Most of all we are grateful to our families for their constant patience, love, and support as we brought the volume to its conclusion.

Contributors

Adrian Blackledge is a Senior Lecturer in the School of Education, University of Birmingham, Birmingham, UK. His publications include *Teaching bilingual children* (Trentham Books, 1994), *Literacy, power, and social justice* (Trentham Books, 2000), and *Multilingualism, second language learning, and gender* (co-edited with Aneta Pavlenko, Ingrid Piller, and Marya Teutsch-Dwyer, Mouton de Gruyter, 2001). His main area of research is multilingualism and social justice in linguistic minority settings, including political and institutional discourse.

Suresh Canagarajah is an Associate Professor in the English Department of Baruch College, City University of New York, New York City, US. He teaches postcolonial writing, ethnic literature, ESL, and composition. His research interests span bilingualism, discourse analysis, and critical pedagogy. His book *Resisting linguistic imperialism in English teaching* (Oxford University Press, 1999) won the 2000 Mina P. Shaughnessy Award of the Modern Language Association. He is also the author of *A geopolitics of academic writing* (University of Pittsburgh Press, 2002) and *Critical academic writing and multilingual students* (University of Michigan Press, 2002).

Meredith Doran is an Assistant Professor of French and applied linguistics at the Pennsylvania State University, State College, US. Her areas of specialization include sociolinguistics, second language acquisition, discourse analysis, and contemporary French language and culture. Her current research focuses on youth language and identity in France, language ideologies, and the use of personal narratives of cultural difference as a tool in second language pedagogy.

Benedicta Egbo is an Associate Professor of Education at the University of Windsor, Windsor, Ontario, Canada. Her research interests include literacy, gender and education, critical pedagogy, educational policy, and education and social justice. She has published widely in these areas, including a book *Gender, literacy, and life chances in sub-Saharan Africa* (Multilingual Matters, 2000). She is the founding editor of the *Journal of Teaching and Learning* (an international journal published by the University of Windsor).

Frances Giampapa is completing her doctorate on Italian Canadian youth, identity politics, and language practices at the Ontario Institute of Studies in Education/University of Toronto, Toronto, Canada, in 2003. Her areas of research include sociolinguistics, bilingualism, cultural studies, and second language education. Her work has previously appeared in the *International Journal of Bilingualism*.

Melissa James studied history in the School of Slavonic and East European Studies at University College of London, London, UK, and then completed a Master's degree in race and ethnic relations. She obtained her Ph.D. in the Department of Language and Communication Science at City University of London, under the supervision of Professor Bencie Woll. Her research explores issues of language, race, and identity in relation to Britain's Black Deaf Community.

Yasuko Kanno is an Assistant Professor of TESOL at the Department of English, University of Washington, Seattle, US. Her main research interests are in the areas of language and identity and bilingual education. She is the author of *Negotiating bilingual and bicultural identities: Japanese returnees betwixt two worlds* (Lawrence Erlbaum Associates, 2003) and the co-editor (with Bonny Norton) of the special issue on 'Imagined communities and educational possibilities' for the *Journal of Language, Identity, and Education* (2003). She is currently working on an ethnographic project on bilingual education in Japan.

Celeste Kinginger is an Associate Professor of French and applied linguistics at the Pennsylvania State University, State College, US, where she teaches in the Linguistics and Applied Language Studies Program and conducts research in collaboration with the Center for Language Acquisition. Her research program focuses on qualitative variation in learning experiences and its developmental consequences for language learners and teachers. Her publications have appeared in the *Modern Language Journal, Applied Linguistics, Foreign Language Annals*, the *Canadian Modern Language Review*, and the *French Review*.

Jennifer Miller is a Lecturer in the School of Education at the University of Queensland, Queensland, Australia, where she teaches undergraduate and postgraduate courses in the TESOL area, and is involved in pre-service teacher education. Her research and publications are in the areas of language acquisition and identity, qualitative methodology in applied linguistics, and teachers' work. Miller also teaches ESL in an intensive reception program for immigrant high school students. Her book, *Audible difference: ESL and social identity* (Multilingual Matters, 2003) explores the politics of speaking and representation for immigrant students in high schools.

Jean Mills is a Senior Lecturer in the School of Education, University of Birmingham, Birmingham, UK. She has taught since the 1970s in multi-lingual schools in England and lectured in higher education in Canada and Australia. She is author/editor of several books and articles on education and multilingualism. Her research focuses on the bilingual perspectives of women of Pakistani heritage and of their children.

Aneta Pavlenko is an Associate Professor of TESOL at the College of Education, Temple University, Philadelphia, US. Her research examines the relationship between language and cognition, emotions, and identity in bi- and multilingual individuals. She has published numerous scientific articles and co-edited two volumes, *Multilingualism, second language learning, and gender* (with Adrian Blackledge, Ingrid Piller, and Marya Teutsch-Dwyer, Mouton de Gruyter, 2001) and *Gender and English Language Learners* (with Bonny Norton, TESOL Inc., 2004).

Bencie Woll came to the Department of Language and Communication Science at City University, London, in 1995 to take up the newly created Chair in Sign Language and Deaf Studies, the first chair in this field in the UK. She was previously at Bristol University where she pioneered Deaf Studies as an academic discipline. Her research and teaching inter-ests embrace a wide range of topics related to sign language, including the linguistics of British Sign Language (BSL) and other sign languages, the history and sociolinguistics of BSL and the Deaf community, the development of BSL in young children, and sign language and the brain. She is the co-author of *The linguistics of BSL: An introduction* (Cambridge University Press, 1999), the winner of the 1999 Deaf Nation Award and 2000 BAAL Book Prize.

Introduction: New Theoretical Approaches to the Study of Negotiation of Identities in Multilingual Contexts

ANETA PAVLENKO AND ADRIAN BLACKLEDGE

Introduction

In her memoir *My life*, Golda Meir (1975: 242) recalls how, during her stay in Moscow in 1948, a well-known Russian writer of Jewish origin, Ilya Ehrenburg, approached her at a party and started speaking Russian to her: ' "I'm sorry, but I can't speak Russian," I said. "Do you speak English?" He looked at me nastily and replied, "I hate Russian-born Jews who speak English." "And I am sorry for Jews who don't speak Hebrew or at least Yiddish!" I answered.' In our view, this brief exchange perfectly exemplifies negotiation of identities that takes place every day in multilingual contexts, where different ideologies of language and identity come into conflict with each other with regard to what languages or varieties of languages should be spoken by particular kinds of people and in what context. For Ehrenburg, a Soviet writer, Russian was the primary language of all Russian-born Jews, while, for Meir, the first Israeli ambassador in Moscow, Jewish identity was intrinsically linked to Hebrew, the language of the newly formed state of Israel, and to Yiddish, the lingua franca of Eastern European Jews.

The confrontation between Meir and Ehrenburg poignantly illustrates the fact that, in multilingual settings, language choice and attitudes are inseparable from political arrangements, relations of power, language ideologies, and interlocutors' views of their own and others' identities. Ongoing social, economic, and political changes affect these constellations, modifying identity options offered to individuals at a given moment in history and ideologies that legitimize and value particular identities more than others. In the case in question, Ehrenburg was familiar with two identity options offered by the Soviet government to its Jewish population, concentrated in urban centers: complete assimilation/Russianization, or migration to the Yiddish-speaking area of Birobidzhan in Siberia. The arrival of Meir and her team pointed to a new, previously unimaginable, identity option of being a citizen of an independent Jewish state – but more than a quarter of a century would pass before this option became a reality for thousands of Soviet Jews.

The shifts and fluctuations in language ideologies and in the range of identities available to individuals have become particularly visible in the light of recent sociopolitical and socioeconomic trends: globalization, consumerism, explosion of media technologies, the postcolonial and postcommunist search for new national identities, formation of new regional coalitions, such as the European Union, dissolution of former coalitions, such as the Soviet Union, repatriation of former colonies, such as Hong Kong, and increased transnational migration. A close look at the links between language and identity in contexts affected by these phenomena demonstrates the complexity of these links: in some settings languages function as markers of national or ethnic identities, in others as a form of symbolic capital or as a means of social control, and yet in others these multiple roles may be interconnected, while multilingualism is appropriated to construct transnational consumer identities (Piller, 2001).

If we trace, for instance, the shifts in the status of Russian in the former USSR, we will see that, after the Second World War, Russian was imposed on the population of the newly appropriated Baltic republics in order to transform Latvians, Lithuanians, and Estonians into Soviet citizens. Fifty years later the tabs have changed and it is now members of the Russian diaspora that have to learn the formerly devalued Estonian, Latvian, or Lithuanian in order to become legal citizens of the Baltic countries. This and other instances of the use of language as a means of social control of minority or immigrant populations are becoming a major concern for scholars in the field of bilingualism (cf. May, 2001; Skutnabb-Kangas & Phillipson, 1995). Consequently, while acknowledging that cultural and linguistic diversity in educational and work contexts around the world is progressively increasing and the range of available identity options is becoming wider, we use this volume as a vehicle to express our commitment to social justice and the notion of linguistic human rights (cf. also Blackledge, 2000). We also use it to express our concerns about the use of languages as a means of social control, about the growing dominance of English as a supranational language, about linguistic nationalist movements which suppress bilingualism and linguistic diversity, and, most importantly, about ways in which language and literacy are at times used to marginalize and disempower particular individuals or minority groups. To emphasize that in most contexts these groups and individuals find some means to resist linguistic impositions and to subvert dominant discourses, we decided to make negotiation of identities the common thread which unites the diverse chapters in this volume.

The fact that languages – and language ideologies – are anything but neutral is especially visible in multilingual societies where some languages and identity options are, in unforgettable Orwellian words, 'more equal than others.' Negotiation is a logical outcome of this inequality: it may take place between individuals, between majority and minority groups, and, most importantly, between institutions and those they are supposed to serve. The goal of this volume is to examine negotiation of identities in multilingual societies where some identity options are more valued than others, and where individuals and minority groups may appeal to – or resist – particular languages, language varieties, or linguistic forms in the struggle to claim the rights to particular identities and resist others that are imposed on them. Clearly, identities can be negotiated in numerous ways, starting with public debates over political alliances or educational and economic policies and ending with private decisions about religious affiliations, celebration of particular holidays, and even food choices and clothing. The focus of this volume is exclusively on ways in which identities are negotiated in and through linguistic practices.

This focus is not new to the fields of bilingualism and sociolinguistics – over the years numerous studies have addressed the relationship between language and identity in multilingual settings. We believe, however, that, until recently, this complex relationship has been significantly undertheorized, with the focus being on negotiation of language choice, or on performance and indexing of identities. Consequently, the present chapter has three aims. First, we will examine three alternative paradigms which theorize negotiation of identities in multilingual settings. We will argue that a poststructuralist framework allows us to examine and explain negotiation of identities as situated within larger socioeconomic, sociohistoric, and sociopolitical processes, and thus in more nuanced and context-sensitive ways than approaches offered by social psychology or interactional sociolinguistics. Second, we will outline the poststructuralist approach adopted in this volume and grounded in the work of Bourdieu (1977, 1982, 1991), Davies and Harré (1990), Hall (1990), Heller (1992, 1995a,b), and Woolard (1985, 1989, 1998). We will show that this framework is well equipped to capture the complexity of identities in postmodern societies, where languages may not only be 'markers of identity' but also sites of resistance, empowerment, solidarity, or discrimination. And, finally, we will show how the chapters in the present volume contribute to this emerging field. In the discussion that follows, in accordance with the proposed approach and with unfailing interest in social justice in mind, we will use the somewhat problematic and dichotomizing terms 'minority' and 'majority,' not to draw attention to numerical size of particular groups, but to refer to situational differences in power, rights, and privileges (Grillo, 1989; May, 2001).

Sociopsychological and Interactional Approaches to the Study of Negotiation of Identities in Multilingual Contexts

Sociopsychological approaches

The first paradigm that examines negotiation of identities in multilingual contexts is known as *sociopsychological*. It consists of a number of inter-group approaches, which draw on Tajfel's (1974, 1981) theory of social identity and/or on Berry's (1980) theory of acculturation to explain language contact outcomes through group memberships (cf. Agnihotri *et al.*, 1998; Giles & Byrne, 1982; Kim, 1988, 1996). Researchers working in this paradigm commonly assume a one-to-one correlation between language and ethnic identity and, thus, examine 'ethnolinguistic groups' and measure their 'ethnolinguistic vitality,' defining *ethnic identity* as 'a subjective feeling of belongingness to a particular ethnic group' (Noels *et al.*, 1996: 246). *Negotiation*, in turn, is viewed as a transactional inter-action process, in which individuals attempt to evoke, assert, define, modify, challenge, and/or support their own and others' desired self-images, in particular ethnic identity (Ting-Toomey, 1999).

Drawing on Tajfel's framework, Giles and Byrne (1982) developed a theory of ethnolinguistic identity which considers language to be a salient marker of ethnic identity and group membership. The researchers identified a number of factors that contribute to a group's ethnolinguistic vitality and conditions under which members of the group were most likely to acquire the language of the dominant group. They suggested that members of groups where the in-group identification is weak, in-group vitality low, in-group boundaries open, and identification with other groups strong may assimilate and learn the second language (L2) rapidly. In turn, members of the groups whose ethnolinguistic vitality is high (e.g. strong in-group identification, hard in-group boundaries etc.) may experience a fear of assimilation and achieve a low level of L2 proficiency, as the L2 is seen as detracting from their ethnic identity. These conclusions were borne out in the work of Clément and associates, which shows that members of linguistic minority communities identify either with the first or the second language community but rarely with both (Clément, 1987; Noels *et al.*, 1996). In contrast, the work of Berry and associates (Berry, 1980; Berry *et al.*, 1989) suggests that immigrants have at their disposal four different modes of acculturation and typically prefer the integration of their two ethnolinguistic identities.

Criticisms of inter-group approaches are typically directed at the over-simplification and essentialization inherent in their conceptual premises (Hamers & Blanc, 2000; Hoffman, 1989; Husband & Saifullah Khan, 1982; Pavlenko, 2002; Syed & Burnett, 1999; Williams, 1992). The cornerstone of the approach, the one-to-one correlation between language and identity, is criticized for its monolingual and monocultural bias, which conceives of individuals as members of homogeneous, uniform, and bounded ethnolinguistic communities and obscures hybrid identities and complex linguistic repertoires of bi- and multilinguals living in a contemporary global world. Ethnographic investigations of multilingual contexts challenge the homogeneous view of minority communities and show significant in-group differences in patterns of language contact and social organization. For example, Li Wei (1998) demonstrates that, among the British-born children of Chinese immigrants in the Tyneside area in the UK, there are two distinct sub-groups, Cantonese Punti families and Ap Chau families. The Ap Chau families have many more opportunities to maintain their ethnic contacts; consequently, children from these families are able to maintain more knowledge of Chinese language, culture, and history than their peers and use more Chinese in interactions with their parents and grandparents.

The monolingual bias also obscures the fact that, in many cases, languages may be linked to professional, rather than national or ethnic, identities. For instance, Iranian immigrants in the US display high degrees of linguistic competence in English and high levels of structural assimilation; at the same time, they exhibit low degrees of identification with the US society (Hoffman, 1989). For many of them, English is not a marker of an 'American identity,' rather it is a language in which they perform their professional duties; it is also a lingua franca, which in the pre-revolutionary times of Westernization in Iran was used by members of the Iranian upper class not only with foreigners but also with each other. Similarly, in many postcolonial contexts, world languages, such as English, French, or Portuguese, are appropriated as a means of expressing new national, ethnic, and social identities, rather than as a means of assimilating to former colonial powers (Breitborde, 1998; Jacobson, 1998; Stroud, 2002).

The monolingual bias inherent in sociopsychological approaches is also visible in assumptions that high linguistic competence comes first to individuals whose in-group identification is weak and that it is often accompanied by the loss of the native language and culture (Clément, 1987; Giles & Byrne, 1982; Schumann, 1986). These assumptions have been challenged by numerous studies, which demonstrated, on the one hand, that some minority communities with high levels of ethnolinguistic vitality also exhibit high levels of linguistic competence in the majority language (oftentimes, without identifying with its speakers, cf. Hoffman, 1989) and, on the other, that individuals with high levels of identification with the target language group may exhibit low levels of linguistic proficiency (cf. Schmidt, 1983). Recent research in second language acquisition clearly demonstrates that the relationship between individuals' multiple identities and second language learning outcomes is infinitely more complex than portrayed in the sociopsychological paradigm and cannot be reduced to a few essentialized variables (McKay & Wong, 1996; Norton Peirce, 1995, 2000; Pavlenko, 2000, 2002). The problem is further compounded by the fact that inter-group approaches portray learning trajectories as linear and unidirectional, with little acknowledgment of the fact that, over a single lifetime, and over the lifetime of an immigrant group, certain events may send people back to a prior language and a prior identity. In Israel, for instance, the 1990s' wave of Russian immigrants led to a revival in Russian-language cultural activities and prompted many of the immigrants who arrived in the 1970s to embrace their Russian identities once again.

Several scholars also point out that the categories adopted in sociopsychological research, such as 'acculturation' or 'ethnolinguistic vitality,' are oversimplified, ambiguous in their specification, and detached from real-life contexts. As a result, they reduce diverse contexts to a few ad hoc dimensions and ignore power relations and complex sociopolitical, socioeconomic, and sociocultural factors which shape interactions between various groups in multilingual societies. Consequently, the critics argue, intergroup approaches to language and identity are weak theoretically, since they lack a coherent theory of language and power and are based on a social identity theory which itself requires a sociological grounding (cf. Husband & Saifullah Khan, 1982: 196). They also suggest that the aim for a high level of analysis and generalization in order to identify 'common processes underlying diverse speech strategies' (Giles & Byrne, 1982: 18) prevents inter-group theorists from understanding ways in which various language varieties function in local contexts and ways in which local hegemonic structures may oppress or legitimize particular ethnic groups or identities. In other words, such approaches prevent scholars from seeing multiple ways in which social contexts constrain or prevent individuals from accessing linguistic resources or adopting new identities (Pavlenko, 2000, 2002).

With regard to methodology, inter-group approaches are criticized for the inherent belief that the richness of human experience may be reduced to a few constructs and numbers and for resulting over-reliance on self-evaluation, questionnaires, and numerical scales that may reflect ways in which the individuals would like to portray themselves but obscure actual behaviors and contexts that shape them. The use of questionnaires has also been criticized for implicit assumptions that individuals responding to a particular questionnaire operate with relatively similar understandings of 'culture,' 'identity,' or 'language competence.' It was also pointed out that sociopsychological measures and assessments operate with the standard language notions in mind, ignoring the full range of individuals' linguistic repertoires.

It is important to acknowledge here that some recent sociopsychological studies recognize the importance of power relations in acculturation of newcomers (Birman & Trickett, 2001; McNamara, 1987), attempt to supplement the use of the questionnaires with the interviews (Birman & Trickett, 2001), and even try to bring together inter-group approaches and social constructionist and poststructuralist views (Armour, 2001; McNamara, 1997). Nevertheless, they continue to exhibit the over-simplifying and reductionist tendencies for which the paradigm originally came under fire. As a result, even though sociopsychological approaches clearly deserve credit for pioneering important questions and agendas in the study of language contact between minority and majority groups, we believe that theoretical and methodological weaknesses outlined above render them less than useful for exploring complex sociopolitical and socioeconomic issues in the shaping and negotiation of multilinguals' identities.

Interactional sociolinguistic approaches

While sociopsychological approaches examine negotiation of identities in second language learning and language use, *interactional sociolinguistics* focuses on negotiation of identities in code-switching and language choice. Two volumes which appeared in the 1980s – Gumperz's (1982) collection on language and social identity and Le Page and Tabouret-Keller's (1985) ethnographic study of language use in the Caribbean – signified the beginning of a transition from sociopsychological approaches (that originally inspired Le Page) to ethnographically-oriented inter-actional sociolinguistics, which views social identities as fluid and constructed in linguistic and social interaction. Gumperz's (1982) ground-breaking work drew on earlier insights of Fishman (1965) and pioneered an understanding of code-switching as yet another resource through which speakers express social and rhetorical meanings and index ethnic identities. Heller's (1982) explorations of negotiations of language choice in Montreal and Le Page and Tabouret-Keller's (1985) investigation of the complex linguistic repertoires of West Indian communities demonstrated that multilingual speakers move around in multidimensional social spaces and that each act of speaking or silence may constitute for them an 'act of identity.'

Over the years, several sociolinguists examined negotiation of language choice and identities in multilingual contexts; only a few, however, attempted to theorize it. The best-known sociolinguistic model of nego-tiation of identities through code-switching is the markedness model, proposed by Myers-Scotton (Myers-Scotton, 1998; Scotton, 1983, 1988). This framework views talk as a negotiation of rights and obligations between speaker and addressee and assumes that speakers have a tacit knowledge of indexicality, i.e. of marked and unmarked language choices in a particular interaction. According to Myers-Scotton, speakers opt for a language that would symbolize the rights and obligations they wish to enforce in the exchange in question and index the appropriate identities. In making the unmarked choice, the speakers recognize the status quo as the basis for the speech event. In contrast, making a marked choice indi-cates an attempt to negotiate a different balance of rights and obligations. If such choice is indexical of solidarity it can narrow the social distance between the interlocutors. In turn, if it is used to index the power differ-ential, anger or resistance, it could serve to increase the social distance. In addition, people may also make marked choices to encode deference and also because of the inability to use the unmarked choice.

In contexts where one language is dominant, this language may be more closely associated with the in-group membership and thus become the unmarked choice, indexical of solidarity. In other contexts, code-switching itself serves as a means of in-group communication and is thus the unmarked choice. For example, Mexican-Americans may use English–Spanish code-switching to convey the sense of their dual iden-tity (Jacobson, 1998). In contrast, in Belgium the polarization between the speakers of French in the south and the speakers of Dutch in the north reached such a degree that Brusselers no longer consider a mixed code to be an appropriate expression of their identity (Treffers-Daller, 1992). Consequently, in societies marked by inter-group tensions, code-switching may be used as a marked choice to negotiate a change in social distance. In this view then, language choice and code-switching are indexical of identities, i.e. 'codeswitching patterns may be indicative of how speakers view themselves in relation to the socio-political values attached to the linguistic varieties used in codeswitching' (Myers-Scotton, 1998: 99).

Over the years, assumptions about identities and indexicality made in early code-switching research and, in particular, in Myers-Scotton's markedness theory have been subject to a number of criticisms. First of all, critical sociolinguists argue that identity cannot and should not be used as an explanatory concept in the study of linguistic practices, as it is itself in need of explanation (Cameron, 1990; Johnstone, 1996; Tannen, 1993). Second, they criticize the essentialized links between languages and specific national or regional groups which obscure the fact that individuals may also construct particular identities through linguistic resources of groups to which they do not straightforwardly belong (most recently this phenomenon was explored in studies of code-crossing, cf. Cutler, 1999; Lo, 1999; Rampton, 1995, 1999a,b). Third, many researchers express concerns about the notion of indexicality and the unproblematic links it posits between languages, identities, and speech events. Alvarez-Caccamo (1998) argues that the indexical value of code-switching is not necessarily a compound of social-indexical values of the two languages in use. Auer (1998a) and Li Wei (1998) question whether a static notion of indexicality, which draws on the analysts' perceptions rather than on local meanings, has potential to capture the diversity of interactions in multilingual settings. Auer (1995) points out that many speech events are not tied to a particular language, and even among those where certain tendencies are observed, these tendencies are never strong enough to predict language choice in a probabilistic way. In turn, Heller (1982, 1988, 1992, 1995a,b) demonstrates that, during the time of francophone mobilization in Quebec, all assumptions about speech events were suspended and the code of each interaction had to be negotiated anew. Many scholars also acknowledge that identity is not the only factor influencing code-switching and that in many contexts the alteration and mixing of the two languages are best explained through other means, including the linguistic competencies of the speakers (cf. Auer, 1998b; Jacobson, 1998).

We fully agree with Auer's (1995, 1998a) suggestion that the analysis of macro-sociolinguistic aspects of the speech situation will never predict or determine patterns of code-switching and language choice. These patterns can be uncovered and explained only through close attention to interactional aspects of bilingual conversation (Auer, 1995, 1998a; Li Wei, 1998). The agenda for the present volume is a different one – we aim to examine instances of negotiation of identities that are not necessarily limited to code-switching and to explain what identity options are available to speech event participants, what shapes these options, and which identities are being challenged and why. In other words, rather than examining reasons for the choice of particular languages, we will consider how languages are appropriated in construction and negotiation of particular identities. To do so, we will appeal to poststructuralist theory which recognizes the sociohistorically shaped partiality, contestability, instability, and mutability of ways in which language ideologies and identities are linked to relations of power and political arrangements in communities and societies.

Poststructuralist Approaches to Negotiation of Identities

Poststructuralist and critical theory in sociolinguistics of multilingualism

Due to the pioneering efforts of Gal (1989), Heller (1988, 1992, 1995a,b), and Woolard (1985, 1989, 1998), in the past two decades, sociolinguistic and anthropological research on multilingualism received solid grounding in poststructuralist and critical theory and in political economic analysis, which led many scholars to consider language choices in multilingual contexts as embedded in larger social, political, economic, and cultural systems. In many ways this reconceptualization was inspired by the influential work of French sociologist, Pierre Bourdieu (1977, 1982, 1991), who viewed linguistic practices as a form of symbolic capital, convertible into economic and social capital, and distributed unequally within any given speech community (linguistic stratification). The value of a particular language variety in a symbolic market place derives from its legitimation by the dominant group and the dominant institutions, in particular schools and the media. Bourdieu's model of symbolic domination rests on his notion that a symbolically dominated group is complicit in the misrecognition (*meconnaissance*), or valorization, of that language and variety as an inherently better form. In other words, the official language or standard variety becomes the language of hegemonic institutions because both the dominant and the subordinated group misrecognize it as a superior language. In this view, ideologies of language are not about language alone (Woolard, 1998), but are always socially situated and tied to questions of identity and power in societies. While modern linguists may regard all languages and language varieties as equal in value, political and popular discourse often comes to regard official languages and standard varieties as essentially superior to unofficial languages and non-standard varieties (Collins, 1999).

Adopting the basic premises of Bourdieu's model, Gal (1989), Heller (1992), and Woolard (1985) noted that Bourdieu's view of symbolic domination is flawed in that it does not accommodate the possibility for resistance and links the hegemonic power to relative numbers of speakers of a particular variety. The three scholars expanded his theory in slightly different ways. Woolard (1985) pointed out that symbolic domination is grounded in the wide acceptance of the value and prestige of a particular linguistic variety, rather than in numerical disparities between majority and minority communities. She also expanded Bourdieu's marketplace metaphor, showing that, in any given context, there may be several alternative market places which assume different language norms and assign different values to particular language behaviors and linguistic varieties. In local markets, local linguistic variants may be seen as solidarity-based linguistic practices and as a form of opposition to symbolic domination. Gal (1989) similarly noted that speakers may use the microstructures of interaction to transform linguistic norms and their own stigmatized social identities. Her analysis also revealed differences between ethnic groups and classes which may be related to the political economic systems in different ways.

Heller's (1982, 1988, 1992, 1995a,b) work played a critical role in attracting the field's attention to the fact that conventional language practices represent relatively stable power relations. In contrast, in the context of sociopolitical change, language norms – oftentimes monolingual – are no longer shared and 'in the place of unconscious, or semi-conscious, use of language in everyday life is an extreme awareness of language, a new way of holding conversations that involves the negotiation of language choice in every interaction' (Heller, 1982: 109). Heller's ethnographic investigations of language choice in public and private settings in Canada from 1978 to 1990 laid the foundation of the poststructuralist study of negotiation of identities, showing that languages can no longer be seen solely as unproblematic markers of particular ethnic identities. In Quebec, in the context of francophone resistance to English domination, language choices came to signify a complex set of assumptions about the interlocutors' mother tongue, ethnicity, linguistic competence, political position (federalist vs. separatist), and even open-mindedness and politeness, as seen in the following exchange:

> I stopped in a garage . . . and struggled to explain . . . that my windshield wipers were congelé and I wanted to make them fonctionner. He listened in mild amusement and then said: 'You don't have to speak French to me, madame. I am not a separatist.' (cited in Heller, 1982: 108)

Heller (1982) interpreted frequent conversation breakdowns she observed as a sign that the renegotiation of shared social knowledge and norms of language use was under way in Quebec. To challenge the dominance of English, francophones flouted the prevailing conventions, speaking French where English was expected. In turn, some anglophones insisted on their right to maintain conversation in English, while others attempted to speak French and saw their attempts rebuffed as in the conversation above. Emerging new conventions required bilingualism from all participants and members of both anglophone and francophone elite rushed to learn the valued variety of the other language in order to gain or retain privileged access to the same kinds of education, workplace opportunities, and socioeconomic positions (Heller, 1992).

Drawing on her ethnographic explorations, Heller (1992, 1995a,b) developed a theoretical framework for exploring ways in which language practices and negotiation of identities are bound in power relations. This framework links language and power in two important ways. On the one hand, language is seen as part of processes of social action and interaction and in particular as a way in which people influence others. On the other, it is a symbolic resource which may be tied to the ability to gain access to, and exercise, power. Consequently, any analysis of language practices needs to examine how conventions of language choice and use are created, maintained, and changed, to see how language ideologies legitimize and validate particular practices, and to understand real-world consequences these practices have in people's lives. Methodologically, this implies that code-switching needs to be examined not as a unique phenomenon but as a part of a range of linguistic practices which people employ to achieve their goals and to challenge symbolic domination (Heller, 1992).

It is this range of practices that will be explored in this volume in order to see how, in the context of shifting power relations and the renegotiation of 'game rules,' new identity options come into play and new values are assigned to identity options which have previously been legitimized or devalued by dominant discourses of identity. In what follows, we will outline our own framework for the study of negotiation of identities in multilingual contexts. This framework emerged over several years in collaboration with participants in several conference panels on the topic, contributors to the special issues of the *International Journal of Bilingualism* (Pavlenko & Blackledge, 2001) and *Multilingua* (Blackledge & Pavlenko, 2002), as well as through discussions of the chapters in the volume with contributors and reviewers. To embed linguistic practices in the context of power relations, this framework draws on insights from Bourdieu, Gal, Heller, and Woolard. Unlike these scholars, however, we do not aim to explain linguistic stratification in multilingual settings. Our interest is in how languages are appropriated to legitimize, challenge, and negotiate particular identities and to open new identity options for oppressed and subjugated groups and individuals. To offer a more nuanced under-standing of identites, we appeal to insights from social constructionist and poststructuralist thinking on the politics of identity and to contributions to this volume which offer fresh, innovative, and intriguing perspectives on negotiation of identities in a variety of multilingual settings around the world. In doing so, we will integrate references to the volume chap-ters in our discussion rather than present them as a traditional summary.

Identities

While variationist and sociopsychological approaches view identities as relatively stable and independent of language, social constructionists conceptualize identities as an interactional accomplishment, produced and negotiated in discourse (Davies & Harré, 1990; Edwards, 1997; Gergen, 1994; Harré & van Langenhove, 1999). In turn, poststructuralists argue that the social constructionist agenda underemphasizes the role of power in the process of categorization; their work illuminates ways in which particular identities are legitimized or devalued in the context of global and local political economies (Bourdieu, 1991; Cerulo, 1997; Weedon, 1987). Recent poststructuralist thought points to splits and fissures in categories previously seen as bounded or dichotomous and brings into focus hybrid, transgendered, and multiracial identities that have previously been ignored (Bammer, 1994a,b; Bhabha, 1990; Brah, 1996; Hall, 1990). Our own framework combines aspects of both approaches, appealing to the social constructionist focus on discursive construction of identities and to the poststructuralist emphasis on the role of power relations. Below, we will discuss five characteristics of identities particularly important for the proposed framework: (1) location within particular discourses and ideologies of language; (2) embeddedness within the relations of power; (3) multiplicity, fragmentation, and hybridity; (4) the imagined nature of 'new' identities; and (5) location within particular narratives.

Identities, discourses, and language ideologies

In agreement with a social constructionist view, we see identity options as constructed, validated, and offered through discourses available to individuals at a particular point in time and place (Davies & Harré, 1990; Edwards, 1997; Gergen, 1994; Harré & van Langenhove, 1999; Tabouret-Keller, 1997). This discursive approach views the relationship between language and identity as mutually constitutive in at least two ways. On the one hand, languages, or rather particular discourses within them, supply the terms and other linguistic means with which identities are constructed and negotiated. On the other, ideologies of language and identity guide ways in which individuals use linguistic resources to index their identities and to evaluate the use of linguistic resources by others.

All of the volume contributors share our commitment to locating identities discussed within particular discourses and ideologies of language and identity. Giampapa, for instance, situates the identities of her Italian Canadian participants within the discourses of *italianità* (Italianness) prevalent in Toronto's Italian Canadian and Canadian worlds. In doing so, she shows that youths in her study resist normative representations of what it means to be Italian Canadian with regard to linguistic competence, religious affiliation, or sexual identity. Mills locates the beliefs and identities of immigrant mothers in Britain within the ideologies of 'mother tongue,' which dictate a particular version of what it means to be a good mother. She demonstrates that these ideologies impose a conflicting set of norms on minority mothers: on the one hand, good mothering involves fostering the mother tongue as well as religious and cultural values, and, on the other, it means promoting English, which alone has the power to ensure the children's educational and later professional success. Torn between the two sets of values, some participants are unable to find the time and resources to support the mother tongue and thus feel that they failed as good mothers.

As seen in the examples above, to say that identities are discursive constructions does not imply that they are not 'real' in the material world. As pointed out by Bammer (1994b: xvi), 'the discursive nature of cultural formations is often eclipsed by the palpable experience of their force.' In fact, it is precisely the power of identities to unite and divide individuals, groups, communities, and societies that fuels our and our contributors' interest in the subject.

Identities as embedded within power relations

Poststructuralist thinking, and in particular Bourdieu's model of symbolic domination, allow us to analyze the real-life impact of discursive categories as embedded within local and global relations of power. In Bourdieu's terms, those who are not speakers of the official language or standard variety are subject to symbolic domination, if they believe in the legitimacy of that language or variety. As mentioned earlier, these beliefs are shaped in the process of *misrecognition*, which, according to Gal and Irvine (1995), often contributes to the indexical linking of linguistic varieties with character types and cultural traits, whereby linguistic behaviors of others are seen as deriving from speakers' social, political, intellectual, or moral character, rather than from historical accident. A corollary of such linguistic ideology is that speakers of official languages or standard varieties may be regarded as having greater moral and intellectual worth than speakers of unofficial languages or non-standard varieties. Thus, according to Bourdieu (1991), we have to examine power in places where it is least visible, because symbolic power 'is that invisible power which can be exercised only with the complicity of those who do not want to know that they are subject to it or even that they themselves exercise it' (p. 163).

The volume contributors are fully committed to investigating how languages and identities are embedded within the relations of power. Blackledge's analysis highlights ways in which British politicians link the use of Asian languages in the home to educational underachievement of minority children and ultimately to violence and social disorder on the streets. Instead of acknowledging the link between the ongoing riots and racism and Islamophobia, parliamentary speakers collaborate in the process of normalization, in which it comes to appear natural that British English dominates other languages, is more legitimate, and provides greater access to symbolic resources. It is from this position then that they call for compulsory enrollment in English classes and demand naturalization language testing for those who seek permanent settlement in Britain as spouses (usually wives) of British citizens.

Kanno and Miller illuminate the role of schools in reproduction of social inequality. The respective descriptions of an elementary school in Japan and a high school in Australia show that second language learners in these contexts are subject to unequal power relations and are often unable to achieve the 'right to speak' and 'impose reception' (Bourdieu, 1991). The authors argue that schools should become more active in recognizing, challenging, and reversing social inequality, shifting in the process from 'coercive' to 'collaborative relations of power' (Cummins, 2000: 44).

Egbo's and Canagarajah's chapters discuss some ways in which this shift can be achieved. Egbo shows how women in rural Nigeria are empowered by English literacy, which offers them a greater power within the household, more opportunities in the labor market, and increased respect from the villagers. While not a panacea per se, Egbo argues that literacy is a necessary prerequisite for enabling women to understand and transform their social world and their place within it. In turn, Canagarajah pays close attention to negotiation of textual identities in academic discourse. He shows how two strategies, appropriation and transposition, allow second language users of English to challenge dominant discourses and to bring in alternative discourses and values in ways that preserve the writers' authority and legitimacy and allow them to be heard on their own terms.

Multiplicity, fragmentation, and hybridity

Another important aspect of identities in the present framework is their *multiplicity*. While early studies of language and identity privileged a single aspect of identity – most commonly ethnicity or gender – at the expense of others, poststructuralist inquiry highlights the fact that identities are constructed at the interstices of multiple axes, such as age, race, class, ethnicity, gender, generation, sexual orientation, geopolitical locale, institutional affiliation, and social status, whereby each aspect of identity redefines and modifies all others. Since individuals often shift and adjust ways in which they identify and position themselves in distinct contexts, identities are best understood when approached in their entirety, rather than through consideration of a single aspect or subject position.

James and Woll offer an excellent example of what such consideration involves in their chapter on the interplay of identities of Black Deaf individuals. Dislocation is a fact of life for their participants. Growing up Deaf in hearing families, many of them experienced feelings of loneliness which separated them from their hearing relatives and led them to self-identify primarily as Deaf. In turn, racial discrimination in the workplace and in the larger, predominantly white, Deaf community prompted the growth of racial awareness and the desire, for some individuals, to self-identify as Black or Black Deaf. Other informants talk about being marginalized within the Black hearing community, and position themselves as Deaf Black. The authors explore the shifting landscape of this repositioning and conclude that, at every point, the participants' positioning depends upon the level of inclusion, acceptance, and equality that they feel among Black people and in the Deaf community.

At times, fragmentation and splintering give birth to new, hybrid, identities and linguistic repertoires. New discourses of gender, sexuality, class, or ethnicity may bring with them new identity options, just as other options may be fading into the background. In Czarniawska's (2000) words, identities are susceptible to fashion and individuals and institutions reform themselves according to identity options that dominate at certain times and places. The recognition of the emerging nature of identity, and of identity fragmentation, de-centering, multiplicity, and shifts, oftentimes exacerbated by transnational migration, led poststructuralist philosophers to posit the notion of *hybridity* as the 'third space' that enables the appearance of new and alternative identity options (Bhabha, 1990).

The notions of hybridity and 'third space' are productively explored by several authors in the volume. James and Woll point to the emerging Black Deaf community with its own organizations and clubs, and with its own communicative repertoire, a Black variant of the British Sign Language. Doran argues that Verlan, a sociolect of Parisian suburbs, creates a similar 'third space' for low-income multi-ethnic minority youths, marginalized in French society. She shows that the use of a sociolect located outside of the prescriptive norms of Standard French allows these youths to construct an alternative 'universe of discourse,' one in which they can negotiate identities distinct from those imposed on them by the hegemonic and assimilationist discourses of the mainstream. 'Third space' also figures in Giampapa's account of the Italian Canadian diasporic experience, allowing her to illuminate ways in which Italian Canadian youths create hybrid identities negotiated both locally, within the spaces of the Italian Canadian and Canadian worlds, and transnationally, in an Italian world.

Identities and imagination

Imagination plays a crucial role in the process of creation of new identity options, or, in Hall's (1990) terms, in the process of imaginative production of identity. This process is often aided by new linguistic terms, by visual art, and by literary narratives, which together create new practices of self-representation and thus new 'imagined communities' (Anderson, 1983; Hall, 1990). Notions of imagination dominate Blackledge's, Pavlenko's, and Kinginger's chapters. Blackledge investigates how particular symbolic links, associations, and meanings are discursively created – and thus imagined – in British political discourse, which ties social cohesion to monolingualism and imagines a British self against an undesirable non-English-speaking Other. He argues that this language ideological debate is not a struggle over language alone, but over the kind of society that Britain imagines itself to be: either multilingual, pluralist, and diverse, or ultimately English-speaking, assimilationist, and homogeneous. Pavlenko explores the search for social cohesion in the early twentieth-century US, where the country fathers, dealing with an overwhelming influx of immigrants from Eastern and Southern Europe, reimagined the country as one where the national identity was conceived in English monolingualism.

Kinginger shifts the focus to a single individual and portrays a clash of images in a study abroad situation. Her participant, Alice, an American learner of French, embarks on the trip in order to acquire a new cultural capital, consciousness, and refinement, and to leave behind her identity as a low-income wage earner and daughter of a migrant worker. Her quest is informed by the romanticized discourses of francophonie, which portray France as a picturesque and bucolic place studded with archi-tectural monuments and populated by cultivated, refined, and elegant people. The real France encountered by Alice is so unlike the imaginary one that she becomes depressed to the point of contemplating suicide. It is only with time that she manages to re-narrate her experience and trans-form her goals and objectives, adapting them to her new image of France.

Identity narratives

Narratives play a particularly important role in our account of negoti-ation of identities. Unprecedented transnational migration and displace-ment (Bammer, 1994a) and creation of new diasporas (Brah, 1996; Hall, 1990) are the hallmark of the twentieth century. These phenomena often lead to tension between fragmented, decentered, and shifting identities experienced by groups and individuals and their desire for meaning and coherence. Identity narratives offer a unique means of resolving this tension, (re)constructing the links between past, present, and future, and imposing coherence where there was none (Czarniawska, 2000; Hall, 1990; Pavlenko, 1998, 2001). New narratives and images 'offer a way to impose an imaginary coherence on the experience of dispersal and frag-mentation, which is the history of all enforced diasporas' (Hall, 1990: 224).

We see this view of identities, as located not only within particular discourses and ideologies but also within narratives, as immensely enriching in that it gives our perspective a diachronic dimension. Consequently, identities are no longer just discursive options – they are also 'the names we give to the different ways we are positioned by, and position ourselves within, the narratives of the past' (Hall, 1990: 225), as well as the narratives of the present and future. And thus, following Ricoeur (1988: 246), we suggest that 'To answer the question "Who?" . . . is to tell a story of a life.' This perspective privileges a dynamic view of identities, with individuals continuously involved in production of selves, positioning of others, revision of identity narratives, and creation of new ones which valorize new modes of being and belonging.

The narrative view of identity informs all of the chapters in the volume. While Blackledge explores the dominant narratives of identity imposed on minority speakers in multilingual Britain, the rest of the contributors examine personal narratives of multilingual speakers who search for ways to resist normative identities and in the process create different narratives of the self. Pavlenko underscores the important role literary texts play in the creation of the national identity narrative which aims to impose and preserve a particular version of the nation's collective experience. She shows that, at the turn of the twentieth century, Eastern and Southern European immigrant writers in the US managed to rewrite the 'national text' and to present America as a nation of immigrants, rather than of white Anglo protestants. In doing so, they created new identity options, in particular new ways of being American, which became available for appropriation by their fellow immigrants.

In sum, we view *identities* as social, discursive, and narrative options offered by a particular society in a specific time and place to which individuals and groups of individuals appeal in an attempt to self-name, to self-characterize, and to claim social spaces and social prerogatives. We also want to underscore that, while we recognize the intrinsic links between languages and identities, identity is not always an interesting or relevant concept for investigation of language use in multilingual settings. As pointed out earlier, in some contexts, where power relations are relatively stable, dominant interpretations and identity options may reign uncontested, at least temporarily. As a result, linguistic practices in these contexts may be better understood in sociopolitical and economic terms, rather than in terms of identity. For us, identity becomes interesting, relevant, and visible when it is contested or in crisis. In other words, we see identity as particularly salient in contexts where multiple interpretations or meanings collide, resulting in a power struggle as to whose interpretation prevails. This said, however, we do not mean to imply that identities are negotiated only where there are relatively unstable relations of power. As will be shown later, identities are often imposed and contested even in societies where an apparently liberal ideology is dominant. What do we mean then by negotiation of identities?

Negotiation of identities

To make the process of negotiation visible, we differentiate between the ongoing construction and performance of identities in multilingual contexts (cf. Auer, 1998b) and the negotiation of identities which takes place only when certain identities are contested. In the present volume we limit our discussion to struggles which occur when certain identity options are imposed or devalued, and others are unavailable or misunderstood. This focus stems from our interest in human agency, and thus in instances where individuals resist, negotiate, change, and transform themselves and others. This attention to negotiation and agency echoes similar movements in other subfields of sociolinguistics, in particular the study of language and gender, where the focus on normative femininities and masculinities has recently expanded to embrace transgressive subjects who defy conventional practices and engage in resistance, subversion, and reinvention of gendered selves (Bucholtz *et al.*, 1999).

To analyze how identities are shaped, produced, and negotiated, we adopt 'positioning theory' (Davies & Harré, 1990; Harré & van Langenhove, 1999), which allows us to bring together the views of identities as located in discourses and as situated in narratives. *Positioning*, for Davies and Harré (1990: 48), is the process by which selves are located in conversation as observably and subjectively coherent participants in jointly produced story lines, informed by particular discourses. Interactive positioning assumes one individual positioning the other, while reflective positioning is the process of positioning oneself. Although Davies and Harré (1990) see positioning as largely a conversational phenomenon, in the present volume we expand the meaning of positioning to all discursive practices which may position individuals in particular ways or allow individuals to position themselves.

While agency and choice are critical in positioning, it is important to underscore that instances of reflective positioning are often contested by others and many individuals find themselves in a perpetual tension between self-chosen identities and others' attempts to position them differently. Therefore, in the present collection *negotiation of identities* will be understood as an interplay between reflective positioning, i.e. self-representation, and interactive positioning, whereby others attempt to position or reposition particular individuals or groups. Such negotiation may take place in oral interaction where an attempt at a controversial reflective positioning may be immediately challenged, or in print whereby the challenge in the form of repositioning may be temporally delayed. Moreover, in a heteroglossic Bakhtinian view assumed here, negotiation does not necessarily involve two or more physical parties – it may also take place 'within' individuals, resulting in changes in self-representation.

The framework we propose differentiates between three types of identities: *imposed identities* (which are not negotiable in a particular time and place), *assumed identities* (which are accepted and not negotiated), and *negotiable identities* (which are contested by groups and individuals). Clearly, all three categories acquire a particular status within unique sociohistorical circumstances. Options that are acceptable for and, there-fore, not negotiated by some groups and individuals, may be contested by another group, or even the same group at a different point in time. In this view then, imposed (or non-negotiable) identities are the ones that individuals cannot resist or contest at a particular point in time. For instance, in Nazi Germany, individuals may have disagreed with being identified as Jews, but their opinions did not matter much in the process of extermination. Immigrants arriving in the US in the early twentieth century may have resented compulsory name changes imposed by local authorities, but were unable to refuse them. And nowadays, as seen in Blackledge's chapter, 'common-sense' discourse dictates that immigrant wives and husbands who wish to apply for British citizenship must learn sufficient English to fulfill their duties as citizens. These contenders may take issue with citizenship-related language testing, but are powerless to resist it.

In turn, assumed (or non-negotiated) identities are those that many – albeit not all – individuals are comfortable with and not interested in contesting. Oftentimes, these identities are the ones most valued and legit-imized by the dominant discourses of identity (e.g. heterosexual white middle-class males or monolingual speakers of the majority language). Thus, Giampapa's chapter highlights the fact that the links between Italianness, machismo, and heterosexuality are contested only by one of her study participants, a gay man. In turn, another participant questions the links between Italianness and Catholicism, unproblematic for some of the others.

Finally, negotiable identities refer to all identity options which can be – and are – contested and resisted by particular individuals and groups. In the present volume these identity options are negotiated in the areas of ethnicity and nationality (Blackledge, Giampapa, Mills, Pavlenko), gender (Egbo, Mills, Pavlenko), race (James and Woll), class and social status (Doran, Egbo, Kinginger, Miller, Pavlenko), (able)bodiedness (James and Woll), sexuality (Giampapa), religious affiliation (Giampapa,

Pavlenko), and, last but not least, linguistic competence and ability to claim a 'voice' in a second language (Blackledge, Canagarajah, Kanno, Kinginger, Miller, Pavlenko). These identities are negotiated in a variety of sites, which include the family (Egbo, Giampapa, James and Woll, Mills), peer group interactions (Egbo, Doran, Giampapa, James and Woll, Kinginger, Miller), educational contexts, such as schools and universities (James and Woll, Kanno, Kinginger, Miller), workplace (Giampapa, James and Woll), and public discourses on educational, language, and immigration policies (Blackledge, Pavlenko).

Pavlenko's chapter also underscores that the notion of 'negotiation of identities' needs to be approached from a sociohistorical perspective: identities considered to be negotiable at present may have been assumed or non-negotiable 100 years ago. Her analysis of turn-of-the-century immigrant memoirs demonstrates that European immigrant writers, drawing on the rhetoric of individual uplift, successfully reimagined American national identity in a way that would make it negotiable for new European arrivals. At the same time, racial minorities, in particular large numbers of Asian immigrants, had no access to the negotiation process and were not 'imagined' as legitimate Americans. Furthermore, she shows that subject positions renegotiated and reimagined by the immigrant writers included national, ethnic, cultural, gender, and religious identities, but not linguistic ones. The right of new immigrants to write in English appeared uncontested and in fact they were encouraged to do so. In contrast, many contemporary immigrant and bilingual writers are thrust into positions where they have to defend their linguistic rights and ownership of English; consequently, their memoirs foreground negotiation of linguistic identities.

Linguistic means of negotiation

Traditionally, the key linguistic means of negotiation of identities discussed in the bilingualism literature include code-switching, or code-alternation, code-mixing, and language choice (Auer, 1998b; Bailey, 2000; Heller, 1988; Scotton, 1983), and, more recently, crossing (Rampton, 1995, 1999a,b). Eastman and Stein (1993: 187) alternatively categorize these means as language display, or 'a language-use strategy whereby members of one group lay claims to attributes associated with another, conveying messages of social, professional, and ethnic identity.' The present volume expands this understanding of negotiation and illuminates a wide variety of linguistic practices which individuals and minority groups may appropriate – or even invent – to position and (re)position themselves, examining not only code-switching and code-mixing, but also invention and use of new linguistic varieties, second language learning, literacy learning, appropriation of new rhetorical strategies, and creation of new identity narratives.

James and Woll show how the Black Deaf in Britain, who often experience discrimination both on the part of the Black hearing community and the white Deaf community, build a group identity through the use of a Black variant of the British Sign Language (BSL). This variant incorporates facial expressions, gestures, and body language typical for interaction styles in the Black community, especially those associated with Black youth culture. It also includes new signs for 'Black' and 'white' and for various aspects of Black cultural life. These innovations prompted scorn in the white Deaf community, where some members refuse to accept the new ways in which the Black Deaf express themselves.

In turn, Doran's chapter explores Verlan, a language variety spoken primarily among multi-ethnic youth living in disadvantaged neighborhoods outside Paris. In recent decades, this 'street language' has become a recognizable sociolect in the low-income housing projects. Characterized by various alterations of Standard French and by incorporation of borrowings from Arabic, English, Wolof, and other languages, it is a kind of linguistic *bricolage* which expresses the multilingualism and multiculturalism present in the communities where it is spoken. Doran argues that Verlan is best understood as an alternative code that allows its users to delineate a peer universe in which their complex, multilingual, multicultural, working-class identities can be performed and recognized in a way they are not within the larger society.

Linguistic innovation is not the only way in which identities can be negotiated. Kinginger and Pavlenko point to second language learning as another arena in which new identities can be sought out and constructed. The participant in Kinginger's study, Alice, goes to France because of her desire to imagine herself anew in a context where her social options are broadened. Her learning trajectory is shaped by her history of hardship, homelessness, and transience, and her choice of France, influenced by American cultural mythology, is a bid for a new respectable social identity. Kinginger emphasizes that, in this sense, Alice's efforts toward French language competence are just as much an 'investment' in social identity as those of the immigrant women in Canada in Norton's (2000) study.

Egbo and Canagarajah showcase literacy as another domain in which new, more powerful identities can be constructed (Egbo) and the dominant discourses successfully challenged through the use of particular rhetorical strategies (Canagarajah). Pavlenko's analysis of turn-of-the-twentieth-century immigrant memoirs also pays close attention to rhetorical strategies. She points out that, to inscribe European immigrants into the American national identity narrative, immigrant authors appealed to two dominant tropes of the time, the trope of the 'self-made man' and the opposition between the Old and the New World. These tropes allowed them to position themselves and fellow immigrants as legitimate Americans who achieved this status by 'luck and pluck.'

Audibility and visibility

While all of the authors in the volume are concerned with what it means to be heard, Miller successfully theorizes the negotiation of voice through the notion of *audibility*, namely the degree to which speakers sound like, and are legitimated by, users of the dominant discourse. In her view, audibility is co-constructed and requires a collaboration between the speaker and the listener. At the same time, Miller and others acknowledge that visibility, namely race and ethnicity, play a major role in this co-construction, whereby some speakers are more easily imaginable than others as authoritative, competent, and legitimate.

Both race and ethnicity are at the foreground in the creation of 'imagined communities' (Anderson, 1983) of contemporary nation-states, where prototypical British, Australian, French, or US citizens are imagined as white. Blackledge and Mills point to the exclusion of immigrants, whose dress, customs, and skin color signal their Asian heritage, from being truly British in public terms. Oftentimes, these immigrants are not recognized as legitimate speakers of English and are urged to 'acquire more competence.' Similarly, Doran's chapter brings to the foreground multi-ethnic and multilingual Parisian youths who struggle against racist discourses that portray working-class immigrants from North and West Africa and Southeast Asia as thugs, junkies, prostitutes – and deficient speakers of Standard French.

Miller and Kanno explore the relationship between visibility and audibility in educational contexts. Miller's study is conducted within the context of one Australian high school. It highlights differences between the integration of white Bosnian students, who easily make Australian friends and get to be heard by the teachers, and that of Chinese students, who are – sometimes literally – positioned as incompetent and inaudible speakers of English. Miller argues that the school did not offer these students sufficient opportunities to develop independent and audible voices and suggests that one reason for this may have been their relative invisibility. In turn, Kanno's study portrays a group of linguistic minority students in Japan who can visually 'pass' as Japanese. She recognizes the possibility that the ability to 'pass' visually makes 'mainstream' Japanese identities more accessible to many language minority students.

Not surprisingly, identity options are most often contested and resisted by the most marginalized and discriminated against segments of the population, which in multilingual societies often consist of linguistic minorities. How much room for resistance to particular positioning individuals and groups may have will depend on each particular situation, the social and linguistic resources available to participants, and the balance of power relations which sets out the boundaries for particular identity options. This complex and delicate balance cannot be adequately explored through methodologies used in early research, which oftentimes relied exclusively on questionnaires or interaction analysis. Consequently, we will offer a brief discussion of methodological and analytical choices made by the volume contributors.

Methodological choices

All of the volume contributors acknowledge the political nature of the research process and share a commitment to an emic, i.e. participant-relevant, perspective which acknowledges the views and opinions of people formerly known as 'research subjects' and leads researchers to collaborate with, rather than investigate the practices of, the study participants. In order to reflect the participants' voices, opinions, and beliefs, the authors appeal to semi-structured interviews (Egbo, Doran, Giampapa, James and Woll, Kanno, Kinginger, Miller, Mills) and to written reflections in the forms of e-mail messages, journals, diaries, letters, essays, or questionnaire responses (Canagarajah, Giampapa, Kinginger, Miller). The interviews were conducted in a way that gave participants most control over the process. In some cases, the participants were invited to go over the interview texts and to discuss the preliminary findings in order to create additional opportunities for reflection and to allow them to retain the authorship over the texts (Kinginger, Mills). And in order to bring in the voices of those who, for some reason or another, could not be interviewed directly, some authors analyzed public speeches (Blackledge) and published academic and literary texts (Canagarajah, Pavlenko).

While participant perspectives are privileged in the volume, they are not necessarily made into the cornerstone of analysis. The contributors take a critical stance with regard to all texts and appeal to critical ethnography, which allows them to triangulate the data, and to critical discourse analysis, which enables them to uncover hidden ideological meanings that inform particular views and statements. Critical ethnography is the most common approach taken in the volume (Egbo, Doran, Giampapa, Kanno, Miller). Acknowledging the social and political nature of research, this approach views the researcher and research participants as affiliates in the co-construction of meaning and prompts researchers to combine multiple methods of data collection. In the present volume these methods included participant observation, videotaped or tape-recorded (individual and focus group) interviews with the study participants and, where appropriate, with their teachers or school administrators, as well as written reflections in the form of journals, diaries, or written responses to open-ended questionnaires. In addition, Doran and Giampapa also audiotaped and analyzed naturally occurring speech. The triangulation allowed the authors to highlight discontinuities and tensions in the participants' accounts and to offer complex accounts of negotiation of identities in specific contexts.

In their analysis of the data, many authors appealed to discourse analysis to identify the semiotic processes and rhetorical means by which identities are constructed and negotiated in linguistically diverse contexts. Content analysis allowed Doran, Giampapa, James and Woll, and Mills to identify common issues and patterns of experience of their participants. In turn, critical discourse analysis and Bakhtinian theory of heteroglossia and dialogic discourses illuminated intertextuality, namely ways in which participants incorporate and engage with other texts, discourses, and ideological positions (Blackledge, Miller, Mills, Pavlenko). For instance, Blackledge's analysis of British politicians' statements and interviews, following the so-called 'race riots' in the north of England in the summer of 2001, shows how, in the chain of discourses that emerged in the wake of the riots, *understanding English* became iconically linked with *good race relations* and ultimately with *social cohesion*. Canagarajah and Pavlenko also appealed to rhetorical and literary analyses. Canagarajah manages to showcase rhetorical strategies that offer second language users of English opportunities to challenge dominant discourses. Pavlenko uses literary and rhetorical approaches to examine how sociohistorical circumstances and ideological forces shaped the content, dominant tropes and metaphors, and silences and omissions in immigrant autobiographies, and to understand how some turn-of-the-twentieth-century immigrants managed to make their voices heard, while others never got a chance.

Conclusions

While the issues discussed above are only some of many tackled in the volume, this discussion has helped us to illuminate the central themes of *Negotiation of identities in multilingual contexts*: (1) that linguistic and identity options are limited within particular sociohistoric contexts, even though continuously contested and reinvented; (2) that diverse identity options and their links to different language varieties are valued differently and that sometimes it is these links rather than the options per se that are contested and subverted; (3) that some identity options may be negotiable, while others are either imposed (and thus non-negotiable) or assumed (and thus not negotiated); and, finally and most importantly, (4) that individuals are agentive beings who are constantly in search of new social and linguistic resources which allow them to resist identities that position them in undesirable ways, produce new identities, and assign alternative meanings to the links between identities and linguistic varieties.

The papers collected here portray groups and individuals that (re)negotiate their identities in response to hegemonic language ideologies which demand homogeneity. The different ways in which they do so exemplify the complexity involved in attempts to 'negotiate' identities in multilingual states which are underpinned by implicit monolingual ideologies. Examining ways in which language practices are bound up in relations of authority and power, and in larger socioeconomic and sociopolitical processes, the contributors ask: What identity options are offered in particular contexts for particular groups and individuals? How are they valued by competing ideologies, in particular by the dominant ones? Which options are negotiable and which are not? Where, when, why, and how do certain identities become contested? Who negotiates them and how are they negotiated? Specifically, what is the role of language and particular language structures, forms, and practices in the negotiation process? And, most importantly, who gets to impose meaning in the process of negotiation, that is, what are the power relations between the negotiating parties and how do they impact the outcome of the negotiation process?

Many of these questions were difficult or impossible to ask within sociopsychological and variationist paradigms. Consequently, we argue that a poststructuralist approach to the study of negotiation of identities in multilingual contexts, pioneered by Gal, Heller, and Woolard and expanded in this volume, is much more nuanced and allows for a more complex and rich understanding of particular negotiations. The present volume demonstrates how such understanding can be employed in a variety of contexts, including the study of second language learning in which poststructuralist approaches have not yet been widely used. The distinguishing features of this theoretical approach are its attention to the sociohistorical dimension of identity options and the resulting challenge it poses for the false macro/micro dichotomy. In full agreement with this view, the papers in the present volume convincingly demonstrate that, when identities are negotiated, interactional strategies are informed by and understood through larger societal ideologies of language, power, and identity, specific to a particular time and place.

Despite the fact that all papers in the volume are written within a particular theoretical paradigm, they are distinguished by geographical, linguistic, and disciplinary diversity. Geographically, the studies in the volume span five continents, from Africa (Egbo), to North America (Canagarajah, Giampapa, Kinginger, Pavlenko), to Australia (Miller), to Europe (Blackledge, Doran, James and Woll, Mills), to Asia (Canagarajah, Kanno). These chapters examine a variety of languages and linguistic modalities, which include not only English, French, Italian, or Japanese, but such rarely discussed linguistic varieties as Verlan (Doran) or Black Sign Language in the UK (James and Woll).

At the same time, all papers are powerfully united by the common aim of making visible the hidden symbolic power which underpins an ideological drive toward homogeneity, a drive which potentially marginalizes or excludes those who either refuse, or are unwilling, to conform. The contributors argue that social injustice through symbolic domination continues to occur in hyper-modern, neo-liberal democratic states and their institutions, which respond variously to their increasingly diverse populations. In asking questions about social justice, about who has access to symbolic and material resources, about 'who is in' and 'who is out,' they take account not only of localized linguistic behaviors, attitudes, and beliefs; they also locate them in wider social contexts, which include class, race, ethnicity, generation, gender, and sexuality. In doing so, the papers collected here make a significant contribution to the understanding of the relationship between identity negotiation and social justice in multilingual contexts around the world.

Acknowledgments

We would like to thank Deborah Golden, Stephen May, Ron Schmidt, and Li Wei for their insightful comments on an earlier version of this manuscript. All remaining errors and inconsistencies are exclusively our own.

References

Agnihotri, R., Khanna, A., and Sachdev, I. (eds) (1998) *Social psychological perspectives on second language learning.* London: Sage.

Alvarez-Caccamo, C. (1998) From 'switching code' to 'code-switching': Towards a reconceptualization of communicative codes. In P. Auer (ed.) *Code-switching in conversation: Language, interaction, and identity* (pp. 29–48). London/New York: Routledge.

Anderson, B. (1983) *Imagined communities.* London: Verso.

Armour, W. (2001) 'This guy is Japanese stuck in a white man's body': A discussion of meaning making, identity slippage, and cross-cultural adaptation. *Journal of Multilingual and Multicultural Development* 22 (1), 1–18.

Auer, P. (1995) The pragmatics of code-switching: A sequential approach. In L. Milroy and P. Muysken (eds) *One speaker, two languages: Cross-disciplinary perspectives on code-switching* (pp. 115–135). Cambridge: Cambridge University Press.

Auer, P. (1998a) Introduction: *Bilingual conversation* revisited. In P. Auer (ed.) *Code-switching in conversation: Language, interaction, and identity* (pp. 1–24). London/New York: Routledge.

Auer, P. (1998b) *Code-switching in conversation: Language, interaction, and identity.* London/New York: Routledge.

Bailey, B. (2000) Language and negotiation of ethnic/racial identity among Dominican Americans. *Language in Society* 29, 555–582.

Bammer, A. (ed.) (1994a) *Displacements: Cultural identities in question.* Bloomington, IN: Indiana University Press.

Bammer, A. (1994b) Introduction. In A. Bammer (ed.) *Displacements: Cultural identities in question* (pp. ix–xx). Bloomington, IN: Indiana University Press.

Berry, J. (1980) Acculturation as varieties of adaptation. In A. Padilla (ed.) *Acculturation: Theory, models, and some new findings* (pp. 9–25). Boulder, CO: Westview Press.

Berry, J., Kim, U., Power, S., Young, M., and Bujaki, M. (1989) Acculturation attitudes in plural societies. *Applied Psychology* 38 (2), 185–206.

Bhabha, H. (1990) The third space: Interview with Homi Bhabha. In J. Rutherford (ed.) *Identity: Community, culture, difference* (pp. 207–221). London: Lawrence and Wishart.

Birman, D. and Trickett, E. (2001) Cultural transitions in first-generation immigrants: Acculturation of Soviet Jewish refugee adolescents and parents. *Journal of Cross-Cultural Psychology* 32 (4), 456–477.

Blackledge, A. (2000) *Literacy, power, and social justice.* Stoke-on-Trent: Trentham.

Blackledge, A. and Pavlenko, A. (2002) Ideologies of language in multilingual contexts: Special issue. *Multilingua* 21 (2/3).

Bourdieu, P. (1977) The economics of linguistic exchanges. *Social Science Information* 16, 645–668.

Bourdieu, P. (1982) *Ce que parler veut dire.* Paris: Fayard.

Bourdieu, P. (1991) *Language and symbolic power.* Cambridge: Polity Press.

Brah, A. (1996) *Cartographies of diaspora: Contesting identities.* London/New York: Routledge.

Breitborde, L. (1998) *Speaking and social identity: English in the lives of urban Africans.* Berlin: Mouton de Gruyter.

Bucholtz, M., Liang, A.C., and Sutton, L. (1999) *Reinventing identities: The gendered self in discourse*. New York/Oxford: Oxford University Press.

Cameron, D. (1990) Demythologizing sociolinguistics: Why language doesn't reflect society. In J. Joseph and T. Taylor (eds) *Ideologies of language* (pp. 79–93). London/New York: Routledge.

Cerulo, K. (1997) Identity construction: New issues, new directions. *Annual Review of Sociology* 23, 385–409.

Clément, R. (1987) Second language proficiency and acculturation: An investigation of the effects of language status and individual characteristics. *Journal of Language and Social Psychology* 5, 271–290.

Collins, J. (1999) The Ebonics controversy in context: Literacies, subjectivities, and language ideologies in the United States. In J. Blommaert (ed.) *Language ideological debates* (pp. 201–234). Berlin: Mouton de Gruyter.

Cummins, J. (2000) *Language, power and pedagogy*. Clevedon: Multilingual Matters.

Cutler, C. (1999) Yorkville Crossing: White teens, hip hop, and African American English. *Journal of Sociolinguistics* 3 (4), 428–442.

Czarniawska, B. (2000) Identity lost or identity found? Celebration and lamentation over the postmodern view of identity in social science and fiction. In M. Schultz, M. Hatch and M. Larsen (eds) *The expressive organization: Linking identity, reputation, and the corporate brand* (pp. 271–283). New York/Oxford: Oxford University Press.

Davies, B. and Harré, R. (1990) Positioning: The discursive production of selves. *Journal for the Theory of Social Behaviour* 20 (1), 43–63.

Eastman, C. and Stein, R. (1993) Language display: Authenticating claims to social identity. *Journal of Multilingual and Multicultural Development* 14 (3), 187–202.

Edwards, J. (1997) *Discourse and cognition*. London: Sage.

Fishman, J. (1965) Who speaks what language to whom and when? *La Linguistique* 2, 67–88. Reprinted in Li Wei (ed.) (2000) *The bilingualism reader* (pp. 89–106). London/New York: Routledge.

Gal, S. (1989) Language and political economy. *Annual Review of Anthropology* 18, 345–367.

Gal, S. and Irvine, J. (1995) The boundaries of languages and disciplines: How ideologies construct difference. *Social Research* 62 (4), 967–1001.

Gergen, K. (1994) *Realities and relationships: Soundings in social construction*. Cambridge, MA: Harvard University Press.

Giles, H. and Byrne, J. (1982) An intergroup approach to second language acquisition. *Journal of Multilingual and Multicultural Development* 3 (1), 17–41.

Grillo, R. (1989) *Dominant languages: Language and hierarchy in Britain and France*. Cambridge: Cambridge University Press.

Gumperz, J. (ed.) (1982) *Language and social identity*. Cambridge: Cambridge University Press.

Hall, S. (1990) Cultural identity and diaspora. In J. Rutherford (ed.) *Identity: Community, culture, difference* (pp. 222–237). London: Lawrence and Wishart.

Hamers, J. and Blanc, M. (2000) *Bilinguality and bilingualism* (2nd edn). Cambridge: Cambridge University Press.

Harré, R. and van Langenhove, L. (1999) *Positioning theory: Moral contexts of intentional action*. Oxford: Blackwell.

Heller, M. (1982) Negotiations of language choice in Montreal. In J. Gumperz (ed.) *Language and social identity* (pp. 108–118). Cambridge/New York: Cambridge University Press.

Heller, M. (1988) *Code-switching: Anthropological and sociolinguistic perspectives.* Berlin: Mouton de Gruyter.

Heller, M. (1992) The politics of codeswitching and language choice. *Journal of Multilingual and Multicultural Development* 13 (1/2), 123–142.

Heller, M. (1995a) Language choice, social institutions, and symbolic domination. *Language in Society* 24, 373–405.

Heller, M. (1995b) Code-switching and the politics of language. In L. Milroy and P. Muysken (eds) *One speaker, two languages: Cross-disciplinary perspectives on code-switching* (pp. 158–174). Cambridge/New York: Cambridge University Press.

Hoffman, D. (1989) Language and culture acquisition among Iranians in the United States. *Anthropology and Education Quarterly* 20, 118–132.

Husband, C. and Saifullah Khan, V. (1982) The viability of ethnolinguistic vitality: Some creative doubts. *Journal of Multilingual and Multicultural Development* 3 (3), 193–205.

Jacobson, R. (ed.) (1998) *Codeswitching worldwide.* Berlin/New York: Mouton de Gruyter.

Johnstone, B. (1996) *The linguistic individual: Self-expression in language and linguistics.* New York/Oxford: Oxford University Press.

Kim, Y. (1988) *Communication and cross-cultural adaptation: An integrative theory.* Clevedon: Multilingual Matters.

Kim, Y. (1996) Identity development: From culture to intercultural. In H. Mokros (ed.) *Interaction and identity* (pp. 347–369). New Brunswick, NJ: Transaction Books.

Le Page, R. and Tabouret-Keller, A. (1985) *Acts of identity: Creole-based approaches to language and ethnicity.* Cambridge/New York: Cambridge University Press.

Li Wei (1998) Banana split? Variations in language choice and code-switching patterns of two groups of British-born Chinese in Tyneside. In R. Jacobson (ed.) *Codeswitching worldwide* (pp. 153–175). Berlin/New York: Mouton de Gruyter.

Lo, A. (1999) Codeswitching, speech community membership, and the construction of ethnic identity. *Journal of Sociolinguistics* 4 (3), 461–479.

May, S. (2001) *Language and minority rights: Ethnicity, nationalism, and the politics of language.* London: Longman.

McNamara, T. (1987) Language and social identity: Israelis abroad. *Journal of Language and Social Psychology* 6 (3/4), 215–228.

McNamara, T. (1997) What do we mean by social identity? Competing frameworks, competing discourses. *TESOL Quarterly* 31 (3), 561–567.

McKay, S. and Wong, S. (1996) Multiple discourses, multiple identities: Investment and agency in second-language learning among Chinese adolescent immigrant students. *Harvard Educational Review* 66 (3), 577–608.

Meir, G. (1975) *My life.* New York: Dell.

Myers-Scotton, C. (1998) Structural uniformities vs. community differences in codeswitching. In R. Jacobson (ed.) *Codeswitching worldwide* (pp. 91–108). Berlin/New York: Mouton de Gruyter.

Noels, K., Pon, G., and Clément, R. (1996) Language, identity, and adjustment: The role of linguistic self-confidence in the acculturation process. *Journal of Language and Social Psychology* 15 (3), 246–264.

Norton Peirce, B. (1995). Social identity, investment, and language learning. *TESOL Quarterly* 29 (1), 9–31.

Norton, B. (2000) *Identity and language learning: Gender, ethnicity, and educational change*. London: Longman.

Pavlenko, A. (1998) Second language learning by adults: Testimonies of bilingual writers. *Issues in Applied Linguistics* 9, (1) 3–19.

Pavlenko, A. (2000) Access to linguistic resources: Key variable in second language learning. *Estudios de Sociolinguistica* 1 (2), 85–105.

Pavlenko, A. (2001) 'In the world of the tradition I was unimagined': Negotiation of identities in cross-cultural autobiographies. *International Journal of Bilingualism* 5 (3), 317–344.

Pavlenko, A. (2002) Poststructuralist approaches to the study of social factors in second language learning and use. In V. Cook (ed.) *Portraits of the L2 user* (pp. 277–302). Clevedon: Multilingual Matters.

Pavlenko, A. and Blackledge, A. (eds) (2001) Negotiation of identities in multilingual contexts: Special issue. *International Journal of Bilingualism* 5 (3).

Piller, I. (2001) Identity constructions in multilingual advertising. *Language in Society* 30, 153–186.

Rampton, B. (1995) *Crossing: Language and ethnicity among adolescents*. London: Longman.

Rampton, B. (1999a) Styling the Other: Thematic issue. *Journal of Sociolinguistics* 3 (4).

Rampton, B. (1999b) Styling the Other: Introduction. *Journal of Sociolinguistics* 3 (4), 421–427.

Ricoeur, P. (1988) *Time and narrative III* (Kathleen Blarney and David Pellauer, trans.). Chicago, IL: University of Chicago Press.

Schmidt, R. (1983) Interaction, acculturation, and the acquisition of communicative competence: A case study of an adult. In N. Wolfson and E. Judd (eds) *Sociolinguistics and language acquisition* (pp. 137–174). Rowley, MA: Newbury House Publishers.

Schumann, J. (1986) Research on the acculturation model for second language acquisition. *Journal of Multilingual and Multicultural Development* 7 (5), 379–392.

Scotton, C. (1983) The negotiation of identities in conversation: A theory of markedness and code choice. *Journal of the Sociology of Language* 44, 115–136.

Scotton, C. (1988) Codeswitching as indexical of social negotiations. In M. Heller (ed.) *Codeswitching: Anthropological and sociolinguistic perspectives* (pp. 151–186). Berlin/New York: Mouton de Gruyter.

Skutnabb-Kangas, T. and Phillipson, R. (eds) (1995) *Linguistic human rights: Overcoming linguistic discrimination*. Berlin/New York: Mouton de Gruyter.

Stroud, C. (2002) Framing Bourdieu socioculturally: Alternative forms of linguistic legitimacy in postcolonial Mozambique. *Multilingua* 21 (2/3), 247–274.

Syed, Z. and A. Burnett, (1999) Acculturation, identity, and language: Implications for language minority education. In K. Davis (ed.) *Foreign language teaching and language minority education* (Technical report N 19) (pp. 41–63). Honolulu: University of Hawaii, Second Language Teaching and Curriculum Center.

Tabouret-Keller, A. (1997) Language and identity. In F. Coulmas (ed.) *The handbook of sociolinguistics* (pp. 315–326). Oxford: Blackwell.

Tajfel, H. (1974) Social identity and intergroup behavior. *Social Science Information* 13, 65–93.

Tajfel, H. (1981) *Human groups and social categories*. Cambridge: Cambridge University Press.

Tannen, D. (1993) The relativity of linguistic strategies: Rethinking power and solidarity in gender and dominance. In D. Tannen (ed.) *Gender and conversational interaction* (pp. 165–188). New York/Oxford: Oxford University Press.

Ting-Toomey, S. (1999) *Communicating across cultures*. New York: Guilford Press.

Treffers-Daller, J. (1992) French–Dutch codeswitching in Brussels: Social factors explaining its disappearance. *Journal of Multilingual and Multicultural Development* 13, 143–156.

Weedon, C. (1987) *Feminist practice and poststructuralist theory*. London: Blackwell.

Williams, G. (1992) *Sociolinguistics: A sociological critique*. London: Routledge.

Woolard, K. (1985) Language variation and cultural hegemony: Towards an integration of sociolinguistic and social theory. *International Journal of the Sociology of Language* 66, 85–98.

Woolard, K. (1989) *Double talk: Bilingualism and the politics of ethnicity in Catalonia*. Stanford: Stanford University Press.

Woolard, K. (1998) Introduction: Language ideology as a field of inquiry. In B. Schieffelin, K. Woolard and P. Kroskrity (eds) *Language ideologies: Practice and theory* (pp. 3–47). New York/Oxford: Oxford University Press.

Chapter 1

'The Making of an American'[1]: Negotiation of Identities at the Turn of the Twentieth Century

ANETA PAVLENKO

Introduction

In the past decades, narratives and, in particular, stories people tell about their lives, have gained increasing stature outside the fields of literature and folklore and have become the focus of the evolving inter-disciplinary field of narrative study, which posited narrative as the central means by which people construct identities and give their lives meaning across time. Consequently, scholars in a variety of disciplines expressed new interest in autobiographies as a unique, 'rich and unsurpassed resource for an understanding of the inward experience of how social and individual forces may interact' (Sollors, 1990: xi). The fields of second language acquisition (SLA) and bilingualism are no exception to this trend: lately, several researchers have turned to stories people tell about their language learning and use (Kramsch & Lam, 1999; Pavlenko, 1998, 2001a,b,c; Pavlenko & Lantolf, 2000; Schumann, 1997; Tse, 2000; see also Kinginger, this volume). All of these investigations, however, examined contemporary stories, either published or elicited by the researchers. The goal of the present study is to see how sociohistoric circumstances impact ways in which people view the relationship between their languages and identities and construct their language learning stories. In order to answer this question, I will examine negotiation of identities in a corpus of narratives that has not previously been discussed in the field: immi-grant autobiographies from the turn of the twentieth century. I will then compare narrative identities negotiated in this corpus to the ones constructed and negotiated in cross-cultural memoirs published in the past two decades.

In what follows, I will first introduce the theoretical framework and methodological approaches to narrative inquiry adopted in the present investigation. Then, I will examine which identities were negotiated in early-twentieth-century immigrant narratives. I will argue that these memoirs differ from contemporary immigrant autobiographies as far as the relationship between language and identity is concerned, and will attempt to explain the differences through ideologies of language and identity dominant in the early twentieth century. In doing so, I will show how sociopolitical, sociohistoric, and sociolinguistic circumstances shape individuals' understandings of themselves and their relationships with the languages in their environment.

Theoretical Framework

The theoretical framework adopted in the present paper is situated at the nexus of critical and poststructuralist theories (Anderson, 1991; Bourdieu, 1991; Weedon, 1987), with the focus on autobiography and narrative identity construction (Green, 2001; Hokenson, 1995). In this perspective, identity is viewed as a dynamic and shifting nexus of multiple subject positions, or identity options, such as mother, accountant, heterosexual, or Latina. At various points in history different societies make somewhat distinct identity options available to their members (for instance, being anything but heterosexual may not be a legitimate option in some societies). Furthermore, at different times these options are negotiable to a different degree. Narrative identities, constructed in fiction and non-fiction writing, often emerge as reactions to available identity options, reproducing some and rejecting or reimagining others. Autobiographies play a central role in the process of identity negotiation in writing, as they are a prime example of 'identity narratives,' i.e. 'narratives constructed or construed as statements about the identity of the speaker and perhaps about the community of which she or he is a member' (Green, 2001: 8).

The focus of the present paper is on narrative identities constructed in American immigrant autobiographies, i.e. memoirs written by first generation immigrants who had arrived in the US as children or adults and who discuss the story of their assimilation. The aim of the paper is to examine sociohistoric constraints on these identity narratives and, consequently, on immigrant identity options seen as 'imaginable' or 'negotiable' in the US at the turn of the century. To explore ways in which European immigrants used the genre of autobiography to imagine and legitimize new identities for themselves and fellow immigrants, I will draw on Anderson's (1991) notion of nation-states as imagined communities. This notion is particularly apt for discussions of the encounter between new arrivals and the country they had imagined and in which they now had to imagine themselves. In addition to the notion of imagination, I will also appeal to Bourdieu's (1991) concept of speaking rights that will allow me to analyze which new immigrants had 'the right to speak' and the right 'to impose reception' in the process of identity negotiation. Finally, to explain why turn-of-the-twentieth-century immigrant memoirs may depict second language learning and the relationship between language and identity differently from contemporary cross-cultural autobiographies, I will resort to a sociohistoric analysis of the circumstances in which the two sets of narratives were produced and to a rhetorical analysis of tropes and narrative plots available to early- and late-twentieth-century immigrant autobiographers. I will argue that history has a profound impact on identity stories, not only in terms of material, social, and political circumstances in which they take place, but also in terms of ideologies of language and identity dominant in a particular place and time and in terms of identity options considered negotiable, legitimate, or particularly desirable.

Methodology and Research Questions

The present study will analyze 11 full-length immigrant memoirs and one collection of essay-length immigrant autobiographies. The memoirs were published between the years of 1901 and 1935 and written by (or in case of Holt's (1906) volume, collected from) immigrants who had arrived in the US between 1870 and 1913, mainly during the Great Migration wave. While many other memoirs were published at the time, I chose the autobiographies below on the grounds of representativeness and visibility. In other words, I aimed to include memoirs that were well known and widely discussed at the time of publication. In order to offset the bias of focusing exclusively on narratives of successful middle- and upper-middle-class professionals, I also chose to analyze an edited collection which contains autobiographies of working-class immigrants from a variety of backgrounds (Holt, 1906). Below, I list the memoirs in the corpus in the chronological order in which they were originally published. To facilitate subsequent discussion, I offer a brief commentary on each author's ethnic, social, and linguistic background.

(1) Riis, J. (1901) *The making of an American*. Born in 1849 in a middle-class family in Denmark, Jacob Riis emigrated to the US in 1870. In 1873, after

a series of jobs in the shipyards and in the ironworks, he became an editor of a weekly paper in Long Island City and, in 1878, a police reporter for the *New York Tribune* (Holte, 1988). His articles, dramatic photographs, and books, in particular the widely-acclaimed *How the other half lives* (1890), exposed the impoverished conditions under which immigrant workers labored and lived in the urban slums. Riis also led a number of urban renewal projects which positively transformed some of the communities described in his work. His autobiography was immensely popular at the time of appearance and went through 12 editions in seven years, even though some reviewers criticized its writing style and the amount of self-praise (Holte, 1988; Hutner, 1999).

(2) Antin, M. (1912) *The Promised Land.* Mary Antin, a Russian Jew from the small town of Polotzk, arrived in Boston in 1891 at the age of 10, fluent in Yiddish, Hebrew, and Russian. She soon distinguished herself as a good student, a writer, and a poet, and published her first account of her journey in 1899 with a preface by Israel Zangwill. *The Promised Land,* her best-known memoir, met with an enthusiastic reception and sold 85,000 copies in 34 printings (Handlin, 1969). Afterwards, Antin spent several years giving public lectures on Americanization all over the US and received many literary and civic honors (Hutner, 1999).

(3) Steiner, E. (1914) *From alien to citizen: The story of my life in America.* Edward Steiner was born in 1866 in Slovakia, in a multilingual German-Jewish family. He arrived in the US in the late 1880s as a well-educated young man who, in his student days, visited Tolstoy in his estate in Yasnaya Polyana. For several years Steiner travelled around the US, working with immigrants wherever his journey took him. His budding interest in Christianity and knowledge of Judaism brought him to a seminary at Oberlin College, Ohio. Eventually, he converted to Christianity and became first a minister, and then a professor at Grinnell College, Iowa. Steiner put a lot of time and energy into the study of immigration, publishing 15 books on the topic.

(4) Ravage, M.E. (1917) *An American in the making: The life story of an immigrant.* Marcus Ravage, a multilingual Romanian Jew, arrived in New York City in 1900 as a young man. He tried a number of occupations and eventually graduated from Missouri State University. As a public figure, Ravage participated in numerous debates on immigration.

(5) Bok, E. (1921) *The Americanization of Edward Bok: The autobiography of a Dutch boy fifty years after.* Edward Bok arrived in the US from Netherlands in 1870 at the age of six together with his upper-middle-class family.

At the age of 13 he quit school to work as an office boy at the Western Union Telegraph Company. While working there, he wrote for several magazines and in 1884 became the editor of *Brooklyn Magazine*. In 1889 he was appointed the editor of the *Ladies' Home Journal* and remained in that position for 30 years, becoming one of the most influential journalists in the United States. His autobiography won the Pulitzer Prize for biography in 1921 and went through over 30 editions in four years (Holte, 1988).

(6) Panunzio, C. (1921) *The soul of an immigrant*. Born in southern Italy in 1885, Constantine Panunzio arrived in the US in 1902 as a sailor. Three years later he went to Maine Wesleyan Seminary, then to Wesleyan University, and then to Boston University School of Theology. Just before the First World War, he converted to Methodism, became ordained as a minister, and worked in several eastern cities as a mediator between Italian immigrants and surrounding communities. He went on to become a professor of sociology at the University of California and was honored at the 1939–1940 New York World's Fair as a foreign-born citizen who had made outstanding contributions to American culture (Hutner, 1999).

(7) Yezierska, A. (1925) *Bread givers*. A Jew, born in Russian Poland, Anzia Yezierska disembarked at Ellis Island at the age of eight in 1890. She left home at the age of 17 and worked in sweatshops and laundries while going to school and then university. In 1915 she began publishing short stories about immigrant life in the Lower East Side, the struggle against poverty, and Jewish women's experience of reconciling the New World with the Old. Her first collection was made into a Hollywood film which brought her wealth and fame. She went on to publish more stories and several novels until the topic went out of vogue in the 1940s and 1950s.

(8) Cahan, A. (1926) *The education of Abraham Cahan*. Abraham Cahan, a revolutionary Jewish refugee from tsarist Russia, landed in Philadelphia in 1882 at the age of 22. He is best known for founding in 1897 the *Jewish Daily Forward*, a popular Yiddish newspaper which he edited for the rest of his life. Cahan also gained respect as a writer, in both Yiddish and English, in particular for the acclaimed novel *The rise of David Levinsky* (1917). He publicly criticized Riis's 'other half' approach that, in his view, unnecessarily otherized and exoticized the incoming immigrants, in particular Eastern European Jews.

(9) Bartholdt, R. (1930) *From steerage to Congress: Reminiscences and reflections*. Richard Bartholdt arrived in the US from Germany in 1872, at the age of 17; he spoke German, English, French, and a smattering of other languages. A few weeks after landing in New York City he was already

working in a Brooklyn printing office. Eight years later he was a legislative correspondent in Albany, New York, for a German-American newspaper. In 1892, he became a Congressional representative from Missouri, the first German-American to become a member of Congress. He retired from Congress in 1915. Even though earlier Bartholdt had planned to run for Senate, the First World War and resulting anti-German feelings killed this ambition.

(10) Adamic, L. (1932) *Laughing in the jungle: The autobiography of an immigrant in America*. Louis Adamic arrived in the US from Slovenia in 1913 at the age of 14. He started out working for a Slovenian newspaper, *Narodni Glas (People's Voice)*. Later, he became a journalist and a writer, authoring a number of books on various social issues and participating vigorously in public debates on assimilation and Americanization.

(11) Nielsen, T. (1935) *How a Dane became an American, or Hits and misses of my life*. Nielsen came to the US from Denmark in 1890 at the age of 15, along with his brother and father. The family joined relatives in a little town in Iowa where Nielsen went to school. Eventually, he graduated from Cornell College, married an American woman and became an English-speaking Methodist minister, giving up the Lutheran faith and his native language, which aroused strong resentment from the local Danish community.

(12) Holt, H. (1906/1990) *The life stories of undistinguished Americans (as told by themselves)*. These stories first appeared separately in Holt's newspaper *The Independent*. Then a representative selection of the life stories was published together as a collection.

The methodology chosen to analyze the texts is informed by Denzin's (1989) sociohistorical approach to the study of personal narratives, which sees autobiography as a 'literary and sociological form that creates particular images of subjects in particular historical moments' (p. 35). This approach leads me to consider personal narratives not simply as ethnographic data, subject to content analysis, but rather as a genre which is shaped by local contexts, as well as by social, historical, cultural, and linguistic influences. Thus, I will look not only at the content of the stories, but also at the sociohistorical contexts in which the narratives were created, at the ideological forces which shaped particular tellings, as well as particular silences and omissions, and, finally, at the voices which were – and weren't – being heard. Current literary scholarship also acknowledges that autobiographies produced in different literary traditions may be very distinct in shape and scope (Hokenson, 1995; Wong, 1991). Several authors who compared personal narratives written and published in English in the US with those constructed in other languages and for other audiences – even though at times by the same authors – found that these stories have different storylines and different foci, and are performed through distinct linguistic means (Pavlenko, 2001a; Taubenfeld, 1998; Wong, 1991; Yin, 1998). Consequently, the arguments in the present paper will be limited to the corpus of narratives written and published in English in the US in the early twentieth century.

Three questions will be asked in the present study: (1) which identities were negotiated in the immigrant narratives in the corpus; (2) what is the role of language and linguistic identities in these narratives; and (3) whether portrayals of second language learning and use in the early twentieth century narratives differ from those in contemporary immigrant autobiographies.

Negotiation of Identities in Immigrant Memoirs

'The making of an American'

Consistent with the theoretical and methodological framework of the study, prior to analyzing the narratives, I will discuss the sociohistoric context which shaped the life trajectories of their authors. In the 44 years between 1880 and 1924, often termed the Great Migration, approximately 24 million immigrants entered the United States (US Bureau of the Census, 1975). The vast majority of these immigrants came from Southern and Eastern Europe. These new arrivals were often negatively compared to 'old immigrants,' who came to the US prior to 1880s, predominantly from Northern Europe, and were perceived to be relatively assimilable. In contrast, the 'new immigrants' were considered distinct from the mainstream Anglo population ethnically, culturally, and linguistically, with differences often described in terms of racial, intellectual, and moral inferiority. The overwhelming influx of new arrivals raised numerous concerns about national unity and the capacity of American society to assimilate such a large body of newcomers, leading to national anxiety as to what was meant by 'We the People of the Unites States' (Boelhower, 1991). These concerns resulted in a search for new means of ensuring social cohesion and fashioning national identity. The resulting movement, which aimed to assimilate immigrants through instruction in English, civics, and oftentimes personal hygiene, eventually became known as Americanization. While a more detailed discussion of Americanization of

European immigrants can be found elsewhere (cf. Hartmann, 1948; Weiss, 1982), the present paper will examine how negotiation of who is to become an American and on what terms took place in immigrant autobiographies.

Anderson (1991), Boelhower (1991), and Green (2001) underscore the key role literary texts play in the identitary project, i.e. the creation of the 'national text,' which aims to impose and preserve a particular version of the nation's collective experience. Thus, it is not surprising that, among other projects which promoted Americanization, the country's leaders strongly encouraged publication of immigrant memoirs, which served as testaments of the authors' thorny yet successful paths toward assimilation. Over the years, numerous immigrant authors responded to the call of times, producing Americanization stories which aimed to justify immigration in the face of a rising sentiment for restriction, to inspire fellow immigrants, to educate mainstream America (while being accepted by it), and to contribute to the ongoing national identity project. Some authors explicitly acknowledged the fact that their work responded to sociopolitical demands and concerns of the time. Thus, Constantine Panunzio (1921) revealed in his foreword that, while initially he was hoping to leave his humble beginnings behind, with the end of war

> and with the unprecedented way in which the American public has turned its attention to the all-important question of the assimilation of the immigrant, it became increasingly clear to me that I owed it to my adopted country to give the story to the public. (Panunzio, 1921: x)

Several prominent public figures aided in bringing this work – and the plight of the immigrants – to the public's attention. Thus, many of the memoirs in the corpus initially appeared as separate chapters in periodical publications – Riis's (1901) story in *The Outlook, The Churchman*, and *The Century Magazine*, and Antin's (1912) in *The Atlantic Monthly*. A prominent journalist, Hamilton Holt, made a concerted effort to publish interviews with recent immigrants in his newspaper, *The Independent*, and several other newspapers and periodicals published similar accounts (Sollors, 1990). The genre even inspired simulation and a writer, Broughton Brandenburg, wrote up a memoir, *Imported Americans* (1904), posing as an Italian immigrant (Sollors, 1990). Several of the memoirs, in particular work by Mary Antin, Edward Bok, Jacob Riis, and Anzia Yezierska, became immediate bestsellers. The fact that Yezierska's first book was made into a Hollywood movie brought additional recognition to the author and further raised the public's awareness of challenges faced by immigrants. Some of the authors, including Louis Adamic,

Mary Antin, and Constantine Panunzio, also became popular on the lecture circuit where they familiarized their audiences with immigrants' needs and concerns. Americanization brochures often included references to this body of literature, recommending the use of the memoirs for the purposes of teaching English and civics (cf. Bach, 1923; Roberts, 1920). Together, these facts suggest that, with the growing interest in the issues of immigration and assimilation in the first two decades of the century, immigrant memoirs were part of the mainstream literature, read and responded to by the general public.

What identities were negotiated in these memoirs? The analysis of the autobiographies in the corpus suggests that, in addressing the themes of immigration, readjustment, and assimilation, the authors engaged in renegotiation and reimagining of national, ethnic, cultural, gender, and sometimes even religious identities. Ethnic identities play a particularly prominent role in these autobiographies, since for many European arrivals ethnicity was a relatively new concept, oftentimes imposed on them by the new environment against their will. Some authors, like Panunzio (1921), recall ethnic slurs they experienced or witnessed and stereotypes they had to struggle against. In turn, Louis Adamic (1932) perceptively points out that America not only promotes stereotypes but in fact constructs ethnicity, with ethnic identification and self-identification being another outcome of the immigrant experience. Oftentimes, the identification is non-negotiable and first generation immigrants have no choice but to accept the label forced upon them. To give an example, Adamic brings up Slavic immigrants, who, in the old country, used to define themselves in terms of obscure provinces rather than nation-states, and in the new were often 'assigned' an ethnic label that was more familiar to their American interlocutors:

> If a Slovenian was asked what his nationality was, he very likely replied that he was a Kranjec or Krainer or Carniolan, from Kranjsko. . . . If he really knew what he was, he declared himself a Slovenian, but that, to the average American, Irishman, or Scandinavian, meant no more than Carniolan . . . before he was through explaining, presto! he was an 'Austrian'. (Adamic, 1932: 101)

Yet another experience common for many immigrants was that of modernization, industrialization, and urbanization, whereby previous peasants, villagers, and small-towners became urban dwellers. This transition also entailed new social identity options, which had to be understood, internalized, and inhabited. For instance, Marcus Ravage recalls that his community relied on a social dichotomy of 'intelligents' vs. 'clodpates,' which assigned distinct behaviors and values to the two characteristics:

> I continually heard people in the shop, and in the quarter generally, referred to as 'clodpates' and 'intelligents', and I knew that an intelligent was a person who went to lectures and read books and preferred tragedy to vaudeville, and looked upon America as a place which afforded one an opportunity to acquire and express ideas, while a clodpate cared more for dollars than for ideas. . . . I was already being classed as an intelligent among the hands at the shop. (Ravage, 1917: 153)

Not all identities were necessarily new or imposed – the immigration experience also offered a perfect chance to reject some subjectivities and allegiances seen as constraining. Both Antin's and Yezierska's stories describe a rebellion of young Jewish women against gender roles prescribed for them by Orthodox Judaism. Antin recalls that

> in the mediaeval position of the women of Polotzk education really had no place. A girl was 'finished' when she could read her prayers in Hebrew, following the meaning by the aid of the Yiddish translation especially prepared for women. (Antin, 1912: 111)

It is not surprising then that she was quite excited about joining her father in America, where, according to him, 'all the children, boys and girls, Jews and Gentiles, went to school' (Antin, 1912: 148). There, Antin longed for opportunities offered by the American womanhood:

> A long girlhood, a free choice in marriage, and a brimful womanhood are the precious rights of an American woman. (Antin, 1912: 277)

For some immigrants then, as for these Jewish women, assimilation also involved secularization. For others, it involved a change of a religious affiliation, often from a more marginal religious identity to a more mainstream one. Thus, Steiner (1914) abandoned Judaism to become a Protestant minister, while Panunzio (1921) and Nielsen (1935) gave up, respectively, Catholic and Lutheran faiths to become Methodist ministers. In his lectures, Steiner often framed his story as that of conversion and assimilation through faith, arguing that 'a Christian America could melt all people into one strong society' (Hutner, 1999: 169).

These and other authors also describe transformations of identity that take place in political, socioeconomic, and cultural realms, oftentimes involving names, appearance, clothing, values, and behavior. The main purpose of their books, however, is not merely to describe what they had seen or experienced with regard to their own and others' multiple identities. The key goal for early immigrant writers is to rewrite the American national identity narrative so that it would become available for appropriation. They do so by appealing to the dominant master trope of the time – that of the 'self-made-man.' Decker (1997) argues that, in the early twentieth century, the archetypal myth of a 'self-made man' became vital in the construction of American identity, linking national character and individual success. Consequently, American autobiography took a shape of a 'rags-to-riches' narrative à la Horatio Alger (Boelhower, 1991; Decker, 1997; Hokenson, 1995; Sollors, 1990). In contrast to earlier Protestant rhetoric of moral character and inner virtue, which privileged white middle-class Anglo-Saxon men, the new 'luck and pluck' plot was available for appropriation by women, immigrants, and racial minorities who managed to succeed in the marketplace. The analysis of the memoirs in the corpus demonstrates that, in order to position themselves as Americans, immigrant authors continuously appeal to the metaphors of individual uplift:

> I began to realize that, even with the serious handicap placed upon me by my foreign birth and lack of language, work would win; that I was, after all, the 'captain of my soul.' I really began to believe, what I had seriously questioned before, that if a 'foreigner' really tries to make good, recognition will come. (Panunzio, 1921: 171)

The 'self-made-man' rhetoric also appears in Antin's tract, *They who knock at our gates* (1914), where she uses the trope to write new immigrants into the canon of national character:

> There is a phrase in the American vocabulary of approval that sums up our national ideal of manhood. That phrase is 'a self-made man.' To such we pay the tribute of our highest admiration, justly regarding our self-made men as the noblest product of our democratic institutions. Now let any one compile a biographical dictionary of our self-made men, from the romantic age of our history down to the prosaic year of 1914, and see how the smell of the steerage pervades the volume! (Antin, 1914: 76)

The rags-to-riches formula is also manifested in recurrent descriptions of job interviews, employment opportunities, and advancement and, in particular, in a continuous bookkeeping urge reminiscent of Benjamin Franklin's memoirs (cf. Holt, 1906: 24, 54–58; Ravage, 1917: 227). The importance of financial success for realization of the American Dream was reinforced not only in public discourses of the time, but also in

Americanization materials and English textbooks which devoted numerous chapters to discussions of the virtue of thrift, to descriptions of banking and savings procedures, and to the planning of family budgets (cf. Beglinger, 1922).

Even the titles of the autobiographies in the corpus make the ritualistic nod toward the trope of 'self-making' and the narrative of 'luck and pluck': Riis's (1901) memoir is entitled *The making of an American*, Steiner's (1914) *From alien to citizen*, Ravage's (1917) *An American in the making*, Bok's (1921) *The Americanization of Edward Bok*, Nielsen's (1935) *How a Dane became an American*, and Bartholdt's (1930) *From steerage to Congress*. 'I was born, I have lived, and I have been made over' are the first words in Antin's (1912: xix) autobiography. And while some authors, like Bok (1921) or Riis (1901), simply position themselves as 'remade' Americans and tell their story, others offer an argument as to why they should be considered American. Thus, an Italian immigrant, Constantine Panunzio, poignantly states:

> I have now been in America for nineteen years; I have grown up here as much as any man can; I have had my education here; I have become a citizen; I have given all I had of youthful zeal and energy in serving my adopted country; I have come to love America as I do my very life – perhaps more and yet they still call me a 'foreigner.' (Panunzio, 1921: 328)

Notably, these narratives are not written simply as an enthusiastic monologic pledge of allegiance, which reaffirms an American identity and tries to sneak in a few Eastern European Jews and Italians who 'transformed themselves' into Anglo-Saxons. While, as will be shown later, some narratives do exhibit an implicit belief in Anglo-Saxon superiority, the immigrant authors in the corpus use their mastery of the key tropes of American autobiography not only to demonstrate the efficacy of the 'melting-pot' success, but also to revise the national identity narrative, to create space for 'new Americans,' and to bring in new cultural scenarios, typically taking place outside of the normative American space and unfamiliar to the general reader (Boelhower, 1991). In doing so, they appeal to yet another popular American trope, the opposition of the Old and the New World. Thus, in proclaiming their rights to the designation of an American, these authors offer their own understanding of what makes an American and what differentiates Americans from the inhabitants of other countries. Some, like Richard Bartholdt, point out that the newly emerged American does not have to be made in an Anglo-Saxon mold:

America cannot be made Anglo-Saxon any more that it can be made Irish, German, French, or Italian. We must cultivate a type of our own, the American type . . . and no one race should be allowed to be the sole judge of what is good and what is evil. (Bartholdt, 1930: 85)

Other authors problematize a superficial view of Americanization as a 'two-hundred-hour course' (Panunzio, 1921: 184) or 'an affair of a rubber stamp and an oath of allegiance and bath tubs' (Ravage, 1917: 137). Panunzio suggests that America cannot content itself

by delegating to a few hundred public school teachers the enormous task of transforming fourteen millions of 'foreigners' into Americans, a task which belongs to the whole citizenry. (Panunzio, 1921: 184)

In turn, Bartholdt (1930) points to a coercive and ultimately futile nature of such an enterprise and instead tries to present Americanization not as a task, but as a process that involves all citizens. Edward Bok also suggests that it is the American-born who may be in need of insight and reform, while Marcus Ravage argues that immigrants are the truest Americans of all:

One fundamental trouble with the present desire for Americanization is that the American is anxious to Americanize two classes – if he is a reformer, the foreign-born; if he is an employer, his employees. It never occurs to him that he himself may be in need of American-ization. (Bok, 1921: 445)

It is the free American who needs to be instructed by the benighted races in the uplifting word that America speaks to all the world. Only from the humble immigrant, it appears to me, can he learn just what America stands for in the family of nations. The alien must know this, for he alone seems ready to pay the heavy price for his share of America. . . . Yes, we immigrants have a real claim on America. Every one of us who did not grow faint-hearted at the start of the battle and has stuck it out has earned a share in America by the ancient right of conquest. (Ravage, 1917: ix, xii)

And, just as they are critical of mainstream America's desire to assim-ilate the immigrant into the Anglo-Saxon mold, these authors are also disapproving of their compatriots who adopt new values and behaviors wholesale. Rather than being enthusiastic about the speedy assimilation of their countrymen and women, Cahan (1926) points to the losses involved in the process, while Ravage (1917) ridicules such behavior as a 'degeneration':

> Even their names had become emasculated and devoid of either char-
> acter or meaning. Mordecai – a name full of romantic association –
> had been changed to the insipid monosyllable Max. . . . Whole battal-
> ions of people were called Joe; the Harrys alone could have
> repopulated Vaslui; and of Morrises there was no end. With the
> women-folks matters went even worse. It did not seem to matter
> at all what one had been called at home. The first step towards
> Americanization was to fall into one or the other of the two great
> tribes of Rosies and Annies. This distressing transformation, I discov-
> ered before long, went very much deeper than occupation and the
> externals of fashion. It pervaded every chamber of their life. . . . Good
> manners and good conduct, reverence and religion, had all gone by
> the board, and the reason was that these things were not American.
> (Ravage, 1917: 78–79)

These arguments show that early immigrant writers were not
uncritically accepting of the America they encountered; on the contrary,
their narratives demonstrate a complex interplay of consent and dissent
(Sollors, 1986). How successful were these authors in negotiating
membership in the new community or, in Bourdieu's (1991) terms, in
'imposing reception'? In view of the differences in positioning of 'old' and
'new immigrants,' it is not surprising that Northern Europeans led among
those who managed to be heard, to enlist support from public figures for
their causes, and to become visible as 'exemplary Americans.' Three of
the authors in the present corpus, Richard Bartholdt, Edward Bok, and
Jacob Riis, count American president Theodore Roosevelt among their
personal friends. Riis and Roosevelt had met in 1890, after the publication of Riis's revolutionary book, *How the other half lives* (1890), which
brought attention to the horror of life in New York slums. Shortly after
the book was published, Riis received a scrawled note from Roosevelt,
who then served as the city police commissioner: 'I have read your book,
and I have come to help' (Crichton, 1998). Crichton (1998: 126) states that,
before his term with the city was over, 'Roosevelt has come to see Riis
as "the most useful citizen in America," and Riis had acquired enormous
respect and affection for the reform-minded police commissioner.' Many
years later, Roosevelt said the following about Riis in an issue of *The
Outlook*, published on June 6, 1914:

> He did not come to this country until he was almost a young man;
> but if I were asked to name a fellow-man who came nearest to being
> the ideal American citizen, I should name Jacob Riis. (Roosevelt, in
> Riis, 1901/1961: xi)

Riis, Bok, and Bartholdt are not the only ones, however, who managed to capture the public imagination and Roosevelt's attention. Antin's (1912) and Yezierska's (1925) work turned out to be equally, if not more, successful in appealing to the masses. Louis Brandeis noted that Antin's (1912) message rekindled the latent patriotism in many a native American (Handlin, 1969: vii); later on, Antin also managed to help convert Roosevelt to the cause of women's suffrage. Thus, we can see that, as individuals, some, if not all, of the authors in the present corpus were extremely successful, with Mary Antin, Edward Bok, and Jacob Riis lauded by the press as exemplary American citizens who inspired fellow immigrants and raised patriotic feelings in the American-born. The authors' key achievement, however, is not the individual one – it is the fact that they had made the American national identity negotiable for other European immigrants, turning the United States from an Anglo-Saxon into 'an immigrant nation.'

Clearly, most of first generation and at times even second generation European immigrants were not as successful in being accepted by mainstream America and continued to live in what were seen as 'foreign' or 'ethnic' enclaves. At the same time, they now had a blueprint of an identity narrative at their disposal to which they could appeal in their quest for a place in the United States. In contrast, thousands of immigrants from various parts of Asia, who settled in the US at the same time, were not considered eligible for American citizenship and, as a result, were segregated from the mainstream of American social and economic life. In light of this racial bias, it is not surprising that the corpus does not contain any identity memoirs by Asian authors. As Kim (1982) points out, early Asian immigrants did not see the American culture as something that belonged to them and to which they could contribute. Moreover, in many Asian cultures autobiographical writing was virtually unknown, since for a scholar to write a book about himself would be considered egotistical in the extreme (Kim, 1982). Consequently, while a few autobiographies written by Chinese and Japanese authors were published at the time, they did not engage in identity negotiation along the lines described above – instead, the authors aimed to educate the general public about life in their home country (cf. Wing, 1909; see also Hutner, 1999; Kim, 1982). In Bourdieu's (1991) terms then, not all immigrants had 'the right to speak': while European arrivals were 'allowed' to make a bid for an American identity, immigrants from racial minority groups were notably absent from the negotiation process.

The analysis of the narratives also underscores the inequities existing between immigrants from Northern Europe and Eastern and Southern

Europeans. Professionally successful Northern Europeans from Denmark (Nielsen, Riis), or the Netherlands (Bok), who arrived in the US between 1870 and 1890 as a part of the 'old migration,' did not see the need to establish or argue their Americanness – they simply told the reader that this was who they were. An intriguing exception here is Richard Bartholdt (1930). While his initial political career attests to a high degree of social acceptance, this acceptance of Bartholdt and other German-Americans came to an end, at least temporarily, when the anti-German movement during and after the First World War challenged the legitimacy of hyphenated Americans (Luebke, 1974, 1980; Pavlenko, 2002; Wiley, 1998). His memoir is an attempt to re-establish this legitimacy and to argue that a hyphenated American can nevertheless be a valuable citizen. Similarly, Eastern European Jews (Antin, Cahan, Ravage, Steiner, Yezierska), a Slovenian (Adamic) and an Italian (Panunzio), who had come to the US between 1882 and 1913 as a part of the 'new migration,' felt the need to explain to the general public what made them and fellow immigrants American.

In sum, the analysis of the autobiographies in the corpus suggests that the main goal of immigrant memoirs, published in the US in the first quarter of the twentieth century, was to inscribe European immigrants into the American national identity narrative. The authors managed to do so by appealing to two dominant tropes of the time. The rhetoric of individual achievement allowed them to position themselves and fellow immigrants as legitimate Americans who achieved this status by 'luck and pluck.' In turn, the opposition between the Old and the New World allowed them to contest the Anglo-Saxonization of the American national identity and to argue for new approaches to Americanness that would be closer to the forefathers' vision. With time, narratives of successful assimilation created by Riis (1901), Antin (1912), and Bok (1921) became 'the immigrant canon' and images of enthusiastic voluntary Americanization displaced other, more problematic and ambivalent, narratives that depicted Americanization as an enforced and coercive process (cf. Bartholdt, 1930). They also obscured racial inequities in American identity politics and the fact that the immigrant myth applied only to Europeans. In other words, the national identity at the time was negotiable for European immigrants (more so for Northern Europeans), but non-negotiable for members of racial minorities. The analysis of the memoirs in the corpus also shows that negotiation of identities was discussed by the authors in terms of national, as well as ethnic, gender, cultural, and religious identities, but rarely if ever in terms of language. Considering the fact that English was seen as the key to assimilation then

– just as it is now – this omission is intriguing. Consequently, in what follows I will examine how linguistic identities were constructed in the immigrant narratives in the corpus.

Individual language learning trajectories

Steiner (1914: 173) terms English the most vital force in the process of Americanization, one that 'is not foisted upon the stranger by any official decree, but which has back of it a still greater compulsion.' How, then, is the learning of English discussed in the memoirs in the corpus? To begin with, with the exception of Antin's (1912) and Ravage's (1917) memoirs, the references to language learning are few and far between. Riis (1901) does not devote more than two or three sentences to the fact that he had to study English to transform himself from a Danish carpenter into an American writer and journalist. It is only from Nielsen (1935) that we find out that, in his later years, the Great Dane, Riis, still had a Danish accent. Yezierska (1925), so intent on preserving the colorful vernacular of her characters, acknowledges that her protagonist had to study English, but does not describe when and how the learning took place. Others make brief and often joking references to the challenges posed by English. In other words, while they provide lengthy discussions of the protagonists' negotiation of political, social, and economic realities of American life, immigrant authors in the corpus rarely discuss the intricacies of mastering English grammar, pronunciation, or rules of politeness.

If depicted at all, second language learning is portrayed as an enterprise which proceeds through a series of comic blunders to a happy conclusion. Thus, Ravage states tongue-in-cheek that his acquisition process started out with a purchase of a dictionary:

> As it was my purpose to learn the whole English language and nothing less, I meant to start at the letter A and proceed alphabetically right through to the end. . . . But when I beheld that bulky volume, and found on the title-page something about thirty thousand words, my enthusiasm got a little chilled. I had never realized that Americans were so loquacious. (Ravage, 1917: 104)

Nevertheless, the protagonist perseveres in memorizing words, reading the Bible and the newspapers, and interacting with his native and non-native interlocutors. In fact, he soon starts offering English lessons to the less accomplished and fortunate. Then, he goes off to college in Missouri and there realizes that, despite his native-like pronunciation and significant ease with writing, his English 'was still the very grammatical and very clumsy book-English of the foreigner' (Ravage, 1917: 220). Marcus also sees that the stories and jokes he tries to tell fall flat, because of subtle shades of meaning that still escape him, and that his colloquial and idiomatic vocabulary is rather impoverished compared to that of his jolly and vivacious Midwestern friends, who 'had command of a whole vast and varied vocabulary of which not a trace could be found in any dictionary, no matter how diligently I searched' (Ravage, 1917: 222). Eventually, however, through the friendship with his college classmates, he masters the skills of convivial self-expression and ends his memoir on a high note:

> I had become one of them. I was not a man without a country. I was an American. (Ravage, 1917: 266)

An even more rapid and much more romanticized trajectory is depicted in Antin's (1912) autobiography. This optimistic narrative portrays a happy immigrant child, hungry for education, who welcomes the educational and linguistic challenge offered by the public school and produces her first literary essay after only four months of English instruction. After that, Mary, supported by an open-minded father, a caring family, and an array of adoring teachers, proceeds to win multiple prizes, kudos, and acclaim for her poems and essays in a newly acquired language. Her celebratory account ends in an appropriately star-spangled fashion:

> And I am the youngest of America's children, and into my hands is given all her priceless heritage. . . . Mine is the whole majestic past, and mine is the shining future. (Antin, 1912: 364)

While other autobiographers in the corpus are more reticent when it comes to discussions of learning English, the stories they do tell strongly resemble Antin's (1912) and Ravage's (1917) narratives in the speed of acquisition and in its successful outcome. With little variation, the learning trajectory described proceeds from the purchase of a dictionary, to the reading of shopsigns, billboards, newspapers, and magazines, to the Bible and literary texts (Adamic, 1932; Cahan, 1926; Nielsen, 1935; Panunzio, 1921; Steiner, 1914). Bok (1921) mentions that he learned English through immersion in a public school; others, including Steiner (1914), Ravage (1917), and Adamic (1932), note that they briefly attended evening schools. Antin (1912), Panunzio (1921), Ravage (1917), Steiner (1914), Yezierska (1925), and Nielsen (1935) also give some credit to their college experiences, which allowed them to further polish their linguistic abilities. In fact, it appears that language learning proceeds successfully for all, regardless of the environment and oftentimes thanks to the efforts of relatives, friends, and acquaintances. Thus, Panunzio (1921) takes private lessons from a grade school teacher, Miss Richmond, Adamic (1932) is helped by the three children of his landlords, Riis (1901: 25) in his 'observations on the American language' finds 'a volunteer assistant in Julia, the pretty bare-footed daughter of a coal-miner,' while Ravage (1917) recalls grumpy assistance offered to him by fellow immigrants.

One may point out that it is not surprising that immigrant children and adults who had the advantage of comprehensive education and middle-class upbringing were successful in learning English. Interestingly, language learning is also portrayed as a successful enterprise by Panunzio (1921) and Ravage (1917), born in small European villages, and by working-class immigrants whose stories were collected by Holt (1906). There, an anonymous Lithuanian worker states, four years after his arrival in America:

> I help the [union] movement by being an interpreter for the other Lithuanians who come in. That is why I have learned to speak and write good English. The others do not need me long. They soon learn English, too, and when they have done that they are quickly becoming Americans. (Holt, 1906: 20)

Similarly, a young Polish girl, a worker in a sweatshop, proudly acknowledges:

> For the last two winters I have been going to night school. I have learned reading, writing, and arithmetic. I can read quite well in English now and I look at the newspapers every day. I read English books, too, sometimes. (Holt, 1906: 27)

A Greek peddler complains that his boss didn't want him to learn English, so, instead, he asked his relatives in Greece to send him a Greek–English dictionary:

> when it came I studied it all the time and in three months I could speak English quite well. (Holt, 1906: 45)

The acquisition process appears to be similarly fast for the Swedish farmer:

> I studied English coming out on the vessel, but I was here six months before I could speak it well. (Holt, 1906: 58–59)

The narrative of second language learning as a speedy enterprise is not limited to the stories in the corpus – it can also be encountered in newspaper articles published in the 1920s and in the accounts of Americanization professionals and educators eager to celebrate rapid linguistic assimilation of immigrant children and young adults. For instance, a Portland, Maine, local newspaper once published a story entitled 'Greek pupils at Staples School learn to speak English in a few months,' while school principals in Gary, Indiana, told visitors that, after the first semester, they could not differentiate between the foreign-born and local children (Olneck, 1989).

Whatever difficulties in the language learning process are reported, they are usually of a transitional nature. For instance, a French dress-maker states that, in the beginning of her American employment, she and her friend were taken advantage of and it took them six months to learn 'enough of the English' to start negotiating better payment (Holt, 1906: 74). The only instance of linguistic discrimination encountered in the corpus is described by Nielsen (1935), who talks about his struggle to become an English-speaking minister serving English-speaking congregations:

> The ministry seems the only place where it is written on the door, 'All who have been brought up in any other language than the English cannot enter here.' (Nielsen, 1935: 263)

Nevertheless, Nielsen proceeds in his chosen career and is ultimately successful in establishing a personal and professional identity in the new language. Neither for him nor for others is the learning process linked to pains or losses; if anything, the transformations involved appear to be joyful, as in Panunzio's memoir:

> I am in a special way happy to have learned the English language and through its medium to have become acquainted with the stal-wart thought of the Master minds of the Anglo-Saxon race. (Panunzio, 1921: 294)

Panunzio is not the only one who uses the printed page to profess his love for English – similar declarations come from Antin and Nielsen:

> I am glad, most of all, that the Americans began by being Englishmen, for thus did I come to inherit this beautiful language in which I think. It seems to me that in any other language happiness is not so sweet, logic is not so clear. (Antin, 1912: 208)

> soon I made a discovery. I liked English better than I did Danish. I liked it better, not simply because I was in America, but because of the power and beauty of the language. To me, English seems more euphonious, in some ways softer, with more of a variety of shades and notes and tones. As for power of expression and

pungency, I think the English language has almost unlimited possibilities. (Nielsen, 1935: 121–122)

In sum, it appears that early-twentieth-century immigrant authors devote little time to discussions of second language learning and use in their portrayals of Americanization. When they do mention English learning, it is commonly described as a rapid and successful process, devoid of any but the most trivial challenges. And, while immigrant authors are keen on positioning themselves in terms of their new national, social, or cultural identities, they – and others in their environment – seem to take their new English-speaking identity for granted. This is especially intriguing, since language is crucial for performance of their professional and public identities as journalists, writers, editors, politicians, ministers, and public lecturers. And yet, except for Nielsen, we do not hear from them about any linguistic discrimination, that is, instances where their accents or grammatical and semantic errors would be used to contest their legitimacy as professionals or Americans.

Comparative analysis of immigrant identity stories

How does negotiation of identities in early immigrant memoirs compare to that in contemporary immigrant autobiographies? To begin with, similar to the memoirs discussed above, present-day immigrant authors use their autobiographies to create new national, ethnic, racial, social, cultural, and gender identities for themselves and for public imagination (Pavlenko, 2001c). In contrast to their predecessors, however, contemporary authors do not necessarily aim to create all-American identities for themselves and opt for hybrid, hyphenated, or transnational and cosmopolitan identities. Linguistic identities occupy a primary position in these narratives: several recent memoirs and edited collections focus exclusively on second language learning (Hoffman, 1989; Lvovich, 1997; Ogulnick, 1998, 2000; Rodriguez, 1982; Stavans, 2001), or at least assign linguistic construction of identity a significant role (Danquah, 2000; Dorfman, 1998; Mori, 1997). The authors appeal to the safety and authority of writing to claim ownership of their new language and to construct legitimate linguistic identities for themselves and their fellow bilinguals, challenging the native/non-native speaker dichotomy which grants unique authority to monolingual native speakers of English (Pavlenko, 2001c).

Recent analyzes of contemporary immigrant memoirs also show that these narratives often depict second language learning as an excruciating and anguishing journey, a painful process of self-translation, in which some identities may be lost forever and others acquired and constructed anew (Pavlenko, 1998, 2001a,b,c; Pavlenko & Lantolf, 2000). In contrast, as argued above, turn-of-the-twentieth-century memoirs rarely deal with language per se and, if so, portray language learning as a rapid and joyful process. On the other hand, they privilege lengthy discussions of one's employment and financial standing, which rarely if ever appear in contemporary memoirs, even those that deal with class and poverty. And, while early immigrant authors clearly do aspire to literary expressiveness and aim to show off their superior, and in many cases superb, mastery of English, these attempts are distinct from the explicit arguments offered in contemporary work. For instance, after recalling a number of incidents where she and her family members had to defend their right to legitimacy as English speakers, Julia Alvarez, a Dominican-American writer working in English, bluntly states that she refuses to imagine herself as anyone else but a legitimate speaker of English and an American writer:

> The truth was I couldn't even imagine myself as someone other than the person I had become in English, a woman who writes books in the language of Emily Dickinson and Walt Whitman, and also of the rude shopper in the grocery store and of the boys throwing stones in the schoolyard, their language, which is now my language. (Alvarez, 1998: 72)

In contrast, when we look at turn-of-the-twentieth-century memoirs, we don't see anyone denying the writers the right to be legitimate speakers of English in the same way as some deny them – and their fellow immigrants – the right to call themselves Americans. How should we understand these differences? How could we interpret the repeated tale of outstanding and rapid linguistic progress when, 50 years later, second language learning appears to take years or even decades? And how could we explain the relatively painless nature of turn-of-the-twentieth-century learning that is in contradiction with later accounts, which associate second language learning and socialization with losses, ambiguities, and linguistic discrimination of non-native speakers of English?

One possibility is that the only stories published at the time were those of happy linguistic assimilation and the ones depicting linguistic discrimination and difficulties never saw the light. Clearly, we may never know which memoirs did not get published, and we have definitely lost the stories that weren't written down in the first place. At the same time, the analysis of the narratives in the corpus shows that many immigrant authors take an explicitly critical stance toward their new country, criticizing ethnic and racial discrimination (Panunzio, 1921; Steiner, 1914), exploitative working conditions in the sweatshops and a dehumanizing living situation in boarding houses (Adamic, 1932; Panunzio, 1921; Riis, 1901), negative consequences of the assimilation process (Adamic, 1932; Ravage, 1917), and the attitudes of the native-born toward 'the foreigners.' Panunzio (1921: 207), for example, points out that many Americans would prefer to Americanize 'the foreigner' at a distance, at the same time drawing a sharp line between 'us' and 'them' and, thus, encouraging the creation of little Italies and Polands. Bok (1921) criticizes the public school system for paying insufficient attention to increasing numbers of foreign-born children, while Adamic (1932: 73) ridicules the English class he took from a teacher who was clearly less educated in his native language than many of his Italian, Jewish, Dutch, and Eastern European students were in theirs. Ravage (1917: 59–61) talks about multiple ways in which immigrants are invariably disappointed in America. This explicitly critical stance is not unique to well-educated middle-class immigrants – several autobiographies in Holt's (1906) collection also voice some form of social criticism. This stance did not go ignored by the reviewers, one of whom inquired upon the publication of the volume

> there is not in a single one of these histories of life, a word of acknowledgment or gratitude to the country which gave them the chance and the success. Why is this? Was there anything lacking in the gift? (as cited in Sollors, 1990: xxiii–xxiv)

In other words, it seems that, if the narrators were not afraid to criticize major flaws in the social fabric of American life, they would not have had a problem evoking ways in which Americans discriminate against immigrants with limited English proficiency or with an accent. Perhaps, with the exception of Nielsen (1935), these authors were simply not attentive enough to language? This possibility is not borne out in the examination of the corpus either: as writers and journalists, many authors display an outstanding sensitivity to language, using a rich variety of linguistic devices to portray the speech of their characters and offering explicit criticisms of the linguistic 'impurities' in the speech of their fellow immigrants. Ravage, for instance, is critical of the transfer of Yiddish and Romanian patterns into the speech of his countrymen:

> My friends were finding English contemptibly easy. That notion of theirs that it was a mixture of Yiddish and Rumanian, although partly justified, was yielding some astonishing results. Little Rumania was

in throes of evolving a new tongue – a crazy-quilt whose prevailing patches were, sure enough, Yiddish and Rumanian, with here and there a sprinkling of denatured English. They felt no compunction against pulling up an ancient idiom by the roots and transplanting it bodily into the new soil. One heard such phrases as 'I am going on a marriage,' 'I should live so,' 'a milky dinner.' (Ravage, 1917: 103)

His sentiments are echoed by Cahan, who criticizes the Yiddish used by the fellow immigrants:

I have already described how the Yiddish of American-born children grated on my ears. The Americanized Yiddish of the immigrants, studded with English expressions, was no better. My anger rose when I heard such expressions as 'er macht a leben' (he makes a living) or 'er is vert tsehn toisend dolar' (he is worth ten thousand dollars). Or such horrors as 'vindes' (windows) or 'silings' (ceilings) and 'pehtaytess' (potatoes). (Cahan, 1926: 241–242)

It appears, however, that these new speakers of English are also the ones most critical of the speech of other second language users. In turn, they themselves encounter little if any criticism and linguistic discrimination. Even Nielsen (1935: 263) who complains that people are critical of his performance from the pulpit, acknowledges that 'there is no such discrimination in other vocations in America.' The absence of incidents of linguistic discrimination in the narratives suggests that the authors' linguistic identities were rarely contested. Consequently, they did not feel the need to negotiate this identity and to argue their rights to legitimate ownership of English. To find reasons for such dramatic differences in the portrayal of second language learning, I will examine the sociohistoric, sociopolitical, and socioeconomic circumstances that influenced autobiography as a genre and linked American identity and English in distinct ways in the beginning and at the end of the twentieth century.

Language and Identity in the US in the Twentieth Century

Language ideologies during the Americanization era

As already pointed out, turn-of-the-twentieth-century immigrant narratives were written at a time of a national crisis, engendered by the unprecedented influx of the 'new immigrants' that started in the 1880s. As time went by, individual philanthropists and charity organizations started looking for ways to facilitate the transition and assimilation of the new arrivals. Eventually, it became clear that these efforts were insufficient and that many immigrants and naturalized citizens were still unable to speak English. The separation between the mainstream society and the ethnic enclaves and availability of jobs for which English was unnecessary account for some of this lack of proficiency. For some immigrants, the reluctance to learn English was also compounded by their real or perceived sojourner status. Interested in earning some money, but not in becoming Americans, these new arrivals did not consider it practical to devote time to English and citizenship classes (Wyman, 1993). To respond to the problem, in 1906 Congress approved a major change in the US naturalization policy, the Nationality Act, which required aliens seeking citizenship to speak English, and thus further reinforced the importance of language in the public mind. Even this measure did not prove to be entirely effective and large numbers of aliens continued to live in the US without naturalizing their status or acquiring English proficiency. The census of 1910 revealed that 13 million, or 14.8% of the total population, were foreign-born persons and, of these, 23% of people 10 years of age and over were unable to speak English (Macias, 2000).

While worrisome, this slow assimilation was seen as a temporary condition, which could eventually be remedied with the immigrants' children. Consequently, at least until the beginning of the First World War, liberal Americanization efforts often focused on obligations of citizenship and participation in the American system of self-government (often taught in multiple languages), rather than on native-like mastery of the English language. It is quite possible that, if not for the war, assimilation efforts would have remained the domain of various agencies and philanthropists, rather than the government and the wider public (Hartmann, 1948). The conflict in Europe heightened the sense of American nationalism and highlighted the persistence of Old World ties, language among them, among the European-born. With patriotism on the rise, immigrants were noticed by the previously indifferent public, and Americanization began to assume the proportions of a national crusade (Hartmann, 1948). Now, however, it was no longer enough for the immigrants to learn English and to assimilate: the political climate of the era required them to discard hyphenated identities and with them all other languages and all other allegiances but to America (for an in-depth discussion, see Pavlenko, 2002). This new attitude was particularly evident in two types of legislation adopted between the years of 1917 and 1922. More than 30 states passed Americanization laws, which obligated aliens unable to speak or read English to attend public evening schools and, in some cases, authorized funding for such schools and imposed fines on non-compliant aliens. Thirty-four states also passed official English-language policies, which declared English the only language of instruction and effectively terminated bilingual education and foreign language education in elementary schools, a blow from which the German-American community – which took significant advantage of dual-language instruction – never recovered.

And so it is within this particular, and shifting, constellation of language ideologies and identities that immigrant writers had to position themselves. They did so in different ways, depending both on the time of their arrival in the US and on the time in which their memoirs were published. In the relatively tolerant atmosphere of the nineteenth century, the quality of 'old immigrants'' English was rarely scrutinized and so it is not surprising that Bartholdt (1930), Bok (1921), and Riis (1901), who came to the US in 1870s, evoke few, if any, difficulties in learning or using English. More attention was paid to English learning by the 'new immigrants,' who were the target of the Americanization efforts, and thus Antin (1912) and Ravage (1917) discuss language learning at length, while several others mention attending, and later on teaching, Americanization classes. It is important to remember, however, that the overwhelming concerns of the time were not with the quality of the immigrants' English, but with the basic proficiency. Little if any attention was paid to the 'non-native-speakerness' of immigrants who did manage to master English. On the contrary, oftentimes their achievements were applauded and glorified as a model for others. Clearly, not everyone was thrilled by the 'aliens' who claimed the rights to the Anglo-Saxon linguistic inheritance, and several public figures did step up to defend the English language. The most prominent among them was Henry James, who, in 1905, after 'traumatic' visits to Ellis Island and to the Lower East Side, delivered an impassioned speech to the graduating class of Bryn Mawr, warning the students against an imminent threat to the civilized tongue from

> the vast continent of aliens whom we welcome, and whose main contention . . . is that, from the moment of their arrival, they have just as much property in our speech as we have, and just as good a right to do what they choose with it. (James, 1905, cited in Brumberg, 1986: 6–7)

Not many immigrants, however, interacted with either James or like-minded individuals, and, overall, as compared to the vast majority that still had to acquire even a basic level of proficiency, those who could function in English had all reasons to consider themselves – and to be considered – successful. The key factor that significantly contributed to this situation is the industrial economy, where many jobs required minimal or basic proficiency only. A similar situation existed in the service economy, and Antin recalls that her mother, who went to work immediately upon arrival, made quick progress due to the interaction with the store customers:

> as she could perform the acts of weighing, measuring, and mental computation of fractions mechanically, she was able to give her whole attention to the dark mysteries of the language, as intercourse with her customers gave her opportunity. In this she made such rapid progress that she soon lost all sense of disadvantage. (Antin, 1912: 196)

The third factor that worked to the advantage of the new arrivals was their multilingualism. Looking at the authors in the present corpus, we can see that Bartholdt (1930) came to the US speaking German, English, French, and a smattering of other languages; Ravage (1917) arrived from Romania fluent in Romanian and Yiddish, with some German in the mix; Antin (1912) had been educated in Hebrew, Yiddish, and Russian; while Cahan (1926) came from Lithuania fluent in Yiddish, Hebrew, Russian, Lithuanian, Polish, and familiar with German, Latin, and Greek. While the knowledge of classical languages may be limited to well-educated members of the middle- and upper-middle-class, multilingualism in general was quite common among the European arrivals. Cahan (1926: 225) recalls that 'even the uneducated immigrants could speak Russian, although they preferred Yiddish.' Similarly, a Polish sweatshop girl talks of her mother, who worked in a grocer's shop in a little village in Poland and could speak Russian, German, Polish, and French (Holt, 1906: 21).

The multilingualism of the immigrant writers explains not only the ease with which they acquired yet another language, but also the fact that this acquisition did not seem to produce any internal conflicts. In the pre-First World War atmosphere of linguistic tolerance, where bilingual education, ethnic press, and mother tongue literature, entertainment, and religious service were the order of the day (Kloss, 1977; Pavlenko, 2002; Wiley, 1998), English learning did not necessarily entail any losses. During and after the First World War, the attitude toward native language maintenance changed and this shift was reflected in the memoirs by Bartholdt (1930) and Nielsen (1935). The two authors take opposing positions on the issue of native language maintenance. Nielsen (1935) opts to give up his Danish and to live his personal and professional life in English only. He explains his decision both through the low prestige of Danish in

America and through the way in which his own variety of Danish positioned him as an individual:

> In Danish I spoke the low language. That had been the language of my stepmother, and though I could speak the high, it was very awkward for me. I found that most of the Danes in America spoke the high language, and so I was often a sort of stray sheep and the butt end for jokes, even among Danes. I think that was one reason why I started to go the American way so soon after arriving in America. (Nielsen, 1935: 123)

While Nielsen (1935) is glad to give up his native language and negotiate a more advantageous social position through the use of English, Bartholdt (1930) mounts a spirited defense of the right of any ethnic American to use his or her language alongside English:

> The right of the German, the Dutchman, the Scandinavian, the Italian, the Greek, the Slav, to live up to his racial traditions (which include the privilege of using the mother tongue in family, school and church), is a fundamental one, and the moment we proceed to abridge it, we depart from American principles and ideals. (Bartholdt, 1930: 31)

His dissent, however, was lost in a sea of consent, either voluntary or, in Chomskian words, 'manufactured' and, with time, monolingualism in English became inextricably bound to American national identity. In what follows, I will argue that it is this reinforced link between monolingualism and Americanness that prompted late-twentieth-century immigrant writers to see their second language learning as painful, to negotiate their linguistic identities, and to defend – or in Rodriguez's (1982) case, give up – their right and desire to be bilingual.

Assimilation in immigrant memoirs

After an almost 40-year respite, in the 1970s and 1980s, US society witnessed a new influx of immigrants, predominantly Latin American and Asian in origin. Similar to the Great Migration, the appearance of these immigrants led to a renegotiation of the American national identity, with race and ethnicity coming to the foreground of discussion (Schmidt, 2000). Once again, immigrant and bilingual writers occupied a central role in raising public awareness of the issues implicated in linguistic and cultural transitions. The renewal of interest in immigrant and ethnic lifewriting was marked by the appearance of such acclaimed literary masterpieces as Kingston's (1975) *The woman warrior*, Rodriguez's (1982) *Hunger of memory*, and Hoffman's (1989) *Lost in translation: A life in a new language*, all of which dealt with the role of language in the shaping of identity, and viewed language socialization as intrinsically related to race, ethnicity, class, and gender. These narratives, in turn, inspired an explosion of cross-cultural lifewriting with the focus on language, evident in numerous recent memoirs and collections (e.g. Danquah, 2000; Dorfman, 1998; Lvovich, 1997; Mori, 1997; Ogulnick, 1998, 2000; Stavans, 2001).

Representative of the new immigrant demographics, many of the contemporary authors are either Latino (Alvarez, 1998; Dorfman, 1998; Rodriguez, 1982; Stavans, 2001) or Asian and Asian-American (Kingston, 1975; Mori, 1997). Influenced by the 1970s' revival of ethnic and racial consciousness, these writers challenge the racial biases permeating American identity and language politics. A few, in particular Rodriguez (1982), still view assimilation as the only desired or possible outcome, but most of them question this assumption, offering new and hybrid linguistic identities for public imagination. Rather than portraying straightforward trajectories, they focus on contradictions and multiplicities of contemporary existence, privileging the role of language in the shaping and reshaping of linguistic, racial, ethnic, class, and gender identities (Fischer, 1986; Hokenson, 1995; Pavlenko, 2001a,b,c). This disjunction is recognized by the Polish-American writer, Eva Hoffman (1989), who acknowledges that 'the postmodern condition' requires a different narrative than the one written by her predecessor, Mary Antin:

> A hundred years ago, I might have written a success story, without much self-doubt or equivocation. A hundred years ago, I might have felt the benefits of a steady, self-assured ego, the sturdy energy of forward movement, and the excitement of being swept into a greater national purpose. But I have come to a different America, and instead of a central ethos, I have been given the blessings and the terrors of multiplicity. . . . If I want to assimilate into my generation, my time, I have to assimilate the multiple perspectives and their constant shifting. (Hoffman, 1989: 164)

To sum up, I suggest that the links between language and identity depicted – or omitted – in the two sets of immigrant autobiographies are critically influenced by the sociohistorical contexts in which the authors learned and used their languages and produced their narratives. In the turn-of-the-twentieth-century atmosphere of relative linguistic tolerance, the immigrants' rights to English were, for the most part, uncontested. Thus, linguistic trajectories in their narratives were depicted as rapid and successful, and Americanness was constructed primarily through the rhetoric of individual achievement. In contrast, several decades later, when the national identity became strongly bound to monolingualism in English, second language learning was transformed into a painful journey, involving a loss of primary identities linked to the mother tongue (Hoffman, 1989; Rodriguez, 1982). In the atmosphere of linguistic intolerance of the late twentieth century, immigrant authors in the US strive to defend their rights to legitimate ownership of English and, consequently, create Americanness out of linguistic hybridity.

Conclusions

In the present paper, I argue that the notion of 'negotiation of identities' needs to be approached from a sociohistorical perspective, which illuminates how identities considered to be negotiable at present may have been non-negotiated or non-negotiable in the past. The analysis of turn-of-the-twentieth-century immigrant memoirs demonstrates that European immigrant writers, drawing on the rhetoric of individual uplift, successfully reimagined American national identity in a way that would make it negotiable for new arrivals not only from Northern, but also from Southern and Eastern Europe. At the same time, racial minorities, in particular large numbers of Asian immigrants, had no access to the negotiation process and were not 'imagined' as legitimate Americans.

Moreover, while national identity was a subject of heated contestation, linguistic identities do not appear to be contested in the same way in the memoirs of the era. Even though some of the writers in the corpus still had accents and at times produced an unfortunate turn of phrase, in an atmosphere of linguistic tolerance and of concern over basic levels of English proficiency, their errors were generally ignored and linguistic achievements celebrated as a model for other immigrants. In contrast, at present immigrants find themselves in a position where learning the second language implies losing or giving up the first and thus contemporary language learning stories are often accounts of painful experiences. Many contemporary immigrant and bilingual writers are also thrust into positions where they have to defend their linguistic rights and ownership of English; consequently, their memoirs foreground negotiation of linguistic identities. The shifts in negotiable identity options examined in the present study offer a unique opportunity to understand how sociohistoric circumstances impact negotiation of identities and remind us that personal narratives of individuals are not simply individual performances, but also complex stories written by and for individuals 'by law, literature, politics, and history' (Zaborowska, 1995: x).

Acknowledgements

I would like to thank my reviewers, Celeste Kinginger and Yasuko Kanno, and my co-editor, Adrian Blackledge, for their insightful, generous, and constructive comments on the earlier versions of this manuscript. I would also like to thank my research assistant, Bei Zhou, for her invaluable support. Any remaining errors or inaccuracies are strictly my own.

Note

1. I fully realize that there is more to America than the United States. In the present chapter, I will use the term 'America' to refer to the United States exclusively in a poetic and historic sense, in order to faithfully reflect the discourses of the immigration and Americanization era.

References

Adamic, L. (1932) *Laughing in the jungle. The autobiography of an immigrant in America*. New York/London: Harper and Brothers.
Alvarez, J. (1998) *Something to declare*. Chapel Hill, NC: Algonquin Books.
Anderson, B. (1991) *Imagined communities: Reflections on the origin and spread of nationalism* (revised edn). London/New York:Verso.
Antin, M. (1912/1969) *The Promised Land*. Princeton, NJ: Princeton University Press.
Antin, M. (1914) *Those who knock at our gates: A complete gospel of immigration*. Boston: Houghton Mifflin.
Bach, E. (1923) *Americanization in Philadelphia*. Philadelphia, PA: Philadelphia Chamber of Commerce.
Bartholdt, R. (1930) *From steerage to Congress: Reminiscences and reflections*. Philadelphia: Dorrance and Company.
Beglinger, N. (1922) *Constructive lessons in English for the foreign-born*. Boston: The Gorham Press.
Boelhower, W. (1991) The making of ethnic autobiography in the United States. In J.P. Eakin (ed.) *American autobiography: Retrospect and prospect* (pp. 123–141). Madison, WI: University of Wisconsin Press.
Bok, E. (1921) *The Americanization of Edward Bok: The autobiography of a Dutch boy fifty years after*. New York: Charles Scribner's Sons.
Bourdieu, P. (1991) *Language and symbolic power*. Cambridge: Polity Press.
Brumberg, S. (1986) *Going to America, going to school: The Jewish immigrant public school encounter in turn-of-the-century New York City*. New York: Praeger.
Cahan, A. (1926/1969) *The education of Abraham Cahan*. The Jewish Publication Society of America.
Crichton, J. (1998) *America 1900: The sweeping story of a pivotal year in the life of the nation*. New York: Henry Holt and Company.
Danquah, M.N. (ed.) (2000) *Becoming American: Personal essays by first generation immigrant women*. New York: Hyperion.

Decker, J. (1997) *Made in America: Self-styled success from Horatio Alger to Oprah Winfrey*. Minneapolis: University of Minnesota Press.

Denzin, N. (1989) *Interpretive biography*. Newbury Park, CA: Sage.

Dorfman, A. (1998) *Heading South, looking North: A bilingual journey*. New York: Farrar, Straus, and Giroux.

Fischer, M. (1986) Ethnicity and the post-modern arts of memory. In J. Clifford and G. Markus (eds) *Writing culture: The poetics and politics of ethnography* (pp. 194–233). Berkeley: University of California Press.

Green, M.J. (2001) *Women and narrative identity: Rewriting the Quebec National Text*. Montreal: McGill-Queen's University Press.

Handlin, O. (1969) Foreword. In M. Antin (1912/1969) *The Promised Land* (pp. v–xv). Princeton, NJ: Princeton University Press.

Hartmann, E. (1948) *The movement to Americanize the immigrant*. New York: Columbia University Press.

Hoffman, E. (1989) *Lost in translation: A life in a new language*. New York: Dutton.

Hokenson, J. (1995) Intercultural autobiography. *a/b: Auto/Biography Studies* 10 (1), 92–113.

Holt, H. (ed.) (1906/1990) *The life stories of undistinguished Americans (as told by themselves)*. New York/London: Routledge.

Holte, J. (1988) *The ethnic I: A sourcebook for ethnic-American autobiography*. New York: Greenwood Press.

Hutner, G. (1999) *Immigrant voices: Twenty-four narratives on becoming an American*. New York: Signet Classic.

Kim, E. (1982) *Asian American literature: An introduction to the writings and their social context*. Philadelphia, PA: Temple University Press.

Kingston, M.H. (1975) *The woman warrior: Memoirs of a girlhood among ghosts*. New York: Vintage.

Kloss, H. (1977/1998) *The American bilingual tradition*. Washington, DC: Center for Applied Linguistics.

Kramsch, C. and Lam, W. Sh. E. (1999) Textual identities: The importance of being non-native. In G. Braine (ed.) *Non-native educators in English language teaching* (pp. 57–72). Mahwah, NJ: Lawrence Erlbaum Associates.

Luebke, F. (1974) *Bonds of loyalty: German-Americans and World War I*. De Kalb, IL: Northern Illinois University Press.

Luebke, F. (1980) Legal restrictions on foreign languages in the Great Plain states, 1917–1923. In P. Schach (ed.) *Languages in conflict: Linguistic acculturation on the Great Plains* (pp. 1–19). Lincoln, NE/London: University of Nebraska Press.

Lvovich, N. (1997) *The multilingual self*. Mahwah, NJ: Lawrence Erlbaum Associates.

Macias, R. (2000) The flowering of America: Linguistic diversity in the United States. In S. McKay and S.C. Wong (eds) *New immigrants in the United States* (pp. 11–57). Cambridge, MA: Cambridge University Press.

Mori, K. (1997) *Polite lies: On being a woman caught between cultures*. New York: Henry Holt and Company.

Nielsen, T. (1935) *How a Dane became an American, or Hits and misses of my life*. Cedar Rapids, IA: The Torch Press.

Ogulnick, K. (1998) *Onna rashiku (Like a woman): The diary of a language learner in Japan*. Albany, NY: SUNY Press.

Ogulnick, K. (ed.) (2000) *Language crossings: Negotiating the self in a multicultural world*. New York: Teachers College Press.

Olneck, M. (1989) Americanization and the education of immigrants, 1900–1925: An analysis of symbolic action. *American Journal of Education* 97 (4), 398–423.

Panunzio, C. (1921/1926) *The soul of an immigrant*. New York: Macmillan.

Pavlenko, A. (1998) Second language learning by adults: Testimonies of bilingual writers. *Issues in Applied Linguistics* 9 (1), 3–19.

Pavlenko, A. (2001a) Language learning memoirs as a gendered genre. *Applied Linguistics* 22 (2), 213–240.

Pavlenko, A. (2001b) 'How do I become a woman in an American vein?': Transformations of gender performance in second language learning. In A. Pavlenko, A. Blackledge, I. Piller, and M. Teutsch-Dwyer (eds) *Multilingualism, second language learning, and gender* (pp. 133–174). Berlin: Mouton de Gruyer.

Pavlenko, A. (2001c) 'In the world of the tradition, I was unimagined': Negotiation of identities in cross-cultural autobiographies. *The International Journal of Bilingualism* 5 (3), 317–344.

Pavlenko, A. (2002) 'We have room for but one language here': Language and national identity in the US at the turn of the 20th century. *Multilingua* 21 (2/3), 163–196.

Pavlenko, A. and J. Lantolf (2000) Second language learning as participation and the (re)construction of selves. In J. Lantolf (ed.) *Sociocultural theory and second language learning* (pp. 155–177). New York: Oxford University Press.

Ravage, M.E. (1917) *An American in the making: The life story of an immigrant*. New York/London: Harper and Brothers Publisher.

Riis, J. (1901/1961) *The making of an American*. New York: Macmillan.

Roberts, P. (1920) *The problem of Americanization*. New York: Macmillan.

Rodriguez, R. (1982) *Hunger of memory*. New York: Bantam.

Schmidt, R. (2000) *Language policy and identity politics in the United States*. Philadelphia: Temple University Press.

Schumann, J. (1997) *The neurobiology of affect in language learning*. Boston: Blackwell.

Sollors, W. (1986) *Beyond ethnicity*. New York: Oxford University Press.

Sollors, W. (1990) From the bottom up: Foreword. In H. Holt (ed.) *The life stories of undistinguished Americans (as told by themselves)* (pp. xi–xxviii). New York/London: Routledge.

Stavans, I. (2001) *On borrowed words: A memoir of language*. New York: Viking.

Steiner, E. (1914) *From alien to citizen: The story of my life in America*. New York/London: Fleming Revell Company.

Taubenfeld, A. (1998) 'Only an "L"': Linguistic borders and the immigrant author in Abraham Cahan's *Yekl* and *Yankel der Yankee*. In W. Sollors (ed.) *Multilingual America: Transnationalism, ethnicity, and the languages of American literature* (pp. 144–165). New York: New York University Press.

Tse, L. (2000) The effects of ethnic identity formation on bilingual maintenance and development: An analysis of Asian American narratives. *International Journal of Bilingual Education and Bilingualism* 3 (3), 185–200.

US Bureau of the Census (1975) *Historical statistics of the United States: Colonial times to 1970*. Washington, DC: US Bureau of the Census.

Weedon, C. (1987) *Feminist practice and poststructuralist theory*. Oxford: Basil Blackwell.

Weiss, B. (1982) Introduction. In B. Weiss (ed.) *American education and the European immigrant: 1840–1940* (pp. xi–xxviii). Urbana/Chicago: University of Illinois Press.

Wiley, T. (1998) The imposition of World War I era English-only policies and the fate of German in North America. In T. Ricento and B. Burnaby (eds) *Language and politics in the United States and Canada: Myths and realities* (pp. 211–241). Mahwah, NJ: Lawrence Erlbaum Associates.

Wing, Y. (1909) *My life in China and America*. New York: Henry Holt and Company.

Wong, C.S.L. (1991) Immigrant autobiography: Some questions of definition and approach. In J.P. Eakin (ed.) *American autobiography: Retrospect and prospect* (pp. 142–170). Madison, WI: University of Wisconsin Press.

Wyman, M. (1993) *Round-trip to America: The immigrants' return to Europe, 1880–1930*. Ithaca, NY/London: Cornell University Press.

Yezierska, A. (1925/1999) *Bread givers*. New York: Persea Books.

Yin, X. (1998) Worlds of difference: Lin Yutang, Lao She, and the significance of Chinese-language writing in America. In W. Sollors (ed.) *Multilingual America: Transnationalism, ethnicity, and the languages of American literature* (pp. 176–187). New York: New York University Press.

Zaborowska, M. (1995) *How we found America: Reading gender through East European immigrant narratives*. Chapel Hill, NC: University of North Carolina Press.

Chapter 2

Constructions of Identity in Political Discourse in Multilingual Britain

ADRIAN BLACKLEDGE

Introduction

As we saw in the introduction to this volume, identities of linguistic minority speakers are constantly constructed and reconstructed in discursive interactions. When the dominant majority insists that the ideal model of society or nation is monolingual, we immediately encounter questions about identity and group membership (Blommaert & Verschueren, 1998a). If the majority language is endowed with a symbolic status which asserts its superiority over minority languages, there are issues of social justice, as linguistic minority speakers may be excluded from access to, or membership in, the more powerful group. In this chapter I review recent research which has illuminated understanding of the ways in which identities are either negotiated, or found to be non-negotiable, in multilingual states. I will then present an analysis of a current language ideological debate in political discourse which followed the so-called 'race riots' in the north of England in the summer of 2001. This debate focused on the perceived symbolic association between minority Asian languages and social disorder, and on ways of controlling the monolingual use of such languages in Britain. Based on Critical Discourse Analysis (Fairclough, 1989, 1995a,b; Fowler, 1991; Wodak *et al.*, 1999), and dialogic discourse (Bakhtin, 1986, 1994; Voloshinov, 1973), the analysis is informed by Bourdieu's (1990: 68) notions of *habitus* and *field*. My analysis will also be located in Irvine and Gal's (2000) model which sets out the semiotic processes by which identities are constructed and negotiated in linguistically diverse contexts.

Language Ideologies in Multilingual Contexts

Recent studies have recognized the social positioning, partiality, contestability, instability, and mutability of the ways in which language uses and beliefs are linked to relations of power and political arrangements in societies (Blommaert, 1999; Blommaert & Verschueren, 1998a; Gal, 1998; Gal & Woolard, 1995; Irvine & Gal, 2000; Kroskrity, 1998, 2000; Woolard, 1998). In Bourdieu's model of language and symbolic power, the social order is produced and reproduced in 'an abundance of tangible self-evidences' (2000: 181), which give the illusion of common-sense reality. The inscription of *habitus*, or way of being, is inculcated through ongoing acts of recognition and misrecognition in the social arena (*field*). The relation between *habitus* and *field* creates the conditions in which existing shared self-evidences are produced and reproduced. This process of *symbolic violence*, of production and reproduction of common-sense consensus, occurs in discourses in the media, education, politics, the economy, and the law, to mention only institutional contexts. In an increasingly globalized environment, the State is not necessarily involved in this process at all levels. However, 'the State makes a decisive contribution toward the production and reproduction of the instruments of construction of social reality' (Bourdieu, 2000: 175). In this chapter I examine political discourse which appears to make self-evident a 'common-sense' reality that languages other than English are associated with disorder in an English state. Such discourse is endowed with symbolic power and is the more effective when supported in law:

> The form par excellence of the socially instituted and officially recognized symbolic power of construction is the legal authority, law being the objectification of the dominant vision recognized as legitimate, or, to put it another way, of the legitimate vision of the world, the orthodoxy, guaranteed by the State. (Bourdieu, 2000: 186)

The State has the power to distribute identities, through setting criteria for the award of certificates which bring benefits and privileges (for example, the award of Social Security numbers, the award of citizenship, the award of right of stay for refugees). At the same time, the State has the power to set criteria for the award of such certificates which are exclusionary. The establishment in law of *social frontiers* enables the State to play a part in the social distribution of privileges. Laws are not, of course, either natural or uncontested. In democratic societies they emerge from chains of political discourses (Wodak, 2000). Such discourses act hand-in-hand with the law to create 'common sense' realities which are held to be self-evident. It is 'common-sense' that not all refugees should be allowed entry, so a law is required to prevent this. It is 'self-evident' that people who do not speak the majority language impoverish the nation, so laws are required to prevent their settlement. Political discourse and the law act (alongside other discourses) to create a social world which is self-evident, natural, taken for granted, and which reproduces the social order.

Gal and Irvine (1995) note that there are striking similarities in the ways ideologies misrecognize differences between linguistic practices, often identifying linguistic varieties with 'typical' persons and activities and accounting for the differentiation between them. In these processes the linguistic behaviors of others are simplified and are seen as deriving from speakers' character or moral virtue, rather than from historical accident. In their later paper, Irvine and Gal (2000) illustrate their point with an analysis of the ways in which identities were constructed in linguistic practices in nineteenth-century Macedonia. The region was unusually multilingual, with language use not falling within expected ethnic bound- aries, and was often described in historical documents as 'primitive' and 'barbaric.' Imposing their own ideologies, which viewed nations as essen- tially monolingual, visitors to Macedonia considered that the linguistic heterogeneity of the region had consequences for the moral reputation of Macedonians, because 'multiple languages were assumed to indicate multiple loyalties and thus a temperamental flaw, a lack of trustworthi- ness' (Irvine & Gal, 2000: 65). Irvine and Gal consider that linguistic features are often seen as reflecting and expressing broader cultural images of people and activities:

> Participants' ideologies about language locate linguistic phenomena as part of, and evidence for, what they believe to be systematic behav- ioral, aesthetic, affective, and moral contrasts among the social groups indexed. (Irvine & Gal, 2000: 37)

They point to three semiotic processes by which languages are indexed to the essential nature of their speakers: *iconization, fractal recursivity,* and *erasure.* They describe these processes as follows:

> *Iconization* involves a transformation of the sign relationship between linguistic features (or varieties) and the social images with which they are linked. Linguistic features that index social groups appear to be iconic representations of them, as if a linguistic feature somehow depicted or displayed a social group's inherent nature or essence.
>   *Fractal recursivity* involves the projection of an opposition, salient at some level of relationship, onto some other level.

Erasure is the process in which ideology, in simplifying the sociolinguistic field, renders some persons or activities (or sociolinguistic phenomena) invisible. (Irvine & Gal, 2000: 37–38)

These categories will provide a useful model in my analysis of the construction of identities in political discourse in the second half of this chapter.

Language and National Identity

Bourdieu's notion of symbolic violence is consistent with the Gramscian notion of *hegemony*, which emphasizes that dominant ideas are particularly powerful because they are the assumed, implicit aspects of a more explicit ideology. Gramsci (1971) proposed that state control could not be sustained over time without the consent of the polity through ideological persuasion; that is, through hegemony (Philips, 1998). Although Gramsci did not insist that such persuasion was necessarily implicit more than explicit, in post-Gramscian writings the term *hegemony* has come to mean the taken-for-granted, almost invisible, discourse practices of symbolic domination. Hegemony is about domination as well as about integration. That is, it is about the process of a dominant group exerting power over society as a whole, but it is also about making alliances, and achieving consent from subordinated groups (Fairclough, 1995a). Hegemonic struggle takes place at a range of sites, from local (e.g. family, workplace, community), to national (e.g. education policy, welfare policy, naturalization testing) and international (e.g. globalization). However, while hegemony is a recognizable process, it is neither stable nor monolithic. Rather, it is constantly shifting, being made and remade, characterized by contradiction and ambiguity, productive of opposing consciousnesses and identities in subordinate populations, and always exposed to the possibility of alternative counterhegemonies (Blommaert, 1999; Gal, 1998; Williams, 1977). The achievement of domination through hegemony is always complex and problematic, usually only partially achieved, and often fragile. When a language is linked to national identity, the symbolic status of a language can create identity and discontinuity, and can both unite and divide, as it can become a battleground, an object of oppression and a means of discrimination (Blommaert & Verschueren, 1998a). It is more than a simple national symbol, like a national anthem or a national flag (Bokhorst-Heng, 1999). Rather, its symbolic status occurs within the larger process of imagining the nation (Anderson, 1983).

In the face of hegemonic ideologies of homogenization, it is not surprising that those who are subject to the 'symbolic violence' of

monoglot standardization appear to comply with their symbolic domination. A process of normalization occurs, in which it comes to appear
natural that one language, or one variety, dominates others, is more legitimate, and provides greater access to symbolic resources. This process can
be made visible through close scrutiny of public discourse, and in particular through analysis of the creation and reproduction of language
ideologies:

> Cultural and linguistic unification is accompanied by the imposition
> of the dominant language and culture as legitimate and by the rejec-
> tion of all other languages into indignity. (Bourdieu, 1998: 46)

Bourdieu further characterizes the unification of the cultural and
linguistic market as contributing to the construction of 'national identity,'
or 'legitimate national culture' (1998: 46). The 'homogenization of all
forms of communication' (1998: 45) contributes to a national habitus,
which implicitly shares common principles of vision and division. That
is, division not only by class, but also by gender, race, ethnicity, age, sexuality, and linguistic background. Thus, in asking questions about who has
access to symbolic and material resources in Britain, about who is 'in' the
imagined community of the nation and who is 'out,' we need to take account
not only of localized linguistic behaviors, attitudes, and beliefs; we must
also locate them in wider discourses of education, politics, economics, the
law, and the media.

Anderson (1983) suggests that nations are imagined political communities, imagined as both inherently limited and sovereign. In Anderson's
analysis, the development of print capitalism led to a literate bourgeoisie
who could now *imagine* themselves as part of that (national) community.
Thus nations are *imagined* because most of their members will never meet
each other, 'yet in the minds of each lives the image of their communion'
(1983: 6). Irvine and Gal (2000) and Silverstein (2000) argue, however, that
Anderson's analysis assumes that linguistic homogeneity is a 'real-world
precondition' (Irvine & Gal, 2000: 76), rather than a social construction
which may have succeeded (and even been a consequence of) print
capitalism. Thus Anderson's analysis may ignore the heterogeneity of
multilingual states. That is, while nations are imagined as cohesive monolingual communities, speakers of minority languages or varieties may be
unable to gain access to membership of such communities (whether 'real'
or imagined). Grillo (1998) points out that, while modern nation-states
were conceived as ideally homogeneous, seeking from their citizens
uniformity and loyalty, this ideology was constantly confronted with
the reality of social, cultural, and linguistic heterogeneity. This tension

between a dominant ideology of national homogeneity and actual hetero-geneity has important implications for multilingual identities and social justice in liberal democratic states. In Western democracies the response to diversity in society has often been to unite around the hegemony of the majority, standard language (Hymes, 1996). The monolingualizing tendencies (Heller, 1995, 1999) of state, social, media, and economic institutions produce and reproduce this dominant ideology of homo-geneity. The analysis in the second half of this chapter will address questions related to the ways in which national identities are constructed in public discourse, and whether linguistic minority speakers are able to gain access to communities which are imagined as monolingual nation-states.

Language in the Construction of 'Self' and 'Other'

It has often been the expectation in the United States that immigrants should replace whatever traits make them different with characteristics which make them appear more 'American.' Among these characteristics are spoken and written English. Allowing languages other than English to flourish appears to jeopardize the status quo of the dominance of English and those who speak it. Schieffelin and Doucet (1998) note that language ideologies are often the location of images of 'self/other' or 'us/them.' That is, the 'official English' debate in the United States is a contest about political identity, about who is allowed to be 'American' and who is not, and about who is 'in' and who is 'out.' Recent research has found that the process of self-translation for second language learners is far from straightforward, as identities have to be renegotiated, and some may possibly be lost forever (Pavlenko, 2001a,b,c). Grillo (1998) recalls that, after mass immigration to the United States in the early twentieth century, the 'Americanization' movement insisted that all immigrants must achieve proficiency in English if they were to be American citizens. To be a 'good American' required proficiency in English, and language and literacy tests for immigrants were introduced (see also Pavlenko's chapter). This dominant ideology of homogeneity is not uncontested in the United States. It sits in tension with a more liberal ideology which supports linguistic heterogeneity. Schmidt (2000, 2001, 2002) analyzes the two sides of the *assimilationist* versus *pluralist* debate in the United States, and finds that language is deeply connected to 'race,' in that both are embedded in the politics of identity. The debate over bilingualism in the United States is in fact a debate over 'race' – at present most non-English speakers in the US are members of *racialized* minority groups, whose languages are often stigmatized as markers of those racialized identities. English language dominance is thus intimately linked to racialized dominance of the 'white' majority group.

In many European countries, as in the United States, an ideology of monolingualism as the norm – or at least an ideology which privileges certain languages over others – prevails. This is in spite of considerable evidence of the linguistic heterogeneity of European communities (Gardner-Chloros, 1997). Especially in Europe, state monolingualism is a cultural construction embedded in broader discourses about the bases of social stratification and the nature of persons. In Belgium recently, in local elections in Antwerp (October 2000), the ultra-Right Vlaams Blok party won 20 of the city council's 50 seats, demonstrating that an explicitly liberal, multilingual nation-state ideology is contested by ideologies of monolingualism which are evident in discourses on the politics of immigration. Blommaert and Verschueren (1998b) studied the 'rhetoric of tolerance' in public discourse in Belgian newspapers, documents issued by political parties, and communications from government agencies. Rather than discover the self-evident ideologies of minority, ultra-Right political groups, the researchers set out to identify the taken-for-granted, common-sense views and attitudes of the majority. Their analysis reveals that, in Belgium, the non-acceptance of diversity predominates, even among the majority, which tends to view itself as the embodiment of openness and tolerance. Blommaert and Verschueren conclude that, for (at least partly) historical reasons, a key aspect of homogeneity and national belonging in Flanders is the Flemish language: 'language is the essence of identity' (1998b: 128). This ideology relies on the notion of an immutable unity between language and the cultural identity of a population group. Blommaert and Verschueren (1998a) further demonstrate that, in Germany, an apparent acceptance of 'foreignness' is contradicted by an ideology which seeks to deny voting rights to immigrant groups. Their analysis of the European press finds that, in the print media, there is a theory which 'revolves around the impossibility of heterogeneous communities and the naturalness of homogeneous communities' (Blommaert & Verschueren, 1998b: 207).

Piller's (2001) study of recent (January 1, 2000) changes to naturalization legislation in Germany reveals that, when the coalition government of Labour and Greens attempted to simplify the naturalization process, a central plank of the new criteria for acquisition of German citizenship was proof of German language proficiency. Accordingly, the authorities are now required to test whether naturalization candidates can cope with daily life in their German environment, can conduct a conversation in

German, and can read and understand a German text. Piller's analysis demonstrates that the newly-imposed, arbitrary language testing practices lack both democratic and linguistic validity, as knowledge of the German language functions as an exclusionary gatekeeping device. Piller (2001) shows that the tests were often conducted by officials who had little or no linguistic knowledge or experience, and were used as a basis for discrimination. In Germany these naturalization language tests are used in exclusionary ways because they are completely arbitrary. In Piller's analysis nations are not only 'imagined communities,' which allow people to imagine a shared experience and identity; they are also exclusionary domains, to which access is restricted via citizenship. Of course it is not only in Germany that language testing is part of the process of application for naturalization. The classic immigration countries, Australia, Canada, and the US, all demand some proficiency in English from applicants for citizenship (for a detailed discussion, see Piller, 2001).

In Britain the current language requirement (that is, as the law stood before the introduction of the new *Nationality, Immigration and Asylum Act,* 2002) for citizenship applicants is laid out in the *British Nationality Act,* 1981 as follows:

> 6 – (1) If, on application for naturalisation as a British citizen made by a person of full age and capacity, the Secretary of State is satisfied that the applicant fulfils the requirements of Schedule 1 for naturalisation as such a citizen under this subsection, he may, if he thinks fit, grant him a certificate of naturalisation as such a citizen. (2) If, on application for naturalisation as a British citizen made by a person of full age and capacity who on the date of the application is married to a British citizen, the Secretary of State is satisfied that the applicant fulfils the requirements of Schedule 1 for naturalisation as such a citizen under this subsection, he may, if he thinks fit, grant him a certificate of naturalisation as such a citizen. (Home Office, 1981)

Schedule 1 states that, in addition to residential requirements (*a*) and (*d*):

> The requirements for naturalisation as a British citizen under 6 (1) are, in the case of any person who applies for it –
> (*b*) that he is of good character; and
> (*c*) that he has a sufficient knowledge of the English, Welsh or Scottish Gaelic language. (Home Office, 1981)

It is clear that applicants for naturalization as British citizens are required to demonstrate *sufficient knowledge* of the English (or other indigenous British) language. The *Act* does not expand on what is meant by *sufficient knowledge.* However, Home Office leaflet BN7, *Information about natural-isation as a British citizen,* offers the following gloss:

> The person applying must have a good enough knowledge of the language to deal with everyday situations. He or she does not have to be able to read or write the language. The Home Secretary may decide that the person does not have to meet this requirement if he or she is old or physically or mentally disabled. (Home Office, n.d.a)

Home Office Guide AN, *Naturalisation as a British citizen: A guide for applicants,* adds the following note:

> - Your knowledge of the language does not have to be perfect, but it must be sufficient for you to fulfill your duties as a citizen, and to mix easily with the people with whom you work.
> - If because of disability you cannot speak the language, it will be sufficient if you can communicate by, for example, writing or using British sign language.
> - If you are old or suffer from physical or mental handicap you may not have to meet this requirement. (Home Office, n.d.b)

Whereas the government department explains *sufficient knowledge* in terms of *everyday situations* in leaflet BN7, in AN the requirement is more specifically related to the duties of citizenship and to the workplace. It would be interesting to speculate about what criteria would be set if applicants' knowledge of the language did have to be *perfect.* Returning to the *Act* itself, we find the following note appended to Subsection (2):

> Note that knowledge of one of English, Welsh or Gaelic is not required of the spouse of a British citizen as a pre-requisite to the acquisition of British citizenship by naturalisation. (Home Office, 1981)

This distinction between the language requirements for general applicants for British citizenship, and applicants for the same who are married to British citizens, will be a key factor in the analysis of political discourse in the second half of this chapter. As the law stood before November 2002, whereas applicants for naturalization as British citizens had to satisfy some (vague) requirement to be able to speak English, this did *not* apply when the applicant was already the spouse of a British citizen. The new *Nationality, Immigration and Asylum Act* legislates to amend this exception. It is here that a language ideological debate has recently been fought in political discourse in the United Kingdom – a language ideological debate which symbolically links language, race, and culture.

Language Ideological Debates and Social Unrest in Northern England

The data for analysis in the remainder of this chapter are related to the so-called 'race riots,' which occurred in the north of England during June and July 2001, and to a legislative change in the *Nationality, Immigration and Asylum Act*, 2002. The social unrest mainly involved running battles between young 'white' men, young 'Asian' men, and the police. The data presented here include transcripts from *Hansard* (the text of parliamentary debates in the British Parliament in London) of politicians' statements to Parliament, a web-based interview with a Home Office minister, and a statement from the Home Secretary. Each of these texts was a link in the chain of discourses which led to legislative change in 2002.

'Let us consider the causes': Language as cultural marker

On July 17, 2001, in the aftermath of a summer of social unrest in the towns of Bradford, Oldham, and Burnley in northern England, Ann Cryer, Labour Member of Parliament (MP) for Keighley, made a speech in the House of Commons during the Westminster Hall debate on Urban Community Relations (Bradford, Oldham, Burnley, and Keighley are towns in the north of England with multiethnic populations). In the course of the speech she addressed what she saw as the causes of the social unrest in the areas neighboring her constituency:

> We need to examine why those young Asian men were so keen to join in the criminal activity. Let us consider the causes. There is little point in blaming the situation simply on racism and Islamophobia. We must instead consider in detail what causes the under-achievement that I have mentioned. The main cause is the lack of a good level of English, which stems directly from the established tradition of bringing wives and husbands from the sub-continent who have often had no education and have no English. As a result, the vast majority of Keighley households have only one parent with any English and children go to school speaking only Punjabi or Bangla. That frequently gets children off to a slow start, which can damage their progress and mean that they leave school with few, if any, qualifications. Many cannot get paid work or find only poorly paid jobs. (*Hansard*, 2001a)

This section of the speech begins by constructing an opposition between the apparently inclusive, deictic *We* (in *We need to examine*), and *those young Asian men.* It is not immediately clear to whom the inclusive *We* refers, although it seems to exclude young Asian men in the north of England. The social context of the speech, made in the House of Commons, implies that *We* includes other Members of Parliament; but it may also include the broader liberal establishment, policy-making bodies, and, perhaps, all 'right-thinking' people who want to remove social disorder from the streets. Thus *We* here also implies *you.* The inclusive pronoun and obligational modal auxiliary verb (*We need*), repeated in *We must*, implies that what is required, and what will follow, is a full and thorough analysis of the causes of the riots:

We need to examine

Let us consider

We must . . . consider in detail

In foregrounding her list of causes of violence on the streets in such terms, Ann Cryer lays the foundations for an apparently unshakeable argument. The imperative *Let us* implies an instruction, and is endowed with some authority and gravitas. The word *cause* or *causes* appears three times here, to emphasize the politician's view of cause and effect in the background to the riots. Between the first and second *causes* is the following sentence:

There is little point in blaming the situation simply on racism and Islamophobia.

Here Ann Cryer is engaging in a discourse which marginalizes contrary views by naturalizing her own, as she responds to an assumed argument which *simply* blames racism and Islamophobia for the rioting. This argument is presupposed to come from beyond, as well as from within, the House of Commons. In Bakhtin's terms, this is hidden polemic, in which the discourse 'sharply senses its own listener, reader, critic, and reflects in itself their anticipated objections, evaluations, points of view' (1994: 108). Ann Cryer dismisses the possibility that racism and Islamophobia are causes of the rioting, and paves the way for her own analysis. In the phrase *There is little point*, she creates an emphatic presupposition that racism and Islamophobia are not to blame. She alludes to opposition texts, but reformulates them, substituting the wording of her opponents with an ideologically revised wording of her own (Fairclough, 1989: 188). Key here is the word *simply*. In none of the texts surrounding the riots (e.g. David Aaronovitch, *The Independent*, 2001a; Faisal Bodi, *The Guardian*, 2001b; Ian Herbert, *The Independent*, 2001c; Simon Hughes, MP, *Hansard*,

2001a) did commentators state that the causes of the rioting were 'simply' racism or Islamophobia. Yet Ann Cryer's intertextual negative assertion would certainly imply this.

In what follows, Ann Cryer identifies eight causes of the rioting. Linking violence to *under-achievement*, she lists the following as reasons for young Asian men to join in *criminal activity*:

(1) *the lack of a good level of English;*
(2) *the tradition of bringing wives and husbands from the sub-continent;*
(3) *only one parent with any English;*
(4) *children go to school speaking only Punjabi or Bangla;*
(5) *children off to a slow start;*
(6) *which can damage their progress;*
(7) *few, if any, qualifications;*
(8) *cannot get paid work or find only poorly paid jobs.*

Each of these apparent causes of criminal activity is linked to language ideological debates about the role of minority languages in Britain. Fairclough (1989: 188) suggests that 'Where one has lists, one has things placed in connection, but without any indication of the precise nature of the connection.' While Ms Cryer suggests a kind of 'common-sense' logic to support her argument that the violence of young Asian men is caused by their (or their parents'? or their wives'?) inability to speak English, this is little more than a list of apparently connected factors. The speaker suggests logic with the constructions *which stems directly, As a result, That frequently gets, and mean that.*

The first of the eight *causes* listed, *the lack of a good level of English*, is said to be the main one. Although there is no definition here of what *a good level of English* means, a lack of it is iconically associated with a predisposition to be *keen* to join in with violent criminal activity. The second cause links people with *no education* and speakers of *no English* with social disorder; the third cause associates with the rioting all households where there is *only one parent with any English*; the fourth cause links children who speak *only Punjabi or Bangla* with the unrest; the fifth, sixth, seventh, and eighth causes are associated with children who go to school unable to speak English. All of these stated causes of the rioting identify linguistic features that index the (so-called) Asian group and 'appear to be iconic representations of them' (Irvine & Gal, 2000: 37), as if linguistic features could somehow depict or display a social group's inherent nature or essence. This list of causes of the riots creates an ideological context which privileges English above other languages in society. This ideology is not only linguistic, however. In maintaining established traditions, in speaking languages other than English, in allowing a situation where only one parent speaks English, in sending children to school as speakers of other languages, Asian people are regarded as being 'to blame' for the disorder in the streets. In a process of what Irvine and Gal (2000: 37) call *fractal recursivity*, a dichotomy which exists at the linguistic level recurs at other levels.

'Some remedies': language as iconic representation

In the next section of Ann Cryer's speech, she proposes solutions to the problems she has identified. These can be listed in six sections. The first *remedy* is as follows:

> I should like to suggest some remedies, which I know will be regarded as controversial by many of the self-styled Asian leaders in Bradford. Asian parents should consider arranging marriages for their children with Asian Muslims brought up and educated in the United Kingdom. That would avoid the present importation of poverty into their families and the problems that I mentioned for the next generation when the children go to school, and would also stop the increasing number of cases of young men and women having extremely unhappy and difficult marriages with spouses from the sub-continent with whom they have nothing in common. I have dealt with such cases, and they are a growing problem in Keighley. (*Hansard*, 2001a)

Ann Cryer prefaces her list of *remedies* with an acknowledgment that her views will be *regarded as controversial by many of the self-styled Asian leaders in Bradford*. The phrase *self-styled* here undermines the authority of the Asian leaders. Having acknowledged the probable opposition to her case, in 'internally polemic discourse' (Bakhtin, 1994: 108), Ann Cryer continues to identify what *should* be done to remedy the current situation. In each case the modal auxiliary verb *should* is used, emphasizing the authority of the speech, and the logical basis of the solutions proposed. In the first proposed remedy Ann Cryer refers back to what she sees as the major cause of under-achievement, and therefore rioting, which is *bringing wives and husbands from the sub-continent*. Asian parents are here asked to consider arranging marriages with British Asian Muslims, which would avoid the *importation of poverty*. It is not clear how *poverty* is necessarily imported into families in this way. The immediate implication is that Asian languages are associated with economic poverty. However, as Ann Cryer's point was about *the lack of a good level of English*, it is possible that she is implying 'linguistic poverty' here. At the same time, the ambiguity of this phrase could be interpreted as an iconic association between lack of English and social, cultural, or moral poverty. Although the *causes* of the riots had been identified in linguistic terms, this first 'remedy' for these perceived linguistic difficulties seems to pay little attention to language. Instead, Ann Cryer's focus is on intercontinental arranged marriages. Here the MP claims her credentials by saying *I have dealt with such cases, and they are a growing problem in Keighley*. It is notable that, on three other occasions in her speech, Ann Cryer seeks to establish her 'right to speak' on issues affecting the Asian community. Indeed, the MP is widely considered to be a liberal spokesperson for her Asian constituents.

Ann Cryer's second *remedy* is as follows:

> Months off school for extended holidays in the sub-continent should be avoided. At the moment, there seems to be little regard for the problems that this can cause. Instead, people in the Asian community could add a week before and after the long summer holiday, because I would be the last person to suggest that they sever their links with the sub-continent. (*Hansard*, 2001a)

None of the eight *causes* of under-achievement and criminal activity identified by Ann Cryer refer to the practice of taking extended holidays in the sub-continent. Yet the second of the proposed 'remedies' for these perceived problems suggests that such holidays *should be avoided* because of *the problems this can cause*. There is no indication here of what these problems may be. However, the word *cause* refers cohesively to the eight points which linked language ideologies with street rioting. There is a presupposition here that extended holidays in the sub-continent cause problems in children's learning of English. This does not need to be said explicitly, because it has been said elsewhere (for example, Margaret Eaton, leader of Bradford City Council, quoted in *The Guardian*, 2001a; former Bradford headteacher, Ray Honeyford, 1988; Herman Ouseley, 2001: 14). Intertextual understanding – what Fairclough calls 'the already-said-elsewhere' (1995a: 6) – shapes the discourse, implying that visits abroad will lead to linguistic and academic problems of the sort that will cause under-achievement and, ultimately, violence. Despite lack of support from linguistic research, discourse is here dialogically penetrated by a presupposition which appears to be 'common-sense.' It is notable that Ann Cryer retains her liberal status here, saying that she *would be the last person to suggest that they sever links with the sub-continent*.

Ann Cryer's third 'remedy' for the social unrest in the north of England refers more explicitly to language ideological debates:

> When possible, English should be used and encouraged in the home in addition to Punjabi and Bangla. (*Hansard*, 2001a)

Notable here is the absence of agency in Ann Cryer's statement. It is not clear *who* should be using English, or whether those who should be using English at home are the same as those who should be encouraging the use of English. There is a cohesive link here to the earlier sentence beginning *As a result*, which suggests that households in which only one parent has *any English* lead to children going to school speaking *only Punjabi or Bangla*. The cohesive link (through repetition of *Punjabi and Bangla*) has two ideological functions: first, the implication is that parents should both speak English at home and encourage their children to do so; second, the apparently positive *in addition to Punjabi and Bangla* is less positive when set alongside the earlier *only Punjabi and Bangla*. Whereas in the second instance Asian languages seem to be equal to English, in the first example they are not sufficient. The absence of agency in this sentence implies blame of Asian families for failing to speak sufficient English (although a failure to *encourage* English-speaking in the home may also be directed at professionals). A further ideological effect of this obfuscation is to leave a space within which a 'common-sense' discourse is allowed to emerge. This discourse states that, in order to be successful learners of English, children (and adults) should speak English at home.

The fourth 'remedy' proposed by Ann Cryer is as follows:

> Much more should be provided in further education colleges and community centres for non-English speakers by way of high-quality teaching of English as a second language. That should include crèche provision, with the funding coming from both central and local government. Such projects would be much better than channelling finance towards extra policing, as we have seen over the past few weekends. (*Hansard*, 2001a)

Again Ms Cryer's proposal is characterized by a non-agentive construction. It is not clear who should provide the services she calls for, although the sentence which refers to funding suggests that the audience for this section is central or local government, rather than Asian families. However, in the context of this section of the speech as a whole, it may be that the fourth 'remedy' is doing no more than paving the way for the fifth 'remedy':

> Sponsors should be encouraged to enrol husbands and wives who enter from the sub-continent in full-time English courses. (*Hansard*, 2001a)

Here again an absence of agency creates ambiguity: there is no indication
of exactly who should *encourage* sponsors to enroll their newly-arrived
spouses in full-time English courses. This ambiguity causes obfuscation,
and throws the onus back on the *sponsors*. In fact the words *be encouraged
to* may be superfluous, as they are directed at no one in particular. The
ideological function of this proposal is to directly tell Asian people to
enroll their newly arrived husbands and wives in full-time English
courses. Notable here is the lack of agency accorded to the newly arrived
husbands and wives, semantically as well as syntactically. There is no
sense in which they may choose to enroll themselves in English courses:
the fact that they cannot speak English seems to imply that they do not
have the right to choose.

The fifth 'remedy' links cohesively with the sixth and final proposal
from Ms Cryer:

> My most controversial point is one that I have made previously. It
> has not gone down terribly well, although I have had support from
> hon. Members. I will repeat what I said, so that I place on record
> precisely what I mean. If, after possibly five years, we are no nearer
> to achieving the solutions and ambitions, and the deprivation with
> all that flows from it continues, the Government should consider
> having an element of English as an entry clearance requirement for
> husbands and wives who seek permanent settlement. There should
> be a further requirement for them to take a full-time English
> course to reach a reasonable level. The conditions should apply to
> all applicants outside the European Union. My proposals are in line
> with immigration requirements in many countries, including the
> United States of America, Canada and the Netherlands. (Hansard,
> 2001a)

Ann Cryer prefaces this proposal by saying that it is her *most controversial point*. In doing so, she makes a cohesive link to the *self-styled Asian
leaders* to whom she referred earlier. Once again the ideological effect
of this is to position as extremist any criticism of her view. When
she proposes her remedy, the deictic *we* reappears for the first time in
the 'remedies' section of the speech. The apparently inclusive *we* is
ambiguous here: it may refer to the Members of the House of Commons;
at the same time, it includes a wider audience of policy makers and
concerned people, who would in due course read reports of the speech
in the broadsheet newspapers. Ambiguity is a further feature of the statement in the phrase *the solutions and ambitions*. It is not clear what *solutions*
are to be achieved; nor is it clear who has *ambitions* even less so what

these are. *Solutions* is semantically linked to *remedy*, so it may be that this word refers to the five preceding proposals from Ms Cryer.

In the next clause, *deprivation* is linked to *poverty*, and implies that, if the importation of (linguistic, cultural, moral, economic) poverty cannot be stopped, the Government should prevent the permanent settlement of those who do not have *a reasonable level* of English. The proposed demand for *a reasonable level* of English echoes the existing requirement in law for general applicants for naturalization to have *sufficient knowledge* of English. It is not clear who decides what constitutes a *reasonable level* of English, or according to what criteria such a judgment is made. Here the phrase *husbands and wives* links this sixth remedy with the first. Ann Cryer proposes a further requirement for *them to take a full-time English course*. She claims authority and status for her proposals by stating that they are consistent with *immigration requirements in many countries*. While it is true that Britain is constrained by European law, it is not clear why the extension of language testing should apply to all applicants *outside the European Union*. It may be that there is a 'racialized' dimension here (Schmidt, 2000, 2001, 2002).

It is possible to identify in Ann Cryer's proposals ideological representations of linguistic differences. These can be further analyzed with reference to the three semiotic processes outlined by Irvine and Gal (2000: 37). In this section of the speech, when taken together with the earlier section in which *causes* of rioting are identified, linguistic features are iconically associated with elements of Muslim Asian cultural, moral, and social characteristics which are to be 'remedied.' A lack of 'good' English is iconically linked to the cultural practices of intercontinental arranged marriages and extended holidays to the sub-continent, and to the importation of poverty. Linguistic poverty depicts the essentially poor moral and cultural traits of those who engage in these practices. Linguistic features represent cultural features, and *both* are to be remedied. Similarly, monolingual (or at least non-English-speaking) speakers of Asian languages in the home are positioned as deficient. The linguistic ideology expounded here is one which does not accept non-English speakers. This ideology *erases* the possibility of monolingualism in an Asian language in Britain, insisting that such speakers transform themselves into bilingual, multilingual, or monolingual speakers of English. The dominant ideology here appears to deny the possibility that bilingual speakers can have 'reasonably' good English. This process of erasure underlies the call for compulsory enrollment in English classes, and the demand for naturalization language testing for those who seek permanent settlement in Britain. Adopting Irvine and Gal's analysis, then, the linguistic ideology which is proposed and expounded by Ann Cryer erases any possibility of citizenship for non-English speakers in Britain.

Language testing for British citizenship

The MP for Keighley is happy to propose the extension of language testing for all applicants who seek permanent settlement in Britain, because this practice fits with what Irvine and Gal call a 'totalizing vision' (2000: 38) of England for English speakers; any alternative is a recipe for social unrest. Here she conceives of British citizenship being available only to speakers of English. The speech was widely reported in the national print media and, shortly after Ann Cryer's speech in Parliament, the Minister of State for the Home Office, Lord Rooker, supported her in the House of Lords (*Hansard*, 2001b) and made the following statement during an interview for ePolitix.com on August 17, 2001:

Interview: Do you agree with Ann Cryer that new citizens should learn to speak English?

Lord Rooker: I am on record in the House of Lords as supporting exactly what Ann Cryer said about this issue, based on constituency experience. There is a real problem she has identified. There are situations, this has got nothing to do with asylum seekers, where sometimes people are not encouraged or persuaded to learn English by their family. The men say 'they don't need it.' I don't accept that because it's people being denied their civil rights. The question arises do we require people to learn English as a consequence of applying for nationality, which you've got to do in English anyway. We're looking at this. We're looking at the issue of citizenship. People must maintain their culture, maintain their religion and live in peace and tranquillity but they must not be denied their opportunity to participate properly particularly in the employment market. (Rooker, 2001)

In this response Lord Rooker adopts a similar strategy to that of Ann Cryer in establishing his 'right to speak' on the issue (*based on constituency experience*). Lord Rooker picks up the word *encouraged* from Ann Cryer's speech, making a cohesive tie between the two. The rather oblique *people* here is as ambiguous as the non-agentive sentence on the same subject in Cryer's speech. Here *the family* appears to be at fault for failing to persuade or encourage *people* to learn English (Rooker changes Cryer's *used* to *learn*). However, in the next sentence *The men* appear to be the villains of the piece, as they reportedly say *'they don't need it.'* The implication therefore is that *people* refers to Asian women, and presumably Asian women who are not English speakers. The next sentence confirms this. Lord Rooker invokes the phrase *civil rights* (which he also used in his speech in the House of Lords) to support his argument. In using this term Rooker asserts that his argument is unimpeachable: no one can argue with civil rights, as they just are a good thing. The ideological effect of using this phrase is to establish a liberal tone in his illiberal statement. However, there is no reference here to the civil rights of those (men or women) who wish to become British citizens, but are unable or unwilling to score highly on an arbitrary English language test. It is notable here that the definite article (*The men*) does ideological work, grouping together what we suppose to be all Asian men, or perhaps all Muslim Asian men, or even all Muslim Asian men in Britain. In Lord Rooker's reply there is no mention of Asian groups; however, intertextual references to Ann Cryer's speech suggest that *The men* are indeed Asian. In these latter two sentences Lord Rooker engages in dialogic discourse (Bakhtin, 1994: 108), directing his argument against the supposedly authoritarian statement of *The men*. The discourse takes a presupposed statement by Asian men, reworks it, and simplifies it, contrasting it with the phrase *civil rights*. In doing so, the discourse lays the apparently liberal foundation for an illiberal proposal.

The next sentence begins *The question arises*, as if the question of naturalization language testing had agency of its own, and had not emerged from a language ideological debate located in the context of 'race riots.' The deictic *we* in *do we require people* is ambiguous: it could refer to the government alone; at the same time, it can include the wider British public, or anyone concerned to deal with the recent social disorder. In this sentence Lord Rooker's rationale for revising the law on naturalization language testing is based on rather unwieldy logic. As we have seen, the current legislation requires applicants to have *sufficient knowledge* of the language to deal with work and/or everyday situations. However, the legislation does not currently include any language requirement for a person applying as the husband or wife of a British citizen. This being the case, it would appear that Lord Rooker and Ann Cryer are proposing a change to the law particularly as it affects naturalization requirements for spouses (usually wives) of British citizens. The deictic *We* in *We're looking at this*, and in the following sentence, is less inclusive than before, referring to the Government, or perhaps the Home Office. In the final sentence of his response, Lord Rooker refers once more to *People*. Again this probably refers to Asian women in Britain (it is difficult to see why he uses such a euphemism), and probably Asian immigrant women in Britain. The obligational auxiliary modal verb is emphatic in insisting that such *People must* maintain their culture and religion and live in *peace and tranquillity*. The connective (*but*) seems to create an oppositional discourse, however, implying that the maintenance of culture and religion, and living in peace and tranquillity, are somehow opposed to *proper* participation in employment. In the context of the main point of the response, which addresses naturalization language testing, and in the intertextual context of Ann Cryer's speech, it is likely that 'proper participation' is here a metaphor for learning and speaking English. That is, maintenance of culture and religion, and what Ouseley (2001: 24) refers to as 'self-segregation,' *must* not stand in the way of linguistic homogeneity.

Taking Irvine and Gal's (2000) model of semiotic processes in the analysis of linguistic ideologies, a lack of English, and a failure to encourage others to speak English, are iconically associated with the presupposed oppressive, regressive values and practices of Asian men. At the same time, a lack of English is associated with self-segregation of communities and individuals. In Irvine and Gal's terms, these politicians define the 'self against some imagined Other' (2000: 39), as the linguistic behaviors of others are simplified and seen as if deriving from those persons' essences rather than from historical accident.

On August 19, 2001, two days after Lord Rooker's interview was published on the ePolitix.com website, *The Observer* and *The Independent on Sunday* reported a statement released by the Home Secretary, David Blunkett. Both (liberal) newspapers quoted the Home Secretary, saying that he supported Lord Rooker's comments, and sought debate

> on the important and central part an understanding of English plays in developing good community and race relations, and the chances of obtaining both education and employment.

Although his statement masquerades as liberal and egalitarian, it is clear that, in supporting Lord Rooker, the Secretary of State is bringing one step closer the institutionalization in law of an ideology which blames non-English-speaking women for their children's educational under-achievement, and ultimately for the violence and social disorder on the streets. This apparently common-sense ideology – that, when all members of a nation-state speak the same language, social cohesion automatically follows – is established as self-evident 'reality' in the discourse of politicians, and is converted into the potential for the legal legitimation of exclusionary practices. Alongside the potential for actual exclusionary practices, through creating what Bourdieu calls 'social frontiers' (2000: 187) inscribed in law, a less tangible process of *symbolic violence* is reiterated. When one of the three most powerful politicians in Britain implies that non-English-speaking immigrants are to blame for a breakdown in social cohesion, the mass media listen and report, and symbolic violence is done to those who are either second language learners or recent arrivals in the country. For example, following the Home Secretary David Blunkett's statement in an interview in December 2001 that naturalization candidates should have 'a modest grasp of the English tongue, so they can feel and become English' (*The Independent on Sunday*, 2001), every national newspaper in England featured the story. In such chains of discourses (Fairclough, 1995a) realities are constructed which suggest that the only way to be British is to be an English (or possibly Welsh or Gaelic) speaker. This discourse is common-sense, self-evident, and oppressive.

In 2002 the Secretary of State introduced into Parliament the *Nationality, Immigration and Asylum Act*, in which he set out government plans for new legislation for citizenship and nationality, which extends the requirement to have sufficient knowledge of English (or Welsh or Scottish Gaelic) to those applying for naturalization on the basis of marriage. That is, following the passing into law of the *Act* language testing requirements extend to the spouses of applicants who are married to British citizens. For all applicants, including spouses of British citizens, the *Act* adds a requirement that applicants should demonstrate 'sufficient knowledge about life in the United Kingdom' (1, 1, (ca)). The *Act* further legislates for new powers allowing the Secretary of State to test applicants' knowledge of English (or Welsh or Scottish Gaelic), and their knowledge of life in the United Kingdom. These are set out in terms of new regulations which refer to:

(1) possession of a specified qualification;
(2) possession of a qualification of a specified kind;
(3) attendance on a specified course;
(4) attendance on a course of a specified kind;
(5) a specified level of achievement
(6) a person designated by the Secretary of State to determine sufficiency of knowledge in specified circumstances;
(7) the Secretary of State being enabled to accept a qualification of a specified kind as evidence of sufficient knowledge of a language.

At the time of writing it is not known how these powers will be exercised in practice. The provisions of the *Act* appear to be quite specific in their focus, but in fact leave considerable room for maneuver on the part of the Secretary of State. It is not yet clear how *sufficient knowledge of English, Welsh or Scottish Gaelic* and *sufficient knowledge about life in the United Kingdom* will be tested – whether by arbitrary tests, or by simple attendance on one of a range of courses. What is clear, though, is that a language ideological debate which began with the apparently absurd notion that social disorder and civil unrest are linked to, if not caused by, some groups' use of Asian languages rather than English, has been transformed into new legislation which requires all applicants for citizenship to prove that they have sufficient knowledge of the language of the dominant host group.

Conclusion: Language, Logic, and Moral Conformism

It seems clear that, in the chain of discourses which emerged in the wake of the riots in northern England, *understanding English* is iconically linked with *good race relations*, even at the highest level of government. The opposite of good race relations is perceived to be the kind of rioting witnessed during the summer of 2001. In the linguistic ideology emerging in these discourses, 'good English' has become a precondition for social cohesion. Proficiency in Asian languages, on the other hand, is iconically linked with a predisposition to violence and social disorder. This language ideological debate is about more than language: it appears to be about the viability of the multicultural state.

In Bourdieu's terms, the debate which links the lack of English proficiency of the spouses of British citizens with social disorder creates a natural, self-evident discourse which is 'the foundation of a logical conformism and a moral conformism' (2000: 172). The social world is experienced as a common-sense reality in which it is accepted (by dominant and dominated groups alike) that all citizens of Britain must have sufficient knowledge of the indigenous language. In this logical, moral discourse, common sense dictates that immigrant wives and husbands who wish to apply for British citizenship must learn sufficient English to engage in everyday work and social practices (neither of which necessarily require use of English), and to fulfill their duties as citizens (whatever they may be). This language ideological debate is a struggle not over language alone, but over the kind of society that Britain imagines itself to be: either multilingual, pluralist, and diverse, or ultimately English-speaking, assimilationist, and homogeneous. In the debate analyzed and reported here, the strongest voices represent the most powerful institutions, and belong to those who see the future of Britain as a homogeneous, monolingual state.

References

Anderson, B. (1983) *Imagined communities*. London: Verso.

Bakhtin, M. (1986) *Speech genres and other late essays*. In C. Emerson and M. Holquist (eds) Austin, TX: University of Austin Press.

Bakhtin, M. (1994) Problems of Dostoevsky's Poetics. In P. Morris (ed.) *The Bakhtin reader: Selected writings of Bakhtin, Medvedev, Voloshinov* (pp. 103–113). London: Arnold.

Blommaert, J. (1999) The debate is open. In J. Blommaert (ed.) *Language ideological debates* (pp. 1–38). Berlin: Mouton de Gruyter.

Blommaert, J. and Verschueren, J. (1998a) The role of language in European nationalist ideologies. In B. Schieffelin, K. Woolard, and P. Kroskrity (eds) *Language ideologies: Practice and theory* (pp. 189–210). New York: Oxford University Press.

Blommaert, J. and Verschueren, J. (1998b) *Debating diversity: Analysing the discourse of tolerance*. London/New York: Routledge.

Bokhorst-Heng, W. (1999) Singapore's *Speak Mandarin Campaign*: Language ideological debates in the imagining of the nation. In J. Blommaert (ed.) *Language ideological debates* (pp. 235–266). Berlin: Mouton de Gruyter.

Bourdieu, P. (1990) *The logic of practice*. Cambridge: Polity Press.

Bourdieu, P. (1998) *Practical reason*. London: Polity Press.

Bourdieu, P. (2000) *Pascalian meditations*. Cambridge: Polity Press.

Fairclough, N. (1989) *Language and power*. London: Longman.

Fairclough, N. (1995a) *Critical discourse analysis: The critical study of language*. London/New York: Longman.

Fairclough, N. (1995b) *Media discourse*. London: Arnold.

Fowler, R. (1991) *Language in the news: Discourse and ideology in the press*. London: Routledge.

Gal, S. (1998) Multiplicity and contention among language ideologies: A commentary. In B. Schieffelin, K. Woolard, and P. Kroskrity (eds) *Language ideologies: Practice and theory* (pp. 3–47). New York: Oxford University Press.

Gal, S. and Irvine, J. (1995) The boundaries of language and disciplines: How ideologies construct difference. *Social Research* 62 (4), 967–1001.

Gal, S. and Woolard, K. (1995) Constructing languages and publics: Authority and representation. *Pragmatics* 5 (2), 129–138.

Gardner-Chloros, P. (1997) Vernacular literacy in new vernacular settings in Europe. In A. Tabouret-Keller, R. Le Page, P. Gardner-Chloros, and G. Varro (eds) *Vernacular literacy: A re-evaluation* (pp. 189–221). Oxford: Clarendon Press.

Gramsci, A. (1971) *Selections from the prison notebooks*. New York: International.

Grillo, R. (1998) *Pluralism and the politics of difference*. Oxford: Clarendon Press.

The Guardian (2001a) Bradford's painful future, July 13, 17.

The Guardian (2001b) Old hatred, new style, July 27, 17.

Hansard (2001a) Commons *Hansard* Debates text for July 17, 2001, Volume No. 372, Part No. 22. On WWW at http://www.publications.parliament.uk/pa/cm200102/cmhansrd/cm010717/hallindx/10717-x.htm.

Hansard (2001b) Commons/Lords Debates text for July 19, 2001, Volume No. 626, Part No. 20. On WWW at http://www.publications.parliament.uk/pa/ld200102/ldhansrd/vo010719/text/10719-18.htm#10719-18_spmin0.

Heller, M. (1995) Language choice, social institutions and symbolic domination. *Language in Society* 24, 373–405.

Heller, M. (1999) *Linguistic minorities and modernity: A sociolinguistic ethnography.* London/New York: Longman.

Home Office (1981) *British Nationality Act.* London, HMSO.

Home Office (2002) *Nationality, Immigration and Asylum Act.* London, HMSO.

Home Office (n.d.a) *Information about naturalisation as a British citizen.* On WWW at http://www.ind.homeoffice.gov.uk/default.asp?PageId=151.

Home Office (n.d.b) *Naturalisation as a British citizen: A guide for applicants.* On WWW at http://www.ind.homeoffice.gov.uk/default.asp?PageId=119.

Honeyford, R. (1988) *Integration or disintegration?: Towards a non-racist society.* London: Claridge.

Hymes, D. (1996) *Ethnography, linguistics, narrative inequality: Toward an understanding of voice.* London: Taylor and Francis.

The Independent (2001a) David Aaronovitch: Forget political correctness – racism causes racial tensions, June 29, 10.

The Independent (2001b) David Aaronovitch: Forget political correctness – racism causes racial tensions, July 13, 12.

The Independent (2001c) Ouseley claims Bradford is city gripped by fear and prejudice, July 13, 3.

The Independent on Sunday (2001) If we want social cohesion we need a sense of identity, December 9, 20.

Irvine, J. and Gal, S. (2000) Language ideology and linguistic differentiation. In P. Kroskrity (ed.) *Regimes of language: Ideologies, polities and identities* (pp. 35–84). Santa Fe, NM/Oxford: School of American Research Press.

Kroskrity, P. (1998) Arizona Tewa Kiva speech as a manifestation of a dominant language ideology. In B. Schieffelin, K. Woolard, and P. Kroskrity (eds) *Language ideologies: Practice and theory* (pp. 103–122). New York: Oxford University Press.

Kroskrity, P. (2000) Regimenting languages: Language ideological perspectives. In P. Kroskrity (ed.) *Regimes of language: Ideologies, polities and identities* (pp. 1–34). Santa Fe, NM/Oxford: School of American Research Press.

Ouseley, H. (2001) *Community pride, not prejudice: Making diversity work in Bradford.* Bradford: Bradford Vision.

Pavlenko, A. (2001a) Language learning memoirs as a gendered genre. *Applied Linguistics* 22, 213–240.

Pavlenko, A. (2001b) 'How do I become a woman in an American vein?': Transformations of gender performance in second language learning. In A. Pavlenko, A. Blackledge, I. Piller, and M. Teutsch-Dwyer (eds) *Multilingualism, second language learning, and gender* (pp. 133–174). Berlin: Mouton de Gruyter.

Pavlenko, A. (2001c) 'In the world of the tradition, I was unimagined': Negotiation of identities in cross-cultural autobiographies. *The International Journal of Bilingualism* 5 (3), 317–344.

Philips, S. (1998) Language ideologies in institutions of power: A commentary. In B. Schieffelin, K. Woolard, and P. Kroskrity (eds) *Language ideologies: Practice and theory* (pp. 211–222). New York: Oxford University Press.

Piller, I. (2001) Naturalisation language testing and its basis in ideologies of national identity and citizenship. *International Journal of Bilingualism* 5 (3), 259–278.

Rooker, Lord (2001) Interview with Rt Hon. Lord Rooker, August 17, 2001. On WWW at http://www.ePolitix.com.

Schieffelin, B. and Doucet, R. (1998) The 'real' Haitian Creole: Ideology, metalinguistics and orthographic choice. In B. Schieffelin, K. Woolard, and P. Kroskrity (eds) *Language ideologies: Practice and theory* (pp. 285–316). New York: Oxford University Press.

Schmidt, R. (2000) *Language policy and identity politics in the United States.* Philadelphia: Temple University Press.

Schmidt, R. (2001) *Racialization and culture in language policy conflict: A perspective from the USA.* Paper presented at the Third International Symposium on Bilingualism, Bristol, UK, April 18–20, 2001.

Schmidt, R. (2002) Racialization and language policy: The case of the USA. *Multilingua* 21 (2/3), 141–162.

Silverstein, M. (2000) Whorfianism and the linguistic imagination of nationality. In P. Kroskrity (ed.) *Regimes of language. Ideologies, polities and identities* (pp. 84–138). Santa Fe/Oxford: School of American Research Press.

Voloshinov, V.N. (1973) *Marxism and the philosophy of language* (L. Matejka and I.R. Titunik, trans.; first published 1929). London/New York: Seminar Press.

Williams, R. (1977) *Marxism and literature.* Oxford: Oxford University Press.

Wodak, R. (2000) Recontextualization and the transformation of meanings: A critical discourse analysis of decision making in EU meetings about employment policies. In S. Sarangi and M. Coulthard (eds) *Discourse and social life* (pp. 185–206). London: Longman.

Wodak, R., de Cillia, R. Reisigl, M., and K. Liebhart, (1999) *The discursive construction of national identity.* Edinburgh: Edinburgh University Press.

Woolard, K. (1998) Introduction: Language ideology as a field of inquiry. In B. Schieffelin, K. Woolard, and P. Kroskrity (eds) *Language ideologies: Practice and theory* (pp. 3–47). New York: Oxford University Press.

Chapter 3

Negotiating Between Bourge and Racaille: Verlan as Youth Identity Practice in Suburban Paris

MEREDITH DORAN

On commence à le parler . . . parce qu'on se cherche et on se trouve pas, et on arrête de le parler quand on s'est trouvé, et quand on s'est donné une autre identité. Mais je sais pas, moi je le parle encore. (Dalila, age 19[1])

(You start speaking it [Verlan] . . . because you're looking for yourself and you aren't finding yourself, and you stop speaking it when you've found yourself, when you've given yourself another identity. But I don't know, I'm still speaking it.)

Introduction

For several centuries, the French State has enacted numerous policies to construct a French 'imagined community' (Anderson, 1991) which is monocultural, monolingual, monoethnic (*nos ancêtres les Gaulois* 'our ancestors the Gauls'), monoideological, and shares a common national identity (Blommaert & Verschueren, 1998; Marconot, 1990). However, as Bourdieu (1991, 1993) and other analysts of language and society have pointed out, the consolidation of such a mythically homogeneous community depends in part on the exclusion or suppression of populations and characteristics which do not fit into its ideal self-definition. In other words, while the 'ideology of the standard' may foster nationalistic unity, at the same time it militates against recognizing a sociocultural reality which is in fact heterogeneous and multiform. In France specifically, the dominance of this ideology has meant that the linguistic, cultural, and ethnic diversity present within France's borders has tended to be obscured or outright denied in order to reinforce a homogeneous vision of what it means to be 'French' (Ager, 1999; Boyer, 1996, 1997; Durand, 1996; Grillo, 1985; Weber, 1976). In keeping with a long tradition of monolingual policies in France, as recently as 1994 the Toubon Act institutionalized the dominant ideology of language and identity in a legislation which made the use of French obligatory in many public domains. The rationale for this legislation clearly stated that 'French is a fundamental element of the personality and heritage of France' (preamble to the Toubon Act, 1994, cited in Ager, 1999: 10). Blommaert and Verschueren (1998: 194–195) have referred to this kind of republican ideology as 'the dogma of *homogeneism*: a view of society in which differences are seen as dangerous and centrifugal and in which the "best" society is suggested to be one without intergroup differences.'

It is in the context of such dominant language ideology that this chapter explores a particular aspect of linguistic diversity in contemporary France: the use of a language variety called Verlan. Spoken primarily among multiethnic youth populations living in disadvantaged neighborhoods outside Paris (and several other major French cities), this 'street language' has become in recent decades a recognizable sociolect in *la banlieue* (the suburbs) and, more specifically, in the low-income housing projects referred to collectively as *les cités* (the cities). Characterized by various alterations of Standard French terms, borrowings from such languages as Arabic, English, and Romani, and certain distinctive prosodic and discourse-level features, Verlan is a kind of linguistic *bricolage* marked by the multilingualism and multiculturalism present in the communities where it is spoken, which include immigrants from North Africa, West Africa, Portugal, Asia, and the Caribbean. Given the marginal status of these communities vis-à-vis elite Parisian culture, Verlan can be viewed as an alternative code which stands both literally and figuratively outside the hegemonic norms of Parisian culture and language.[2]

Not surprisingly, the emergence of this non-standard language variety on France's linguistically normative landscape has piqued the interest of linguistic and cultural commentators alike. In the past 15 years, a number of studies have examined the formal properties of Verlan as a divergence from Standard French (Azra & Cheneau, 1994; Bullock, 1996; Fabrice, 1998; Goudaillier, 1998; Lefkowitz, 1989, 1991; Méla, 1988, 1991, 1997; Petitpas, 1998; Plénat, 1993, 1995; Sewell & Payne, 2000; Valdman, 2000; Weinberger & Lefkowitz, 1992) and several popular 'decoding' dictionaries of Verlan have appeared on the public scene (Aguillou & Saïki, 1996; Andreini, 1985; Bézard, 1993; Goudaillier, 1998; Merle, 1997; Pierre-Adolphe *et al.*, 1998).

However, in focusing largely on the structural properties of Verlan, much of the existing research has tended to leave aside questions of the possible social meaning of the emergence and use of this language variety, or of how its use might be tied to questions of identity among marginalized minority youths whose 'mixed' identities (tied to both family minority and French cultures) find little room for expression or recognition within the larger imagined community. Indeed, the same ideological hegemony which has undergirded the construction of a monolithic French identity has also traditionally denied the possibility of 'non-standard' identities within its borders (Ager, 1999; Souilamas, 2000), placing minority youths in a kind of 'no man's land' of identity, caught at a crossroads between 'immigrant' and 'French' (Hargreaves, 1997).[3]

With the goal of exploring these identity issues, this chapter will present the findings of a study of the use of Verlan in a suburban youth community. This study examined how this language variety – an alternative to the Standard French of *L'Académie* – serves as a tool for minority youths to enact social realities and perform identities which diverge from the models offered by mainstream French society and its language. Based on interviews and observational data, I will argue that, by using their own local language, with its own in-group meanings, young people in this community were able to delineate a 'third space' (Bhabha, 1994) for identity in which their complex, multilingual, multicultural, working-class identities could be both performed and recognized in a way that they were not within the larger society.

The chapter will be divided into four major sections: first, a brief presentation of the major theoretical concepts which inform this study; second, an overview of the major research on Verlan to date, including its treatment of language and identity; third, an introduction to the specific research project I carried out, describing its major goals, community of study, and methodology; and, finally, an analysis of the research data, centering on the ways in which speakers' choices to use, or not to use, Verlan in particular settings were tied to various aspects of identity, including ethnicity, class, cultural values, and relation to the stereotypical figure of suburban youth street culture, *la racaille*.

Theoretical Framework

This study draws on recent poststructuralist paradigms that treat identity as multidimensional, contingent, and subject to negotiation across contexts (Blackledge & Pavlenko, 2001; Bucholtz, 1999; Eckert & McConnell-Ginet, 1999; Hill, 1999; Lo, 1999). From this perspective, language is recognized as a central tool for the strategic enactment of multiple subject positions; individuals are seen as activating different parts of their linguistic repertoires selectively in order to highlight particular aspects of their social identities (and to downplay others) in particular settings. At the same time, it is also acknowledged that, while certain aspects of identity may be negotiable in given contexts, others may be less so, since individuals may be positioned (Davies & Harré, 1990) by dominant groups in ways they did not choose. In these situations, individuals or groups may seek to challenge, resist, or transform accepted identity categories to allow for greater identity options.

Also important to the analysis in this chapter is Rampton's (1995) work on youth language practices in a multiethnic community in England. Challenging dichotomous notions of 'dominant' vs. 'marginalized' linguistic identities, he explores the dynamic of language crossing, by which adolescents take up out-group minority languages present in the community as a means of 'cultivating alternative minority solidarities' (Rampton, 1995: 294) and demonstrating anti-racism. Rampton's (1995) *Crossing* provides a useful analytical model for this project, both because his object of study bears similarities to Verlan, and because his approach validates such factors as race, class, inter-ethnic relations, and dominant discourses as important for understanding the meaning of non-standard linguistic practices, both among their users, and in relation to the larger society.

Finally, the analysis in this chapter will take up postcolonial theorist Homi Bhabha's (1994) notion of the 'third space' as a metaphor for understanding the dynamics of identity negotiation in minority communities. For Bhabha, the negotiation of identity for minority populations involves creating an in-between or liminal space of culture – a 'third space' – in which the fixed identities of the traditional societal order do not hold sway, and hybrid identities can be performed and affirmed. Such a space is constituted temporally through the re-appropriation and transformation of cultural symbols, including language, which are made to mean in new ways.

Verlan as a Linguistic Phenomenon

Linguistic description of Verlan

Although the term 'Verlan' originally referred to a French language game involving syllabic inversion (*Verlan* is derived from *l'envers*, meaning 'backwards')[4], it now serves as an umbrella term for a more elaborated code which has become a recognizable sociolect over the past two decades. The characteristics of this code have been well studied in both lexicographic studies, which have documented sets of the most recent Verlan terms (Aguillou & Saïki, 1996; Bézard, 1993; Demougeot *et al.*, 1994; Goudaillier, 1998; Pierre-Adolphe *et al.*, 1998), and broader descriptive studies, which have analyzed a wide range of linguistic features that distinguish Verlan from Standard French (SF) (Azra & Cheneau, 1994; Lefkowitz, 1991; Méla, 1988, 1997).[5] These works allow for the following basic description of the major linguistic characteristics of contemporary Parisian Verlan:

Syllabic inversion

As reflected in the original definition of the term *Verlan*, the most canonical procedure for forming an item in Verlan involves the reversing of syllables in a word or short expression from SF, as in the following examples (Verlan terms appear in bold):

méchant 'mean' ⇒ **chanmé**

soirée 'a party', 'an evening ' ⇒ **résoi**

fatigué 'tired' ⇒ **guétifa**

louche 'suspicious' ⇒ **chelou**

tout à l'heure 'just now' ⇒ **leurtoute**

Though the above transformations reflect a fairly neat transposition of syllables, others involve more complex modifications of the original term, including the alteration of medial vowels and/or truncation, meaning greater divergence from the original SF item, and therefore greater incomprehensibility to non-initiates:

flic 'cop' ⇒ **keuf**

femme 'woman' ⇒ **meuf**

parents 'parents' ⇒ *renpa* ⇒ **renp**

disque 'record' ⇒ *dis-que* ⇒ *skeudi* ⇒ **skeud**

Borrowings

Borrowings are drawn from minority languages present in the community – such as Arabic, Wolof, and Portuguese – as well as from Romani (the language of the Rom, or Gypsies) and English (primarily from rap, hip-hop, or reggae music). These borrowings are typically either conversational discourse markers, or else terms relating to music, illicit activities, or taboo topics, such as drugs, theft, sex, or gang culture:

chouia (Arabic) 'a little'

bedave (Romani) 'to smoke'

posse (English) 'gang, group'

joint (English) 'marijuana or hashish cigarette'

Verlan terms may also be taken from archaic or old-fashioned French slang (including criminal *argot*). In this sense, these terms are 'borrowed' from the language of *la culture populaire* (blue-collar culture), which is itself often treated as a variety distinct from SF:

Schmitt, condé 'cop'

baston 'fight'

daron 'father' / *daronne* 'mother'

maille 'money'

These revived slang terms may also be 'verlanized,' or inverted, rendering them even more opaque in form and meaning to outsiders:

faucher 'to steal' ⇒ *chéfo*

tune 'money' ⇒ *neutu*

placard 'prison', literally 'closet' ⇒ *carpla*

Verlan is further characterized by the inclusion of calques (direct translations of idiomatic expressions from other languages), such as the following from Arabic:

sur le Koran '[I swear] on the Koran'

sur la tête de ma mère '[I swear] on my mother's head'

Prosodic and phonemic differences

In addition to its lexical differences from SF, Verlan is characterized by particular prosodic and phonemic patternings which differ from those of the standard language. The processes of truncation and medial vowel alteration illustrated above produce phonemic distribution patterns atypical for French; similarly, the inclusion of foreign borrowings *in toto* contributes certain non-French phonemes, lending Verlan a 'foreign' sound (Tifrit, 1999). In terms of prosodic differences from SF, stress may be placed in non-standard ways within breath groups, making word boundaries difficult to decipher (Méla, 1997). Finally, Verlan is characterized by a distinctive vocalic quality, due both to the frequent reduction of SF medial vowels to [oe] in the process of syllabic inversion, as well as to features of what Calvet (1994: 84) calls a 'suburban accent,' involving lax articulation and backing of vowels. Thus, even though Verlan is sometimes classified as a partial slang, since not all words in a given phrase are 'verlanized' (i.e. lexically distinctive from SF), these prosodic and phonemic features serve as additional distinctive features which signal utterances as Verlan. Due to the variety of linguistic levels on which Verlan diverges from SF, and its association with particular sociocultural groups, it may be classified as a *sociolect* rather than simply a slang lexicon (Bachmann & Basier, 1984; Boyer, 1997).

It is important to point out here that the preceding description of Verlan constitutes only the tip of the linguistic iceberg, since researchers are quick to note that, while certain basic Verlan terms are widely known (*meuf* 'woman' and *keuf* 'cop' being some of the most recognizable), there are always local variations and constant innovations in each particular youth community, including the phenomenon of re-verlanization (Méla, 1988), in which existing Verlan terms undergo further inversions or modifications, as a form of re-encoding (e.g. *Arabe* 'Arab' ⇒ *beur* ⇒ *reubeu* ⇒ *reub*). Consequently, linguists have had to recognize that an exhaustive description of Verlan will always be elusive, since, just like any other language, it is in continual evolution.

The speakers of Verlan[6]

In the mainstream French media, Verlan has tended to be particularly associated with the North African-origin youth population in *les cités*, referred to as *les beurs* (*beur* is the Verlan term for 'Arab'). However, researchers have established that the use of Verlan is not limited to *beur* youths alone, having become a more generalized phenomenon within the project suburbs at large (Aguillou & Saïki, 1996; Bachmann & Basier, 1984; George, 1986, 1993; Goudaillier, 1998; Lepoutre, 1997).[7] Verlan is spoken by youths from a number of ethnic backgrounds represented in the *banlieue* (suburbs), including North Africa, Spain, Portugal, West Africa, Poland, Pakistan, and Southeast Asia, as well as by those from rural and suburban France (Calvet, 1993b; Lepoutre, 1997).

To date, Verlan has been classified as an adolescent phenomenon, used primarily among the junior high and high school population (Bachmann & Basier, 1984; George, 1993; Lefkowitz, 1991; Lepoutre, 1997). The existing literature on Verlan represents it as a predominantly, if not exclusively, male practice (Aguillou & Saïki, 1996; Méla, 1988, 1991). Bachmann and Basier (1984), in fact, refer to Verlan as *la langue des keums* (the guys' language), and nearly all samples of Verlan cited in scholarship are from male speakers. Though the issue of differential usage according to gender has not been taken up per se in the existing literature, most studies suggest that Verlan's association with tough street culture and even criminal activity may make it socially off-limits for females.[8]

A number of studies (Bachmann & Basier, 1984; Calvet, 1993a; Lefkowitz, 1989; Marconot, 1990; Méla, 1988) emphasize that Verlan use is also correlated with the social status of the speaker, being most pronounced among more marginal youths: 'the most competent speakers of Verlan are often the most "awful" students . . . they are the most deviant in regard to social rules in general, and to school norms in particular' (Bachmann & Basier, 1984: 178). This presumed link between marginality and Verlan use is one reason that the sociolect is often linked to a tradition of criminal slang, or *argot* (a 'secret' language used by criminals to hide their discussion of illicit activities) (Calvet, 1990; Guiraud, 1956).

As for the situations in which Verlan is typically used, Paul (1985) and Méla (1997) maintain that it is mainly a language of peer-group interaction, often used to discuss taboo topics (such as crime, sexual activity, and drug use), though it may also be used at times with authority figures as a form of resistance. Ultimately, though, there has been little systematic analysis of the specific social contexts or speech situations in which Verlan is spoken, in part due to the difficulty of collecting adolescent peer-group conversational data.

Verlan and identity

Alongside the lexicographic and descriptive studies, there is a body of research that includes an interpretive, or sociolinguistic, component in its analysis of Verlan. Several studies raise the issue of identity in relation to Verlan: Bachmann and Basier (1984), Goudaillier (1998), and Méla (1997) propose a *fonction identitaire* (identity function) for Verlan, calling it an 'instrument in the quest for identity' (Bachmann & Basier, 1984: 183) and 'an important component of social identity' (Méla, 1988: 59). Lepoutre's (1997) ethnographic study of a suburban *cité* discusses various aspects of identity among youths who use Verlan and highlights ways in which this sociolect is linked to the performance of a street-wise adolescent persona.

However, while these studies suggest links between Verlan use and identity, ultimately they do not delve deep in this area. In particular, they do not include youths' own perspectives on their sense of identity, and do not provide specific, contextualized examples of Verlan use in interaction to illustrate exactly how youth identities might be solidified, or supported, through the use of Verlan. Moreover, in light of the poststructuralist view of identity put forth earlier in this chapter, which sees identity as fluid, dynamic, and performed in interaction, questions are raised about whether it is possible to speak in terms of 'an' identity connected to Verlan at all.

Indeed, given the racially, culturally, and linguistically heterogeneous nature of the adolescent population in *la banlieue*, it seems appropriate to explore the possibility of multiple orientations to Verlan use which are themselves tied to different identity positions among youths in various contexts. In fact, if identity is conceived of as emerging through a process of negotiation among interlocutors, then Verlan might be viewed as a kind of social practice through which youths can position themselves in relation to their peers and to the dominant discourse in a variety of ways. Taking seriously this multiple perspective on identity, several major questions emerge regarding the relationship between Verlan use and identity. These questions, which furnish the basis for the study, will be discussed in the next section.

Research Project

Research goals

The central questions guiding my research project were the following: which facets of identity are linked to Verlan use? How are these enacted in everyday social interaction using Verlan? Are youths who use Verlan aware of any identity stakes connected with Verlan, and if so, how do they define them?

In order to address these questions – and in the light of the relative lack of longitudinal studies of Verlan use in a single community – one of the major design goals of this project was to ensure the opportunity for the researcher to observe and interact with minority youths in a suburban community where Verlan is used alongside other linguistic repertoires. I also hoped to gain some insight into how the use of Verlan might fit into the way the youths viewed their own identities and, more specifically, their relationship to Standard French language and culture.

Research site

My research focused on the minority youth community in Les Salières, a town located about one hour south of Paris by train. Though the tough *cités* to the north of Paris are most associated with Verlan use in media representations, I chose to focus instead on a smaller, lower-profile neighborhood in the southern suburbs with a more economically and ethnically mixed population. In doing so, I hoped to gain insight into how Verlan might be used and viewed in a more liminal *cité* area. As a way of participating in the community, I volunteered as a tutor in an after-school program administered by L'ASTI (*L'Association de Solidarité avec les Travailleurs Immigrés* 'The Association for Solidarity with Immigrant Workers'), a local, primarily volunteer immigrant-support association. The association provided tutoring in various academic subjects to junior high and high school students and offered adult literacy courses, legal advocacy services, intercultural community events, and youth recreational activities. Since this particular association had a reputation in the community as being warm and supportive, I felt that it was likely to be a good environment for developing more extensive relationships with youths, which would allow me to observe and interact with them in other settings.

The tutoring center itself (the office of L'ASTI) was located in a neighborhood called L'*Île* (The Island), a relatively isolated strip of land which was home to most of the immigrant population in Les Salières, and thus constituted the center of minority culture in the town. The majority of immigrants in this neighborhood lived in government-subsidized housing units, often in cramped conditions. Their national origins were varied: of the youths who regularly attended the *soutien scolaire* (school support) program, about 50% were of North African origin (mainly from Morocco and Algeria), about 20% French, and the remaining 30% were a mix of African, Indian, Portuguese, Caribbean, and Spanish origin. On Wednesdays, the tutoring sessions were conducted in a local school and were more formal in nature; on those days, the ethnic mix was about 50% French/50% ethnic minority youth, allowing me contact with a broader youth population from the town. Because of the change in locale, atmosphere, and student population, these Wednesday sessions provided an informative contrast to the language and general behavior patterns observed during the rest of the week at L'ASTI.

Data collection

Drawing on the strategies adopted in previous studies of youth language and code-switching (Eckert, 1989; Rampton, 1995; Torres, 1997;

Zentella, 1997), data were collected by three major means: participant observation, interviews, and audiotaping of natural speech. Observation took place at a variety of locations throughout the town, including the tutoring center and the local shopping mall, and later, as I came to know the adolescents better, in their homes. In addition to listening for Verlan use, I was interested in examining patterns of inter-ethnic relations, gender relations, age mixing in social groups, and types of marginality in the community, all factors identified in previous research as germane to Verlan use.

After several months of working in the community, I began to conduct semi-structured tape-recorded interviews with adolescents. Discussion centered on both social and linguistic life within the local youth community, including youths' knowledge of Verlan and other languages. Interviews were also carried out with the directors of the association (one Algerian-born French, one Moroccan), and with four of the local youth activity directors. These interviews concerned Verlan use among youths, overall language patterns within the community, and social issues affecting suburban youths in general.

Tutoring sessions and interaction among youths at L'ASTI were recorded on an ongoing basis. Small tape recorders were also loaned to several youths for self-taping of peer interaction when socializing with friends, as a way of assessing whether their verbal behavior in peer-only contexts was different from that observed in other settings, such as the tutoring environment, the home, etc. A total of 45 one-hour audio cassettes were recorded in the course of the project.

Analysis of Research Findings: Negotiating a 'Third Space' for Identity Through Verlan

The observations, interviews, and audio recordings confirmed that Verlan was indeed used within the local youth community and in quite specific ways. This context-dependent usage made clear the strategic aspect of Verlan use, that is, that youths saw it as a particular kind of linguistic tool to be used in selective ways, in specific settings, for particular purposes. In this sense, Verlan constituted one element among several within youths' linguistic repertoires, alongside *le français ordinaire* (everyday spoken French) (Gadet, 1997), Standard French (academic French) and, in many cases, family minority languages, such as Arabic, Urdu, or Spanish, used primarily in the home. In this way, the use of Verlan was similar to the code-switching frequently observed in multi-lingual communities, particularly those in which national, ethnic, or regional identity is displayed by the use of a given language or language variety (Hill & Hill, 1986; Woolard, 1989; Zentella, 1997).

The analysis below draws on interview and interaction data to highlight the ways in which minority youths in Les Salières used Verlan to construct and participate in an alternative social sphere, in which their hybrid identities – ones that did not correspond to the mono norms of the hegemonic imagined community – could find expression and validation. (For a key to the transcription conventions used in the interview material, see the Appendix on p. 121.)

Negotiating a 'we': Verlan as peer-group language

Clearly, a key characteristic of Verlan within the youth community was its status as a peer-group language, a language both created by, and belonging to, the local group: youths frequently referred to it as *notre langage à nous* (our language for us). In contrast to media portrayals of Verlan as a contestatory language used by rebellious youths, young people in Les Salières emphasized that Verlan was above all a language meant to be used *entre potes* (among buddies) in peer social situations – *quand on galère, pour s'amuser* (when we are hanging out, to have fun) – and not one to be used with adults or in more formal situations. Consequently, as a language which belonged neither to the home sphere (where family minority languages were often the norm), nor to the school sphere (where academic French was required), Verlan was the language of an in-between social space, the 'free zone' of peer interaction.

In calling it their language, youths signalled their sense of ownership of the local code, and expressed pride in its creative divergences from the standard language. Nassim, an 18-year-old born in Pakistan, emphasized the creativity and localness of the peer-group language:

> **N:** *bon* on se latchave *ça veut dire 'bien on y va, on part,' ça c'est un mot inventé ça, c'est un mot de . . . de chez nous quoi . . . ça c'est pas un mot écrit dans les dictionnaires . . . c'est pas un mot, c'est seulement inventé. C'est bien quoi.*
>
> (like *on se latchave* that means 'well, let's go, we're leaving,' that's an invented word, a word from . . . from our community, you know . . . that word's not listed in the dictionary . . . it is not a [regular] word, it's just invented. It's cool, you know.)

> **N:** *il y a plein plein de mots inventés. C'est des mots euh des fois ça veut rien dire . . . mais nous on a un sens à ce mot-là entre nous il a un sens.*

(there are lots and lots of invented words. It's words that sometimes don't mean anything . . . but we have a meaning for those words, among us there's a meaning.)

As something creative and original not shared by dominant society, Verlan was perceived as a defining element of the we-group, a means of demarcating the peer circle in relation to other groups. Nassim and Dalila, a 19-year-old born to Moroccan parents in France, described the in-group and identity functions of their local sociolect in these terms:

> **N:** *on a notre code, un langage codé quoi comme ça on se comprend au moins. Des fois on parle et les gens ils comprennent pas . . . il y que nous qu'on comprend.*
> (we have our code language, a code language, you know, that way we understand each other at least. Sometimes we talk and people don't understand . . . it's only us who can understand.)
>
> **D:** [le langage] *c'est pour se distinguer des autres . . . c'est pour se donner une identité quand on se trouve pas, et . . . il faut donner justement une âme au groupe . . parce que . . . il* [le langage] *donne déjà une raison d'être à leur groupe . . comme cercle qui n'est pas de Paris . . . c'est le **cercle des racailles.***
> (it [the language] is to distinguish yourself from the others . . . it's to give yourself an identity when you haven't found yourself, and . . . you really have to give a soul to the group . . . because . . . it [the language] gives a 'raison d'être' to their [young people's] group . . as a social circle that's not from Paris . . . it's a **circle of 'street kids.'**)

The youths stated that the boundary-drawing function of Verlan had less to do with excluding others and more with reinforcing the bonds within the peer group itself. They stressed that using Verlan was a means of affirming solidarity and a sense of mutual understanding among friends. Given the insider status of the language, youths showed a sensitivity to not using it with people outside the peer group. Karim, an 18-year-old born to Moroccan parents in France, and Nassim both described the language as appropriate only among close friends:

> **K:** *c'est un langage pour parler entre potes . . . Pour la personne tu la connais pas, ou c'est pas intime . . . tu dois lui parler correctement. Mais après, si c'est des liens qui se créent tu peux . . . ça c'est autre chose quoi.*
> (it's a language to speak with your buddies . . . When you don't know the person, or it's not intimate . . . you have to talk to the

person correctly. But later, if some bonds develop, you can
[speak in Verlan] . . . it's a totally different thing.)

N: *on sait qu'il faut parler correctement et avoir un langage soutenu*
quand on va . . . quand on va chercher du travail, avoir un entretien,
ça c'est evident. Mais c'est quand on est entre nous on parle comme
on veut, et c'est pas un problème.
(we know that you have to speak correctly and use 'elevated'
language when we go . . . when we go to look for work, have
an interview, etcetera, that's clear. But it's when we're among
ourselves we speak the way we want to, and it's not a problem.)

Framed in these terms, the choice to speak Verlan was, among these
young people, an 'act of identity' (LePage & Tabouret-Keller, 1985),
signalling a symbolic alignment with the local peer group. By using a
language which was outside the norms of the dominant language, youths
constructed an alternative universe of discourse, one in which they could
define and express themselves in their own terms – as local peer-group
members – rather than being positioned by the discourses of either dominant or minority family cultures. In the broadest sense, then, Verlan was
a tool for enacting a 'third space' (Bhabha, 1994) of social interaction in
which youths could negotiate identities which diverged from those available in dominant French society. Indeed, for youths whose mixed
identities (tied both to their home cultures and to the surrounding French
culture) were not recognized within the discourse of the larger French
imagined community, the existence of the peer group and its alternative
language had particular symbolic value, delimiting a space in which
particular aspects of their identities could be normal, and were not subject
to the normative judgments of hegemonic society.

Let us now look at some of the major identity characteristics connected
to the 'we-group' constructed through Verlan use, both in terms of its
'positive identity' characteristics (those youths embraced) and its 'negative identity' characteristics (those they rejected) (Bucholtz, 1999). What
will be shown is that both the structures and uses of Verlan provide clues
to the cluster of issues related to the negotiation of identity for these
minority youths.

Negotiating race and ethnicity: Claiming difference without stigma

Clearly, one important aspect of the local peer-group identity was its
sense of ethnic difference in relation to the homogeneous French imagined

community. The youths who participated in the activities of L'ASTI were well aware of their status as *immigrés de deuxième génération* (second generation immigrants) in the eyes of mainstream French society, whether they were born in France or not. Many were reminded of their ethnic difference every day, be it in the form of increased surveillance when they entered a store, derogatory comments about their racial traits from passers-by, or random checks of their identity papers by police. In this sense, their difference from an unmarked 'ethnically French' norm was a source of differential positioning, regardless of their behavior as individuals.

Among the adolescents I worked with, the heightened awareness of racial and ethnic specificity was expressed linguistically through their frequent use of Verlan terms related to race, ethnicity, and immigration status. These terms included the following:

Arabe 'Arab' ⇒ *beur, reub, reubeu, rabzouille, crouille* (from Arabic *rouilla* 'brother')

Africain 'African' ⇒ *cainf*

Américain 'American' ⇒ *ricain, Mickey* (from 'Mickey Mouse')

Chinois 'Chinese' ⇒ *noiche*

Juif 'Jew' ⇒ *feuj*

Pakistanais or *Indien* 'Pakistani' or 'Indian' ⇒ *big-bang, indou*

Marocain 'Moroccan' ⇒ *camaro*

Noir 'Black' ⇒ *renoi, black*

Tunisien 'Tunisian' ⇒ *zien*

race 'race', 'ethnicity' ⇒ *cera*

clandestin 'illegal alien' ⇒ *clandé, clandax, clando*

These terms were often used in peer conversation, both simply to refer to another person's origins and in frequent teasing or mock insulting rituals within the group. In the exchange below, which took place during a tutoring session at L'ASTI, 13-year-old Loukmane rebuffs 15-year-old Adel's request to borrow a pencil by teasing him in Verlan about his immigration status, to which Adel responds by insulting Loukmane's national origins (even though both are born to Moroccan parents):

L: *Tu n'es qu'un pauvre clandé!*
(You're nothing but a poor illegal alien!)

A: *Et toi, qu'est-ce que tu en sais – tu n'es qu'un sale Camaro!*
         (And what do you know about it – you're just a dirty Moroccan!)
         [followed by Loukmane handing Adel a pencil]

Similarly, in a casual conversation among friends, Samir, 19, born to Algerian parents in France, interrupts his friend Yacine's joke with an insult involving his national origin, to which Yacine, 18, born to Moroccan parents in France, responds in kind:

S: *Tête de Maroc ça pue.*
         (Your Moroccan head stinks.)

Y: *Oh maintenant il fait Rachid Taha.*
         (oh now he's acting like Rashid Taha [a well-known Algerian-born singer in France].) [followed by laughter from the whole group]

While, to outsiders, this kind of teasing about ethnic origins might appear racist and be seen as evidence that ethnic differences were a source of tension among youths, adolescents themselves saw these kinds of exchanges (which they referred to as *les vannes* 'jibes') as an important part of peer bonding, and therefore as playful and 'not mean.' Bahia, 18 (born in Morocco), Jamila, 18 (born in Algeria), and Nassim described teasing in Verlan about race, ethnicity, and national origin in these terms, emphasizing its humour:

B: *c'est normal – c'est pour s'amuser.*
         (it's normal – it's to have fun.)

J: *quand on se charrie comme ça, c'est pas méchant, c'est que pour rigoler.*
         (when we tease each other like that, it's not mean, it's just for laughs.)

N: *c'est juste pour rigoler – on sait très bien comment ça se passe pour chaque bled . . . C'est juste comme ça . . un charriage de euh bon entre cultures de race quoi.*
         (it's just for laughs – we know very well how it is in each country [*bled*] . . . It's just what it is . . a kind of teasing between, well, ethnic cultures, you know.)

They were quick to point out that the Verlan racial terms they used carried a different semantic weight than their SF equivalents, lacking the racist connotations they associated with the French terms. Bahia and Jamila, for example, described their use of the term *clandé* (from *clandestin* 'illegal alien') as a joke rather than an epithet:

B: *clandé, c'est presque un diminutif.*
        (*clandé*, it's almost a diminutive.)

J: *c'est une manière de parler, parce qu'il a l'accent arabe . . . alors tu
        dis c'est un clandé, quoi, c'est juste une blague.*
        (it's a figure of speech, because he has an Arab accent . . . so you
        say that he's a *clandé*, you know, it's really a joke.)

Similarly, Nassim explained the neutrality of various Verlan terms for
black people:

N: *c'est c'est la même chose pour renoi* [from SF *noir* 'black'], *ou les
        blacks ou euh négro, il y a pas de propos raciste là.*
        (it's it's the same thing for *renoi* or *les blacks* or even *négro* [all
        terms meaning 'black'], there's no racist intention there.)

Overall, it was clear from observing peer-group interaction and from
interviewing youths about its meaning, that both the act of noting racial
and ethnic difference, and the terms used to do so, meant different things
within the peer group and outside it. In mainstream French discourse, the
strength of the traditional republican assimilationist ideology means that
ethnic 'particularisms' (Ager, 1999) are not to be discussed, since such
emphasis on difference is viewed as socially divisive. In contrast, within
the youth community, being ethnic was the unmarked case, and thus the
acknowledgment of particular ethnicities was simply a way of affirming
ethnicity as a legitimate aspect of identity. By reconfiguring terms for race
and ethnicity, and using them in playful ways, youths divested them of
the negative social judgments attached to them in mainstream French
discourse, creating a parallel semantic system within which ethnic origins
could be recognized without being a source of stigma or alienation.[9]
    In this sense, both the verlanization of racial terms, and their frequent
use in peer conversation, were ultimately a means of reversing dominant
culture's 'ethnic cleansing' by making diversity a normal part of the peer
universe. Such a move corresponds to what sociologist Souilamas (2000:
183) has described as the transformation of *l'identité subie* (assigned identity), that is, the essentialized identity assigned by the dominant culture,
into *l'identité subjectivée* (self-defined identity), that is, defining oneself in
one's own terms.

Negotiating a multicultural identity: 'We're all the same . . . we're "the foreigner"'

Indeed, it seemed clear that the recognition of racial and ethnic 'difference' within the group was intended less as a way of emphasizing

particularisms of origin than of affirming the bonds of shared membership in a multiethnic community. Thus, while the participants in this
study at times described themselves in specific national terms like
'Moroccan,' 'Pakistani,' or 'Portuguese,' ultimately they stressed their
sense of belonging to a common multicultural group. As Bahia put it,
their specific differences in family origin were ultimately less important
than their shared status as 'foreign':

B: *Marocain, Algérien, Tunisien, pour nous on est tous les mêmes, on
croit qu'on est tous pareil, on croit il y a beaucoup d'unité puisque on
est pareil quoi.*
(Moroccan, Algerian, Tunisian, for us it's all the same, we think
we're all the same, we think there's a lot of unity [among us]
because we're the same, you know.)

B: *pour nous, on dirait pas que vous êtes mieux que l'autre, tu vois? On
dit qu'on est pareils, on est l'étranger. Il n'y a pas d'hostilité entre nous.*
(among us, we would never say that one person's better than
the others, you see? We say we're the same, we're 'the foreigner.'
There's no hostility among us.)

For Nassim, growing up in a diverse group fostered assimilation to a
'multi' norm:

N: *si tu grandis avec des Algériens des Noirs et des Marocains, t'es
comme eux quoi. Des gens ils prennent la qualité des autres . . . on
sait s'apprécier.*
(if you've grown up with Algerians, Blacks and Moroccans,
you're like them, you know. People take on the qualities of
others . . . we know how to appreciate each other.)

Consequently, using the language of the group – Verlan – was seen as
a means of performing solidarity with, and belonging to, a specifically
'multi' youth community. Fatya, one of the directors of L'ASTI, herself of
Moroccan origin, stressed the role of Verlan as a constitutive element of
multicultural identity for adolescents in the neighborhood:

F: *[le Verlan] c'est une particularité qu'ils [les jeunes] veulent avoir en
tant que groupe, une appartenance mais pas à une communauté
d'origine précise . . . mais à une communauté des jeunes issus de l'immigration . . . donc moi je pense que . . . ce langage il regroupe toute
une jeunesse qui est vraiment multiculturelle et multi-etcétera.*
(it [Verlan] is a kind of distinctiveness they [young people]
want to have as a group, a kind of belonging which is not to a

particular community of origin, but to a community of second generation immigrants . . . so I think that . . . the language draws together a whole youth generation which is really multicultural and multi-etcetera.)

Dalila also viewed the use of Verlan as tied to the affirmation of identity rooted in the local second generation community, over and above any particular national origin:

D: [le Verlan] *c'est vraiment pour se donner une identité, c'est de dire 'ouais moi je suis un **mec**, un mec qui vient d'une **cité**, alors je vais parler comme ça pour me démarquer des autres jeunes.' Parce qu'en fait, c'est vraiment s'accorder son ethnie, mon ethnie c'est ma cité . . . c'est mon pays . . . c'est mes origines.*
(it [Verlan] is really to give yourself an identity, it's to say 'yeah, I'm a **guy**, a guy who's from a *cité*, so I'm going to talk like **that** to mark my difference from others, from other young people.' Because in fact, it's really like giving yourself an ethnicity . . . my ethnicity is my *cité* . . . it's my country . . . my [point of] origin.)

In this sense, the Verlan-speaking community of practice (Holmes & Meyerhoff, 1999; Wenger, 1998) among these youths in Les Salières was characterized by an ethnicity-bridging dynamic similar to that described in Eckert and McConnell-Ginet's (1999: 186) study of a northern California high school, in which adolescents of varying origins formed a Pan-Asian group out of 'a shared need to construct a commonality around which to join forces.' For the minority youths in Les Salières, then, Verlan was a tool of marking the boundaries of a common ethnic community, of validating the existence of a local multi-culture within which they could affirm the hybridity of their own identities, tied both to their particular family origins, and to the local neighborhood and its diverse population.

In terms of language, this sense of multi-ness was signalled in part by the incorporation of borrowings from family and other minority languages, including Arabic, Berber, English (particularly from rap music), and Romani. The heteroglossia of youths' local code served as a means of indexing their ties to (and solidarity with) a variety of languages and cultures, allowing them to express their own sense of cultural and linguistic hybridity, tied both to France as a literal home, and to other cultures within and outside it. This dynamic of language mixing – in which youths borrowed from languages which were not necessarily 'theirs' through family heritage – constitutes a form of what Rampton (1995) has called language crossing, where youths take up the use of languages which 'are not generally thought to belong' to them for purposes of demonstrating anti-racism and creating 'alternative minority solidarities' (p. 280).

Negotiating difference from ethnic Frenchness: Positioning 'the French' as Other

As discussed above, one feature of these youths' ethnically-based self-identification was their sense of being perceived as 'Other' by the French on the basis of their ethnic, racial, and cultural difference from the unmarked hegemonic norm. In interviews, the adolescents talked about their direct experiences of racism and a more general awareness of (and frustration with) the generally negative portrayal of ethnic minorities in media representations. Nassim and Dalila described these experiences and perceptions as follows:

> **N:** *avec l'ASTI je suis parti plusieurs fois au ski, et chaque année je me suis embrouillé, chaque année on m'a sorti 'ouais espèce de sale basané,' et euh, personnellement, je le prends mal ça.*
> (I've gone skiing several times with L'ASTI, and every year I've had trouble, every year someone has come out with a 'hey, you dirty darkie,' and, personally, I take it badly.)

> **D:** *la réputation . . . que la plupart des médias accordent à notre commu-nauté fait que nous on est que des **sauvages**, on est des **dealers**, on est des **drogués**, on est des **prostituées**. Je continue ou je m'arrête?*
> (the reputation . . . that most media attributes to our community [Arab] is that we're just **savages**, we're **dealers**, we're **drug addicts**, we're **prostitutes**. Should I continue or stop?)

> **D:** *selon leur discours et leurs propos, euh les Arabes c'est des porcs qui ont été élevés sans éducation, des extremistes radicaux.*
> (according to their [bourgeois French high school students] discourse and their ideas, Arabs are swine who have been raised without education, [who are] radical extremists.)

> **D:** *il y a du racisme au niveau de l'embauche. C'est sur le physique qu'on t'embauche pas. C'est sur le physique et la façon de parler . . . Maintenant les Maghrébins francisent leurs noms pour être embauchés, mais en fait à l'entretien ils se font recaler.*

(there's racism in hiring. It's based on how you look that they won't hire you. It's based on how you look and how you talk . . . Now North Africans 'frenchify' their names to get hired, but in fact at the interview they get rejected.)

Perhaps not surprisingly, given their sense of being discriminated against by mainstream French society, minority youths used a number of Verlan terms for *les Français* which had pejorative connotations. Many of these items played on stereotypical French traits:

les fils de Clovis 'sons of Clovis' (the fifth-century king of the Franks)

les Gaulois 'the Gauls'

les Céfrans (Verlan for *français* 'French')

les fromages blancs 'white cheeses'

les pâté-rillettes 'pâté-spread'

les froms (from *fromage* 'cheese')

les babtous, les babs (from Arabic *toubab* 'white person')

The caricatured quality of these terms suggests that the kind of Frenchness they framed as negative Other is not that of any and all French people (who, youths acknowledged, varied in their attitudes and behaviors), but of the image of the French person held forth in dominant culture as traditional, the ethnically French *français de souche*, whose cultural values and attitudes minority youths perceived as intolerant of difference. Karim, 18, born in France to Moroccan parents, described the (stereo)typical Frenchman as:

> **K:** *c'est une baguette sur le vélo . . . il n'aime pas les étrangers, ils viennent piétiner sur son terrain . . . Les Français ils ont peur de la différence. Le Français typique il fait tout et tout bien . . . c'est un Français Français.*
> ([he's] the baguette on the bicycle . . . he doesn't like foreigners, they've come to tread on his territory . . . The French are scared of difference. The typical Frenchman does everything and does it all well . . . that's a real 'French' French guy.)[10]

Within the peer group, then, these Verlan terms that other the French in the way youths themselves often felt othered, served as a means of negotiating their difference from, and rejection of, a kind of idealized ethnic, traditional Frenchness which they could neither identify with, nor feel accepted by.

Negotiating class and cultural values: 'We're not *bourge*'

While ethnicity was clearly an important aspect of identity among these youths, it was certainly not the only one. As Blommaert and Verschueren (1998) note, questions of social difference, exclusion, and group identity are rarely reducible to ethnicity alone: social class, economic status, and access to resources are also important determiners of the demarcations among groups. For many of these minority youths, their sense of difference from *les Français* was not simply about a difference in skin color, but also about a relation of alterity to the class status and value system of *le bourgeois*, the idealized figure of the French *citoyen*. Minority youths in Les Salières identified themselves as working-class and generally perceived a certain class conflict between their group and the *bourgeois* (upper-class) population in town, who they felt judged them negatively. As Adel, a 15-year-old born to Moroccan parents in France, put it: *je suis un fils d'immigré ... fils d'ouvrier* (I'm an immigrant's kid, a factory worker's kid).

But perhaps more importantly than differences in income per se, these youths' sense of difference from *les bourgeois* was intimately bound up with questions of cultural difference. Specifically, they saw their local, multi-ethnic culture as having different values than those of the imagined bourgeois French society, in particular being less individualistic, more communitarian, more friendly, and less snobbish than that of the typical *bourgeois*. Nacira, 18, born to Moroccan parents, made these comparisons between her values and those of 'the French':

> N: *le système, j'aime pas. En France, c'est un pays où c'est chacun pour soi. Les Arabes, jamais on laissera tomber quelqu'un.*
> (I don't like the French system. In France, it's each person for himself. Arabs will never let anyone down.)

> N: *nous on ne dirait pas qu'on est mieux que les autres, mais les Français ils sont, ben, ils sont hautains on va dire.*
> (we [minority youths] we wouldn't say we're better than anyone else, but the French are, well, let's say they're haughty.)

This sense of difference (and even alienation) from *les bourgeois* and their values had the specifically linguistic consequence of making youths reject the kind of language stereotypically associated with this group – *le français soutenu* (elevated French) – at least in the free zone of peer interaction, where youths had the power to define their own norms. As a result, while acknowledging the need to use *le français soutenu* in more formal settings (such as job interviews and administrative encounters), the minority youths in the study accused friends who used too much of this upper-class language of *se la raconter bourge* (putting on bourgeois airs), an expression which connoted acting inauthentically, that is, trying to be something one was not. In other words, since this kind of official language was associated with a *bourge* culture they rejected, youths saw speaking like a *bourge* as a betrayal of the group identity. Philippe, a 28-year-old local youth director of French origin, described how overuse of formal French with friends could, in fact, have dire social consequences:

> P: *tout de suite tu as quelqu'un qui parle en français soutenu . . . dans le dans le groupe d'appartenance, 't'arrête de te la raconter euh . . . tu te la racontes bourgeois?' . . . il passe à un autre groupe . . . c'est plus dans le groupe.*
>
> (if all of a sudden you have someone who starts speaking in 'elevated French' . . . in the group he belongs to, [the others will say] 'stop showing off, huh . . . you're acting *bourge*? . . . he's on to another group . . . he's no longer in the group.)

Refusing the official language in intimate peer interaction, then, was a rejection of a particular bourgeois Frenchness, which they associated with unattractive values, including snobbery, individualism, and a sense of superiority to others. Speaking Verlan, on the other hand, served as a means of displaying one's class allegiance and adherence to the local value system, which involved group solidarity, generosity, hospitality, and respect for others. In fact, to be included in the peer universe, using at least some Verlan was essentially a requirement. Youssef, a local youth activity director of Berber origin, talked about language pressures within the peer group:

> Y: *oui il y une pression sociale . . . il y en a qui aimeraient à la limite pas parler comme ça . . . mais euh ils sont bien obligés d'apprendre pour pas passer pour un idiot . . . sinon on va être un peu à l'écart.*
>
> (Yes, there's a social pressure [to use the language] . . . there are some [youths] who would really prefer not to speak that way . . . but um they're quite obligated to learn to so as not to look like an idiot . . . if not you're going to be sidelined a little.)

This group pressure to use the alternative language echoed the dynamic identified by Woolard (1989), where members of a minority group essentially enforce a certain use of the minority language as a means of asserting group identity and solidarity, and simultaneously resisting the authority (and hegemonic ideology) of the dominant language. For these minority youths in France, then, using Verlan was not only tied to belonging to a local peer group, but more specifically to a group which defined itself, at least in part, in opposition to a *bourgeois* majority culture, perceived as different both in socioeconomic position and cultural values.

Negotiating a relationship to street culture: 'I'm not a *racaille*'

We can see, then, that Verlan was embraced as a language of peer inter-action and solidarity and as a way of marking the group's difference from the bourgeois ethnic French ideal (and its language, *le français soutenu*). On the other hand, youths were also well aware of Verlan's stereotypical association – particularly in journalistic accounts of suburban youth life – with *la racaille*, the mythical figure of the tough ghetto youth involved in drug dealing, theft, and other illicit activities.[11] Indeed, some youths in the community were attracted to the external style of *la racaille* (inner-city fashions, street-wise body language, etc.) as a kind of hip fashion. Dalila described her 15-year-old brother Farid's mimetic relationship to the *racaille* style:

> **D:**   *C'est pas une racaille et en même temps c'est en une . . . il prend les petits aspects de la racaille qui lui plaisent, il y a le côté vestimentaire et le côté linguistique.*
> (He's not a *racaille* and at the same time he is one . . . he takes up the little aspects of *les racailles* that he likes, there's the clothing side and the linguistic side.)

> **D:**   *Farid il parle pas comme une racaille à la mairie, mais des qu'il est avec ses copains . . . 'ah ouais zy-va . . . il y a pas de problème.' En fait, tous les jeunes Maghrébins, on a un cliché, et en fait ils rentrent tous dans ce cliché. C'est Reebok Lacoste Nike Adidas.*
> (Farid, he doesn't talk like a *racaille* at the city hall [that is, in formal settings], but as soon as he's with his friends, it's *'ah ouais, zy-va . . . il y a pas de problème'* [Verlan for 'oh yeah, get out of here . . . there's no problem']. In fact, all the young North Africans, there's some kind of stereotype, and in fact they all follow the stereotype. It's Reebok Lacoste Nike Adidas.)

While some youths like Farid take up certain superficial elements of *racaille* style, they are also very critical of what they call real or flagrant *racailles*, which they define in terms as pejorative as those applied to *les bourges* at the other end of the identity continuum. Dalila, Nassim, and Souad, 13, born in France to Moroccan parents, defined *la racaille* in these terms:

D: *Une racaille c'est vraiment un loser. Le côté péjoratif de la racaille, c'est quelqu'un qui a pas eu de vie sociale ... c'est en plus un délinquant, et en plus quelqu'un qui réussit pas ... une racaille c'est le mec qui est complètement inculte et niais.*

(A *racaille* is really a loser. The pejorative side of the *racaille*, it's someone who hasn't had a social life ... who's a delinquent on top of it all, and also someone who doesn't succeed ... a *racaille* is the guy who's totally uneducated and lame.)

N: *Une racaille voilà c'est quelqu'un qui ... qui se prend pour le roi du monde, le nombril de la terre. T'es une vraie racaille t'es en fait un bouffon.*

(A *racaille* is someone who ... who thinks he's the king of the world, the center of the universe. But in fact if you're a real *racaille* you're a loser.)

S: *Une racaille n'a rien dans la tête. C'est un zéro.*

(A *racaille*'s got nothing in his head. He's a zero.)

Given their negative views of *la racaille* – judged to be disrespectful, uneducated, and unsuccessful – it was clear that these youths neither identified with the real version of these 'bad boys,' nor wanted to be labelled as such. Consequently, while youths did want to speak Verlan with friends, they were also careful not to use it in certain 'public' settings and with certain people, to avoid being labelled as *racaille*. Souad and Dalila focused on the increased difficulties that youths of North African origin faced in this regard:

S: *à un ami on peut le dire, tu vois, mais c'est pas à dire à une grande personne âgée, c'est un manque de respect ... ils disent 'c'est quoi ces enfants-là?,' et après, c'est là où on a une sale rumeur nous les Arabes.*

(you can speak that way [in Verlan] with a friend, you see, but it's not to use with a big person who's older, it's disrespectful ... they say 'what's with those kids there?,' and then we have a bad reputation, we Arabs.)

D: *les médias, quand ils montrent la communauté maghrébine, ils montrent pas les gens qui réussissent ... ils montrent que les racailles. Je suis désolée moi chais pas, je suis pas une racaille ... je casse pas des cabines téléphoniques, je deale pas, je ne me drogue pas.*

(when the media presents the North African community, they don't show people who succeed ... they only show *les racailles*. I'm sorry but I don't know, I am not a racaille ... I don't destroy phone booths, I don't deal [drugs], and I don't take drugs.)

Interestingly, a major aspect of what youths rejected in the figure of *la racaille* was its self-isolation as a group, making integration and success in society difficult, if not impossible. For Dalila, *la racaille* constitutes its own mini-society:

> **D:** *Ils se créent leur monde, ils se font leur société à eux . . . ils vivent dans la société mais en même temps ils sont complètement à part dans la société.*
>
> (They create their own world, they make their own society . . . they live in society but at the same time they're completely separate in society.)

For the youths I worked with, the problem was not that *les racailles* used Verlan, but that they were unable to speak any other way. As Suzanne, the director of the association put it:

> **S:** *ils se marginalisent de plus en plus parce qu'ils parlent pas le même langage que les autres.*
>
> (they marginalize themselves more and more because they don't speak the same language as others.)

From their point of view, the fact that *la racaille* (over)used Verlan in all situations, not only with friends but also in public settings (in the bus, in schools, etc.) and with authority figures meant that he locked himself into a fixed oppositional persona, and therefore foreclosed his possibilities for occupying other identity positions in other settings.

In contrast, what these youths valued was flexibility in self-presentation, tied strongly to the ability to use different kinds of language according to situation. Accordingly, while they used Verlan in some settings, they recognized the value of leaving it behind in others. Dalila and Bahia stressed the importance of attending to context in deciding when to use Verlan:

> **D:** *c'est vraiment un langage qui s'adapte à toutes les situations et il s'emploie selon fin un contexte . . . il est mobile quoi. Tu t'en sers et tu l'oublies, tu le ranges dans un placard et tu le ressors quand t'es entre copains, parce que c'est vraiment selon la situation.*
>
> (it's really a language that adapts to any situation and is used according to the context . . . it's flexible, you know. You use it and then you forget it, you put it in the closet and then you take it out again when you're with friends, because it really depends on the situation.)

B: *entre amis, on peut parler verlan, mais si on parle à quelqu'un d'autre*
         il faut parler bien et comme nos amies françaises, nettement, un peu
         genre Jean de la Rue.
         (among friends, we can speak in Verlan, but if we talk to
         someone else we have to speak right and like our French
         [girl]friends, clearly, like 'Jean de la Rue' [a TV talk show host])

These comments illustrate youths' strong awareness of the need to vary
their linguistic codes according to context, in order to perform different
kinds of social identities. In relation to the *racaille* stereotype in particular,
they recognized the dangers of negative labelling inherent in using Verlan
indiscriminately, and therefore managed its use strategically. They spoke
it with friends to index familiarity with local street culture and its style
and therefore to fit into the peer group. They also sought to avoid using
it in settings (or around particular people) where it might earn them the
negative label *racaille*, which they did not want.

Interestingly, what motivated these youths to reject both *bourge* and
racaille as identity positions was a similar underlying characteristic: both
figures represented exaggerated, fixed social personae, which belonged
to restricted social spheres and had undesirable qualities. The *bourge*
was inhospitable, had a superiority complex, and was intolerant of
diversity; equally unattractive, the *racaille* acted disrespectfully, engaged
in delinquent activities, and isolated himself from the rest of society.
Consequently, for these youths, choosing to enact either one of these polar
positions of identity – through an exclusive use of elevated French in all
settings, or else a total adoption of Verlan as one's main language – would
represent an extreme self-positioning, and therefore a loss of other, more
hybrid identity positions.

Conclusions

As we have seen, the existing literature on Verlan has stressed the role
played by such factors as gender, age, geographical location, and social
marginality in determining Verlan use. While, on one level, my field
observations and interviews in a particular youth community confirmed
the validity of these factors as general parameters, the present study
also points toward intersections among them. The portrait of minority
youths' language use turned out to be quite complex, as they were
capable of switching from family language in the home, to Verlan use
among peers, to Standard French when interacting with the larger
society. What the analysis in this chapter has attempted to highlight are
the ways in which the strategic, context-specific choice of Verlan is tied

to the enactment of an interstitial 'third space' – one which is neither family minority culture nor dominant French culture – in which youths can position themselves along an alternative identity continuum, outside the fixed categories available in the standard language.

Thus, Verlan is not a de facto vernacular dialect used always and everywhere by a subset of minority youths, but rather a sociolect available to these young people as one mediational tool among many. Specifically, its use indexes youths' inscription in a particular sociocultural universe, which conceives itself as distinct from that of mainstream French society (the classic 'imagined community'). Within this universe youths can occupy complex, hybrid identity positions situated in the liminal space between the polar identity extremes of *bourge* and *racaille*. In this sense, Verlan, as a divergence from the prescriptive norms of Standard French, provides a means for marginalized adolescents – who are part of the French landscape but struggle for positive recognition within it – to define and express a certain alternative social world within which they could feel at home, in a way they do not when speaking the dominant language.

Notes

1. Throughout this chapter, all study participants have been assigned pseudonyms in order to ensure anonymity.
2. It is important to point out that Verlan use is not limited to *cité* youths alone: both Lefkowitz (1991) and Albert (2000) have documented Verlan use among middle- and upper-class adolescents in France. Further, elements of this sociolect have been commodified and appropriated into mainstream culture to a certain degree, through advertising, popular music, and other media sources, meaning that particular Verlan terms are widely known to the general public. Nevertheless, the most 'authentic' users of Verlan continue to be defined as youths in the *cité* (see Boyer, 1997; Goudaillier, 1998; Lepoutre, 1997; Méla, 1997), and it is the use of Verlan among this type of population that will be treated in the present chapter.
3. The use of the term 'minority' in the French context requires at least two caveats: first, the notion of minorities is itself not current in French discourse, due to a persistent republican ideology in which the recognition of 'minority groups' is viewed as socially divisive (see Dubet & Lapeyronnie, 1992) and is therefore generally avoided even in conceptual terms; and second, it is certainly not the case that 'minorities' form a homogeneous group – it is true that, in France as elsewhere, some groups face greater discrimination than others (Minces, 1997).
4. The practice of inverting syllables in words as a form of wordplay is attested as early as the twelfth century (Azra & Cheneau, 1994); its use as a criminal slang appears to date from the nineteenth century (Calvet, 1990).
5. All of these studies focus on the youth sociolect in the Paris area specifically. Though similar sociolects are spoken in the suburbs of other major French

cities, such as Lyon, Marseille, and Lille, they are outside the scope of the present study.
6. It should be stressed again that this literature review does not attempt to cata-logue all the communities in which Verlan may be used; here, Verlan is treated primarily in terms of its uses in the low-income suburbs around Paris.
7. The association of Verlan with the *beur* population has its roots in a series of sociopolitical events of the early 1980s (including violent protests) in which young *beurs* were major social actors and came to be seen as the representa-tives of an emerging *cité* youth culture, whose emblematic language was Verlan (Dulong & Paperman, 1992; Jazouli, 1992).
8. For a more detailed discussion of female adolescents' use of Verlan, and the issues surrounding it, see Doran (2002).
9. This observation is consistent with Lepoutre's (1997) analysis of ritual teasing in Verlan among male adolescents in a *cité* in the northern Parisian suburbs. For Lepoutre, racialized teasing among minority youths 'constitutes a way to create a social bond between stigmatized individuals and in so doing to cancel out or neutralize the stigma' (1997: 79).
10. Jean-Marie Le Pen (and his xenophobic political party, the Front National) are representative of this kind of intolerant attitude.
11. For more detailed discussions of *la racaille*, and of French suburban *cité* condi-tions in general, see Boyer (2000), Dubet (1987), Dubet and Lapeyronnie (1992), Garnier (1996), Giudicelli (1991), Jazouli (1992), Lepoutre (1997), Mangez (1999), Schnapper (1991), Seguin (1994), Seguin and Teillard (1996), Vieillard-Baron (1996).

Appendix

Key to transcription conventions

,	Continuing pitch contour
.	Pause shorter than two seconds
...	Pause greater than two seconds
[...]	Material omitted
'words'	Quotation
words	Emphatic utterance (i.e. with raised pitch or volume)
[words]	Clarification/elaboration of non-specific referent defined in previous utterances
[words]	Description of non-linguistic action occurring during interaction

References

Ager, D. (1999) *Identity, insecurity, and image: France and language*. Clevedon: Multilingual Matters.
Aguillou, P. and Saïki, N. (1996) *'La Téci à Panam': Parler le langage des banlieues*. Paris: Michel Lafon.

Albert, S. (2000) *One Verlan or many? Social meanings of a French language game.* Paper presented at the Annual Conference of the American Association of Applied Linguistics, Vancouver, Canada.

Anderson, B. (1991) *Imagined communities: Reflections on the origin and spread of nationalism.* London: Verso.

Andreini, L. (1985) *Le verlan: Petit dictionnaire illustré.* Paris: Henri Veyrier.

Azra, J.-L. and Cheneau, V. (1994) Jeux de langage et théorie phonologique: Verlan et structure syllabique du français. *French Language Studies* 4, 147–170.

Bachmann, C. and Basier, L. (1984) Le Verlan: Argot d'école ou langue des Keums? *Mots* 8, 169–187.

Bézard, C. (1993) Le langage de jeunes: À décrypter avec décodeur. *L'Événement du Jeudi* 457, August 5–11.

Bhabha, H. (1994) *The location of culture.* London/New York: Routledge.

Blackledge, A. and Pavlenko, A. (2001) Negotiation of identities in multilingual contexts. *International Journal of Bilingualism* 5 (3), 243–259.

Blommaert, J. and Verschueren, J. (1998) The role of language in European nationalist ideologies. In B. Schieffelin, K. Woolard, and P. Kroskrity (eds) *Language ideologies: Practice and theory* (pp. 189–210). New York: Oxford University Press.

Bourdieu, P. (1991) Identity and representation: Elements for a critical reflection on the idea of region. In J. Thompson (ed.) *Language and symbolic power* (G. Raymond and M. Adamson, trans.). Cambridge, MA: Harvard University Press.

Bourdieu, P. (1993) La démission de l'état. In P. Bourdieu (ed.) *La Misère du monde* (pp. 337–350). Paris: Seuil.

Boyer, H. (ed.) (1996) *Sociolinguistique: Territoire et objets.* Lausanne: Delachaux et Niestlé.

Boyer, H. (1997) 'Nouveau Français,' 'parler jeune,' ou 'langue des cités'?: Remarques sur un objet linguistique médiatiquement identifié. *Langue Française* 114, 6–15.

Boyer, J.-C. (2000) *Les banlieues en France.* Paris: Armand Colin.

Bucholtz, M. (1999) Why be normal?: Language and identity practices in a community of nerd girls. *Language in Society* 28, 203–223.

Bullock, B. (1996) Popular derivation and linguistic inquiry: Les javanais. *The French Review* 70 (2), 180–191.

Calvet, L.-J. (1990) L'Argot comme variation diastratique, diatopique et diachronique. *Langue Française* 90, 40–52.

Calvet, L.-J. (1993a) Le Verlan en kit. *Le Français dans le Monde*, April, 42.

Calvet, L.-J. (1993b) The migrant languages of Paris. In C. Sanders (ed.) *French today: Language in its social context* (pp. 105–119). Cambridge: Cambridge University Press.

Calvet, L.-J. (1994) *L'argot.* Paris: Presses Universitaires de France.

Davies, B. and Harré, R. (1990) Positioning: The discursive production of selves. *Journal for the Theory of Social Behaviour* 20 (1), 43–63.

Demougeot, M., Duvillard, J., Laurioz, H. and Marcoz, L. (1994) *Nouveau Français: la compil. Petit dico des mots interdits aux parents.* Paris: J.-C. Lattès.

Doran, M. (2002) *A sociolinguistic study of youth language in the Parisian suburbs: Verlan and minority identity in contemporary France.* Unpublished Ph.D. dissertation, Ithaca, NY: Cornell University.

Dubet, F. (1987) *La Galère: jeunes en survie.* Paris: Fayard.

Dubet, F. and Lapeyronnie, D. (1992) *Les Quartiers d'exil*. Paris: Seuil.

Dulong, R. and Paperman, P. (1992) *La réputation des cités HLM*. Paris: L'Harmattan.

Durand, J. (1996) Linguistic purification, the French nation-state and the linguist. In C. Hoffmann (ed.) *Language, culture and communication in contemporary Europe* (pp. 75–92). Clevedon: Multilingual Matters.

Eckert, P. (1989) *Jocks and burnouts: Social categories and identity in the high school*. New York: Teachers College Press.

Eckert, P. and McConnell-Ginet, S. (1999) New generalizations and explanations in language and gender research. *Language in Society* 28, 185–201.

Fabrice, A. (1998) Des mots et des oms: Verlan, troncation et recyclage formel dans l'argot contemporain. *Cahiers de Lexicologie* 72 (1), 41–70.

Gadet, F. (1997) *Le Français ordinaire*. Paris: Armand Colin.

Garnier, J. (1996) *Des Barbares dans la cité: De la tyrannie du marché a la violence urbaine*. Paris: Flammarion.

George, K. (1986) The language of French adolescents. *Modern Languages* 67 (3), 137–141.

George, K. (1993) Alternative French. In C. Sanders (ed.) *French today: Language in its social context* (pp. 155–170). Cambridge: Cambridge University Press.

Giudicelli, A. (1991) *La Caillera*. Paris: Jacques Bertoin.

Goudailler, J.-P. (1998) *Comment tu tchatches! Dictionnaire du français contemporain des cités*. Paris: Maisonneuve et Larose.

Grillo, R. (1985) *Ideologies and institutions in urban France*. Cambridge: Cambridge University Press.

Guiraud, P. (1956) *L'argot*. Paris: Presses Universitaires de France.

Hargreaves, A. (1997) *Immigration and identity in Beur fiction: Voices from the North African immigrant community in France*. Oxford: Berg.

Hill, J. (1999) Styling locally, styling globally: What does it mean? *Journal of Sociolinguistics* 3, 542–556.

Hill, J. and Hill, K. (1986) *Speaking Mexicano: Dynamics of a syncretic language in Central Mexico*. Tucson: University of Arizona Press

Holmes, J. and Meyerhoff, M. (1999) The community of practice: Theories and methodologies in language and gender research. *Language in Society* 28 (2), 173–183.

Jazouli, A. (1992) *Les Années banlieue*. Paris: Seuil.

Lefkowitz, N. (1989) *Verlan*: Talking backwards in French. *French Review* 63, 312–322.

Lefkowitz, N. (1991) *Talking backwards, looking forwards: The French language game Verlan*. Tübingen: Gunter Narr Verlag.

Le Page, R. and Tabouret-Keller, A. (1985) *Acts of identity: Creole-based approaches to language and ethnicity*. Cambridge: Cambridge University Press.

Lepoutre, D. (1997) *Coeur de banlieue: Codes, rites, et langages*. Paris: Éditions Odile Jacob.

Lo, A. (1999) Codeswitching, speech community membership, and the construction of ethnic identity. *Journal of Sociolinguistics* 3, 461–479.

Mangez, C. (1999) *La Cité qui fait peur*. Paris: Albin Michel.

Marconot, J.-M. (1990). Le Français parlé dans un quartier HLM. *Langue Française* 85, 68–81.

Méla, V. (1988) Parler Verlan: Règles et usages. *Langage et société* 45, 47–72.

Méla, V. (1991) Le Verlan ou le langage du miroir. *Langage*, March, 101, 73–94.

Méla, V. (1997) Verlan 2000. *Langue Française: Les mots des jeunes, observations et hypothèses* 114, 16–34.

Merle, P. (1997) *Argot, verlan et tchatches*. Paris: Milan Éditions.

Minces, J. (1997) *La Génération suivante*. La Tour d'Aigues: Éditions de l'Aube.

Paul, E. (1985) *Étude des regularités morpho-syntaxiques du Verlan contemporain*. Unpublished master's thesis, Université de Paris 3, Paris, France.

Petitpas, T. (1998) Analyse descriptive de trois procédés de codage morphologique français: Javanais, verlan et largonji. *Cahiers de Lexicologie* 73 (2), 149–166.

Pierre-Adolphe, P., Mamoud, M., and Tzanos, G.-O. (1998) *Tchatche de banlieue*. Paris: Mille et une nuits.

Plénat, M. (1993) Notes sur la morphologie du verlan, données et hypothèses. *Cahiers de grammaire* 17, 173–208.

Plénat, M. (1995) Une approche prosodique de la morphologie du verlan. *Lingua*, March, 1–3, 97–129.

Rampton, B. (1995) *Crossing: Language and ethnicity among adolescents*. London: Longman.

Schnapper, D. (1991) *La France de l'intégration: Sociologie de la nation en 1990*. Paris: Gallimard.

Seguin, B. (1994) *Crame pas les blases*. Paris: Calmann-Lévy.

Seguin, B. and Teillard, F. (1996) *Les Céfrans parlent aux Français: Chronique de la langue des cités*. Paris: Calmann-Lévy.

Sewell, P. and Payne, C. (2000) Arrête de me chauffer, tu me laves trop le cerveau avec tes clesarti! *Francophonie* 21, 8–11.

Souilamas, N. (2000) *Des 'Beurettes' aux descendantes d'immigrants nord-africains*. Paris: Grasset/LeMonde.

Tifrit, A. (1999) *Traits phonologiques du français populaire de banlieue: Une analyse sociolinguistique chez de jeunes maghrébins*. Unpublished master's thesis, Université de Paris 10, Nanterre, France.

Torres, L. (1997) *Puerto Rican discourse: A sociolinguistic study of a New York suburb*. Mahwah, NJ: Lawrence Erlbaum.

Valdman, A. (2000). The language of the inner and outer suburbs: From argot to popular French. *The French Review* 73 (6), 1179–1192.

Vieillard-Baron, H. (1996) *Les Banlieues*. Paris: Flammarion.

Weber, E. (1976). *Peasants into Frenchmen: The modernization of rural France*. Stanford, CA: Stanford University Press.

Weinberger, S. and Lefkowitz, N. (1992) Uncovering French syllable structure with Verlan. In C. Laeufer and Morgan, T. (eds) *Theoretical analyses in Romance linguistics* (pp. 37–53). Amsterdam: John Benjamins.

Wenger, E. (1998) *Communities of practice: Learning, meaning, and identity*. Cambridge: Cambridge University Press.

Woolard, K. (1989) *Double talk: Bilingualism and the politics of ethnicity in Catalonia*. Palo Alto, CA: Stanford University Press.

Zentella, A. (1997) *Growing up bilingual*. Oxford: Blackwell.

Chapter 4

Black Deaf or Deaf Black?
Being Black and Deaf in Britain

MELISSA JAMES AND BENCIE WOLL

Introduction

To be deaf is to have a hearing loss; to be Deaf is to belong to a community with its own language and culture. Deaf communities parallel other minority linguistic communities in terms of linguistic and cultural oppression. The existence of the Deaf community, the identity of Deaf people, and the experience of Deafhood (Ladd, 2003) are the consequences of their experiences in the hearing world, not just as a result of exclusion but in equal part stemming from a desire to create structures alternative to those of hearing society. In the Deaf community the problems of communication and interaction with non-signing, hearing people are excluded. Through interaction with other Deaf people the individual is able to develop an awareness and acceptance of self. Through participation in the various organizations that make up the community, individuals are able to acquire a sense of self-esteem, which may be impossible to develop within the hearing world.

The Deaf community represents a most complex response to the threat of social isolation and the difficulties of communication that the Deaf person experiences in the wider community. Its culture comprises a range of activities, which are sufficiently powerful to nullify the negative experiences of daily life and enable Deaf people to develop an acceptance and celebration of both the individual and collective Deaf self. By sealing off those aspects of their lives that really matter, Deaf people have made the existence of a positive Deaf identity possible. There are numerous studies that explore Deaf identities and describe how Deaf people create communities based on three factors: deafness, communication, and mutual support (Higgins, 1980; Lane, 1984; Markowicz & Woodward, 1978; Padden & Humphries, 1988; Woll & Lawson, 1982). Deaf community social and cultural lives are underpinned and driven by the choice of a sign language as a preferred language. The centrality of these languages is reflected not only in the social and political organizations of these communities, but in the strong 'oral' cultural tradition of sign-play, jokes, storytelling, and poetry found in many of them. In the most practical sense the central fact of Deaf community membership is linguistic membership. Membership of these Deaf communities is also determined not by audiological measurement or hearing impairment, but by self-identification as 'Deaf 'and reciprocal recognition of that identification. This self-identification is built on two cornerstones. Deaf residential schools have provided a place where Deaf children could come together, learn sign languages, and begin the process of accessing the wider Deaf community. Despite continued attempts to suppress sign language throughout the twentieth century, schools maintained their role in ensuring the continuity of sign language use and the passing on of Deaf culture and Deaf historical traditions from one generation to another.

The second cornerstone of the Deaf community is the Deaf club. The Deaf clubs which sprang up after the formation of Deaf schools have provided a central focus for Deaf adult life, not merely creating and maintaining the language and culture of childhood, but extending the Deaf experience into all the organizational forms required in adulthood – local, regional, and national; social, cultural, and political.

This chapter is based on James (2000), which explores some of the life experiences of a group of British Black Deaf individuals and the influences affecting their identity development. It highlights the impact of the social environment and social attitudes on their relationship with others and on their personal lives. Much of the literature exploring discourses on identity development, disability, Deaf culture, and issues of race has failed to recognize the complexity of identity development for Black and Deaf people. While the early individual personal identity theories of Winncott (1965) and Erikson (1968) provide an understanding of how individual identities develop and may be understood, they do not explain how group or collective identities develop. This is also true of sociological models, such as those of Cross (1978), Higgins (1980), and Goffman (1968), whose theories also analyze identity development as a psychological process undergone by the individual.

Other approaches have taken into account the relationship between the group and the individual. Black feminist theories (Davis, 1982; hooks, 1982) that use a multiple oppressionist model recognize the need to take into consideration gender, class, race, and disability, while cultural theorists, such as Hall (1992) and West (1995), focus on the wider impact of society and the social issues on the identity development process. Only cultural discourses that treat identities as contradictory and subject to negotiation and change provide an appropriate model for understanding the identity development of Black Deaf people. Our discussion will provide further evidence for this argument by highlighting the diversity of British Black Deaf identities and the multicultural nature of the Black Deaf community. Throughout the chapter, unless otherwise stated, the term Black will be used to denote people of Afro-Caribbean and African origin.

Black Deaf communities

A review of the literature on the British Deaf community reveals few references to Black Deaf people. The focus is predominantly on barriers to accessing services and inappropriate service provision. Studies undertaken by Deaf voluntary organizations have been primarily concerned with the improvement of service delivery practices. The absence of Black Deaf people from Deaf-led initiatives and organizations has led to a lack of information and understanding of their social and cultural lives. The few written treatments available (GLAD 1991; Sharma & Love, 1991) adopt a needs-based approach, suggesting that Black Deaf people's lives can only be understood in relation to these needs. Even the Open University's 'Issues in Deafness' course (Taylor & Meherali, 1991) discusses Black Deaf people as part of 'the other' Deaf community.

Although by virtue of their origins and historical heritage Black Deaf Americans cannot be considered as having an interchangeable history and experience with their Black British counterparts, a substantial literature does exist on Black Deaf people in America. These studies provide an insight into the experiences of Black Deaf people (Hairston & Smith, 1983) and discuss the existence of a distinctive Black variant of American Sign Language (ASL) (Woodward, 1976). American studies have also explored issues of identity (Aramburo, 1989; Valli *et al.*, 1992), examining whether Black Deaf people identify themselves as primarily Black Deaf or Deaf Black. In Aramburo's (1989) study, people who identified primarily with the Black community did so because of the invisibility of deafness and the visibility of race. People who identified themselves as Deaf Black were more often born to Deaf families and had attended residential schools.

Aramburo's study provided an insight into the identity positioning of Black Deaf people and their relationships within the Black hearing community. However, there are few details of how this process occurs or the nature of the relationship of Black Deaf people with white and ethnic minority individuals. Limited information is provided on the impact of the social environment or on how personal experiences influenced identity choices. In turn, Valli *et al.*'s (1992) study describes an 'inside vs. outside' experience. Black Deaf people primarily identified themselves as Deaf, but were aware that they would be treated as Black because of the invisibility of deafness. Valli *et al.* noted that, for some Deaf people, identity was defined depending on those around them. For example, in a Deaf group they identified as Black first, but in a hearing group they felt Deaf first. Similarly, in the company of white people they felt Deaf first, and with Black people they felt Black first. Thus Black Deaf people's dual ethnicity was often negotiated during social interaction. These findings rest on the assumption that Black Deaf people have a developed sense of racial and Deaf identities which are negotiated differently in different situations, and Valli *et al.* acknowledge that further research is needed in this area.

In both Britain and the United States, Black Deaf people are multilingual and multicultural. Multilingualism plays an important role in understanding their collective identity. Through language and communication Black Deaf people have defined their relationships both with other Deaf people and with hearing people. The use of sign language places them within the Deaf community, while the existence of a Black variant also shapes their identities as members of a Black Deaf community. Multilingualism for Black Deaf children is a fact of life. Their communication at home is different from their communication at school and different still among Deaf peers in the playground. Without the ability to communicate within such diverse contexts, Black Deaf people face isolation and dislocation from both Deaf and hearing communities.

This chapter discusses Black Deaf people living in Britain and examines the social, cultural, and linguistic influences on their lives. It focuses on the evidence of an emerging Black Deaf community and considers whether the labels Black Deaf or Deaf Black better suit a description of the identities of Black Deaf people. Special attention is paid to the role of language in identity formation of the individual and the group.

Research Participants

This study was undertaken with 21 British Black Deaf people aged between 18 and 35. They were all of African or Afro-Caribbean origin. Most had been born and raised in the UK, but four had spent part of their childhood in Africa or the Caribbean. All the informants were bilingual to a greater or lesser extent, communicating predominantly through British Sign Language (BSL) and English. There were eight male and thirteen female informants. Fifteen individuals were single and six married or engaged to be married. Ten were employed, seven unemployed, and four were students (Table 4.1).

Recruiting informants

'Snowballing' was the main method used to recruit the participants. This technique involved asking individuals to recommend others as informants. This sampling technique was chosen because of difficulties in identifying and recruiting members of the Black Deaf community. As a group Black Deaf people were not easily identifiable. They had a small presence at Deaf clubs and activities across London, which made it difficult to contact them. Melissa James began the fieldwork by contacting two Black Deaf friends. They provided names and details of other potential Black Deaf informants. This process continued until the desired sample size was achieved.

The snowballing technique was particularly effective for recruiting Black female informants. Black Deaf women were more willing than men to take part in the research and had a more accessible network. They were more active in setting up groups aiming to empower other Black Deaf women and participated in job clubs, Deaf events, and organizations. In contrast, using snowballing techniques to recruit Black Deaf men achieved limited success. Despite the fact that Melissa James renewed contact with each female informant and requested that information be passed to Black Deaf male friends or partners, initially only two Black Deaf men were recruited using this method. To increase the number of male informants, Melissa James made further visits to a Deaf Job Club, distributed posters publicizing the research to both social and voluntary services, and placed advertisements on Deaf community Teletext pages. These efforts achieved only limited success: only one male informant was recruited via the Deaf Job Club. The other seven male informants were recruited by 'snowballing' (furthermore, even though ten male informants were recruited altogether, only eight ended up participating in the study).

Research Design

In order to reduce potential communication barriers or inequalities, before organizing interviews, two Black sign language interpreters, one male and one female, were recruited. Shared gender and racial identities were intended to facilitate more open responses from the informants.

Table 4.1 The informants

	Name	Age	Gender	Level of deafness	Preferred communication	Nature of family unit	Siblings in family unit	Secondary school type	Marital status	Work status
1	Janet	34	F	Profound	BSL	hearing	2 hearing	special class[1]	married	secretary
2	Kathy	23	F	Profound	BSL	hearing	2 hearing	residential[2]	single	shop assistant
3	Amy	32	F	Partial	BSL/ speech	hearing	2 hearing	special class	single	admin assistant
4	Sarah	19	F	Profound	BSL	hearing	6 hearing	day school[3]	single	unemployed
5	Natalie	35	F	Profound	BSL	hearing single parent	2 hearing	day school	single	print operator
6	Shamique	35	F	Profound	speech	hearing	2 hearing	day school	single	admin assistant
7	Derek	31	M	Profound	BSL	hearing	2 hearing	special class	engaged	printer
8	Sandra	33	F	Partial	speech	hearing	1 hearing	special class	engaged	admin assistant
9	Judy	21	F	Profound	speech	hearing single parent	only child	special class	single	student
10	Shola	21	F	Profound	BSL	hearing single parent	only child	day school	single	student
11	Anne	27	F	Profound	BSL	hearing	1 hearing	special class	married	unemployed
12	Maria	29	F	Profound	speech	hearing	1 hearing	special class	single	unemployed
13	Francis	27	M	Profound	speech	hearing	1 deaf	special class	single	unemployed
14	Samuel	32	M	Profound	speech	hearing	2 hearing	special class	single	project officer

Table 4.1 continued

	Name	Age	Gender	Level of deafness	Preferred commu- nication	Nature of family unit	Siblings in family unit	Secondary school type	Marital status	Work status
15	Joshua	20	M	Profound	BSL	hearing	2 hearing	day school	single	student
16	Jason	32	M	Profound	BSL	foster care	only child	day school	single	porter
17	Sharon	35	F	Profound	BSL	hearing single parent	only child	day school	single	student
18	Matthew	31	M	Profound	BSL	hearing	3 hearing	day school	single	unemployed
19	Nicky	32	F	Profound	BSL	hearing	1 deaf	day school	single	unemployed
20	Roy	35	M	Profound	BSL	hearing	2 hearing	day school	married	catering assistant
21	Junior	30	M	Profound	BSL	hearing	2 hearing	special class	single	factory worker

Notes:

1. Special class for Deaf children in mainstream school
2. Residential school for Deaf children
3. Day school for Deaf children

Hence, the male interpreter was recruited to assist with interviewing the male informants and the female interpreter to assist with interviewing the women. Before the interview process began both interpreters were briefed about the research and given a guide to the type of questions that would be asked. Since qualitative research methods were used, a topic guide, rather than a standardized questionnaire, guided the interview. The use of qualitative research methods aimed to facilitate a three-way conversation between the researcher, the informant, and the interpreter, with informants encouraged to speak freely about their life experiences and perspectives. To verify the skills of the interpreters six pilot interviews were videotaped and viewed by the project supervisor, Bencie Woll. She informally assessed the sign language interpreters' accuracy of interpretation from English to BSL and vice versa.

Before the interviews commenced, recorded consent was given by all of the informants to be recorded on video, with the tapes to be kept confidential and used only for transcribing purposes. The interview began by asking the informants to explain their current employment situation. This led to a conversation on the subjects in the topic guide, which covered issues concerned with the family, education and training, employment, the Black community, and the Deaf community. The interviews were conducted mostly in BSL and videotaped. The video recorder had a built-in microphone so that the questions and responses, which the interpreter translated from BSL to spoken English, could be transcribed later.

All interviews were transcribed following their completion. Transcribing was a lengthy process. It took approximately three months to complete the coding of the 21 transcripts. All transcripts were analyzed to identify common issues and patterns of experience. An index was created to categorize this information and highlight new themes. Once the transcripts were indexed, thematic data was inserted into charts, which used thematic headings taken from the transcripts and topic guides. The charts, which were all referenced with a transcript page for easy retrieval, consisted of summaries of the informants' experiences with specific issues and included direct quotations. These charts were then studied and interpreted.

In what follows, we will examine the findings of this research. It begins with an overview of the informants' experiences within the family and the impact of family relationships on their feelings about being Deaf.

The Family

Family relationships and experiences had an important influence on the informants' awareness and feelings about being Deaf. These experiences were responsible for laying both positive and negative foundations in their lives, which were in turn of importance when interacting within the hearing and Deaf communities and in the development of allegiances to specific aspects of their bicultural identity. The informants had diverse family backgrounds: traditional nuclear families, single parent units, and extended families in which relatives, such as aunts and uncles, acted as surrogate mothers and fathers. Some informants had experienced periods of separation from their parents as a result of marital breakdowns, being sent abroad, or by having a boarding school education. The nature of the informants' family relationships was influenced by family attitudes toward deafness. These attitudes were reflected both in communication methods and in the way in which they dealt with having a Deaf child. Some parents sought to have their children cured by visiting spiritualist healers and by encouraging them to attend church. The following excerpt taken from Junior's narrative illustrates his embarrassment, fear, and bewilderment at being sent to a healer. It highlights the power of religion and its impact on his mother's perception and management of his deafness:

> My mum stood up. I was so embarrassed. I was saying to my mum: 'Don't, mum', and the preacher was saying: 'Come down, come down to the front.' My heart was beating. I can't believe this. I explained to him that I was deaf and everyone was looking at me. I closed my eyes and for two or three minutes he touched me and I just fell over. Then there was all that noise and I said to myself: 'What is that noise?' I walked downstairs and there was a man standing behind me and he was calling out my name. He would say 'one' and I would repeat that and then 'twelve' and I repeated that. The audience just cheered. I heard something but now I am not sure what happened. I believe in God but there is no proof that deaf people can become hearing. (Junior, profoundly deaf) (Here and further on all quotes represent English translations from BSL, unless indicated otherwise.)

Other informants described having overprotective parents to the point where they felt trapped and lonely, as evident in Janet's narrative:

> I stayed at home. I couldn't go out. They never encouraged me to go out. It was always boring. I remember in the school holidays being very bored with nothing to do. I wanted to talk to my mum and dad about things but I could not because it was difficult to communicate. (Janet, profoundly deaf)

Three of the informants who described having positive and well-balanced family relationships attributed this to their parents' patience and understanding of their communication and support needs. Positive attitudes to deafness were mirrored by positive communication: these families used English, BSL, gestures, and elements of African and Caribbean languages to communicate. Positive family relationships were described by the informants in terms of their level of empathy with family members rather than definitive actions. This suggests the need to take into consideration atmosphere and feeling responses despite the lack of explicit language to describe what is conveyed (Corker, 1996).

Language served an important role in identity formation, as can be seen in Figure 4.1. Children were exposed to English and sometimes BSL at school. While schools held out the promise of integration with the hearing world through English, this did not necessarily help the child to integrate with the world of his family and home culture, whose language often diverged extensively from the model provided at school.

Some of the informants had difficulty in communicating with family members who lacked Deaf awareness skills or who communicated using non-standard dialects and unfamiliar accents. These difficulties created barriers to developing close family bonds and hindered the informants' understanding and ability to participate in family discussions, experiences, and culture. These communication problems led to socialization occurring mainly in the school environment under the influences of peers and teachers. The long hours worked by many of the parents meant

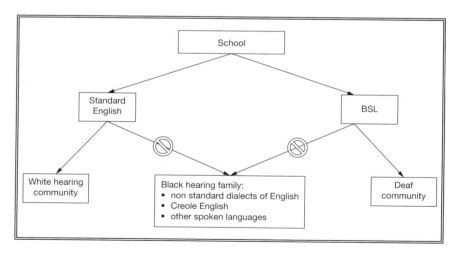

Figure 4.1 Incompatibility of school and family languages

that they had little opportunity to learn to communicate with their deaf children or utilize the support of welfare services, many of which were not culturally sensitive.

Thus the family unit and extended family did not always provide the informants with the opportunity to learn and understand their racial and cultural heritage. Holidays abroad to Africa or the Caribbean may have been part of their parents' attempts to introduce elements of the family heritage, but these holidays were regarded by the informants as a 'waste of time' due to their feelings of isolation.

> I went to visit Jamaica with my family. I was bored. My parents just talked. It was just like a waste of time, a waste of holiday. I was there for a month. I just sat there because I was deaf and everyone was just talking around me. (Janet, profoundly deaf)

During family gatherings and discussions family members talked around them. Only a few informants who were hard of hearing or post-lingually deaf felt able to access information and participate in family activities. For many informants these communication difficulties were a common occurrence, as Kathy's narrative illustrates:

> My family was all together. They were all talking. I wanted to know what they were talking about so I asked my mother: 'What are they talking about?' She said: 'Oh wait, I'm talking', but then after I asked what happened, she'd say 'Oh, I'm busy' or 'I've forgotten what they were saying.' (Kathy, profoundly deaf)

The informants' families played an important role in shaping their feelings about being deaf, through their attitudes and communication patterns. Those who had positive attitudes to deafness and good communication skills tried to include the informants in every aspect of family life. Other families, many of whom lacked support both from external agencies and family members, searched for cures or failed to recognize the special needs of their deaf children. This affected their relationships, which in turn influenced how the informants perceived themselves, forcing them to confront issues of identity early in their childhoods. Being Deaf was the first identity that several informants became aware of, as a result of their feelings of loneliness and inability to share the experiences of other family members. These experiences set the scene for their later interactions with hearing people. They also had an impact on their relationships with other Deaf and hearing people who played a central role in their lives. This is clearly illustrated by the informants' experiences outside the home, which will now be examined.

Education

The informants attended a mixture of mainstream schools and partially hearing units, and residential and non-residential Deaf schools. Fifteen out of the 21 informants chose to continue their studies at further education colleges, which were predominately hearing environments. Here it is important to note that there are no higher education colleges for deaf people in Britain, unlike the US, which has Gallaudet University and the National Technical Institute for the Deaf. Britain only has further education colleges with specialized facilities for deaf people (Doncaster College, Royal School for the Deaf in Derby, and the City Literary Institute in London). Some universities, such as Wolverhampton, Central Lancashire (Preston), and Bristol, offer Deaf Studies courses. Not all of these educational opportunities were available to the informants when they left school – they had rather limited higher educational opportunites and suffered from poor career advice.

The informants' family relationships greatly influenced the nature of their experiences at school. Those who reported having a strong relationship with their families regarded them as a source of support to help them through difficult times. For other informants, particularly those who had weak family bonds, support was sought from friends and teachers. Teachers play a significant role in the life of all young people, but for several informants this relationship was particularly important. For these informants, teachers were the only adults with whom they felt that they could communicate their feelings, because they understood deaf children and the obstacles they faced in the hearing world. The following excerpt from Amy's narrative illustrates how some teachers tried to prepare them for a life outside the school:

> She [the teacher] didn't want us to be stupid or naive or to think that everything comes on a plate. I think of that when I am working with young people and teaching children. I tend to put that into them as well. I say: 'Be realistic. This is not going to be handed to you. You have to work for it.' (Amy, hard of hearing; interviewed in English)

While some teachers supported the informants, others were described as incompetent and oppressive. Many informants described being taught by teachers who practiced favoritism, had poor deaf awareness skills, had low expectations of their pupils, and were insensitive to racial issues. Sharon felt publicly humiliated when one of her tutors ignored her feelings of discomfort and embarrassment, using old-fashioned and offensive terms and signs to denote Black people. This occurred in a racially mixed environment:

A teacher of mine was talking about the Caribbean and about their ways. She was using the old-fashioned signs like the old sign for Black. We don't like that sign. We use the new sign for Black. Then she used the word 'coloured'. I had to stop her and say: 'No, that is wrong. We don't use that any more. We use the word "Black"'; but she carried on using the word 'coloured' so I didn't really say anything more. Those words were a problem. She didn't include me. She didn't have that eye contact so I didn't feel important and that affected me. (Sharon, profoundly deaf)

The informants also described their teachers as having low expectations of them. They were not encouraged to fulfill their ambitions, but were directed toward employment in bars or factories. Some informants were led to believe that Deaf people could not go to university. The following quotation, also taken from Sharon's narrative, shows the lack of support she received from her tutors and its impact on her own expectations:

When I was ready to leave school and was asked what jobs I wanted to do I felt that their [the teachers'] attitude changed. They were frightened because we were facing the real world. I didn't know anything about racism or oppression so sometimes I would wish that there was a role model there. There were no Black teachers or Deaf tutors. There was nothing there like that. When I was at school, if there had been a role model there could have been someone who could have helped me in my chosen job. There were no jobs, only packing boxes, and Deaf people accepted it because they didn't think that they could achieve anything. There was no one there to say that they could do anything better than that. They expected to get the low jobs and just accepted them. .... Architecture was my first dream when I was sixteen. I wanted to do that course, I asked my career teacher for information about architectural courses and they said that I can't do that because I'm deaf. My confidence just dropped. (Sharon, profoundly deaf)

The educational policies in the late 1970s and 1980s, which were marked by changes from assimilationism to cultural pluralism, had little or no impact on the informants' educational experiences. School was not a place where they could formally learn about aspects of minority cultures, including their own. The lack of access to information about Black culture and history, and the absence of contact with Black teachers at school, blocked any opportunities for them to learn about their own cultures, while at the same time, within the family unit, the informants' under-standing of aspects of their cultural and racial heritage was assumed and never explained. Attempts to introduce multicultural educational policies within schools for the Deaf and the mainstream were limited, as Kathy's narrative suggests. Kathy's teachers perceived her requests to introduce a multicultural history curriculum as a challenge to their authority. She was excluded from the classroom like a disruptive child:

> We were taught about Henry VIII. I was bored and asleep and they would try and get my attention. I would tell them that I wanted to learn about Black history. They would send me out of the classroom and I would have to sit outside. They were embarrassed because I wanted to know about Black history. I wanted to know about my past. (Kathy, profoundly deaf)

The difficult relationships that some informants had with their teachers typify much that has been written about Black student–white teacher relationships (Troyna & Carrington, 1990; Wright, 1987, 1992). Some informants suffered from teachers' negative attitudes and were treated in a more restrictive way than other pupils. Teacher insensitivity to the experience of racism was also evident. The informants felt rejected and disillusioned by these attitudes and their inability to progress in the way that they had hoped. The informants' views are supported by evidence of racial stereotyping and unconscious and unintentionally racist attitudes among teachers as a problem affecting the teaching profession (Rampton, 1981; Swann, 1985). Many of the informants believed that their teachers held them back and did not support them. At least half were taught in mainstream schools, where some of these attitudes toward Black hearing pupils were widespread.

While some of the informants described difficult school experiences, many were not able to explain some of the factors which led to their different treatment at school compared to their white counterparts. However, from their narratives, racism was evident in the relationships between some informants and their teachers' practice and behavior. The informants were also taught within an educational environment which failed to embrace multiculturalism and where racial abuse from fellow pupils was a common occurrence. The informants' need to access information about Black culture and contact with Black hearing people was often the result of these negative experiences, as suggested in the excerpt from Shola's narrative:

> My confidence is up and down a bit because some white people have a bad attitude towards me. I prefer to be with a Black person. Not being with a Black person has knocked my confidence. It is a bit like

a roller coaster. The way that they treat me is like to say: 'Go back to Africa.' It is like I am a slave and white people are disrespecting me. They are all achieving but I am not. I want to be achieving. I want to be equal. (Shola, profoundly deaf)

For all informants access to information about the Deaf community and Deaf culture came from friendships and interactions with other Deaf children. They learned what it meant to be Deaf through exposure to sign language and Deaf culture. In addition to initiating them into the Deaf community, learning sign language was for most informants the only way that they could make friends and access information in the wider community. However, the experience of racism was felt both in the mainstream schools and schools for the Deaf. The following excerpt from Sharon's narrative clearly highlights her sense of isolation from fellow Deaf students who were white:

I have been here for a year. They just say: 'Oh hello, how are you?' and that's it. I feel that their attitude is a little bit funny. They talk to the other students but they don't talk to me. They think my brain is okay. They just don't want to talk to me. Maybe they look at me as a challenge. I'm Black. They expect everything to be all white people and suddenly they have this Black person and they are shocked. (Sharon, profoundly deaf)

The limited and ad hoc communication that the informants experienced at home was replaced with a more structured and consistent form of communication at school. This, however, was still often inaccessible, as most schools had a policy of using spoken language only. Most importantly, while the family environment and educational settings contributed to the informants' sense of Deaf identity, an understanding of their racial and cultural heritage remained for the most part unexplored.

Employment and Unemployment

Studies of Britain's Black population show that there has been little change in their economic position since the 1950s (Brown, 1984; Smith, 1976). Black people remain disadvantaged and over-represented in low-paid, low-status jobs compared to their white counterparts. Some of the disadvantages they experience have been attributed to Black workers having poor skills and qualifications, but research has shown that Black people face discrimination at different stages in the employment cycle. Lee and Wrench (1981) identified discriminatory practices at the training stage, while Cross *et al.*'s (1990) study highlighted how career services channel Black people into specific areas of employment. Low expectations led some informants to accept low-paid, menial positions. These jobs offered limited opportunities for personal or professional development and were not in 'Deaf friendly' environments.

Both those informants who were employed and those who were unemployed faced challenges in the employment sector. The informants' experiences of unemployment and employment reinforced their Deaf identity in a negative way, because deafness was seen as the cause of the difficulties they faced. An examination of their experiences clearly demonstrates this. All of the informants described difficulties in obtaining work. While some informants lacked appropriate skills and qualifications, others felt discriminated against for being Deaf. Their experiences are reminiscent of those described by Bannerman *et al.* (1989), who studied discrimination against Deaf people in the job market, in relation to the types of jobs offered and employers' attitudes and expectations. The informants in this study believed that disability discrimination and inexperienced employers were responsible for the problems they faced getting a job. The excerpt taken from Samuel's narrative illustrates how he faced disability discrimination despite being well qualified:

> I was invited to do a test. During the test I said: 'Excuse me, I am deaf.' So they said: 'Oh, you're deaf?' I said: 'Yes, I am.' They said: 'No problems' and wrote all the test questions down. A week later I got a reply back from the company. They said 'We're sorry. We think you are the best person for the job but the problem is you are deaf. You cannot use the telephone so we have given the job to someone else.' (Samuel, profoundly deaf; interviewed in English)

Most of the informants felt that their deafness was the source of discrimination, but a few believed that racism also affected their opportunities to find work. Racial discrimination was seen in the negative attitudes of potential employers, even those who were themselves deaf. Employers generally made no effort to improve communication or access for Deaf workers. Several informants and sympathetic co-workers independently organized Deaf awareness training and sign language classes. Although this resulted in improved communication with colleagues, many of whom continued private sign language lessons, there was a lack of commitment from employers to continue these initiatives. Employers continuously failed to book interpreters for meetings and offered limited access to technological aids and training courses:

The manager complains that my telephone bill is too high, so I have to explain to him that I use a Minicom [text telephone] and it takes a bit longer. He doesn't appear to be supportive or understanding which is a problem sometimes. (Samuel, profoundly deaf; interviewed in English)

Other difficulties facing the informants related to the status and rights that they were accorded. Their work status and pay levels were often lower than those of their hearing co-workers. This is illustrated in Janet's and Shamique's experiences. In Janet's case sexism also influenced how she was treated. Janet was employed as a junior secretary for several years. When she returned from maternity leave she found herself downgraded to an office messenger. Her employers had not negotiated or discussed her job change with her. This demotion left her feeling undermined, undervalued, and powerless:

They changed my job. I never asked to be a messenger. I only wanted to do typing but they changed my job. I was shocked. I didn't expect that but it was too late. They had already done that to me when I went back to work so I had to accept it. (Janet, profoundly deaf)

In addition to poor Deaf awareness and inequalities in status and pay at work, some informants were bullied by their co-workers. Workplace bullying often involved verbal abuse and in some cases physical attacks. The following excerpt from Jason's narrative illustrates how hearing staff treated him with a lack of respect and forced him to undertake tasks which were menial and degrading:

There was no time to relax. Everything had to be done in haste. It was so boring. It was the same thing again and again. They would say: 'You go to the fridge, clean out the fridge, clean out the shelves, clean all the stuff out.' They had a rubber seal around the fridge. I had to clean all that – really detailed work. I had to clean all the shelves and put all the food back and you had to remember where everything was to put it back in the same place. (Jason, profoundly deaf)

The stress faced by many informants at work was exacerbated by communication difficulties with co-workers. Some co-workers were very impatient when conveying information or would shout when the informants could not understand what they were saying. The informants felt that the attitudes of employers exacerbated this as they sent messages through other workers rather than talking to them directly. In some cases they banned the informants from using sign language:

I don't like passing notes. I have to think about how I am going to say something and try to explain myself. I use BSL – that's my language. It's difficult; I get frustrated. How do I write things down? It affects me and makes me angry. Sometimes I just give up. (Janet, profoundly deaf)

Thus, the experiences of the informants demonstrated that job-seekers faced both disability and racial discrimination, and those at work felt 'hired to fail.' Working conditions did not support positive Deaf–hearing interaction, as evidenced by the informants' own attempts to introduce Deaf awareness in the workplace, and the persistent failure of their employers to eliminate workplace bullying and inequality. Most of the informants felt that deafness, not race, was the main disadvantage they faced in the job market. Their educational and home experiences had prepared them to expect disability discrimination, but there was limited communication about racial issues. They had been socialized in environments where deafness was emphasized as the main characteristic by which they would be judged and their own explanations of work difficulties demonstrated that they clearly believed this.

Racial Identity Awareness

Recent research has shown that many sub-communities within the larger Deaf community have difficulties accessing the languages and cultures of their families and maintaining their own ethnic identity. Dively (2001) describes how Native American Deaf people have both limited participation within Native American culture and difficulty in maintaining their Native American identity in the wider Deaf community. These findings are paralleled in Chamba *et al.*'s (1998) research on the experiences of Deaf people of Indian and Pakistani backgrounds in Britain.

In the present study, many informants demonstrated limited awareness of having a racial identity. Four informants had spent the formative years of their childhood (up to the age of 10) living in Africa or the Caribbean, where they had interacted predominantly within Black communities; the remaining 17 informants were born and raised in Britain and lived in ethnically diverse communities. All of these informants encountered members of the Black hearing community, but for many of them contact was limited to family, neighbors, and fellow pupils. The impact of their limited interaction with Black people and the importance of communication in the process of racial identity awareness is clearly exemplified by Janet's comments, where Black people are portrayed as different, almost as a 'race' apart:

> I did not understand what it was to be Black. I heard about Black people but what was it like to be Black? (Janet, profoundly deaf)

Even though the informants lived in multiracial and multicultural communities, they had attended schools which were predominately white and had been taught by white hearing teachers. Most of the Deaf schools and mainstream schools with special classes for deaf children which the informants had attended were located in suburban areas and not in the inner cities where they lived. Mainstreaming thus did not mean a neighborhood education. These informants, like many other Deaf children, were bused to school, which limited their opportunities to develop friendships with local Black children. The informants were thus raised and socialized in predominantly white environments and as a result had fewer problems relating to white hearing people than to Black hearing people, as Francis's comments illustrate:

> I used to get frightened of talking to Black people. They always look so tough – it's true! They would make me nervous the way that they talked. They would tell me what to do like: 'Come here! Go away!' I understand more when I talk to white people. Black people are more tough; white people look weak so it is easier to talk to them; because I know their ways I would always talk to white people. (Francis, hard of hearing)

Most informants who described being aware of having a racial identity while still at school or in further education related this to experiences of racism within these contexts, as a direct response to racial abuse from other children, negative experiences with white teachers, a lack of contact with Black people, and limited access to their cultural heritage. For other informants, particularly those who had been partly raised abroad, racial awareness was attributed to a school curriculum which introduced African and Caribbean culture at an early age and encouraged direct interaction with Black hearing people. The excerpt from Joshua's narrative highlights the impact of first contacts with Black people:

> I was about sixteen and a man came to the school. He was a former student at the school. When he came in, he was talking – really I didn't know about Black Deafness. I knew that I was Deaf but that was it. I was equal. I knew about Deaf rights and how I needed to get more support as a Deaf person and all that sort of thing. He came along and was talking about Black people. Then I really became interested in myself. (Joshua, profoundly deaf)

Having direct interactions with other Black Deaf or Black hearing people led some informants to recognize information needs relating to the Black community. Many female informants felt that a lack of information within the Deaf community on health and personal care issues for Black Deaf women hindered their personal and professional development. They were concerned with how best they could care for their hair and skin, and how illnesses endemic to the Black community, such as sickle-cell anaemia, could affect their health and that of their children:

> They need to know about these things like sickle-cell. How does that affect Black Deaf people? They should know all about these things, and cancer. The doctors should have interpreters because it is part of your cultural health. In hospital, communication was difficult. Because I'm deaf there was no communication. (Janet, profoundly deaf)

Most of the informants, particularly those who were profoundly deaf, experienced difficulties accessing Black hearing events and activities due to a poor level of Deaf awareness among Black service providers. Their interactions with Black hearing people were limited to family activities and open events such as the Notting Hill Carnival, where visual images of Black culture could be enjoyed.

Black Deaf Identity Development

Although all informants recognized that they were Black, they displayed diverse feelings about having a Black identity. These feelings, ranging from positive, through indifference, to negative, have been summarized in Table 4.2. The informants who were uncomfortable being Black had only had limited interactions with the Black hearing community. They had been educated in predominantly white environments with no access to Black teachers or a multicultural curriculum. Many experienced communication barriers within their families and had no desire to mix or interact with Black hearing people. Other informants described feeling a sense of Black pride and desired more contact with Black people and information on Black culture. For these informants, Black pride was strongest when they felt able to access Black events and social activities. These informants had good communication within their families and close family bonds. Amy's sense of pride was evident when she was dancing:

> We go to a club and all these people are dancing and they try dancing to reggae but they can't dance and I'm just swinging in time and they

Table 4.2 Informants' feelings about their racial identity

Positive	Ambivalent	Negative
Black pride – Blackness is an important aspect of identity.	Acknowledge racial identity but display a detachment from it (a color-blind attitude).	A need to escape Blackness because of its stigmatization.
Feel able to access and enjoy Black cultural life.	Limited understanding and knowledge of Black people's experiences.	Unable to access the Black hearing community.
The development of Black consciousness. A desire to learn more about Black people and Black issues. A desire to be involved in Black activities and events.	Life difficulties attributed to experiences of deafness. Few if any life experiences attributed to racial identity. Acknowledge the existence of Black hearing community but have no real desire for involvement.	Poor family relationships influence relationships with other Black hearing people. Feelings of marginalization within the Black hearing community. No opportunities to develop Black pride.
Positive and strong identification with the Black community and Black people.	Weak identification with Black hearing people.	Difficulties relating to Black people.

are looking around and I say: 'Hey I am a Black person.' (Amy, hard of hearing; interviewed in English)

The few informants who were indifferent to having a Black identity stated that race was irrelevant. Most of these informants were unaware of racism and the covert way in which it operated within society. They felt that unless racism was discussed within the Deaf community it did not exist. Maximé (1987) has described how racial identity awareness develops in children as young as three years old. However, with the exception of the four informants who had spent part of their childhood abroad, the informants' narratives suggested that, for the most part, racial identity awareness had occurred much later in their lives. In view of their statements, it is important that racial identity theories consider the role of language and communication in the process of racial identity development. The experiences of these Black Deaf people have shown that communication and interaction are important contributors to developing racial and cultural awareness.

The informants' narratives demonstrated that they did not automatically consider themselves as Black, despite being raised in Black families. Within the family context, racial and cultural issues were rarely discussed in a way accessible to them, and schools failed to incorporate a multicultural curriculum. Direct contact with other Black people, access to information on Black culture, and an understanding and experience of racism were all triggers for the development of the informants' racial identity awareness. The following section provides an exploration of the informants' interactions and experiences within the Deaf community. It demonstrates how audiological deafness did not automatically gain the informants acceptance from other Deaf people or membership in the Deaf community.

The Deaf Community

Approximately 50,000 Deaf people in Britain consider themselves to be members of a cultural and linguistic minority (Corker, 1998). The Deaf community comprises a group of people who have their own language, values, rules of behavior and traditions (Padden, 1989). Deaf culture has at its heart the use of sign language. Members of the Deaf community do not live or work in a specific region, but are spread in small communities across the country. Attitudinal deafness, or 'Deafhood,' was evident among the informants in this study. Several had strong Deaf identities as a result of positive Deaf feelings. For example, several hard of hearing informants displayed more Deaf pride than those who were profoundly deaf. They had higher participation levels in the Deaf community and preferred to communicate using BSL despite possessing good spoken English skills. Like many other deaf people, the informants displayed diverse attitudes toward the wider Deaf community. The Deaf community with its Deaf clubs, pubs, and churches enabled some informants to have a wide network of Deaf contacts and to feel comfortable being Deaf. Deaf pride was particularly strong among the informants who were born deaf or became deaf early in their lives:

I'm only deaf, that's all. There are no other problems with me – everything is all the same. When hearing people see Deaf people they think that brains come out of their ears but we are not stupid. (Kathy, profoundly deaf)

However, this sense of belonging was not universal among all informants, even those who were proud to be Deaf. They described feeling uncomfortable mixing within the Deaf community due to intrusions on privacy, limited social and cultural activities within Deaf clubs, and racism. The following excerpt from Junior's narrative demonstrates the prejudice encountered by some informants at Deaf venues:

Some of them [other Deaf people] would say to me: 'What did you come here for?' I would ask them: 'What do you mean? You should welcome everyone.' It is the same with white people. They are always asking you: 'Where are you from?' and start swearing, all kinds of things. I feel that these people need to welcome everyone. We need to mix. (Junior, profoundly deaf)

Racism within the Deaf community was seen as evident in the refusal of many white Deaf people to accept the new ways in which Black Deaf people expressed themselves through sign language, and in the persistent use of derogatory signs to denote aspects of Black culture. The absence of Black Deaf people within Deaf organizations and institutions and the lack of access by Black Deaf people to charitable and public funds made some informants feel that a 'Deaf Apartheid' existed, fuelled by inter-ethnic antagonism between different Deaf minority groups competing for limited financial resources:

The status of the Black Deaf community is lower than the white community. White Deaf people have more information than the Black community. You look at any of those programs for Deaf people – they are all white people. Where are the Black people? It's all white. I just switch off. I'm not interested. When they start to get Black or Asian people I will start to watch it. (Junior, profoundly deaf)

The informants who had mixed or weak feelings about being Deaf often had difficulties accepting being Deaf and the prospect that they would never hear. Some had been diagnosed late in their childhoods and had been enculturated into the hearing world of family and friends. They often came from families with strong religious backgrounds, as seen in Francis's narrative below:

I came to realize that the Bible said there would be a new system. There would be no war, no suffering, my eyes and ears will be open and deaf people's speech would be normal. It says that in the Bible. That is God's promise. That is his way. (Francis, hard of hearing)

In the experiences of most informants, the prevalence of racism within the Deaf community negated their sense of equality with other Deaf people, and the difficulties of communication with Black people made some of them feel a 'race apart.' The informants' experiences of segregation from white Deaf and other ethnic minority Deaf groups, because of racial, religious, and cultural differences, meant that Black Deaf people did not fit easily into either the wider Deaf community or Deaf ethnic groups with their own organizations.

The Black Deaf Community

The Deaf community comprises native and non-native signers, hard of hearing as well as deaf individuals, having a common language, experiences, and values, and a common way of communicating with hearing people and each other. These characteristics were evident among the informants in this study, clearly making them members of the Deaf community. However, the informants were also members of an emerging Black Deaf community. One of the distinguishing characteristics of this community is the shared use of a Black variant of BSL, saturated with influences of Black hearing culture, and distinctive from the BSL used by the white Deaf community. The Black variant of BSL reflected informants' interactions with Black hearing people, mirroring Black gestures and body language.

Black BSL

The most salient differences between Black and white signers were body movements and facial expressions. Black Deaf signers adopted the interaction style of Black hearing people, especially those associated with Black youth culture. Their facial expressions were more animated and their body movements were described as distinctively Black. For example, Black Deaf people would 'tut' or ' kiss teeth' to convey vexation or annoyance, in the same way as Black hearing people. They also touched fists in greeting.

The existence of a Black variety of BSL created positive feelings of brotherhood and sisterhood. New signs had been created for aspects of Black cultural life, with some local variants in Black districts in London like Peckham, Hackney, and Lewisham. Some of these related to Caribbean food and events like the Notting Hill Carnival. Other new signs included one for 'Black,' which was articulated on the back of the hand.

The new sign 'white' was articulated with the same movement and hand configuration, but on the palm of the hand. Some of the informants objected to the white Deaf sign commonly used for 'Black' – a circular movement of the fist in front of the face. They were annoyed that white Deaf people continued to use the old sign, which they considered offensive and old-fashioned. The following are comments on the Black variant of BSL taken from the informants' narratives:

> Some Black Deaf people will sign in a way that white people don't know. Sometimes they use the signs but they like to make up their own signs so that white people won't know what they mean, so that if Black people are teasing them or making conversation, they won't recognize the signs. (Derek, profoundly deaf)

> Black and white sign language is different. The mannerisms and body language are all different so you know that it is Black. (Kathy, profoundly deaf)

> We've got some cultural signs like 'ackee', and 'Caribbean'. It's got nothing to do with the white Deaf community. They look at those signs and don't like it. The 'ethnic minority' sign – I get angry with that. But that's our sign because we are people of different origin, so that is our sign. (Janet, profoundly deaf)

It was important to these informants that Black Deaf signs and Black Deaf culture be accepted by both the Deaf and hearing worlds. They felt that the field of education, including sign language courses, failed to recognize the existence of Black BSL. Several informants believed that Deaf tutors, most of whom were white, failed to research appropriate signs denoting Black culture. They described white tutors creating their own signs to denote Black culture, which only served to perpetuate signs rejected by Black Deaf people.

Despite the small number of Black interpreters working within the profession (there were only seven registered Black BSL/English interpreters in 2002), the informants considered their presence within the Deaf community as important, particularly in the development and transmission of signs used by Black Deaf people. Black interpreters were seen as having the potential to strengthen and raise the status of the Black Deaf community, as cultural intermediaries with knowledge of both Black and Deaf issues.

While most of the informants considered the racial backgrounds of interpreters as irrelevant, they felt that it was important to have diversity within the profession. The few informants who had used Black interpreters described feeling a sense of empathy with them because of their relaxed and friendly approach. This contrasted with their experiences with white interpreters, who made them feel inadequate, in turn affecting their understanding of the information being conveyed:

> Once I was in a situation where they had a white interpreter. I didn't really understand her signing. She was using her white culture and everything else was inside her. She was very stiff when she was signing, even after they had finished. I didn't know what she was talking about. Her signing just went right over my head. (Sarah, profoundly deaf)

The Black Deaf community: Is there one?

Although there was evidence of a Black variant of BSL, the informants had mixed feelings about the existence of a Black Deaf community. Some believed that the absence of Black Deaf groups and role models was evidence that a community didn't exist, while others felt that the ongoing development of Black Deaf clubs was indicative of an emerging community, even though these clubs moved frequently from one site to another and served a broad membership. In the present study, three types of Black Deaf people were identified on the basis of their attitudes, occupational level, and cultural and linguistic characteristics. These were labelled Aspirers, In-betweeners, and Drifters. Table 4.3 provides a summary of these groups, although it should be noted that the categories are not static and there is movement between the groups.

The informants categorized as Aspirers had either been raised in Africa or the Caribbean, or had spent a significant length of time abroad. They were all employed in skilled or professional jobs, or were continuing their studies in higher education. All Aspirers were ambitious, but the four Aspirers who were raised abroad showed the most determination. They had very clear ideas about what they wanted in life and appeared undeterred by the difficulties they encountered. These informants felt that it was important to complete their education and obtain good jobs. Their experiences of living abroad in an all-Black environment had helped them to develop a strong sense of their own ethnicity. The Aspirers served as leaders in setting up organizations and social activities within the Black Deaf community.

The In-betweeners were all born and raised in Britain, but had travelled abroad. Those who were employed worked in skilled or semi-skilled jobs. They had an awareness of their racial and ethnic identity and participated

Table 4.3 Types within the Black Deaf community

Types of Black Deaf people	Characteristics
Aspirers	Potential Black Deaf Leaders. They have a clear grasp of the politics of the Deaf community and have an active role and interest in setting up Black Deaf-based projects. They are proactive and have aspirations to reach a professional level within the wider Deaf community. They often have a strong racial awareness.
In-betweeners	Tend to be supporters of the Aspirers. They attend Black Deaf events and clubs and support the development of Black Deaf projects and resources. They have latent aspirations, but they are often less confident or appear to be too over-committed in their life to implement them. They tend to involve themselves in the activities of the Aspirers, but also occasionally those of the Drifters. They have a well-developed sense of their racial identity.
Drifters	Comprises those whose lives are immersed in white Deaf cultural and social activities. They are rarely involved in Black Deaf-led initiatives and often attach no significance to their racial identity. They usually follow Deaf friends, both Black and white, and rely on them for direction. They often have no real opinion of their own about the Black Deaf community and have a weak awareness of their racial identity.

widely in both the Deaf and Black Deaf communities. Within the Black Deaf community they played a background role by attending activities and events, and providing moral support to the Aspirers' efforts to develop Black Deaf-led organizations.

The informants who were categorized as Drifters were all unemployed. They stood on the opposite side to the Aspirers, unclear about what they wanted in life, and with little regard for the development of the Black Deaf community. None had lived abroad or had experienced an all-Black environment, and few interacted with Black hearing people. The Drifters had the least developed sense of racial identity awareness and acceptance, and few had positive future expectations.

The Aspirers, In-betweeners, and Drifters also differed in terms of the relationships they had formed with their families. As a group the Drifters had the least contact with their parents. Some had been separated from them at an early age and raised by other family members. Others described having difficult relationships due to poor communication and a non-acceptance of deafness within the family. In contrast, the Aspirers and In-betweeners described having close ties to their families. They had regular contact and good communication with hearing family members.

The informants' attitudes toward the Deaf community also influenced how they were categorized. The Aspirers described themselves as belonging to the Black Deaf community. The In-betweeners also felt part of the Black Deaf community, but moved between the Deaf community and the Black hearing community. The Drifters felt part of the predominantly white Deaf community, participating in mainstream Deaf culture, and not getting involved in the activities of the Black Deaf community. They only aligned themselves with the Black Deaf community when they experienced racial division, hostility, and prejudice. Several informants, particularly the Aspirers, felt that some Deaf people didn't participate within the Black Deaf community because they didn't perceive themselves as Black. These individuals were described as objecting to the use of the label 'Black,' believing it had dangerous and 'bad' connotations.

Black Deaf or Deaf Black?

During the interviews, the informants were asked to describe their identities as Deaf Black or Black Deaf. The final part of this chapter explores their responses. The informants who identified themselves as Black Deaf considered being Black more important than being Deaf. These informants communicated primarily in spoken English and felt able to access the Black hearing community through family and friends. They felt close to Black people and believed that they shared similar experiences with them. They felt that their experiences of racism and discrimination within the Deaf community made it difficult for them to identify primarily with Deaf people or Deaf culture. For these informants,

Deaf culture was an adopted culture which they could abandon at any time, whereas Black culture was perceived to be part of their racial and cultural heritage.

The informants who identified themselves as Deaf Black considered being Deaf central to their identity. They felt that their needs as a Deaf person were far greater than their needs as a Black person. Their involvement in Deaf culture drew them closer to the Deaf community. They felt a strong sense of equality and Deaf pride from interacting with other Deaf people, and believed that the Deaf community offered them access to information and activities. Communicating through sign language linked them to the Deaf community irrespective of their skin color or racial origin:

> If you go for a job interview you have to let them know your needs as a Deaf person. It doesn't matter if you're Black or White. You're Deaf and you have problems with your hearing. If you were a blind man, what would be more important? You're blind. You have to let people know to guide you to sit down. I feel that is the same with deafness. (Derek, profoundly deaf)

Some of the informants had limited interaction with Black hearing people. Their limited interaction and poor access to information on Black issues and culture made it difficult for them to relate to Black people and thus they attached little significance to race. However, a few informants who considered themselves Deaf Black felt closer to the Deaf community because they perceived deafness to be a symbol of failure, particularly in areas of their life where they had underachieved. These informants associated deafness with negative life experiences and believed that describing themselves as Deaf Black reflected this.

Despite informants feeling a close affiliation with other Deaf people, some also wanted to achieve greater acceptance from the Black hearing community. Several talked about redefining their identities once they were able to gain access to Black hearing activities and events. Others resisted any form of categorization, believing Blackness and Deafness to be equally important. These informants felt that Black Deaf and Deaf Black described the same identity. They held no preference for Deaf or Black people, but considered themselves as cosmopolitan, having the ability to occupy a range of identities at any time. A few informants described feeling confused about their identities. They had difficulties filling in ethnic monitoring forms, particularly categories like Black British or Black Caribbean. They often ticked the 'Black Other' category and described themselves as 'Black and Deaf,' believing their Deaf identity was as important as their racial identity. Table 4.4 provides a summary of the main reasons given by the informants for defining themselves as Deaf Black or Black Deaf.

Understanding the Process of Identity Development and Negotiation

The informants were asked how they would define themselves in rela-tion to the categories Deaf Black or Black Deaf. Their responses showed that they were influenced by their feelings toward Deafness and Blackness and also by their experiences of interacting within two different cultural contexts. Table 4.5 represents the diversity of feelings displayed by the informants toward the Deaf Black aspects of their identity.

For many informants, a strong identification with one aspect of their identity often meant that they had negative or weak feelings about the other part. Those informants who had positive Black identity feelings often had negative or intermediate Deaf feelings, while those with positive Deaf feelings had intermediate or weak Black feelings. The infor-mants' narratives indicated that family experiences, interactions with Black and white hearing people, and experiences in the wider Deaf community had a strong influence on how they felt about their identities.

Not all the informants held fixed ideas about Blackness and Deafness. The intermediate position represents the informants who had mixed experiences within both Black and Deaf groups. These informants had ambivalent feelings and in some cases had an alternative dominant iden-tity. For example, one female informant felt that her gender was more important than either race or deafness:

> I try and see myself as just a woman. If I put myself in the category of Black Deaf, I am making my color be the most important thing about me. I am making my color say everything about me. But if I put myself as a woman, you know I am a woman. You don't know anything else. My color should not matter to you; my disability should not matter to you. (Amy, hard of hearing; interviewed in English)

Some informants who had limited contact with both the Black and Deaf communities also occupied an intermediate position. They distanced themselves from either, perceiving themselves as different and consti-tuting a separate and distinctive group. These informants had strong opinions about being Black and Deaf, which influenced their attitudes and interactions with both Black and Deaf people.

Table 4.4 Influences affecting the informants' identity choices

Black Deaf	*Deaf Black*	*Resisting categorization*
Appearance: a black skin color would be the first feature seen by others. Assumptions and stereotypes would be made on physical characteristics. The Black community provides a sense of strength and confidence in their identities. Black Deaf people share common bonds with other Black people: a common racial identity and cultural heritage, similar experiences of racial discrimination. Deaf culture is perceived as artificial; Black culture is perceived as real. Deaf community fails to acknowledge and embrace cultural pluralism and diversity.	Deafness is a central aspect of identity. Important for others to know that needs as a Deaf person are more important than needs as a Black person. Deafhood is the main source of culture with lives immersed in the Deaf community. Sign language is the link to the Deaf community regardless of skin color. Positive feelings about Deafness. Equality and acceptance from other Deaf people. Negative feelings about Deafness. Deafness perceived as a symbol of failure and under-achievement.	Black Deaf or Deaf Black describes the same identity; it is unimportant which aspect comes first. Cosmopolitan identity; there is not one main culture of Black or Deaf. Uncertainty and confusion about identity issues. Categories of Black Deaf or Deaf Black do not take account of gender, which is more important.

Table 4.5 The informants' feelings toward their Black and Deaf identifies

Positive/strong	*Intermediate*		*Negative/ weak*
Positive Black: • Access to Black culture and feelings of inclusion • Knowledge and understanding of Black culture and experiences • Positive inter-actions with Black people • Black pride: positive Black consciousness leading to a desire to learn more about the Black community	Intermediate feelings about Black groups and this aspect of their identity based on mixed experiences or having an alternative Master identity ↓ Mixed feelings	Intermediate feelings about Black groups based on strong Deaf feelings and a sense of having a distinctive Deaf identity ↓ Strong Deaf group feelings	Negative Black: • Feelings of exclusion from the Black community • Stigmatized feelings about being Black • Poor family relationships affecting perceptions of Black people • Difficulties relating to Black people • Negative interactions with Black people
Positive Deaf: • Acceptance of deafness • Preference to be with Deaf people • Deaf pride: recognized positive attributes about being Deaf • Recognize limitations and capabilities	Intermediate feelings about Deaf groups and this aspect of their identity based on mixed experiences ↓ Mixed feelings	Intermediate feelings about Deaf groups based on strong Black feelings and strong sense of having a Black identity ↓ Strong Black group feelings	Negative Deaf: • Difficulties coming to terms with being deaf • Limited contact with the Deaf community; experiencing a sense of isolation from other Deaf people • Negative hearing attitudes toward deafness • Strong religious beliefs in the family influencing perceptions of deafness

The informants rarely achieved an equal balance in their feelings toward their bicultural identities. They negotiated and renegotiated their identities in different situations. Racism and discrimination had an impact on the informants' lives, acting as external influences on their positioning. Experiences of racism and discrimination were common experiences for Black Deaf people, but the informants did not always recognize them as such when they occurred. Instead, racism reinforced feelings and ideas that the informants already held with respect to being Black and Deaf, but did not play a role in identity creation.

The influence of racism and discrimination was most noticeable when the informants positioned and repositioned themselves in different contexts. For example, some informants who experienced racism and discrimination in the Deaf community often identified themselves as Black Deaf because they felt discriminated against on the basis of skin color. Their level of racial awareness, and their ability to recognize racism occurring within the Deaf community, influenced their positioning in the presence of white Deaf people.

Within the Black hearing community, some of the informants positioned themselves as Deaf Black because they felt discriminated against and marginalized for being Deaf. Here their identity positioning depended upon the level of inclusion, acceptance, and equality that they felt among Black people. Knowledge of racism and discrimination did not influence the identity position of the informants who had strong feelings toward Deafness or Blackness or who chose to identify themselves outside the categories of Black Deaf or Deaf Black for other reasons. Thus the 'inside vs. outside syndrome' described by Valli *et al.* (1992) is not applicable to all Black Deaf people. It is only applicable when dealing with Black Deaf people who are conscious of their biculturalism and cannot be taken for granted to exist throughout the British Deaf community.

Conclusions

This study has demonstrated how Black Deaf people are immersed in multicultural and multilingual environments, all of which make conflicting demands on the individual. As a consequence, Black Deaf people assume a diverse range of identities both inside and outside the Deaf community. As the categories of Aspirer, In-betweener, and Drifter represent a continuum, so too the informants could assume different roles within the community and thus move between and create new identities.

For some informants, the terms Black Deaf or Deaf Black had different meanings, while for others these terms were interchangeable. The informants who resisted any attempts to be categorized constructed an identity which did not prioritize either race or deafness. Instead, they negotiated their biculturalism within different contexts. Identity choices were thus based on varying personal experiences of interacting within the Deaf and Black communities. Black Deaf people were immersed in conflicting cultures, and had to constantly negotiate and renegotiate their identities as both negative and positive forces were exerted.

Poor communication, inability to participate in the family's language or culture, use of BSL, and Deaf pride attracted some individuals toward identification with the Deaf community. Racism within the Deaf and wider hearing communities, positive family relationships, and Black pride attracted others toward membership in the Black community. The result is the recent emergence of a British Black Deaf community whose members are not only bilingual but also multicultural. This study of Black Deaf identity development has contested the possibility of a unified Black Deaf identity. It illustrates the complexity of identity formation among Black Deaf people, and the role of language in this process. The model which has emerged is not unique to Black Deaf people but may have implications for the study of emerging minority immigrant groups.

References

Aramburo, A. (1989) Sociolinguistic aspects of the Black Deaf community. In C. Lucas (ed.) *The sociolinguistics of the Deaf community* (pp. 103–119). New York: Academic Press.

Bannerman, C., Miller, J., and Montgomery, G. (1989) *Deaf workers are good workers: An enquiry into opinions and realities about the Deaf workforce*. Edinburgh: Scottish Workshop Publications.

Brown, C. (1984) *Black and white in Britain: The third PSI survey*. Aldershot: Gower.

Chamba, R., Ahmad, W., and Jones, L. (1998) *Improving services for Asian Deaf children: Parents' and professionals' perspectives*. Bristol: The Policy Press.

Corker, M. (1996) *Deaf transitions: Images and origins of Deaf families, Deaf communities and Deaf identities*. London: Jessica Kingsley Press.

Corker, M. (1998) *Deaf and Disabled or Deafness Disabled*. Milton Keynes: Open University Press.

Cross, W. (1978) The Cross and Thomas models of psychological nigresence. *Journal of Black Psychology* 5 (1), 13–19.

Cross, W., Wrench, J., and Barnett, S. (1990) *Ethnic minorities and the career services: An investigation into processes of assessment and placement*. Research paper no. 73. London: Department of Employment.

Davis, A. (1982) *Women, race, and class*. London: Women's Press.

Dively, V. (2001). Contemporary native Deaf experience: Overdue smoke rising. In Bragg, L. (ed.) *Deaf world: A historical reader and primary sourcebook* (pp. 390–405). New York: New York University Press.

Erikson, E. (1968) *Identity, youth and crisis.* New York: Norton.

GLAD (1991) *Race and disability: A dialogue for action.* London: Greater London Association of Disabled People.

Goffman, E. (1968) *Stigma: Notes on the management of spoiled identity.* London: Penguin Books.

Hairston, E. and Smith, L. (1983) *Black and Deaf in America.* Silver Spring, MD: TJ Publishers.

Hall, S. (1992) The question of cultural identity. In S. Hall, D. Held, and T. McGrew (eds) *Modernity and its futures* (pp. 273–326). Cambridge: Polity Press.

Higgins, P. (1980) *Outsiders in a hearing world.* Newbury Park, CA: Sage.

hooks, b. (1982) *'Ain't I a woman?': Black women and feminism.* London: Pluto Press.

James, M. (2000) *Black Deaf or Deaf Black.* Unpublished Ph.D. thesis, City University of London.

Ladd, P. (2003) *Understanding Deaf culture: In search of deafness.* Clevedon: Multilingual Matters.

Lane, H. (1984) *When the mind hears.* New York: Random House.

Lee, G. and Wrench, J. (1981) *In search of a skill.* London: Commission for Racial Equality.

Markowicz, H. and Woodward, J. (1978) Language and the maintenance of ethnic boundaries in the Deaf Community. *Communication and Cognition* 11, 29–37.

Maximé, J. (1987) Some psychological models of Black self-concept. In S. Ahmed, J. Cheetham, and J. Small (eds) *Social work with Black Children and their families* (pp. 100–116). London: Batsford.

Padden, C. (1989) The Deaf community and the culture of Deaf people. In S. Wilcox (ed.) *American Deaf culture: An anthology* (pp. 1–16). Silver Spring, MD: Linstok Press.

Padden, C. and Humphries, T. (1988) *Deaf in America: Voices from a culture.* Cambridge, MA: Harvard University Press.

Rampton, A. (1981) *West Indian children in our schools.* Interim report of the committee of inquiry into the education of children from ethnic minority groups, Cmnd.8273. London: HMSO.

Sharma, A. and Love, D. (1991) *A change in approach: A report on the experiences of Deaf people from Black and ethnic minority communities.* London: The Royal Association in Aid of Deaf People.

Smith, D. (1976) *The facts of racial disadvantage.* London: Political and Economic Planning.

Swann, M. (1985) *Education for all.* Report of the Committee of inquiry into the education of children from minority ethnic groups. London: HMSO.

Taylor, G. and Meherali, R. (1991) Being Deaf: The other Deaf community? D251 Block1 Unit 4. *Issues in Deafness.* UK: Open University Press.

Troyna, B. and Carrington, B. (1990) *Education, racism and reform.* London: Routledge.

Valli, C., Reed, R., Ingram, N., and Lucas, C. (1992) Sociolinguistic issues in the Black Deaf community. In College for Continuing Education, Gallaudet University (ed.) *Empowerment and black deaf persons* (pp. 42–66). Conference Proceedings, April 1990. Washington, DC: Gallaudet University.

West, C. (1995) The new cultural politics. In J. Rajchman (ed.) *The identity in question* (pp. 150–170). New York: Routledge.

Winncott, D. (1965) *The maturational processes and the facilitating environment.* London: Hogarth Press.

Woll, B. and Lawson, L. (1982) British Sign Language. In E. Haugen, J. McClure, and D. Thomson (eds) *Minority languages today* (pp. 218–234). Edinburgh: Edinburgh University Press (revised edition 1990).

Woodward, J. (1976) Black southern signing. *Language in Society* 5, 211–218.

Wright, C. (1987) Black students – White teachers. In B. Troyna (ed.) *Racial inequality in education.* London: Tavistock.

Wright, C. (1992) Early education: Multicultural education in primary school classrooms. In D. Gill, B. Mayor, and M. Blair (eds) *Racism and education: Structures and strategies* (pp. 5–41). London: Sage.

Chapter 5

Mothers and Mother Tongue: Perspectives on Self-Construction by Mothers of Pakistani Heritage

JEAN MILLS

Introduction

This chapter draws upon a larger study which explored language attitudes of 10 bilingual mothers and 10 of their children, all living in the West Midlands, UK (Mills, 2000, 2001a,b,c). The initial aim of this study was to investigate the perceptions the group had of their languages. Preliminary discussions with the mothers raised issues related to gender, self-definition, identity, aspiration, and child rearing, and revealed considerable tensions in their reflections on these areas and their attitudes toward their various languages. Consequently, I became interested in the links between language ideologies (and specifically, mother tongue ideologies), bilingual language practices, the construction of motherhood in linguistic minority communities, and women's responses to their positioning with respect to the languages of their cultural inheritance. In the light of all these considerations, the research questions came to focus more specifically on the relationship between the participants' positioning as mothers and the connotations that the term 'mother tongue' had for them. The focus on the notion of 'mother tongue' was further sharpened by a consideration of relevant literature. Underlying the study was a teasing semantic link between notions of 'motherhood' and 'mother tongue' and how the interaction between these two affected these women's identities.

Mothers and 'Mother Tongue'

Definitions of the phrase, 'mother tongue,' are neither straightforward, nor unproblematic. They encompass particular aspects of the expression in its guise as a metaphor, particularly in relation to the ways in which metaphors both convey and structure attitudes and ways of thinking and enable or constrain linguistic practices. Lakoff and Johnson (1980) have identified a variety of metaphorical practices whereby one area of experience is structured in terms of another; argument, for instance, being constructed in terms of warfare. Within the context of the present discussion, notions of language are metaphorized in terms of mothering. As these metaphorical implications are scrutinized, ways in which mothering and mother tongue relate to each other in terms of gender associations are explored: What are the links assumed in the literature on the topic? What are the connections between the women's identities as mothers and bilingual language transmission? In what ways are both informed – and perhaps even constrained – by gender expectations?

Romaine (1995: 21) and Skutnabb-Kangas and Phillipson (1989: 459) alert us to the need to differentiate between those definitions which are used to apply crude, and possibly inaccurate, labels of ethnicity and linguistic proficiency and those which reveal personal identification with a language. Examples of the former include labelling all people of Pakistani heritage in the UK as Urdu speakers when they may be most accomplished in Punjabi, Mirpuri, or English. In other words, the language one knows best or uses most may not be the one cited as the mother tongue. The focus in my study is on what makes someone identify with a mother tongue and what that reveals of their sense of self, rather than on how to identify what someone's mother tongue is. Consequently, the notion of 'mother tongue' is approached not from the outside, deciding who conforms to particular criteria, but from within, exploring ways in which people relate to a language and the sense of self-definition and identities these relationships convey. I will first consider 'mother tongue' in its gendered or metaphorical sense and, then, in terms of the associations which were most significant for particular speakers in my study.

The language learned from the mother

An exploration of the associations of the phrase 'mother tongue' exposes many features of emotional attachments to particular languages and cultures. In particular, the assumption that this is the language one learns first from one's mother highlights the role of one parent in language acquisition. By implication, the task of the other adult is made to appear almost deviant, since, in English at least, 'father tongue' is not a usual collocation. This can mean, of course, that the father's role may be undervalued or that 'fathers need to be aware of the important role they play in child language development' (Baker, 1995: 16). Put like this in an apparently neutral way, it can seem quite a simple proposition – a readjustment of parenting responsibilities. However, it is not necessarily that straightforward for the families involved. As will be seen later, there are certain ramifications connected with identification of mothers as primary language teachers.

A further exploration brings with it the consideration of context and gender stereotyping. Where, after all, do mothers traditionally operate but in the home and what might be some of the implications of these domestic associations? First, there can be the suggestion that children learn initially within a restricted domain and that the father's role is to offer a different (possibly better) type of interaction. As Baker comments: 'Research has shown that much of mothers' language interaction with their children is about basic housekeeping functions. . . . Many fathers interact with their children in child-centered ways' (1995: 17). In fact, feminist linguists feel the need to address such implicit assumptions and to point out that 'women's language, women's speech, and women's verbal activities are not everywhere socially and culturally inferior, domestic and polite' (Sherzer, 1987: 120).

The associations of mother tongue with primacy, the first language learned, bring a consideration of the potency of early experience and of ways in which a child's personality and emotional development are closely linked to the context in which the first concepts were formed. As Skutnabb-Kangas observes:

> Theodor Kallifatides, a Greek author living in Sweden and writing in Swedish . . . affirms [if] . . . he were even to try to lie in Greek, his mother tongue, all the deep-seated feelings of shame and guilt which his mother had instilled in him when he was a child would be aroused within him. (1981: 50–51)

As Skutnabb-Kangas points out, when one considers how the mother tongue is learned, 'it is easier to see why (it) is so crucial to our personality . . . why it is often difficult to dissociate ourselves from certain values and emotionally charged attitudes bound up with it' (1981: 52).

Gender associations

Speakers, then, may feel particularly closely tied to a language which they designate as their mother tongue. There may also be particular positive, or indeed negative, values associated with it. Some of these values, according to Burton *et al.* (1994), may be related to the gendered nature of the term. In other words, particular female qualities may be allied to certain languages and certain usages. For instance, Liu Hong (1994), one of the contributors to Burton *et al.*'s (1994) volume, describes how a female interpreter in China may play 'a wider feminine role as an intermediary' who 'needs to be flexible and conciliatory, and also to be a willing scape-goat, bearing the brunt of the wrath of both sides' (Burton, 1994: 18).

McDonald (1994), in an echo of Gal's (1979) classic study of language shift in Austria, pursued the relationship between identity and gender vis-à-vis French and Breton. She found that, for peasant women in Brittany, French was associated with femininity and gentility and thus had become opposed to Breton, the language of hard work and farming:

> Femininity and French have arrived, and together they can speak a sophistication that is other than peasant work. . . . Women can define their femininity, and men their masculinity, through the language they use, and language-use has its correlates in social space. The fields and certain bars tend to be male domains. . . . Contrasting with this world of rough and ready masculinity are certain female domains such as the special *salon* or parlour set aside in many farmhouses for guests. (McDonald, 1994: 93)

Moreover, language choice in relation to self-definition does not just appear in physical contexts. It is also apparent in the signals it gives about relationships:

> This is a world where a good mother, by definition, speaks nicely to children, but this can involve a structure of values so strong that in a peasant family . . . where I stayed for a week during my research, the mother spoke French to her two teenage daughters – and then Breton to cows but French to calves, and Breton to hens but French to their chicks, and Breton to pigs and sows but French to piglets. (McDonald, 1994: 103)

In other words, a mother's language choices are related to her notions of mothering. It is particularly ironical and intriguing that, in this situation, it is the imported language, the language of the state, rather than the orig-inal home language, which has come to stand for particular qualities of domesticity.

However, this is not always the case. There is 'the need to examine each case in the light of all its individual peculiarities' (Constantinidou, 1994: 123). Harvey (1994), in an example which is a mirror image of McDonald's, describes the use of the local language, Quechua, as opposed to Spanish, the state language, by women in southern Peru. Here, Spanish is the language of the colonizers, of education, and of work outside the community, and is used more by men, while Quechua is the language of the home, emotions, rituals, networks of kin, and communication with indigenous deities, associated as it is by 'a conquered people with a glorious past – a past that goes back in time beyond the Inkas to the land itself and the original source of productive social life' (Harvey, 1994: 53). Thus, this language choice also makes 'an explicit statement about . . . social identity' (Harvey, 1994: 47), in this case, signalling insider status.

These two examples indicate, once more, the ambiguities related to the notion of mother tongue and emphasize the fact that there may be no direct link between the language first learned and the birth mother. Romaine, for instance, cites Malherbe, who noted 'that it is quite common to find white infants in South Africa who grow up with Zulu nannies and can speak Zulu before they can speak either English or Afrikaans' (1995: 20).

Mothers' language choices

Examples like this apart, however, one's first language may indeed be the mother's tongue, and this, in itself, can have particular effects on which languages children acquire, especially in contexts where 'bilingualism may be associated with inequality and social disadvantage' (Burton, 1994: 4). Thus, in the example of Breton above, it was the peasant mothers who had chosen not to pass the language on to their children (McDonald, 1994). In contrast, younger women who saw themselves as Breton militants had deliberately learned, or relearned, the language and had chosen particular nursery schools which would support Breton for their children. This link between motherhood and responsibility for transmission of a minority language is echoed in Constantinidou's (1994) study, where young women in a village in East Sutherland reproach their mothers for not teaching them Gaelic, saying: '*You* never taught *us*, it was all English you spoke to *us*' (1994: 116).

As these examples indicate, women's responsibilities in nurturing a language within their families may also be equated with a more general responsibility as guardians of a culture. There are numerous examples of just such an equation. For instance, in the former Soviet Union, 'minority languages often became gendered with the imposition of Soviet state power' (Humphrey, 1994: 70), so that 'in Georgian tradition nationalist rhetoric was used for stressing women's traditional role as educators and propagators of the Georgian language and culture' (Chinchaladze &

Dragadze, 1994: 84). Similarly, Constantinidou (1994) describes language death of East Sutherland Gaelic as a decision made by women, part of a 'rejection of older ways of life, extending to their destruction of old furniture – of the kind that was elsewhere being dubbed "antique" and valued accordingly – and its replacement with new' (Burton, 1994: 16).

These examples also remind us of the tension between external and internal identification evoked earlier in this section. There is a feeling in some of these cases that others are imposing an identity on particular groups. In turn, the women may have made a self-determined choice of identity which does not accord with an external ideology. As one of McDonald's respondents notes: 'First they wanted us to speak French, now they want us to speak Breton' (McDonald, 1994: 102). In McDonald's (1994: 102) view, this is 'an apt comment on a situation in which the power and centre of definition are always elsewhere.'

This tension leads us to examine the final aspect of the metaphor which may in fact partially explain it. In fact, mother tongue is often not merely associated with mothers' role in transmitting a culture, but serves as the embodiment of that culture, ethnicity, or sense of nationality. Mackey's description of the monolingual state is particularly apt here: 'The political romanticism of the monolingual nation state . . . imbued the notion of mother tongue with a unique and almost mystical aura' (1992: 45). In this sense, mother tongue becomes a primal term, a metaphor that carries with it the overtones of mother earth, motherland, a crucial identifier of connectedness, rootedness, and belonging. As McDonald notes, 'from early philology to many modern education policies there has been some image of primitive primacy and primordial cultural attachment' (1994: 100). Therefore, choices made in the light of this interpretation are particularly symbolic. The thinking may also be constrained by the parameters of the metaphor. As Mackey puts it: 'If we can have only one mother we can have only one mother tongue' (1992: 45). There is the sense that mother tongue is not simply a set of associations, as outlined previously, but, rather, lies at the core of the personality. For instance, Ketaki Kushari Dyson, a bilingual writer, recalls that for her:

> The bonding with Bengali was . . . very strong. The language expressed our cultural identity as well as, in the early years of my childhood, our political aspirations. (Dyson, 1994:172)

There remains, then, in this discussion, a sense that an individual's relationship with his or her mother tongue defines identity; it is a crucial signal of identity in terms of the choices made and the metaphors used. This study's core metaphor of 'mother tongue,' with its corresponding richness of connotations and associations, alerts us particularly to the fact that mother tongue definitions have not only external considerations but also internal dimensions of self-definition and personality.

Methodology and Research Design

Ten bilingual mothers participated in the study. They were part of 10 families, known to the author on a personal and professional basis. All of the participants were fluent in English; in addition they spoke Punjabi, the language of the Punjab area in Pakistan, or Mirpuri, the language variety of the Mirpur region of northern Pakistan. They also had varying competencies in Arabic, used in reading the Qur'an. Some participants also spoke and had literacy skills in Urdu, the official language of Pakistan with a high level of prestige. Five of the mothers were born in the UK in immigrant families, three came as very young children, and two arrived in early adolescence. Their ages ranged from 29 to 43. The mothers were studying for a range of qualifications, including Bachelor of Arts and Bachelor of Education degrees, and a Post-Graduate Certificate in Education (a UK teaching qualification). Consequently, they had completed a variety of matriculation requirements to enter higher education. All but one of the mothers were mature students, who had completed these qualifications after statutory schooling while also caring for their homes and families.

Over a period of two years, the mothers were audiotaped during semi-structured interviews regarding their views on their own and their children's bilingualism. One school-age child of each mother was interviewed after the mother's first contribution and, in a final interview in the cycle, the mothers were interviewed again after they read their own and their children's transcripts. This approach aimed to give all participants an opportunity for reflection and rumination, while using children's views to inform the mothers' opinions.

The unstructured or semi-structured interview as a method for collecting data was selected partly because of familiarity and custom (see Mills, 1991,1993, 1995, 1996) and also because it related appropriately to methodological issues of subjectivity and gender. Conventionally, the face-to-face interview is cited as a qualitative or *soft* approach (Davies, 1985: 83; Jayaratne & Stewart, 1995: 221), a form of inquiry used by women researchers that has 'become the definitive feminist approach, marginalizing if not excluding (other) work' (Kelly *et al.*, 1995: 236). The interview was deliberately chosen for its qualities of flexibility of operation, sensitivity in acknowledging feelings, and potential delicacy of interpretation.

The interviews were conducted in English, the language in which all participants were fluent; some, namely the children and four mothers, designated it as their most fluent language. Again, this feature was related to the mothers' status as higher education students. Although, of course, this meant that there were no obvious difficulties in communication, it had an interesting effect of highlighting my 'outsider' status as a mono-lingual speaker. Their bilingualism allowed them to bring their position as experts to the fore and to put their other languages in the position of referred 'other' – a topic of discussion (albeit they rarely appeared in the discussion as actual quotations or examples). All the interviews were conducted either in my office or the participants' own homes, on the basis of mutual agreement and convenience.

In effect, the aims and the methodology of the study came together almost at the outset in an intriguing and satisfying way, since they both involved congruent issues of language, identity, and power. The method of the face-to-face interview enabled the respondents to grapple with cru-cial aspects of their identities by working through a dialogic relationship within the text of the interview and between the interviewer and the par-ticipants. Bakhtin's view (1981) of the dialogic quality of language illumi-nates this process as, in Bakhtinian terms, subjectivity is social in nature, since individuals only come to understand themselves through interaction with others. Thus, in my interviews, the respondents revealed themselves and, indeed, came into being by communicating. As Bakhtin explains:

> Nor is it a means of revealing, of exposing the already-formed char-acter of a person; no, here the person is not only outwardly manifested, he becomes for the first time that which he is, not only, – we repeat – as far as others are concerned, but for himself, as well. To be means to communicate dialogically. (1973: 213)

Or, as Moraes puts it: 'Existence (as language) is forged within dialogic social interactions among people' (1996: 10). Thus, in this view, the self is relative; it can 'exist only in relationship to some other, whether that other be another person, other parts of the self, or the individual's society, or her or his culture' (Josselson, 1995: 36).

Notably, dialogues are not just with other people, but also with oneself, in making sense of one's experience. Accordingly, there were many points in the interviews where speakers signalled through a dialogue with them-selves, or by reporting the words of others, that they had come to terms with, or were coming to terms with, a significant aspect of themselves. Indeed, if we view identities as multiple and flexible, we see individuals as always in the process of becoming. It is not surprising, then, that the interviewees' concerns over the relationship between their own identities and language are manifested through a dialogic expression of these identities.

The overt issues of power were addressed by the respondents not merely by owning their words, but also by receiving them in a transcript form and by owning up to those words after scrutinizing them. They retained the words in physical form and in rereading them confirmed or commented further on their views to me. The covert power relationships involved in the whole process were characterized more by certain subtleties and nuances than by the crude stereotype of dominant interviewer and passive interviewee. Positioned as experts on the topic of bilingualism, the respondents often talked at great length and had power over topic control and disclosure. They also expressed and acknowledged features of their multiple identities by engaging with different discourses. In contending with these discourses, they indicated the power which the discourses had over them and also the ways they sought to contest such control.

Accordingly, the research questions, which guided the questions in the semi-structured interview (see Appendix on p. 188), focused on the following areas:

- the relationship between the mothers' attitudes and feelings toward their communicative repertoires and their multiple identities;
- the relationship between 'mother tongue' and mothering;
- the mothers' responses to their positioning as mothers, by themselves and by family members, in terms of their children's language maintenance and development of English;
- their children's attitudes to all the languages in their repertoire and responses to language maintenance issues.

The process of analysis was reflective and cyclical in that it aimed to expose and track particular themes as they arose from the original research questions. The design of the analysis procedure was as follows:

- the transcripts were read several times;
- key themes, generated by the interview questions, were noted in the margins;
- the list of key themes was expanded in detail, after further background reading;
- these themes were then categorized and grouped together, using a tree diagram, into major and subsidiary themes for each set of transcripts; examples of these themes were then sought in the transcript data and highlighted by using different colored pens.

Results and Discussion

The foci of the study framed the data and findings in particular ways. When the issue of terminology in relation to the respondents' languages was introduced, it led to the unsolicited appearance of the favored term 'mother tongue.' Exploration of this phrase with the study participants revealed that 'mother tongue' was a crucial feature of these mothers' sense of their identities. The interview process also served to bring into focus other aspects of the respondents' identities. Thus, the study became an examination of these identities in relation to the respondents' self-realization as mothers and also as aspirant women. Consequently, key motifs in the data were plurality and mutability. As Bhavnani and Phoenix put it, identity is not one thing for any individual; rather, each individual

> is both located in, and opts for, a number of differing, and at times, conflictual identities, depending on the social, political, economic and ideological aspects of their situation: 'identity emerges as a kind of unsettled space ... between a number of intersecting discourses' (Hall, 1991: 10). This concept of identity thus precludes the notion of an authentic, a true or a 'real self'. Rather, it may be a place from which an individual can express multiple and often contradictory aspects of ourselves. (Bhavnani & Phoenix, 1994: 9)

With respect to plurality, the respondents conveyed the notion that they managed multiple identities as mothers, Muslims, British citizens of Pakistani heritage, bilingual speakers, and students. There is a further implication here, then, that, in addition to social identities being neither static nor immutable, they are also 'not fixed prior to the interaction but, rather, emerge within it' (Koven, 1998: 413). The ramification of this is a perception that it is language that constructs identity rather than various social identities being summoned up by language. This introduces the possibility, argued for by Fairclough (1992) and Weedon (1987), that, while individuals are shaped by discursive practices, they are not merely passive transmitters of current procedures, but may be active in being 'capable of reshaping and restructuring those practices' (Fairclough, 1992: 45) and, moreover, 'of negotiating their relationship with the multifarious types of discourses they are drawn into' (Fairclough, 1992: 61).

The mothers in my study expressed a variety of attitudes which could be interpreted as recasting their identities in terms of their own families. Their notions of mothering included educational aspirations, linguistic and cultural transmission, as well as the more familiar affective aspects of mothering. As Weedon observes: 'Social relations ... will determine the forms of subjectivity immediately open to any individual on the basis of gender, race, class, age and cultural background' (1987: 95). Hence, knowledge and experience of different discourses open up the possibility of choice or resistance. In this study, the participants' characteristics as mothers, bilingual speakers, and learners were particularly salient and, indeed, came together in the women's aspirations for themselves and their children. Accordingly, this discussion will begin with the mothers' articulation of the place of 'mother tongue' in the construction of their identities. (All names in the chapter have been changed.)

'Mother tongue' and identity

Respondents introduced the issue of multiple identities as they reflected on their lives and languages, and, in different ways, spoke of contending with these multiple identities and the various challenges they presented in establishing a coherent sense of self. The multiplicity and challenge are reflected in Khalida's comment, '*I suppose it is sort of having a different identity,*' and in Tahera's statement, '*OK we're British but we're still Pakistani.*' Rabia, in talking about her school days, suggested that such identities are managed and that this may occur within particular family constraints:

> *When you were there you still lived these two lives. You lived the life of the school, where you were a student and you were doing well . . . and then you went home and you lived the life that your parents wanted you to live.*

Rubina spoke of the conflict between her public, apparently westernized, self and her private, family, Muslim self, hidden from common view:

> *I'm Muslim, I believe in Islam, but I think there's an inner inside of you. Just because you wear a scarf does not mean that you are a hundred per cent pure or whatever.*

Similarly, Rabia referred to a disjuncture between her legal status and her inability to define her identity precisely, caused by a perceived mismatch between her outward appearance and stereotypes of 'Britishness':

> *R. said to me, 'Well, Rabia, are you a British citizen?' . . . And I sat there and I honestly could not say. I could not answer that question by confidently saying, 'Yes, I'm a British citizen' because what I did say to her, I said, 'Well, who am I really?' That's true like what I've told you, I've lived the two lives. I have got a British passport and all that stuff, but let's turn it the other way. If I was walking down a road who would R. see me as? And then I asked her that and she said, 'British, because you speak English really well.' I said, 'Yeah, but that's because you know me.'*

Rabia's question: *'Who am I really?'* raises a complex of issues and the strong sense that, although she recognizes and manages her multiple identities, she still struggles with her self-definition. She acknowledges two key aspects of British citizenship which she possesses, legal status and English language. At the same time, she cites her Asian appearance in terms of dress and skin color as signalling her Pakistani heritage and, therefore, her exclusion from being truly British in public terms (on public discourses on Britishness, see Blackledge in this volume). Musrat also did not seem to have come to terms with the separation described by Rabia:

> *I never felt that I was British, English and I never felt that I was Muslim. I always felt that I was one in between.*

Alternatively, Tasleem had resolved a similar situation coherently:

> *When I go back other people say to me, 'Oh, you're a white person', because of the way I behave, when I come over here people say to me, 'Oh, you're like a Pakistani person' because I'm floating, I'm not fitting into either. It's only now that I'm deciding you know it doesn't matter for me to fit in anywhere it's who I am and I can go around but I think I've only come to that decision because I've had the choice of both or experience of both cultures.*

In Tasleem's version, identities may be managed on a day-to-day basis. She observes that an individual has control over this situation – it is a site of personal agency. She resolves perceived contradictions by stating her belief that these identities have to be intelligible to oneself in a holistic sense and that they are made intelligible by affiliation and connection. 'Such a position places emphasis on both personal and political agency as key elements within a politics of self-identification, self-definition, and self-actualization' (Rassool, 1997: 191). For Tasleem, to be *floating*, as she terms it, does not seem to impose a particular strain; for Musrat, to be *in between*, does.

Overall, a number of themes emerged from the data concerning the constitution of identity. These were: the construction of a coherent self, the constituents of these respondents' self-definition, and the management and development of multiple identities. During the interviews, the respondents presented various features of their identities which related to each other in particular ways. A very significant aspect of the construction of identity on which all the respondents dwelled was that of education and aspiration. All the respondents referred to their schooling, very often precisely and in detail, and, in particular, in relation to disruption, curtailment of freedom of action and choice, either owing to family circumstances or the school context. Some of the respondents' choices were restricted because they had been required to prematurely curtail their studies by family or school circumstances. Tasleem, for example, had left Pakistan at the age of 14 to come to Britain to look after her sick aunt:

> *I couldn't actually speak any English. I could understand . . . I used to be good at English in Pakistan.*

For others, schooling was interrupted by marriage. Thus, in all these cases, the women's life-chances had been affected by their gender and particular cultural norms:

> *They always said to me if you tried hard, they'd let me carry on, 'cause I could see that girls were* [allowed to carry on with their education]. *I was quite shocked actually when, in the middle of my 'A' Levels, I stopped.* (Rabia)

As a result of these difficulties, most of the students had garnered a variety of qualifications in a painstaking way over a period of years after mandatory schooling, while also managing young children and, in some cases, dependent elderly relatives. These qualifications had eventually allowed them to embark on undergraduate degree courses. At the time of writing, all have successfully completed their studies and gained their degrees. We have here, then, a group who, in common with many other mature students, are particularly persistent, hardworking, and well-organized. The sense of the significance of their own aspirations in relation to education comes across in their comments:

> *I was always eager to study, really eager . . . then after my second child I thought, 'Well I really need to do something.'* (Musrat)

> *When my youngest son came to full time with school I decided I don't want to sit at home and vegetate, I want to go out and enhance my knowledge.* (Shabina)

> *While I was pregnant I thought, 'I'm not going to let the time pass', so I went and did GCSE 'O' Level English.* (Tasleem)

Clearly, mature students who see themselves as having a 'second chance' are not unusual; this detail, however, is notable in relation to other features of these women's identities. In particular, pregnancy was not allowed to be all-absorbing. Thus, Nadia said that she *never sort of left a year blank,* referring not to the production of children but the gaining of academic qualifications. Their accounts of struggles to gain qualifications offered evidence that they were driven to continue their studies and to construct their lives in particular ways, as educated female professionals, as carers in the community, as advisors, and as people who draw on their multilingual resources as part of their work.

'Mother tongue' associations

One of the interview questions asked the respondents which term they used to refer to languages other than English. It was in their responses to this question that their identification with certain languages was brought more sharply into focus. For eight of the respondents, the term was 'mother tongue' and for the remaining two 'home language' and 'first language.' These descriptions, in turn, brought up associations with the respondents' self-definitions, the development of their consciousness in childhood, and feelings of ownership of a particular language. They thus encompass definitions of 'mother tongue' cited by Baker and Prys Jones (1998: 47): the language learned from the mother, the language of an area or country, and the language for which a person has the most allegiance or affection, rather than any notion of proficiency. They also include the language first learned at home (Mackey, 1992: 45):

> *it was the one when I was being brought up associated with my home language. I couldn't say, even now, I couldn't say English is my own language, even though it's more dominantly spoken in my house now.* (Rabia)

> *'Mother tongue' is obviously . . . the one your family has been speaking for many, many years. . . . Your own immediate language.* (Nadia)

> *For me it means the language that you've been communicating . . . actually with your mother or as a child.* (Musrat)

There is here a cluster of attributes linking language, self-consciousness, domestic context, belonging, and nurturing. The language belongs to individuals and also makes individuals belong to a certain community as their sense of self evolves (Tabouret-Keller, 1998: 316). This became particularly clear when two respondents, Khalida and Musrat, had difficulty with a satisfactory definition:

> *I don't know if I would call it mother tongue although, up till the age of five, it was my first language and I had no sort of, no contact with English talk . . . that was my perception that I couldn't speak in my first language, and I adopted English as my language. . . . I really don't consider myself having a mother tongue. . . . 'Mother tongue' is like having roots somewhere, having a root in a language, but I don't think I do.* (Khalida)

Khalida's use of the word *adopted* is particularly telling in implying that the original mother tongue was rejected in favor of the foster child, English. The use of metaphor in the discourse of linguistic mothering is particularly evocative in defining Khalida's relationship with her languages. This is just one of the range of metaphors examined by Fishman (1998) that relate language to collective morality, kinship, the primordial home, and the history of a people. Musrat offered a similar identification of English:

> *I feel that I could never say that Mirpuri or Urdu was my own language because I've communicated in English before I knew Mirpuri or Urdu. Mother tongue, I can't really say it's my mother tongue because I always say my mother communicated to me in English.*

For these two women there is an absence of that sense of affiliation and proprietorship, or perhaps bonding, that seems to set the seal on the close identification of the previous speakers. It is not just that there is a close link here between language and identity, but that language has particular overtones connecting crucially to mothering and nurturing. When that notion is absent, these two speakers have difficulty in readily applying the term.

This sense of unease, of not being able to be definite about one's affiliation was conveyed in other respects, notably in the inconsistencies in different respondents' testimonies, at times citing one language as the mother tongue (Urdu) and at other times unconsciously talking of another (Punjabi). Thus, Khalida, having commented that she wanted her children to know that *their roots are in another language*, shortly after was asked: *if I use the term 'mother tongue' with you, what associations has that term got for you?* She replied, after a significant seven-second pause: ' "Mother tongue" is like . . . having a root in a language, but I don't think that I do.' She hesitated over the choice of a specific appellation – 'I suppose if you said your first language" it would probably be my first language but I don't think of it as such' – and went on to use the phrases *my own home language* and *my first language*. This slippage in terminology accentuated the unresolved relationships that Khalida had with the role that the first language (to avoid, in this instance, as she does, the term 'mother tongue') had in her life.

In other respects, there were, in addition, connotations assigned to specific languages in that each of the minority languages had particular cultural associations and functions. Urdu had associations with aesthetic values, social graces, status, and aspiration and it was these features of higher social class, education, and refinement which were perceived as attractive and related to the respondents' identities as socially and educationally aspirant:

> *Punjabi is a very colloquial language; it's a harsher language and whereas Urdu is very, very polite. You can't even swear, not being polite.* (Shabina)

As for their children, two mothers commented:

> *Urdu. That's what I'd like them to have. . . . To me it's very well, the language is very gentle, not a rough language and whatever . . . because in Punjabi . . . it sounds rude and like for them to have good manners I prefer them to speak Urdu. . . . It just sounds beautiful when you hear it from a little girl or little boy's mouth.* (Tahera)

> *There's two reasons actually. One is that when my children go back to Pakistan people automatically assume that, because they are from a better economic climate, they should be able to speak a different, better language which is like the rich man's language over there.* (Tasleem)

Punjabi, while it was important for conveying values, for cultural maintenance, and for communicating with relatives, lacked cachet, being referred to as 'colloquial,' and in the case of Mirpuri as 'a dialect.' In turn, Arabic was vital for these women as Muslims, in some cases more so than Punjabi or Urdu, as Khalida observed:

> *Then we have the other aspect, which is Arabic, because, being a Muslim, children have to be able to read the Qur'an and, hopefully, understand it as well. . . . For me this is more important than the first language.*

As we can see, each language had different meanings for these women and was linked to different aspects of their multiple identities.

Core values

The interviews revealed several identity markers that contributed to the plurality and mutability of the women's identities. These identity markers included, but were not limited to, multiple languages, religious observance, dress, and skin color. Language particularly was cited as a crucial component of identity. When asked what the loss of the mother tongue would entail, all ten respondents cited it as a vital element of their identity that must not be lost:

> *The language is your identity so to speak and, yes, you do really need to know that. You are identified by your language aren't you?* (Shabina)

*I think it is important . . . for my children to know there is another language.
. . . It's part of their identity.* (Khalida)

For all, as for Musrat in the example below, language appears as a key component in being Pakistani. Musrat also expresses her sense of frustration at superficial external judgments which deny the complexity of her personal struggle:

> *There are some people that I know that will become very westernized and they want to abandon everything even though their mother and father are very typical Mirpuris or from Pakistan. And they become very westernized and the family become angry so they quite often say, 'Can you speak in your own language', because they are cross that the person is trying to reject that part of their identity. . . . I've had people like that quite often who probably think, 'Oh, is she trying to reject her identity and trying to be English?' That's when I get cross . . . thinking I'm trying to reject my identity when, probably, I've got two aspects there to accept.*

Here, as Smolicz (1984: 26) notes, language is seen as vital to the maintenance of the core values of culture, community, and religion for this ethnic group as well as a crucial feature of their multifaceted selves. Similar to dress, cited earlier, it serves as a semiotic signal. Needed to sustain the culture, it is also cited as an important component in identifying oneself as Pakistani by linking to, and making individuals part of, that culture and, therefore, part of that community:

> *I associate it with the culture and just to keep that language as well. . . . They'd lose a sense of touch with their own community, and culture.* (Nasreen)

> *That's the worst thing because they will miss out because those children that have the language when they are adults they will be sitting within the culture.* (Aisha)

This sense of belonging, of identification, of the language enabling affiliation, and of it allowing one to join a group highlighted two other connections. On the one hand, language was presented as a powerful means of exclusion and inclusion. On the other, it was made clear that the loss of a language may lead to exclusion and alienation from groups one wishes to affiliate with or the group that wishes to sustain cross-generational relationships. The potential and actual inability of children to communicate with relatives and, in particular, grandparents, was cited by all respondents.

Musrat, for instance, described her first visit to Pakistan as a young bride and how comments from relatives on her lack of fluency motivated her to be fluent in Mirpuri and Urdu. In making this choice, which was not instrumentally essential for her to carry on her life in England, Musrat powerfully signalled that she wished to join this group, to become part of the family, and, therefore, implicitly endorsed her commitment to her marriage. She, therefore, developed that part of her identity, and in a practical way was able to do so through Punjabi. Rabia introduced a further aspect of this theme in speaking of her son, which similarly highlighted that moment of choice when an individual is suspended between two linguistic worlds and, consequently, alternative identities. In this example there is in addition a version of the common experience of being embarrassed by one's parents:

> *we were walking through the park and I was telling him something and he said, 'Be quiet' and I went, 'Why?' and he went, 'Look, you're speaking different and all these people are looking at me.' And I actually, I sat him down, and I said, 'You must never ever feel like that.' I said, 'You've got to be proud of who you are and what you speak. You can't say, "Be quiet because everyone else is listening."'*

The child here is given very specific guidance and, although not precise in detail, the instruction: *You've got to be proud of who you are and what you speak.* This statement links, for him, language and identity: you are what you speak and it is important for your self-esteem that you recognize that. For this child, the molding of his identity and self-worth explicitly involves his mother tongue, even though he might not be fluent in it.

As a signal and reinforcement of this identification, and as a further aspect of their identities as aspirant women who were committed to education, five of the mothers had gained advanced formal qualifications in Urdu in their own time after they had finished mandatory schooling. The lack of the written language was a cause of great regret to the three not literate in Urdu:

> *I did not learn any text in Urdu . . . and now I feel that I missed out.* (Aisha)

> *I feel that I've lost out because I can't read.* (Rubina)

These respondents felt excluded from aspects of their culture because of this deficiency:

> *it makes so much sense when they read it in Urdu because you get that other, the whole culture and everything flows into it. It's a different feel.* (Rubina)

Language maintenance

It was in their attitudes to language maintenance that the respondents brought together two related areas of identity, aspiration and gender. They consistently affirmed the value of maintaining languages other than English even when experiencing difficulties over practicalities of this maintenance. The issue was also one which brought feelings of regret, remorse, and guilt:

> *It's sad because I really do agree that children should learn Punjabi.* (Shabina)

> *I'm quite sad about it now* [the failure to maintain the mother tongue]. (Rabia)

In addition, in terms of the mothers' own identities, there were sometimes personal reasons for language maintenance:

> *I've had two reasons, for the children and for myself.* (Tasleem)

> *I've wanted them to learn the Qur'an, learn Urdu, so that, basically, they don't have the problems that I've had to put up with.* (Musrat)

There appears to be a link between the attitudes toward the mother tongue noted previously and the reasons given for ensuring that the children developed these skills. The assumption behind a number of the comments appeared to be that respect for the core values of family, community, religion, and moral behavior would be developed in children by adherence to the mother tongue. The language itself would foster particular attributes and attitudes in the children. It was in these respects that the concept of mother tongue was linked with the 'motherly' characteristics of nurturing and became the epitome of some of the aspirations of these mothers for their children. One of these was:

- religious beliefs and moral behavior:

> *I might be speaking to them in English one minute and then explaining things to them sometimes, important, like religion, religious things, I'll definitely go into my own language. Or if there's a concept, like telling lies, or then I try to find out examples in my own language, and explain it to them.* (Rabia)

> *How do you explain to them? That's where I find it's easier. . . . When you explain to them the meaning of the word 'friend' in Punjabi or Urdu it takes a different meaning altogether.* (Tasleem)

Clearly, some concepts do not translate accurately. In another example, quite appropriate for the topic of this study, Tasleem makes the case that the core notion of motherhood, with all its religious, cultural, and moral overtones, can only properly be conveyed in the 'mother tongue':

> *One of the things, one that we are taught in Islam or in Urdu, that heaven is under the foot of the mother, mother's feet . . . so, respect your mother and your life after will be, you know, rewarded and so on. Now if you say that to them in English. 'Son, heaven is at your mother's feet', they just look at you and say 'Mom are you alright?' sort of thing because it just doesn't make any sense to them. . . . I know you can say it in English but it doesn't seem to have the same meaning.*

We can note here, besides other issues of translation, how Tasleem rephrases her own interpretation, to point out the difference in English between 'under the foot' with its overtones of domination, and the second attempt 'at your mother's feet' with its associations of respect and guidance. Finally, the remaining aspects included:

- appreciation of their heritage or culture:

> *I want them to keep their identity and their culture, and I usually like to take them to where I was born.* (Aisha)

> *it is important for, I think, for my children to know that there is another language, that maybe their roots are in another language.* (Khalida)

- affiliation with the family or community. It was this area that was cited most often and the sense of potential loss is quite graphic:

> *They'd lose a sense of touch with their own community.* (Nasreen)

> *I am worried about my boys losing it. Then it's gone, hasn't it, really? It's gone the way of their community. I mean communicating with anybody from Pakistan.* (Rabia)

Gender and subject positions

The sense of loss was among many tensions exhibited during the interviews – tensions that arose from these women's subject positions as wives, mothers, daughters, and sisters. For instance, pursuing educational goals involved, for some, manipulation or negotiation. Musrat, particularly, cited the stages of increasing control over her own life:

> *Initially I used to say to my husband, 'Oh, I'm taking my daughter to the playgroup.' I never said anything about the studying to start off with . . .*

this was a male tutor. I said, 'My husband's not very keen on me having a male teacher, so, if you don't mind, I'll do the work on my own.'

Even when such regulation was not present it was still acknowledged:

It wasn't an issue with him saying 'You don't work.' (Tasleem)

In continuing with their education and trying to forge a career, these women, therefore, confronted and sometimes challenged the expectations and restrictions that could be placed upon them and highlighted the role of initiative and personal agency.

The tensions and conflicts evident in the attitudes to their languages also featured in the respondents' responsibility, or, rather, perceived responsibility, for supporting or promoting languages in the home. For some families, it appeared there had been no conscious decision or discussion between the parents over whether to promote the languages:

It's just happened. It's taken its own course. I've never even said to the children . . . 'You've got to do this'. . . . So it's just been part of life really. (Tasleem)

my husband has always left the children's role on me. (Nadia)

For others, the resolution was more overt:

since the kids have started to grow up he wants to maintain that bit of culture as well. Whereas he started off, when we got married, he started off saying, 'When we have kids, you must speak English with them.' (Rubina)

it was a joint thing. (Shabina)

Nevertheless, as the earlier comments suggest, while there might not be a formal discussion in the family, there was a tacit agreement to sustain the children's languages. However, even when this was so, all the mothers reported that they had taken a significant part in developing the children's languages in the home and, in several cases, had taken the initiative. This was, therefore, a further way in which the appellation 'mother tongue' applied, in that mothers perceived that they took the lead or ensured practical measures were in place. In other words, they were effecting change through their own agency. Musrat, cited above, noted *'all along it's been something . . . that I pushed'* and went on to say:

They pick up all the slang and the rough words and I get very annoyed and I say to my husband, 'Look, this is your fault.' . . . He thinks there's nothing wrong with it, they're speaking their own language.

Musrat, therefore, was not simply interested in communication, but in notions of correctness and appropriate speech. Tahera commented:

> *I think when they were born . . . I just said that I don't want them to learn Punjabi I want them to speak Urdu. . . . I don't think I actually discussed it.*

For Khalida and Rabia, too, this duty seemed to be acquired with little discussion:

> *I think he feels probably a bit more strongly than me because he doesn't have to do it . . . because I do tend to be the educator of the family.* (Khalida)

> *I don't think it bothers him. . . . But I don't think he's adamant. Not like me.* (Rabia)

As Musrat's, Khalida's, and Rabia's comments suggest, within the explicit or the tacit agreement there might be dissent over emphases or orientation in language maintenance between husband and wife. These, however, appeared minimal in comparison to remarks from other relatives which pointedly accentuated the exclusive responsibility of mothers in ensuring that 'mother tongue' was passed on. All respondents voiced the pressure they experienced in this respect, from their parents' or in-laws' expectations:

> *My mom kept telling me off.* (Nasreen)

> *I've been a couple of times reprimanded by my parents.* (Shabina)

There were also expressions of guilt related to their perceived maternal failure within their family or community:

> *people do think that I'm taking aboard the western views a bit more force-fully or strongly so they'll definitely say, 'Oh, her kids can't speak English* [(*sic*) Rabia actually means that her children can't speak Punjabi] *because she never spoke English with them.' It won't ever lie on my husband's shoulders.* (Rabia)

> *I've had that from my mom as well. She says, 'Oh, it's a mother's duty to do this, it's a mother's duty to do that.'* (Rubina)

Khalida emphasized how the joint responsibilities for the children in her marriage ended when it came to their languages:

> *Oh, no. It's my responsibility. Come on, we are talking about the Asian culture. My husband has as much influence on our children's upbringing as I do. He'll change nappies; he'll do anything but, within our culture it is*

the mother's job to do this, even though mummy goes out to work, just as
daddy does. It's just a way you would view it in my culture.

All the mothers were, therefore, alive to the contexts in which their
children might speak their different languages and included special
instructions to them as part of their socialization. There was the perception that not only was it polite and considerate to use different languages
appropriately, but, as noted previously, languages would affiliate the children to particular groups and nurture relationships between generations:

> *I realized that if I was in a situation where I was sitting there and every-*
> *body else was speaking a different language, well, I wouldn't like it at all.*
> *So I explained that to my children just recently. I said, 'When they [visiting*
> *grandparents] come over now you make sure you speak your own language,*
> *especially when you are around them or when they are sitting here. Because*
> *it's just polite.' (Nadia)*

Even more importantly, children needed to realize that the use of a
language conveyed nuances of the culture. Urdu particularly was cited
as the language that could best convey cultural values, particularly what
was termed 'respect,' which appeared to combine deference and esteem.
Linguistic good manners were not only regarded as evidence of respect
for others but were also seen as powerful indicators of satisfactory
upbringing and nurturing. As such, they were subject to judgment by
relatives and others in the community and reflected on the parents, particularly the mother:

> *I mean the other day, like in English you would say 'you' to everybody*
> *whereas in Urdu [and] Punjabi there's a word 'tu' and 'tusi' that's right.*
> *Yes, 'tu' means it's sort of like, if you say it to an adult that's very, very*
> *rude, or somebody you don't know. And my daughter said that to me and I*
> *shouted at her and she says, 'Mom, I didn't mean it.' And I said, 'No, but*
> *I've told you so many times, please don't say that, especially if you say it to*
> *your grandparents . . . it's going to fall back on me.' Especially the mother,*
> *because it's, 'Oh, you didn't train your children properly. They don't know*
> *how to respect the elders.' (Rubina)*

Through the use of a language, particularly Urdu with its high status
connotations, one not only confers respect in this society but can acquire
it oneself. Urdu, as noted previously, in contrast to Punjabi, also had
power as the language of literacy. Of her son, Tasleem said:

> *Now, as he's got older, because a lot of religious literature is written in Urdu,*
> *for him to understand his religion and himself he thinks that he needs and*

he's started to go to the same class as I am as well, to understand what is written and why it is written.

Thus, written language was also directly linked to identity. It was a means whereby this young man could make sense of, and come to terms with, himself.

Educational aspirations

Additional reasons for the participants' children to retain languages other than English concerned educational benefits and potential careers, although these did not figure to any great extent beyond a vague belief that having an additional language was a 'good thing.' The most signifi-cant feature in this regard was the ambivalent attitude of the respondents to the relationship between English and the mother tongue. English was a prerequisite for schooling and, as such, was endorsed as the language of the children's current and future educational success and career advancement:

When they're older in the big wide world, they're going to have to speak English and be able to compete with other people. They're going to have to be just as good as them. (Aisha)

At the same time, there was the desire for the mother tongue to remain alongside:

I do want them to have an education, speak English, but have that behind them as well. (Rubina)

I want my children to be able to communicate in their mother tongue with myself, with others, and also to be able to read and write to understand. But I also want them to learn English. (Aisha)

And yet, alongside the mothers' desire for the children to learn English, there were signals of an ambivalent attitude toward it and regret at its almost predatory nature, the way it had eroded the language in the home. Ironically, as part of their mothering duties the women had promoted English, recognizing it as the route to educational success. Their children's ability in English had become at odds with their desire to maintain the mother tongue. That this is not inconsistent in a strategy which combines apparently opposed discourses has been suggested by Foucault:

There is not, on the one side, a discourse of power, and opposite it another discourse that runs counter to it. Discourses are tactical elements or blocks operating in the field of force relations; there can run different and even contradictory discourses within the same strategy. (cited in Weedon, 1987: 122)

Both positions were, therefore, part of the respondents' discourse of mothering:

> *I don't think I realized it before. I thought, 'Yeah, they're going into school, it's gonna be English, and it's very important. I've got to teach them how to speak English.' And then what happened was they did go into school, came back, knew they could speak to mom in English, knew they could speak to dad in English, and our language started to. . . . It's there for when they need it, but it's like . . . it's bits.* (Rabia)

> *I used to worry they'd have too much Punjabi, and not learn English enough to cope when they get older, but now I feel that now they have picked up the English I wish, that they'd been exposed to some language, so they have a basic knowledge.* (Aisha)

> *I thought, hold on . . . if he's in the white man's system then if he speaks Urdu he's not going to go very far. If that's the only language he's got he's got to get English as well. . . . So I didn't force him into it. I just thought what was spoken was important . . . over the younger ones I've made more of a point from the beginning with the Qur'an alphabet . . . now I'm having that done in English.* (Tasleem)

Tasleem's comment, *if he's in the white man's system*, explicitly acknowledges the discourse of mainstream education that endorses English as the language of schooling, educational success, and job prospects. Here she adjusts her positioning as mother in nurturing Islamic teaching by translating the Qur'an into English for the younger children. Maintaining the discourse of mothering appears to involve many such compromises and adjustments.

There was, then, an intriguing irony in this situation related to the framing of the mothers' identities as aspirant, multilingual people. They have sought educational success for themselves and aspire to it for their children. They also acknowledged identities supported by their multiple languages and wished for the children to develop these identities as well. However, it was seen that educational success would be achieved through English. English, in turn, undermined the maintenance of the mother tongue in the home and, therefore, affected the link between language, identity, and culture that the mothers were keen to promote.

Conclusions

In this discussion I have attempted to show that issues binding together identity and language were very prominent in these data. In reflecting on the relationship between the two at different points, the respondents struggled to come to terms with how aspects of their own identities were partly shaped by their languages. The parts of the interviews that focused on the respondents' attitudes to their different languages indicated ways in which these languages contributed to these individuals' sense of their own identities and reflected their educational aspirations for themselves and their children. In acknowledging these multiple identities, the mothers conveyed certain key points:

- contending with multiple identities involved challenges in establishing a coherent sense of themselves; in several cases this multiplicity involved conflict, struggle, and unresolved tensions;
- there were similar tensions for the mothers seeking to forge a new identity as learners;
- particular core values of religion, dress, and, notably, language, contributed to the plurality and mutability of the women's identities in that choosing to learn a language signalled a particular identity and could affiliate one to a group; at different points in their lives, all the respondents had been faced with language choices and, therefore, choices of identity;
- the associations of the term 'mother tongue' were particularly potent for the mothers, since its maintenance involved fundamental signals of identity through ownership and a sense of belonging to a group, a culture, and a country. It was, therefore, crucial for them, as mothers, to pass on this language to their children. Identity, aspiration, and notions of gender came together in their perspectives on the vital importance of language maintenance.

The metaphor of 'mother tongue' consequently permeated the data as part of a wider discourse of mothering, combining, on the one hand, connotations of domesticity, nurture, ownership, and bonding, and, on the other hand, expression of the mothers' views on communication and networks. Thus, it very aptly expressed the mothers' complex feelings concerning their languages and their hopes for their children. Being a good mother did not just involve physical and emotional care (of which there was considerable evidence in the data), but the inculcation of values in a wide sense. The research brought together in its enquiry questions which attended to notions of mother tongue and also language maintenance in the home. Therefore, it was revealed that mothering involved nurturing the minority languages and ensuring that those languages were passed on as family traits, thus acknowledging respect for the elders and the pressures from relatives.

At the same time, mothering also meant assuring a good start in life for these children, particularly by the promise of a good education which involved fluency in English. This, in turn, had involved acknowledging the power of another discourse, that of mainstream education which transmits the message that a good command of English is essential for educational success. As good mothers, the respondents had incorporated this aspect into their discourse of mothering. While mothering meant fostering the mother tongue in relation to other core values of religion and ethnic markers, it also required promoting English to realize educational ambitions. It was ironic that, at the same time, the mothers were forced to acknowledge that English had had a corrosive effect on the core value of mother tongue which they were so keen to maintain. As the data showed, this led to considerable heart-searching and regret on the part of some respondents, who felt either that they had mistakenly promoted English too strongly or that they were failing as good parents in finding the time and resources to support the mother tongue.

A further and related discourse drawn upon by the respondents, and revealed by the focus on their multiple identities, was that of education and aspiration. Once again, within this discourse there were competing discourses to contend with. For example, all the mothers, in different ways, had been constrained in terms of their own schooling, due to a patriarchal discourse within their own extended family that gave primacy to marriage and the development of household management skills as opposed to formal education. However, the women themselves employed the discourse of educational success and aspiration in confronting this previous set of assumptions, carving out a niche for themselves as learners and working toward a new identity for themselves as well-qualified and ambitious professionals.

Finally, the interview process itself, as a form of communicative practice, impacted these identities in several ways. It allowed them to appear in a particular form, at a particular time and within a particular context. In the dialogue of the interview, and in dialogue with themselves, the respondents created, or added to, aspects of their autobiographies. They incorporated the process into their construction of themselves as learners by reflecting on the interviews per se, on their own learning about themselves and their children, and on the impetus that might be provided for further action.

Appendix

Questions guiding semi-structured interview

Background questions
- Age
- Place of birth
- Educational background
- Number of children
- Employment
- Languages
  - spoken/written
  - used in which circumstances/contexts
  - self-assessment of fluency
  - do you remember learning any of your languages?

Language background
- What term do you prefer to use when describing your other language/s? Why?
- What language do you regard as your mother tongue/first language? Why?
- What does the term 'mother tongue' mean to you?
- How do you feel about being bilingual? Is it an asset? In what ways?
- How important to you is it to keep the/se other languages?
- If the language went, what would be lost?

Home dimension
- Have you maintained your first language? Why/why not?
- Have you maintained your children's additional language? What steps have you taken?
- Why/why not?
- Whose responsibility is this, yours or your husband's?
- What is the attitude of your husband/parents/family members?
- What advice or instructions have you given to your children about their additional language?
- What advice or instructions did your parents give you about the use of your first language?
- Does your family talk about their additional languages?

References

Baker, C. (1995) *A parents' and teachers' guide to bilingualism.* Clevedon: Multilingual Matters.

Baker, C. and Prys Jones, S. (1998) *Encylopedia of bilingualism and bilingual education.* Clevedon: Multilingual Matters.

Bakhtin, M. (1973) *Problems of Dostoevsky's poetics.* Ann Arbor, MI: Ardis.

Bakhtin, M. (1981) *The dialogic imagination.* Austin, TX: University of Texas Press.

Bhavnani, K. and Phoenix, A. (1994) Shifting identities, shifting racisms: An introduction. *Feminism and Psychology* 4 (1), 5–18.

Burton, P. (1994) Women and second-language use: An introduction. In P. Burton, K. Dyson, and S. Ardener (eds) *Bilingual women: Anthropological approaches to second-language use* (pp. 1–29). Oxford/Providence, RI: Berg.

Burton, P., Dyson, K., and Ardener, S. (eds) (1994) *Bilingual women: Anthropological approaches to second-language use.* Oxford/Providence, RI: Berg.

Chinchaladze, N. and Dragadze, T. (1994) Women and second-language knowledge in rural Soviet Georgia: An outline. In P. Burton, K. Dyson, and S. Ardener (eds) *Bilingual women: Anthropological approaches to second-language use* (pp. 80–84). Oxford/Providence, RI: Berg.

Constantinidou, E. (1994) The 'death' of East Sutherland Gaelic: Death by women? In P. Burton, K. Dyson, and S. Ardener (eds) *Bilingual women: Anthropological approaches to second-language use* (pp. 111–127). Oxford/Providence, RI: Berg.

Davies, L. (1985) Ethnography and status: Focusing on gender in educational research. In R. Burgess (ed.) *Field methods in the study of educational research* (pp. 79–96). London: Falmer.

Dyson, K. (1994) Forging a bilingual identity: A writer's testimony. In P. Burton, K. Dyson, and S. Ardener (eds) *Bilingual women: Anthropological approaches to second-language use* (pp. 170–185). Oxford/Providence, RI: Berg.

Fairclough, N. (1992) *Discourse and social change.* Cambridge: Polity Press.

Fishman, J. (1998) Language and ethnicity: The view from within. In F. Coulmas (ed.) *The handbook of sociolinguistics* (pp. 327–343). Oxford: Blackwell.

Gal, S. (1979) *Language shift: Social determinants of linguistic change in bilingual Austria.* New York: Academic Press.

Hall, S. (1991) Ethnicity: identity and difference. *Radical America* 23 (4), 9–20.

Harvey, P. (1994) The presence and absence of speech in the communication of gender. In P. Burton, K. Dyson, and S. Ardener (eds) *Bilingual women: Anthropological approaches to second-language use* (pp. 44–64). Oxford/Providence, RI: Berg.

Hong, L. (1994) A note on my experience as a student, a teacher and an interpreter of English in China. In P. Burton, K. Dyson, and S. Ardener (eds) *Bilingual women: Anthropological approaches to second-language use* (pp. 167–169). Oxford/Providence, RI: Berg.

Humphrey, C. (1994) Casual chat and ethnic identity: Women's second language use among Buryats in the USSR. In P. Burton, K. Dyson, and S. Ardener (eds) *Bilingual women: Anthropological approaches to second-language use* (pp. 65–79). Oxford/Providence, RI: Berg.

Jayaratne, T. and Stewart, A. (1995) Quantitative and qualitative methodology in the social sciences: Feminist issues and practical strategies. In J. Holland,

M. Blair, and S. Sheldon (eds) *Debates and issues in feminist research and pedagogy* (pp. 217–234). Clevedon: Multilingual Matters/Open University Press.

Josselson, R. (1995) Imagining the real: Empathy, narrative, and the dialogic self. In R. Josselson and A. Lieblich (eds) *Interpreting experience: The narrative study of lives* (Vol. 3) (pp. 27–44). London: Sage.

Kelly, L., Regan, L., and Burton, S. (1995) Quantitative methods in feminist research. In J. Holland, M. Blair, and S. Sheldon (eds) *Debates and issues in feminist research and pedagogy* (pp. 235–247). Clevedon, UK: Multilingual Matters/Open University Press.

Koven, M. (1998) Two languages in the self/the self in two languages: French–Portuguese bilinguals' verbal enactments and experiences of self in narrative discourse. *Ethos* 26 (4), 410–455.

Lakoff, G. and Johnson, M. (1980) *Metaphors we live by*. Chicago: University of Chicago Press.

Mackey, W. (1992) Mother tongues, other tongues and link languages: what they mean in a changing world. *Prospects* 22 (1), 41–52.

McDonald, M. (1994) Women and linguistic innovation in Brittany. In P. Burton, K. Dyson, and S. Ardener (eds) *Bilingual women: Anthropological approaches to second-language use* (pp. 85–110). Oxford/Providence, RI: Berg.

Mills, J. (1991) Bilingual children with monolingual teachers: Some implications for assessment. In *Language observed: Approaches to classroom assessment* (pp. 1–7). Oxford: National Primary Centre.

Mills, J. (1993) Language activities in a multilingual school. In R. Mills and J. Mills (eds) *Bilingualism in the primary school: A handbook for teachers* (pp. 9–37). London: Routledge.

Mills, J. (1995) A classroom assistant. In R. Mills and J. Mills (eds) *Primary school people* (pp. 113–128). London: Routledge.

Mills, J. (1996) Nursery partners. In J. Mills (ed.) *Partnership in the primary school* (pp. 13–32). London: Routledge.

Mills, J. (2000) *Mothers and mother tongue: A case study of the bilingual perspectives of educated women of Pakistani heritage in the West Midlands and of their children.* Unpublished Ph.D. dissertation, University of Birmingham.

Mills, J. (2001a) Self-construction through conversation and narrative in interviews. *Educational Review* 53 (3), 285–301.

Mills, J. (2001b) Mothers and mother tongue. *Primary Practice* 28, 4–7.

Mills, J. (2001c) Being bilingual: Perspectives of third generation Asian children on language, culture and identity. *International Journal of Bilingual Education and Bilingualism* 4 (6), 383–402.

Moraes, M. (1996) *Bilingual education: A dialogue with the Bakhtin Circle.* Albany, NY: SUNY Press.

Rassool, N. (1997) Fractured or flexible identities? Life histories of 'black' diasporic women in Britain. In H. Safia Mirza (ed.) *Black British feminism: A reader* (pp. 186–204). London: Routledge.

Romaine, S. (1995) *Bilingualism*. Oxford: Blackwell.

Sherzer, J. (1987) A diversity of voices: men's and women's speech in ethnographic perspective. In S. Philips, S. Steele, and C. Tanz (eds) *Language, gender and sex in comparative perspective* (pp. 95–120). Cambridge: Cambridge University Press.

Skutnabb-Kangas, T. (1981) *Bilingualism or not: The education of minorities.* Clevedon: Multilingual Matters.

Skutnabb-Kangas, T. and Phillipson, R. (1989) 'Mother tongue': The theoretical and sociopolitical construction of a concept. In U. Ammon (ed.) *Status and function of languages and language varieties* (pp. 450–477). Berlin: Walter de Gruyter.

Smolicz, J. (1984) Minority languages and the core values of culture: Changing policies and the ethnic response in Australia. *Journal of Multilingual and Multicultural Development* 5 (1), 23–41.

Tabouret-Keller, A. (1998) Language and identity. In F. Coulmas (ed.) *The handbook of sociolinguistics* (pp. 315–326). Oxford: Blackwell.

Weedon, C. (1987) *Feminist practice and poststructuralist theory.* Oxford: Blackwell.

Chapter 6

The Politics of Identity, Representation, and the Discourses of Self-identification: Negotiating the Periphery and the Center

FRANCES GIAMPAPA

Introduction

The politics of identity,[1] citizenship, and nationhood have garnered much attention in recent years, as discussions have erupted on both the academic and public fronts with regard to the impact of globalization (Chouliaraki & Fairclough, 1999; Giddens, 1991; Quell, 2000). These discussions have moved beyond the essentialist view of identities as fixed and shifted toward an understanding of identities as multiple and intersecting, *inter alia*, with ethnicity, race, gender, and sexuality. To understand the negotiation of these shifting identities, one may ask the following questions: (1) What are the current discourses of identity and representation?; (2) Which identities are negotiable and what 'spaces' are they negotiable in?; and (3) How are identities negotiated in these 'spaces'?

My chapter enters this discussion using the notions of the 'periphery' and 'center' (Giddens, 1984; Grimard, 2000; Grimard & Labrie, 1999; Labrie, 1999) in order to examine how three Italian Canadian youths – Tania, Diana, and Marco[2] – negotiate their identities. A number of themes emerged from the participants' identity narratives, which highlighted their desires to position themselves and be positioned across and within their Canadian and Italian Canadian worlds. To explore these themes, my discussion will focus on the following markers of identity: ethnicity, language, race, gender, sexual orientation, religion, and, in part, citizenship. These become the discursive channels through which one can observe how speakers manage, adapt, and challenge identities through a process of negotiation across spaces and time. The chapter highlights that, as cognizant social agents, these participants challenge the representations and positions of the 'center' in the Canadian and Italian Canadian worlds with respect to what it means 'to be and to become' Italian Canadian in Toronto.

Theoretical Framework

Keith and Pile (1993: 2) suggest that 'space,' whether 'real, imagined, or symbolic,' is neither neutral nor passive, but an active part of the discourse of identity politics. In positioning the self, one is imagining the self in a particular space. Identities and representations are multiple and shifting (Hall, 1990, 1991; Hall & Jacques, 1990) and so are the spaces in which identities are negotiated. Furthermore, these spaces are not created equal or read in one way. They are not only geographical, but also imagined, drawing on transnational connections that function in a unifying way through difference. In this regard, the Italian Canadian diasporic experience is inscribed through the spaces of identities, which are negotiated not only locally, that is, within the spaces of the Italian Canadian and Canadian worlds, but also transnationally, in an Italian world.

Regardless of the particular spatial metaphor one chooses to adopt (e.g. position, location, inside-out, global–local, third space (see Keith & Pile, 1993: 1)), in the discussion of place, politics, and identity, spatial metaphors not only express relations of power and domination, but capture the potential for agency, that is, the possibility of moving from the 'margins' (exclusion) to the 'center' (inclusion) or the reconfiguration and/or establishment of other centers. The act of claiming identities and claiming the spaces of identity is a political act. Using Giddens' (1984) terminology of the 'center' and the 'periphery,' we can say that this act means not only movement from the periphery, but also a reconfiguration of the center. The center is typically seen as a group of people who define and reproduce social, political, institutional, and linguistic norms and have access to symbolic capital and material resources (Labrie, 1999). Grimard (2000: 6) points out that one or more of these defining criteria can describe the inhabitant of the Canadian center:

> White, middle class–upper class, healthy, masculine, heterosexual, married with children, between the ages of 30–65, Canadian born, anglophone, living in an urban milieu, producer of knowledge/ power (e.g. culture, science, political, information, etc.), possessing

neo-liberal values and Christian. Consequently, individuals who do not possess one or more criteria of the center are relegated to the periphery. (My translation)

In addition to these criteria which define the majority community (here, the Canadian world), I would like to highlight that, within the minority community (i.e. the Italian Canadian world), there also exists some 'norm' setting dictating who is in and who is out. The Italian Canadian community is not representationally homogeneous and parallels can be drawn with respect to the hegemonic practices within the spaces of the Canadian world. In addition to the criteria of exclusion noted above, I would include the following:

(1) Age and Generational Status – first/second generation Italian Canadians with wealth and power, as well as native Italians in positions of political power, 'authority,' and with a mandate to promote specific forms of symbolic capital and material resources are heard and given the space to be heard much more than, for instance, Italian Canadian youth.

(2) Linguistic Knowledge/Repertoire – speaking the 'right' kind of Italian, which my research participants refer to as 'standard' Italian, 'real,' 'proper' Italian (Giampapa, 2001), functions in an exclusionary way. Earlier discourses of Italian language learning in Canada typically negated Italian Canadian youth's linguistic knowledge as 'the dialect.' Recently, there has been some change in the dominant discourses of the 'home language' (Cummins, 1983; Cummins & Danesi, 1990) and yet negative perceptions of the 'home language' are still transmitted from generation to generation.

(3) Religion – being Italian Canadian and Catholic is the norm, regardless of whether one is practicing Catholicism or not. This is a representation held not only from within the Italian Canadian community, but also maintained by the Canadian world.

(4) Gender and Sexual Orientation – the dominant discourses of masculinity and heterosexuality, and traditional/patriarchal definitions of gender roles persist and are reproduced within the Italian Canadian world, privileging the voices of heterosexual men over women and sexual minorities.

I will begin to explore the negotiation of Italian Canadian identities through an examination of the spaces of *italianità* (Italianness) and its normative representations within the Italian Canadian and Canadian worlds, which function to maintain the domination and control of the center. Consequently, I will show that it is precisely through the narratives of self-identification that participants articulate a complex discourse of resistance, thus challenging the 'center' with respect to what it means to be Italian Canadian in Toronto.

Methodology

My research is located within a critical ethnographic approach, which acknowledges the political nature of the research process and views the researcher and research participants as affiliates in the co-construction of meaning. Gitlin and Russell (1994: 185) suggest that research conducted in this way:

> allows both participants (i.e., researcher and researched) to become the changer and changed. Central to a dialogical approach is that it can further the aim of developing voice among those who have been silenced historically. The opportunity to speak, to question and to explore issues is an important aspect of this process.

It is through this dialogic process that I explore the negotiation of identities across and within what I call multiple worlds and discourse sites. My participants recognize these as the Anglo-dominant Canadian world and the Italian Canadian world. Embedded within these worlds are the multi-layered and overlapping spaces of interactions in which identities are negotiated. These spaces include the home, the university setting, the peer group social setting, and the workplace. While Giampapa (2001) painted a larger picture of the negotiation that takes place in all of these spaces as well as in the Italian world, the present chapter will explore in-depth negotiation of identities in the workplace and in the peer groups.

The data discussed in this chapter are drawn from a larger corpus collected for my doctoral research from 1998 to 2000 with eight Italian Canadian youths, using multiple methodological tools, such as participant observation, interviews (individual, focus group, and community-based), shadowing, self-taping, questionnaires, and written reflections (see Giampapa, 2001 for a detailed discussion). In this chapter, I draw primarily from the data that emerged from the interviews (see Appendix on p. 217 for transcription conventions), questionnaires, and written reflections. Using identity narratives (or what I call the process of self-identification) as my starting point, I will focus on identity negotiation by three participants – Tania, Diana, and Marco – and explore how they deal with the tensions of living along the periphery within both the Canadian and Italian Canadian worlds. In the following section, I outline my rationale for selecting these three participants and show how their identity narratives reflect their multiple positions and multiple voices (Bakhtin, 1981) from the margins.

The participants

The participants that I focus on in this chapter – Tania, Diana, and Marco – are particularly interesting for a number of reasons. First, in terms of self-identification they all locate themselves within the discourses of Italian Canadianness, thus recognizing the multifaceted and often contradictory nature of being Italian and Canadian at the same time. There is an acknowledgment and acceptance that both 'Canadianness' and 'Italianness' are coterminous factors in their self-identification processes. Second, for different reasons, they are all located along the periphery of their worlds. Tania struggles with the conflictual discourses on language and ethnic identity within the public and private spaces of her life. For Diana, it is religion that is an overriding factor in setting her along the margins, particularly within the Italian Canadian world. For Marco, sexuality and ethnicity conflict and collide, and he struggles to negotiate these identities across worlds in various ways. Third, they are all Canadian born, non-students, in their middle to late twenties, work full-time, and have had diverse linguistic,[3] cultural, and educational experiences and reside in diverse Italian Canadian neighborhoods of Toronto. Thus, they have diverse experiences of *italianità* reflected within the locations in which they live and the network ties that they have forged. Below is an overview of the participants' profiles, which further elucidate the diverse identities and spaces of Italian Canadianness:

- **Tania** (age 27) is single and lives with her family in what is called the 'new' Little Italy (Rapanà, 2001) – Woodbridge – in the township of Vaughan, located north of Toronto. This is an area of middle-class to upper-class homes and incomes. Her father and mother are first generation and 1.5 generation (Lo, 1999) Italian Canadians. They emigrated from Calabria, a southern region of Italy. Tania works full-time in a large financial institution. She has been promoted from a position of a communication facilitator to that of a community relations representative. Her self-identified languages are Standard Italian, English, and a minimal knowledge of her family dialect, Calabrese. She also has a minimal knowledge of French and Spanish.
- **Diana** (age 24) is married and she and her husband reside with her family. They live in a north-western suburb of Toronto. It is an

established area with a large number of Italians. This area borders on one of the older Italian Canadian enclaves, which has become more ethnically and racially mixed with the arrival of new immigrants. This is an area of predominantly working-class and middle-class homes. Her parents are first generation Italian Canadians and emigrated from the Lazio region of central Italy in the 1950s. Diana has held a number of positions within the labor movement. She currently works full-time for a large Canadian union. Her work focuses mainly on educational development and youth issues. She also works as a volunteer for a number of Italian Canadian organizations. She identifies herself as an Evangelical (Christian), and not a Catholic. Her self-identified languages are Standard Italian, English, Portuguese, and no Italian dialect. She also has a minimal knowledge of French.

- **Marco** (age 26) lives with his partner in the west-end of downtown Toronto. This is an area of trendy restaurants, antique stores, and coffee shops with a bohemian and artistic edge. I would call this part the 'Soho of Toronto,' and it attracts students and young urbanites. His family still lives in a north-western suburb of Toronto where a number of Italians reside. This is a predominantly working-class and middle-class area. His parents are first generation Italian Canadians and emigrated from the Abruzzi region of Italy in the late 1950s – early 1960s. He works full-time in the entertainment industry. He is gay and began 'coming out' to his family and close friends in 1996. His self-identified languages are Standard Italian, Abruzzese dialect, and Italiese (Italian/English contact variety, a marker of first generation Italian immigrant speech). He also has a minimal knowledge of French.

To understand ways in which these participants negotiate their identities, it is critical to examine the representations and spaces of *italianità* that have factored into their self-positioning and the way they position others.

The Spaces and Representations of *Italianità* in Toronto

In this section, I will first provide an overview of the shifts within the representations and stereotypes of *italianità* and, second, highlight some of the stereotypes and representations current within the Italian Canadian community, particularly among Italian Canadian youth. These representations and outward expressions of ethnicity (e.g. language, clothing, physical appearance), seen by Bourdieu (1991) as 'the embodiment of identity,' mark identity positions and spaces which function as points of reference that Italian Canadian youth use to locate themselves within their multiple worlds.

Across their multiple worlds, Italian Canadian youth struggle with the varied representations of *italianità*, which are shifting, contradictory, and influenced by specific historical and political moments in time. These representations not only emerge from within the Anglo-dominant Canadian world, but also evolve within the Italian Canadian world. DeMaria Harney (1998) documents how representations of Italian Canadians have been re-articulated within Canadian society since the 1980s. The construction and expression of *italianità* across generations has shifted, not only within the Italian Canadian world, but also within the Canadian world. According to DeMaria Harney (1998), after 1982 the old identities of the *cafoni* (rural louts) and mafiosi were challenged through the claiming of new identities and spaces. He attributes this shift to: (1) the economic emergence of Italy as a dynamic player within the European market, which opened up exportation markets of Italian goods, including food products, textiles, furniture, machinery, and cars; (2) Italy's World Cup soccer victory in 1982, a unifying and 'epiphanic' event, which signified a change in the 'meanings associated with Italy and Italians in Toronto's public culture' (DeMaria Harney, 1998: 158); and (3) the economic, educational, and social upward mobility of first and second generation Italian Canadians during the 1980s.

While the Italian Canadian community in Toronto has gained respect and status within the Canadian landscape as one of its prominent minority communities, stereotyped images of the 'Italian Mamma' or the 'Italian mobster' still exist and are perpetuated through advertisements and film. These representations and identities are not unproblematic and uncontested among Italian Canadians, particularly when they are used within the community itself. For example, the mafia image was used for poster advertisements by an Italian restaurant, Mercatto, located in downtown Toronto. Appearing in the window of the restaurant were two posters: one of a 'bloodied man, his ankles and wrists tied together, his mouth shut with duck tape, stuffed in the trunk of a car, with the caption reading "Authentic Italian Take-Out"' and the second of 'a dead guy in a nice black and white suit lying on the floor next to a spilled cup of coffee with the line "Strong Italian Coffee"' below (Baldassare, 2000: 2). These advertisements garnered attention and criticism, triggering a heated response from the editor and staff of *Tandem*, the lifestyle weekend paper in Toronto. The paper proclaimed these representations to be 'offensive' and 'perpetuating a dangerous stereotype' and called upon Italian Canadians to stop this slandering of the Italian Canadian heritage. The debate demonstrated that the mafia stereotype and its association with being Italian continues to be appropriated and parodied by some young Italian Canadians, while others are outraged and do not see it as a joke.

Another set of stereotypes surviving among Italian Canadian youth concerns those of the 'mangiacake'/'caker' and the 'Gino'/'Gina.' The stereotyped representations of the *mangiachecca* was originally used by first generation Italian Canadians in reference to the white, Anglo-Saxon, English-speaking majority (Danesi, 1986). This was part of a counter-discourse to the marginalizing representations of Italian Canadians as 'dirty WOPs' (without papers) and 'displaced persons' (DPs) (Iacovetta, 1993: 117). Within the current discourses on identity, there are second and third generation Italian Canadians who continue to use 'mangiacake'/'caker' to refer to the Anglo-Canadian center. The term 'cakerized' is also used to refer to Italian Canadians who have undergone a process of ethnic 'dilution' (Giampapa, 2001). It is an identity position that in the past was imposed through the assimilating forces of the center, but has in turn become a contested position and a way for some Italian Canadians to mark their *italianità* through its denial. In turn, the stereotype of 'Gino'/'Gina' refers to a young Italian Canadian who is typically wealthy, spoiled, and lives in Woodbridge.[4] This complex set of images reflects certain values (closed and traditional mindset, patriarchal gender attitudes, no interest in education, expression of *italianità* through commodities) and behaviors (aggressive, loud, flashy) and functions within the Italian Canadian world as a means of social differentiation. In most cases, my participants are very clear on identifying themselves as the antithesis of the 'Gino'/'Gina' representation, which for them does not reflect being an Italian Canadian. The perpetuation of the 'Gino'/'Gina' stereotype has also drawn media attention and sparked heated debates within the Italian Canadian community at large. One example of this is the public reaction to *Eyetalian*'s[5] 'exposé, 'The Armani generation' (Chianello, 1995). This article critiqued Italian Canadian youth and their families in Woodbridge, pointing to their conspicuous consumption, their focus on materialism, and their lack of values for education, to name a few. The article generated an outrage from the Italian Canadian community, particularly the inhabitants of Woodbridge and the high school community, which were the foci of the article. This debate is indelibly imprinted on the collective memory of most Italian Canadians in Toronto (see DeMaria Harney (1998) for a discussion of this debate).

Even in more recent times the focus on Woodbridge has not shaken. This can be observed in a recent *Tandem* article (Rapanà, 2001), which points to the community's 'exclusivity.' This article opens with a melodramatic description of the 'Woodbridge kids':

> They are looked upon with suspicion: they're well dressed, drive fast cars and sport haircuts according to the latest fashion. . . . They're the 'Woodbridge kids,' the grandchildren of Little Italy. Occasionally they feel under scrutiny for their pampered lifestyle, their self assuredness bordering on the ostentatious, but they only care for the moment, then they shrug and go on singing in praise of their kingdom. They stay with their parents until they marry, but even then they don't go far. They buy a house in the area, raise a family and so forth.

These and other representations of Italian Canadians, both within and outside the community, continue to be a source of debates in the media as the varying politicized views of what it means to be Italian Canadian collide among the Italian Canadian intellectual and political elite. In light of the discussion above, I will explore the process of self-identification and the discourses and representations that dictate how Tania, Diana, and Marco negotiate their identities from the margins of the Canadian and Italian Canadian worlds.

The Negotiation of Identities: Speaking From the Margins

Claiming identities: Ethnicity, language, and citizenship[6]

For Tania, Diana, and Marco, being Italian Canadian represents a location in which the identification of an ethnic experience, both past and present, and a revisioning of that experience is tied not only to the multicultural urban landscape of Toronto, but also to the spaces of an imagined and real native Italian world. Ethnicity and language are the entry points in understanding the participants' identity narratives. These are the claims to identities, positions, and spaces within their worlds. Articulating what it means 'to be and become Italian Canadian' reflects the range of identity positions and the negotiability of identities.

In order to understand the connection to language as an avenue for identity performance, one must first understand the participants' views of language and language practices, including code-switching/code-mixing. Language plays a salient and defining role in the way these participants desire to be positioned and position themselves. For Tania, self-identifying as 'Canadian' is not simply the claiming of a position within the center, but a way of shifting the dominant discourse of identity, which exoticizes ethnic difference and pushes it to the periphery. In this way, being Canadian is about difference – it legitimizes Tania's ethnicity as Italian and her right to claim identities beyond her ethnicity. This view is evident in Tania's reflections on Italian citizenship/passport and the references she makes to English and Italian:

> Identity is formed with the influence of many factors, internal and external. Mine has been influenced by my family's background, but also by the 'mindset' of Canadian, although it is difficult to define that mindset. The co-existence of many cultures and the politics of Canada have had as much – actually, more – influence on my life/identity than my Italian heritage. I don't know how to explain this accurately but I think in English, I am insufferably aware of the way that the English language manifests itself. While I also react that way to other languages, English is what I write in – and writing, for me, is where I express myself most succinctly and completely. I am also preoccupied with the relationship between English and the other languages – Italian most notably, I think, because it was passed down from my parents. I guess I don't feel akin to the concerns of Italian citizens – I think it's because I don't feel that way about any other place but Canada . . . I feel more North American – newer, less settled, still defining. I believe that has to do with being Canadian ultimately. (Questionnaire)

As seen in the excerpt, Tania is claiming a Canadian identity not only through ethnicity and birthplace but also through her dominant language, English. In order to capture what she sees as 'still defining' aspects of this identity, she also links it to her Italian heritage and situates it within a much broader frame of reference as 'North American.' Language is also a vehicle through which Tania positions herself in the Italian Canadian world. She speaks what she defines as Standard Italian, the language that was imposed on her at home under the assumption that it would allow her to 'speak to all Italians' (Preliminary interview). This language, however, functions precisely as a tool of exclusion from the most salient relationships in her life – her extended family. She writes:

> At my aunt's funeral, another aunt was speaking to me and I tried to respond in dialect. But I could barely put a sentence together and I didn't feel like myself while speaking it, I thought 'What are these strange sounds coming out of my mouth?' I tried, I guess to connect

with my aunt but I ended up reverting to standard because it was more comfortable. Actually, I ended up speaking more English than anything. (Follow-up interview, written)

Code-switching, which Tania defines as 'completely changing/alternating between English and Italian or using a borrowed phrase' (Questionnaire), becomes, however, impossible. In this instance, her inability to code-switch from Standard Italian to dialect is not simply a result of her lack of linguistic fluency. More importantly, speaking the dialect articulates a position which is foreign to her. As a result, she can neither manage her position as a standard speaker nor shift into dialect. Instead, English offers her a relatively neutral and acceptable position – one that coincides with the positioning of second and third generation Italian Canadian youth as English dominant speakers.

At home, imposing the acquisition of Standard Italian was a means of social differentiation from other Italian Canadians. Tania describes how her parents' own feelings of marginalization were the impetus for them to push her and her sister toward acquiring the cultural capital necessary to belong or attempt to belong to the dominant Anglo-Canadian world:

I feel sometimes like an immigrant but not . . . I have these feelings of inadequacy because I come from an immigrant culture. I come from a culture – I know a lot of people who are awesome people who have done amazing things over the last 35 years but I still feel like people look at me differently, you know, 'She comes from that culture', you know, 'They have tempers and they're not too bright' . . . I think if I can be honest I think it comes from my family. I think it comes from the fact that my parents in order to compensate for these feelings that they had and they still do have, pushed me outside of those stereotypical aspects of the [Italian] culture or just pushed me outside the culture. My dance lessons, my piano lessons, these were all with Anglo-Saxon people and very educated, often well-to-do people and they wanted me to be involved with them almost as much as they appreciated their culture and they love their culture. There was something about being Italian that they knew would make my life, they assumed, would make my life difficult like it made their lives difficult. So they almost wanted me to assimilate to a certain degree and I just feel that I'm not like them. (Follow-up interview)

This discourse counterpoints the stereotyped representations of Italian immigrants from the Anglo-dominant world and the representations of this world in Italian Canadian eyes. In order to become 'Canadian' and gain middle-class status, one must acquire the capital that would allow one to move beyond the periphery. This is not only about 'assimilating' into the Canadian world, but also about defining oneself outside of the stereotype of the 'Woodbridge Italian Canadian' – the 'stereotypical rich Italian kids' with no academic focus (Preliminary interview).

While Tania's positions herself as Canadian, Diana claims a hyphenated identity, which is both Italian and Canadian. The hyphen takes on a symbolic role where 'losing the hyphen' (Preliminary interview) represents for Diana not only a loss of the outward expressions and avenues of Italian Canadian culture (language, radio, television), but also a loss of an important aspect of her identity. She maintains a connection to the Italian Canadian world through her ethnicity and language; at the same time, her religious identity as a non-Catholic keeps her on the margins of this world. She states:

> I think that played a big role in sort of what I did within my community because a lot of my friends weren't Italian, 'cause I went to public schools. So they were everything other than Italian and I went to church which was a large component of my life as well, um, they weren't Italian as well, you know, so . . . but still the identity was STRONG. We had everything else that you can classically consider as culture at home – the language, the food, the, you know, the music. (Specialized interview on religion)

Maintaining her claim to being Italian Canadian means above all else maintaining the language:

> Language is important. I mean if we had, if I had NOTHING else, right, but I spoke the Italian language . . . I would probably still consider myself Italian but if you took the language away then it would not lead me to other things. (Focus group interview with non-students)

Diana sees herself as a speaker of Standard Italian, with no dialect at home. The language remains the constant link in her intimate relationships with family and friends. She claims:

> When I'm around my family and friends . . . I speak Standard Italian. (Questionnaire)

For her, code-switching is the linguistic 'shorthand' within the spaces of the home:

Language switching is when an individual is not comfortable or lacks the vocabulary in the language he/she is speaking then he/she will switch. At home we do it all the time, [we] want to quickly tell the family something but the Italian word escapes us and we use the English or Portuguese word. (Questionnaire)

In the home of Diana's parents, the ideology of language with regard to the learning of Italian went beyond ethnic identity ties. As she was growing up, language was 'sold' to her as a symbolic resource which would open up future employment markets. Diana recalls her grand-mother's mantra:

'It's good to speak Italian because, you know, you're going to get a good job with two languages.' She always sold that to us. (Preliminary interview)

Within this discourse, her linguistic abilities would function as a marketable asset that would allow Diana to negotiate her identity as Italian Canadian and move within the Italian Canadian world even when she is excluded by it. Language maintenance also became the impetus for obtaining an Italian passport, which for Diana is a further claim to a hyphenated identity. The following quote well expresses her desire to be located within the Italian Canadian world and yet to re-imagine the meaning of *italianità*:

I'm really proud that I have the Italian passport and the Canadian citizenship. Yeah, it is part of my identity now . . . I mean, identity is all about what one thinks in their mind . . . and identity can mean different things to different people. (Follow up interview)

In the end, Diana must continually contest the imposed religious iden-tity that is projected on to her by the Italian Canadian world. She challenges this imposition through her involvements with Italian Canadian organizations, where she has taken up a key role, and through her work with the labor movement. And yet, in the Canadian world, she is peripheral as an ethnic and linguistic minority, while in the Italian Canadian world she is marginalized because of her non-Catholic identity.

Marco experiences a similar double marginalization, which stems from his sexual orientation. Marco self-identifies as Italian Canadian and not a 'real' Italian or 'Italian, Italian,' a common reference used to indicate a 'native' Italian – someone 'fresh off the boat,' either literally or figura-tively in terms of behavior (Baldassar, personal communication, 2001). Marco also differentiates himself from what he sees as 'Canadian,' which he uses to refer to the non-Italians of British descent – the 'mangiacakes who come from white families' (Focus group interview with non-students). His definition of the Other calls into play markers of ethnicity and race. However, Marco's reference to race is more a reference to the status and privilege afforded to being Canadian and to the fact that those at the center 'know how to play the game better' (Focus group interview with non-students). It is worth noting, however, that, while today Italian Canadians are not positioned as a visible minority, in the past Italian immigrants, particularly southern Italians, were 'ascribed the status of a visible minority' (Iacovetta, 1993: 106; see also Pavlenko's chapter in this volume).

Marco's self-identification process is strongly connected to his sexuality: as a result of his 'coming out,' he has reached a level of self-awareness and acceptance not only of being gay, but also of being Italian. He states:

> I mean the whole coming [out] thing, you know, all of a sudden you go, 'Okay, this is what I'm about. This is who I am and I don't care who knows' and not only that, that's a good thing and then you start looking at everything not just being gay but, like, you know, like being Italian, being close to my parents, you know. (Preliminary interview)

For Marco, being Italian Canadian means accepting the multiplicity of his identities as Italian, gay, an actor, and Canadian born, and being able to articulate his identities at the same time across his worlds. What becomes painfully clear is that Marco struggles to find a space where he can be gay and Italian Canadian at the same time. His negotiation of these identities is constrained by the dominant discourse on *italianità*, which privileges heterosexuality. The imposed position of the insider/outsider that Marco experiences within the Italian Canadian world is clearly exemplified by the following example:

> When I think about what Italian is to me and my friends who are Italian, I mean it's, like, the fun of the CHIN[7] picnic, it's that, um, just hanging out and speaking a bit of the language . . . you feel like you're walking around in your own backyard. You hear all these familiar voices, you hear everything you heard when you were a kid . . . I kind of miss going, you know, but at the same time it's weird, like, now I go with my boyfriend, what? No. I should get over that, you know. (Preliminary interview)

Within this space, language plays an important part in the negotiation of ethnicity, while sexuality remains non-negotiable. For Marco, language is also critical in the process of self-identification. Even though Marco refers to his parents' Italian as 'not real Italian' (Questionnaire), thus echoing the dominant linguistic discourse which terms Standard Italian as the only 'real' or 'proper' variety, he still claims his family dialect, Abruzzese, as 'valuable' because:

> it is in essence what my history of being Italian is about. (Questionnaire)

In fact, within the focus group interview where Tania, Diana, and Marco reflected upon language use, Italian varieties, and language learning, it is Marco who was most insistent on the importance of the dialect within the family network. This sets him apart from Diana and Tania who are only able to use Standard Italian:

T: I wonder if it has something to do with people who've grown with their grandparents in their homes or have spent a lot of time with them.

D: Depends where you are too from Italy 'cause we don't speak a dialect.

T: We don't – no, my parents speak a dialect to each other and they speak it to my Mom's mother but we never spoke dialect. I – we only – my mother taught me standard and she said she did because she wanted me to be able to speak to a number of Italians, you know, in case if I ever had too. It would be easier and that's why but they do speak a dialect to each other some-times.

M: For me dialect is very important because in terms of the dialect I talk to the most important people in my life when I was growing up, you know, my mom, my dad, my aunts and my uncles and my cousins.

D: It's part of your identity too, right?

M: Exactly. (Focus group interview with non-students)

In sum, Tania, Diana, and Marco position themselves in ways that challenge the dominant discourses of what it means to be Italian Canadian in terms of ethnicity, language use, religious affiliation, and sexuality. In the following sections, I will examine how they negotiate their identities in the public spaces of the workplace and in the private spaces of peer interactions, where the negotiation of identities is contradictory, not always possible, sometimes linguistically articulated, and always imbued with the intention and hope of redefining positions along the periphery.

Public spaces: Negotiating identities in the workplace

Within the workplace spaces of the Canadian world, all three participants experience marginalization based on ethnicity. Tania's workplace
reproduces dominant discourses of the Canadian center and leaves no
room for her to be Italian Canadian. She describes her situation, making
direct references to both language and culture:

> I'm always worried that I sound – that they're not going to take me
> seriously if I don't speak a certain way. If I talk about my culture, if
> I talk about the fact that I still live at home, if I talk about my parents
> in a certain way. I'm always afraid they are going to think of me as
> a – not take me seriously for some reason (Preliminary interview)

Her self-censoring is manifested through her linguistic overcompensation
with regard to English, particularly with her white, male, English-
dominant managers:

> I enunciate and I go out of my way to be grammatically correct.
> (Preliminary interview)

Within this set of power relations, the dominant language of the workplace is 'corporate and professional' English, and ethnicity, language, and
gender are wielded as a marginalizing force (Giampapa, 2001). And yet
Tania refuses to assume the role of the disempowered ethnic female who,
in Tania's words, 'is always in a good mood' (Preliminary interview). She
challenges her marginalized identity within the informal relationships
with non-Italian women in the workplace, doing it through the use of
non-verbal markers and jocular behavior. This behavior is underscored
by the awareness of the way the Other positions her in terms of ethnicity:

> I'm conscious about my hands, you know, but in the office when I'm
> speaking to my friend, to women or just people who are more at my
> level, first of all who are not Italian either I'm very comfortable with
> them, I joke around and I make fun of mobsters and I make fun of
> some of the people I grew up with or I make sure that they under-
> stand I know every stereotype they can think of . . . I want them to
> understand that I'm very smart, I speak well but I'm also Italian.
> (Preliminary interview)

For Tania, who feels that she needs 'to leave her ethnicity at the door'
(Specialized interview on work), the workplace is a constant site of
struggle to negotiate a space to be ethnically and linguistically Italian
Canadian. Ethnicity, language, and gender, as well as age and religion,
are points of negotiation for Diana, who does not feel that there is room

for her ethnicity in her Canadian workplace, nor room for her religion in
the Italian Canadian world. Diana notes that, in a previous workplace,
she never felt compelled to suppress her languages or her ethnicity:

> We did not have to leave it [ethnicity] at the door. . . . We would
> speak Italian and stuff there. (Specialized interview on work)

This is not the norm within the union culture where she is presently
located. There, her ethnicity is challenged and the language of power is
English. Even if she had the opportunity to use Italian, there is no room
for her to do so:

> Ethnicity is not part of the union culture here . . . I don't know where
> I fit in the whole thing. Nobody here speaks Italian. I've never had
> the opportunity to experience THAT. I have to overcompensate
> because I'm young. It has nothing, right now, right NOW, it has
> nothing to do with, yeah, the fact that I'm Italian. I'm very open about
> it. (Specialized interview on work)

Negotiating ethnicity is intertwined with the constant negotiation of age
and gender. Diana refuses to be marginalized, silenced, pushed, or stereotyped based on age, gender, and ethnicity. She explains this through an
example of a work-organized retreat that she attended, where the men
played golf, a sport for 'rich white males' (Specialized interview on work)
and the women went shopping:

> So we went to like a staff retreat and the only organized sport there
> was golf which to me is very UNETHNIC . . . I'm not going to learn
> it . . . when I brought that up one of the French Quebeckers said to
> me, 'What do you mean? Why don't you want to learn golf?', I said,
> 'Why don't I learn golf? My parents came from a country where they
> never played golf.' He says, 'It's good' and I go, 'Why? Because they
> make all the decisions on the golf course? That's why it's good to
> learn it. I'm sorry I refuse to learn it.' . . . In that sort of experience I
> didn't put my ethnicity at the door. I didn't because I spoke out
> against it. I asked why there weren't more organized sports . . . So
> when they would go golfing or shopping I refused to do both.
> (Specialized interview on work)

Diana challenges the exclusiveness and 'unethnic' and gendered practices within this world. She frames her ethnicity and linguistic identities
as assets with which she contests the stereotyped representations that she
encounters. From the periphery of this Canadian world, she defines
herself as

an articulate, young woman who does speak several languages and definitely Italian Canadian. (Specialized interview on work)

Her self-positioning, experience in youth activism, and the knowledge of three languages – Italian, English, and Portuguese – allow her to shift the boundaries of the center. She leans on these identities and takes advantage of what she calls the 'economic value' of her linguistic abilities within the labor movement. The very identities that make her 'stand out' allow her to move beyond the margins of her union workplace and enter other spaces. In particular, her union assigned her to work on political campaigns precisely because of her linguistic capital. She talks with me about these identity shifts as follows:

> D: Well, I definitely – I think I stick out like a sore thumb. I bet you, the first thing people think when they think language skills is Diana.
> F: Really?
> D: Because I speak three.
> F: And that's a rarity in this business.
> D: Oh YEAH . . . Mind you on the political camp, this election that I worked on, it's weird . . . that campaign we were in a very ethnic region and so having somebody who spoke the multi-languages . . . I definitely used my language skills more in the two and half weeks than I have in the past year. (Specialized interview on work)

And yet, while ethnicity, language, gender, and age are negotiated within the spaces of Diana's Canadian world, religion still remains a non-negotiable identity. She describes this with reference to her work as follows:

> D: I found it strange. Why do we even need – I'm not comfortable. To me work is work. Church is church.
> F: There's not an overlap for you?
> D: No.
> F: There's no room for you to overlap.
> D: (laughs) That's right. (Specialized interview on religion)

In her mind, Diana has made a clear distinction between these identity spaces – work and church – and the identities linked to these spaces as well as the negotiability/non-negotiability of these identities. However, Diana is never silent and negotiating other identities becomes a means of resistance. The religious marginalization that Diana experiences is particularly heightened within the work spaces of her Italian Canadian world, where she volunteers within Italian Canadian organizations. She expresses her marginalized position there in terms of two powerful images, one related to race and one related to sexual orientation. First, she compares being non-Catholic in the Italian Canadian world to:

> like, you know, a black person being in the middle of, you know, an assembly of all white people and a white person saying something and it totally not applying to the black person 'cause they're the only black person there. (Specialized interview on religion)

In the second instance, she states that she must attempt to 'come out of the closet' with regard to being an Evangelical Christian:

> Yeah I think I should – out there and come out of the closet. If it comes up to that point I will, where I see that, you know, my boundaries or my space or I'm not being identified or, you know, the minority isn't being – I will, I will say it. (Specialized interview on religion)

In saying so, she not only voices her marginalization, but hints at the fact that she is prepared to take action when necessary. Meanwhile, she takes religion out of the ethnic identity equation:

> My identity unlike other Italian Canadians has nothing to do with my religion, with my faith. I don't see it as, I don't see it as a prerequisite to being Italian Canadian. (Specialized interview on religion)

In doing so, Diana is trying to reconfigure what it means to be Italian Canadian and to push the boundaries of the Italian Canadian center, which in her eyes equates being Italian Canadian with being Catholic and uses religion as a point of exclusion. She manages her religious identity while challenging the definitions that exclude her and contesting her marginalized position. While her ability to speak Italian has allowed her to enter the Italian Canadian world and participate within its volunteer organizations, it is through being defined as the outsider that she challenges the Italian Canadian center:

> Well, I'm more outspoken than the other young people that sit around the table and, um, just plain different, you know, like they're teachers, all teachers in the Catholic board most of them. Whereas my job is protecting workers' rights and I'm sitting around with businesses, so my angle that I bring to the table is really different as well . . . I feel opposite . . . I'm relatively younger compared to everybody else there as well so I guess that puts me out as an oddball . . . And I'm a woman

and wait 'til they hear this / I'm not Catholic. (Specialized interview on religion)

What becomes clear, however, is that, along the periphery, Diana refuses to remain silent and continues to challenge the unfavorable positioning in the workplace. This space is equally challenging for Marco, who experiences double marginalization in terms of his ethnicity and sexuality. He states that he wants to keep his identities as an Italian Canadian and as a gay man quiet for fear of being 'pigeonholed' as an actor, either as the token 'Italian guy' or the 'Italian Canadian gay guy.' He states:

N: And a part of you wants to keep a little quiet?

M: Um, it's more career-wise.

N: Oh yeah?

M: I'm an actor too, so I just don't want anybody to pigeonhole me in just gay parts.

N: Yeah.

M: I love to do gay parts too but as an actor you want to do everything and a lot of times like casting directors want to say, 'Okay, this person,' but even with my name – from the beginning 'cause I'm Italian and Ranelli would come up and they'd just see my name and they go 'Okay, for Italian parts we'll call him.' But they don't know, I look Italian but I can pass for something else too, you know, so, so, they don't, like, pigeonhole [me] into one criterion. I try to keep it quiet. (Specialized interview on sexuality, conducted jointly with Normand Labrie)

And yet he also admits that he is drawn to roles that reflect his *italianità* or his identity as a gay man:

I like to play gay parts a lot 'cause just as I like to play Italian parts too 'cause it is part of my identity but at the same time I want to play stuff that's totally nothing to me. (Specialized interview on sexuality)

At the same time, his choices depend on whether the representations of being gay and/or being Italian are consistent with how he desires to be seen. He states:

Yeah, I've done Italian plays in the past and I like doing stuff that hits home . . . But again it's like everything else. I mean, like, being Italian stuff like that might attract me, IT MIGHT NOT. Stuff about being a young, gay man might attract me but IT MIGHT NOT TOO. I mean sometimes you go, 'Wait a minute. This is, like, not at all [what] it's about for me being gay or it is not at all what it's like being Italian.' (Preliminary interview)

And so, while at times Marco attempts to downplay his identities as an Italian Canadian and as a gay man, at other times he draws on both. He also refuses to change his name, Marco Ranelli, as so many have done in his industry, just because it sounds 'too Italian' (Preliminary interview). For him this would mean 'shedding' a part of his identity and, as noted earlier, denying a salient part of himself. This act of defiance is political as it forces a shift in the representations and identities that are the 'norm' within this space. And yet, where sexuality is concerned, Marco struggles as to whether or not 'to come out.' While he has come out to other actors with whom he has a close working relationship, outside of these relationships, he makes a specific reference to the challenges of negotiating his sexuality within the entertainment industry. He indicates that the 'macho man' stereotype continues to exist within these spaces – 'men being MEN' (Specialized interview on sexuality) – and homophobic comments are rampant. Claiming a gay identity would be paramount to a 'political' statement:

> There's lots of parties to go to for actors where you go meet the casting directors and you talk to directors and producers. I had to go for one. ... there's a part of me that won't go to those parties because if I go I want to bring Stewart but at the same time I don't want to bring Stewart and make a BIG political statement saying, 'I'm gay', you know, so where is that – the middle ground. (Specialized interview on sexuality)

Instead, Marco searches for the 'middle ground,' where his identities can be negotiated. He also explores the potential for leaning on other markers of identity, such as speaking Italian:

> F: Say if [there is] someone who is Italian there, would you go up to that person and speak Italian, is it a situation that you wouldn't want to play up being, you know, your Italianness comes out or-
>
> M: I think if it came out I would, it would be okay to play it up. It's just like another – I don't know like it's just something I connect to somebody else with when you're feeling uncomfortable let's say, you know, even, like not only just Italian but like if I go to another party and there's somebody else who's an actor there, you know, chances are people will talk to you a lot more easily then I would just because you have this, like, point where you can both go, 'Okay, we both have this.' (Preliminary interview)

In sum, Marco's identities as an Italian Canadian and as a gay man are often managed separately in the workplace, and being gay, at times, becomes a non-negotiable identity in the space which privileges discourses of machismo and heterosexuality. In turn language serves as an identity marker, which in certain contexts could connect Marco with other Italian Canadians.

Private spaces: Negotiating identities in the peer group

Within the private spaces of *italianità*, Tania and Marco articulate being Italian Canadian linguistically. Tania also seeks to contest the language values that have been espoused within her home. In interactions with peers, she appeals to language play, or what Rampton (1995) views as ritualized language performance. The use of her Italian Canadian friends' dialects together with the literal translation of Italian phrases in English allows Tania to shift identities and to reclaim, in a sense, her *italianità*:

> Usually with my friends, even with non-Italian friends, I'm very comfortable being Italian. I'm very comfortable speaking. I don't notice – I'm not conscious with my hands. I'm comfortable being aggressive. I'm very comfortable speaking quickly, you know, rolling my consonants, my Rs, just whatever. I have no problem letting myself be, you know, that in between 'cause there's the person at work and there's the in-between and then of course there's the person in Woodbridge (laughs) who doesn't speak proper English sometimes so. (Preliminary interview)

The quote above shows that she is aware of how the embodiment of her identities shifts within this space – 'the person at work, the in-between, the person in Woodbridge' – and it is within the private spaces that Tania produces a counter-discourse to the identities and expectations imposed within the workplace and the home.

Within Marco's private world of the home, family, and peer group networks, language plays a defining role in the articulation of ethnicity. One space where his Italian Canadian identity is negotiable is his volley-ball team, which 'has a lot of Italians on it and there's a part of me that likes it' (Specialized interview on sexuality):

> We're in a volleyball team together and Bruno usually drives Stewart and I home and Bruno and I have this rapport that Stewart and I don't have in the sense of talking to one another in this, I don't know, what we talk about, the context, the context of what we talk about and how

we talk to one another. We throw in Italian words and stuff, I mean it's very, very, it's our own language ... sometimes I wish Stewart could understand that but I don't think he could. At the same time there's a part of me that doesn't want him to 'cause that's mine, you know, this is how we talk. (Specialized interview on sexuality)

Ethnicity is expressed linguistically within this space and Marco views language play with his friend Bruno as a way of performing their *italianità* (Giampapa, 2001). He continues to talk about this with reference to his past university experiences:

I was at university and hanging out with the Italian club we'd speak mainly English but perhaps pepper more Italian in there just because it was the Italian club and it was almost like the secret language. We'd use it if we were talking about somebody in the lounge so they wouldn't understand what we were saying. (Questionnaire)

Within his theater friendship networks in the Canadian world Marco also positions himself both as the 'gay guy' and 'the Italian guy.' In this space he can negotiate both and not have to leave either at the door. He states:

I mean I walk into it with my theater friends and I'm the Italian guy, I'm the gay guy, I'm this and that, I'm whatever, so it's going to be part of this peppering (?) [of] what I'm about there ... everybody comes in with their different stuff and, um, yeah I wouldn't say I consciously leave it at the door. (Specialized interview on sexuality)

While both Tania and Marco find a way of negotiating ethnicity within their private spaces, Diana has moved beyond the Italian Canadian peer network, a space in which she was always considered an outsider. Reflecting upon her university experience in the Italian language classroom, she states:

I went to university and everybody in my class went to the same school or the same Catholic school and it was like a big clique and if you weren't in their club it was horrible, okay. Everybody belonged to St Peter College and, like, I'm the only one who's not ... I was always of different opinion of everybody else and I think that marginalized me. (Preliminary interview)

Marginalized by the Italian Canadian clique, Diana created an alternative space, where Italian became a code used with her closest friend, Lidia, in order to 'play up' their ethnicity:

> When I was in high school I did have a really strong sense that I was Italian because of – I had a friend Lidia and she was Italian . . . and it was a very big thing we would speak Italian to each other . . . we really, really, played up the fact that we were Italian. (Preliminary interview)

The shift in Diana's friendship networks signalled a change in language choice and a forging of ethnic identity beyond the realms of the private:

> See my friends now we speak only English 'cause none of them are purely Italian . . . a lot of my friends in high school they were Italian and different cultures when I went to university they became more English. . . . Some of them I still have but they're the English ones not the Italian ones. (Follow-up interview)

While Diana sees herself as Italian Canadian, she also positions herself – and is positioned – outside of an Italian Canadian group of peers:

> I'm Italian Canadian. I still saw myself different from them. (Preliminary interview)

Unlike Tania and Marco who find solidarity and a way of negotiating their ethnicity within their peer spaces, Diana struggles to be heard and positioned within the Italian Canadian world.

Conclusions

This chapter has attempted to explore the process of 'being and becoming' Italian Canadian through an understanding of the ways in which three Italian Canadian youths negotiate their multiple identities from the 'periphery' of their multiple worlds. The discourses of identity, language, and the representations of *italianità* play a defining role with regard to who is at the 'center' and who is at the 'periphery' of these worlds. The participants' ability to move within and across them is dependent on the valued symbolic capital at play within the worlds, on the negotiability of their identities, and on their decisions to lean on different aspects of their identities in order to facilitate a shift in positioning.

All three study participants have shown that, in different spaces and at different times, they challenge the undesirable imposed identities and attempt to reconfigure what is valued and what is legitimate. They have also positioned themselves as Italian Canadians, albeit in different ways. Tania sees herself as Canadian and yet struggles with this positioning and looks for a place within the Italian Canadian world based on ethnicity and language. Diana clings strongly to a hyphenated identity that leans on her *italianità* and attempts to find a legitimate position in the Italian Canadian world that excludes her on the basis of her religion. In turn, Marco balances being Italian Canadian and gay in the spaces which privilege machismo and heterosexuality.

In exploring the multiple spaces of the workplace and the peer interactions within both Canadian and Italian Canadian world, we see that some identities are negotiable and others are not. The workplace appears to create most problems for the three participants. Tania continuously challenges marginalization based on ethnicity and language. Diana is using her position as an outsider to contest the norm settings of her Canadian workplace. Her languages allow her to transcend the constraints of her Canadian work spaces and to enter the work spaces of the Italian Canadian world. What becomes clear in the process is the non-negotiability of her religious identity within this world. Similarly, Marco is marginalized based both on his ethnicity and sexuality. He finds that, across the various work spaces of his Canadian world, he must manage and downplay both of these identities. Being gay is a non-negotiable identity in these spaces and it also appears to conflict with the Italian Canadian identity, predicated on discourses of machismo and heterosexuality. Within the peer group interactions, however, both Tania and Marco challenge the Italian Canadian norms through linguistic play. This becomes a counter-discourse to the challenges experienced in the public spaces of their lives. For Diana, the challenge is more problematic as she still finds herself on the periphery of these spaces; however, she chooses to forge networks, which in the end allow her to be positioned as Italian Canadian and as non-Catholic. Speaking from the margins, these participants have found ways to re-articulate their identities within the multiple spaces of their multiple worlds and to redefine – at least for themselves – what it means to be an Italian Canadian.

Notes

1. The terms 'identity' and 'identities' will be used interchangeably throughout the paper.
2. All names have been changed to pseudonyms.
3. In this chapter I maintain an emic or participants' view of Italian language varieties (i.e. Standard Italian, dialects, Italiese, etc.) (See Giampapa, 2001, for more details)
4. Woodbridge is a township in the city of Vaughan. It is stereotyped as a neighborhood with large homes and mansions, where one finds gated estates known as 'The Wall.' Within the Italian Canadian community of Toronto, being from Woodbridge immediately conjures up the stereotyped image of

the Gino and Gina. However, this stereotype can also refer to other Italian enclaves in Toronto.

5. *Eyetalian* (1993–1999) was an Italian Canadian magazine featuring Italian Canadian artists, writers, designers, musicians, etc. It touched on a variety of topics and catered to a range of Italian Canadian voices within the community.

6. Marco chose not to contribute to the collection of citizenship data.

7. The CHIN international picnic is a yearly summer event organized by the CHIN radio/television group with a barbecue, musical performances of Italian Canadian artists, and a controversial male and female bikini contest. Despite the fact that it is promoted to all communities, it still remains one of the most prominent Italian Canadian family events.

Appendix

Transcription conventions

/	Short pause (up to five seconds)
IDENTITY	Capitals used for emphasis
[ ]	Author's addition
. . .	Continuing talk edited out as irrelevant to the excerpt
– (dash)	Ellipsis
(?)	Word uncertainty

References

Bakhtin, M. (1981) *The dialogic imagination: Four essays*. Austin: University of Texas Press.

Baldassar, L. (2001) Personal communication.

Baldassare, A. (2000) Much ado about tasteless café ads. *Tandem*, June 4, 2.

Bourdieu, P. (1991) *Language and symbolic power*. Cambridge, MA: Harvard University Press.

Chianello, J. (1995) The Armani generation. *Eyetalian*, Winter, 14–17.

Chouliaraki, L. and Fairclough, N. (1999) *Discourse in late modernity: Rethinking Critical Discourse Analysis*. Edinburgh: Edinburgh University Press.

Cummins, J. (1983) *Heritage language education: A literature review*. Toronto: Ministry of Education, Ontario.

Cummins, J. and Danesi, M. (1990) *Heritage languages: The development and denial of Canada's linguistic resources*. Toronto: Garamond Press.

Danesi, M. (1986) *Teaching a heritage language to dialect-speaking students*. Toronto: OISE Press.

DeMaria Harney, N. (1998) *Eh paesan! Being Italian in Toronto*. Toronto: University of Toronto Press.

Giampapa, F. (2001) Hyphenated identities: Italian-Canadian youth and the negotiation of ethnic identities in Toronto. *International Journal of Bilingualism* 5 (3), 279–315.

Giddens, A. (1984) *The constitution of society: Outline of the theory of structuration.* Berkeley and Los Angeles: University of California Press.

Giddens, A. (1991) *Modernity and self-identity: Self and society in the late modern age.* Stanford: Stanford University Press.

Gitlin, A. and Russell, R. (1994) Alternative methodologies and the research context. In A. Gitlin (ed.) *Power and method: Political activism and educational research* (pp 181–202). New York: Routledge.

Grimard, M. (2000) *Conceptualiser un espace discursif pour les gais et lesbiennes francophones en milieu minoritaire.* (Conceptualizing a discursive space for francophone gays and lesbians in a minority environment). Colloque L'Acadie plurielle en l'an 2000, FORELL et Institut d'Études acadiennes et québécoises à l'Université de Poitiers, Poitiers, France, May.

Grimard, M. and Labrie, N. (1999) *Silence, mots-tabous et hégémonie, ou comment les gais et lesbiennes francophones produisent un discours identitaire.* (Silence, taboo words and hegemony, or how francophone gays and lesbians produce identity discourse). Vingt-huitième Colloque annuel sur l'analyse de la variation linguistique, NWAVE, Toronto, Canada, October.

Hall, S. (1990) Cultural identity and diaspora. In J. Rutherford (ed.) *Identity, community, culture and difference* (pp. 222–237). London: Lawrence and Wishart.

Hall, S. (1991) Ethnicity: Identity and difference. *Radical America* 13 (4), 9–20.

Hall, S. and Jacques, M. (eds) (1990) *New times: The changing face of politics in the 1990s.* London/New York: Verso.

Iacovetta, F. (1993) *Such hardworking people: Italian immigrants in postwar Toronto.* Montreal: McGill University Press.

Keith, M. and Pile, S. (eds) (1993) *Place and the politics of identity.* London/New York: Routledge.

Labrie, N. (1999) *Institutional language policy vs. linguistic minority politics in French speaking communities in Canada.* Second International Symposium on Language Policy, Language Policy at the Millennium, Bar-Ilan University, Israel, November.

Lo, A. (1999) Codeswitching, speech community membership and the construction of ethnic identity. *Journal of Sociolinguistics* 3 (4), 461–479.

Quell, C. (2000) *Speaking the languages of citizenship.* Unpublished Ph.D. dissertation, OISE/ University of Toronto, Toronto, Canada.

Rampton, B. (1995) *Crossing: Language and ethnicity among adolescents.* London: Longman.

Rapanà, A. (2001) Italian-Canadian lifestyle in Woodbridge: With its large homes and growing families many call it the new Little Italy paradise. *Tandem*, August 12, 4.

Chapter 7

Alice Doesn't Live Here Anymore: Foreign Language Learning and Identity Reconstruction

CELESTE KINGINGER

> You said yes, you was going to France. . . . You was going to go where people were gentle, refined and said 's'il vous plaît' instead of 'gimme' and 'merci' instead of 'fuck you' and 'ooh-la-la' instead of 'bullshit'. (Moseley, 1996: 43)

> Now you may not actually be able to get to Paris, or even like the idea of going there, but the important thing is to always have a Paris, France, in your head; a spot that is solely yours – like Paris was mine. A carrot on a stick. A destination that no matter whatever happens to you, you'll be safe there. Some people, I understand, think of heaven that way. (Moseley, 1996: 65)

Introduction

This paper traces four years in the life of Alice, a highly motivated learner who has overcome significant personal, social, and material obstacles to her learning of French. The story of Alice's experience is at once dramatic and mundane, highly idiosyncratic and similar to the stories of numerous other young American women who undertake to learn French. Like the protagonist of Margaret Moseley's feminist mystery novel, *Bonita Faye*, Alice goes to France because of her desire to imagine herself anew in a context where her social options are broadened. Her choice of France, influenced by American mythologies, is a bid for access to a life of cultured refinement. Her story helps to elucidate the importance of personal history, imagination, and desire in the organization of lived experience related to foreign language learning. The story also brings into focus the significance of access to social networks, or of marginality within such networks, in the process of negotiating and (re)constructing a coherent and satisfying identity.

The significance of personal stories of language learning is only beginning to emerge in the research literature of applied linguistics. First-person accounts of language learning have often been received with suspicion, deemed incomplete, biased, unreliable or naïve (e.g. Bailey, 1991; Fry, 1988). Such accounts, it is implied, are unable to yield generalizable insights for the construction of an idealized Everylearner on whose behalf language educators may then construct uniform products, such as learning precepts, or 'strategies,' teaching methods, and standardized tests (e.g. Kasper, 1997; Long, 1997). Many researchers recognize the limitations of this emphasis on uniform practices, but few are overtly critical of its social effects.

One critique of standardization, emerging from a feminist perspective, is offered in Polanyi (1995). Polanyi concludes her paper, which analyzes the personal stories of study abroad participants, with the observation that standard assessments of language ability produce devastating effects. Such procedures can never recognize the achievements of individuals whose profile and experience differ from those of the 'one' standard learner (the white, middle-class male). If what 'one' gets to know inevitably reflects differential learning experiences, it is crucial to consider who 'one' is:

> That impersonal 'one' which 'needs to know' or 'learns a language' is the issue. Who 'one' is is a factor of one's native talent for language learning, one's educational background and motivation but it is also a product of one's gender, one's class, one's race, one's sexual orientation, one's health and degree of abledness. Ultimately, every language learner is alone with a unique experience, an experience tailored to, by and for that individual. (Polanyi, 1995: 287)

An understanding of these unique experiences demands a theoretical apparatus conceived broadly enough to encompass the history, agency, and engagement of language learners, one that values unexpected insights emerging from differential access to learning environments; in short, one that conceives of language learners not as bundles of variables, but as diverse *people* (Lantolf & Pavlenko, 2001). It further requires that the efforts of language learning be situated with respect to the ideological and sociopolitical processes which both constrain and enable (re)negotiation of identity.

Agency and Access in Foreign Language Learning

In the field of second language acquisition (SLA) it is customary to distinguish between foreign and second language learning as a dichotomy. Second language learners are people who are learning the language of the communities where they live, and are assumed to have both stronger motivations and more access to the language than foreign language learners. Foreign language learners are assumed to be people who are studying a language outside of the communities where it is used. Such learners are further assumed to have little access to the language and to harbor instrumental motivations more closely related to school success than to changes in social identity or lived experience.

In a study of second language learning by immigrant women, Norton (2000, 2001) has challenged both of these assumptions. Learners' dispositions toward language learning are indeed highly variable and closely related to both real and imagined belongings within communities of practice (Norton, 2001). Learners have differential access to the social networks providing opportunities for engagement in the interactions so crucial to language development. Access to language is shaped not only by learners' own intentions, but also by those of the others with whom they interact – people who may view learners as embodiments of identities shaped by gender, race, and social class.

It is relatively unusual that issues such as these, or their implications for social justice, come into sharp focus within the field of foreign language education. In the United States, foreign language learning is normally construed as an academic pursuit which is optional at best, and is not seen as a matter of survival. There is no official policy related to foreign language learning at the national level, and foreign language education has never been a high priority of policy makers. Perhaps this occurs because of a widespread and deeply held suspicion toward multilingualism per se (see also Pavlenko's chapter in the current volume), since a foreign language education policy would require an unambiguous and unbiased statement on the value of multilingual competence.

Judd's (1992) review of contemporary policy statements related to foreign and second language learning implicates the national fortress mentality in the construction of attitudes toward competence in multiple languages. Speakers of languages other than English must be assimilated, for their competence is dangerous and divisive. Foreign language instruction may then be reserved for the monolingual elite who have already been Americanized:

Apparently, the underlying philosophy is that a person can study a foreign language post-assimilation but not pre-assimilation. Once someone is acculturated, then foreign language study can begin. In other words, assimilation and Americanization are the overriding concerns of policy makers; foreign language study is secondary. In this way, the elite maintain control over the basic social, political and economic institutions of the country and are not threatened by other groups. (Judd, 1992: 179)

Within this ideological environment, foreign language learning exists as a marginalized add-on to an elite education fundamentally unconcerned by the potential of foreign language competence to expand learners' cognitive and social repertoires. Rarely do US foreign language professionals publicly wonder about the relationship of foreign language study, social identity, and access to resources, or even about the ability of individuals to profit from discursive diversity in general (Harré & Gillett, 1994). After all, such questions imply the existence of gray areas wherein Americanization might be partially compromised and critical reflection on its terms and conditions achieved.

Despite the dominant ideology of monolingualism, foreign language learning in the US is, nevertheless, often an attempt to claim a more complex and more satisfying identity – an attempt that conflicts with implicit monolingual ideologies as well as societal power relations of race, class, and gender. The few studies examining foreign language learning as a phenomenon involving issues of social identity reveal sources of differential success in language learning within the struggle for access to social networks of participation (Wilkinson, 1998, 2001).

In accounts of foreign language learners' sojourns abroad, American women learning foreign languages are shown to confront problems similar to those of Norton's immigrant women. The intentions of study abroad participants conflict with those of others, categories related to social identity are imposed upon them, and their opportunities for language learning are correspondingly restricted. In an analysis of journals recounting experiences of American women studying in Russia, Polanyi (1995) found many instances of direct or indirect sexual harassment functioning to silence these women. Talburt and Stuart (1999) discuss the manner in which an African-American woman studying in Spain was subjected to continuous and humiliating emphasis on race and sexuality in her interactions with Spaniards. Kline (1993) reports that American women studying abroad in France sought refuge in literacy following repeated encounters with sexist and hostile attitudes in the French-speaking community.

Alice

In concluding their statements on the importance of construing language learners as people, Lantolf and Pavlenko (2001: 155) call for 'robust and detailed case studies documenting the activities of people on the periphery of linguistic communities of practice and how they gain or are denied (full) participation in these communities.' This study offers one answer to that call in detailing the experiences of a foreign language learner, Alice. The study traces Alice's experience of foreign language learning at home and abroad over a period of four years, from 1997 to 2000. Data include interviews with Alice before and after her two-year experience as a student in Quebec and France, journals detailing her language learning experience abroad, and e-mails and letters Alice has written to me since 1998 (for interview transcription conventions, see the Appendix on p. 241). The data are analyzed thematically as artful representations, or performances, of reality (Kalaja & Leppänen, 1998) using the HyperQual 3 concept modelling software (Padilla, 1999) to explore and verify themes. The themes are then examined longitudinally, to explore their history over the four-year course of the study. In addition to these sources of triangulation in the data, Alice has participated in an ongoing conversation about the study and has contributed directly to the analysis. This is a collaborative study in the sense that the analysis has emerged from a long-term dialogue between Alice and myself.

The purpose of this paper is to sketch Alice's history as a language learner, focusing on key themes related to foreign language learning as identity reconstruction. The paper treats Alice's dispositions toward language learning and her 'imagined communities' of French language users (Norton, 2001), her accounts of access to social networks at home and abroad, and her use of language learning as a source of coherence and of lessons in persistence.

The perspectives highlighted in this volume suggest particular questions to be addressed in interrogating Alice's experience as a language learner. How can her dispositions toward language learning be characterized in terms of claims to a renegotiated identity? That is, where do they come from and how do they change over time as her access to language learning changes in nature? How does she imagine the communities of French language speakers, her own role within them, and the symbolic capital she will gain through this endeavor? What kinds of communities of practice offer her membership, and how does she gain access to them? Which aspects of her identity are negotiable, and which are not?

Alice's unusual case is distinct from those of many American foreign language learners who are members of the monolingual elite and view their task in ways influenced by the ideologies of language education prevalent in the United States, that is, as a peripheral if not marginal undertaking. Alice's case also differs from the histories presented in literary autobiographies of engaged French language learners such as Alice Kaplan (1993) and Richard Watson (1995), both of whom are of privileged social backgrounds and write from the vantage point of successful professional adults. By contrast, Alice has not enjoyed material, social, or cultural privilege, but nevertheless has constructed a rationale for language learning. Her foreign language learning constitutes a bid for a better life, a theme that gives coherence to her education, and a lesson in persistence that permits her both to profit from the impermanence in her life thus far, and to overcome it.

I met Alice in the spring of 1997, when I had just begun teaching French at a regional state university in the Midwestern United States. Alice came to my office to discuss French courses and programs of study abroad. I had rarely met anyone who seemed as enthusiastic about French as Alice did at that time. Alice reappeared in the fall of 1997 and became my student for the entire academic year, first in a phonetics course, then in a third-year conversation course. She was a diligent, engaged student who earned high grades, though she worked the equivalent of a full-time job. As I got to know her, she began to explain her situation, and to share with me the difficulties she was experiencing in the study abroad office. Her application had met with resistance that Alice attributed to a perceived mismatch between her own simple dress and general appearance and those of the typical middle-class study abroad participant.

In the spring of 1998, Alice convinced the study abroad officials to admit her to the program, and she was granted financial aid for a year in France. I shared with her my aspiration to design and carry out a longitudinal study of foreign language learning experience based on interviews and journals maintained during study abroad. Alice consented to be interviewed in March of that year, and agreed to keep a written record of her experiences during her study abroad program. In the summer of that year, Alice was to begin her study abroad experience with a summer language program in Quebec. She was then to participate in another language program in Caen before she would move to Lille to enroll at the university there.

During that first interview I began to learn about Alice's aspirations, history, and the circumstances of her life to date. Like many of my other students at the regional state university, Alice's past did not conform to that of the implied audience of our French language textbook. The readers of this book were people who lived in 'maisons,' 'appartements,' or 'pavillons,' – people who had the means to envisage France in the modern-day version of the Grand Tour, ordering wine at refined cafés, buying silk scarves from obsequious salespeople, and contemplating celebrated works of art. At the time I interviewed Alice, in fact, my French 1 class had just completed a unit on housing, during which I had naively required the students to ask and answer personal questions about where they lived using the book's vocabulary. Before the exercise began, one of them had said: 'Comment dit-on *trailer park*? 'Cause I don't live in no, like, château.'

Alice was born in Ohio to a family she characterized as 'lower class with a high class mind, kinda.' Her mother was single and had a peripatetic lifestyle as an itinerant tree planter, so, along with a younger sister, the family had moved continually, particularly between Georgia and Arkansas. She claimed that she had 'lived all over the place' but had 'never lived anywhere' in particular until that time when she was enrolled at the university. Much of her experience of schooling took place via correspondence in a home school program, ACE (Accelerated Christian Education). In the ACE program, Alice had studied French for the equivalent of one grade level, using books, tapes, and a series of 12 unit assessments. She had quit public school when she was nine years old, because her mother 'had to do this moving around stuff' in connection with her work. At that time she had attended a Christian school for several years, living in the home of the school pastor while her mother travelled. When she was 15 she moved to her grandfather's home, where she finished two and a half grades within nine months and graduated from the home schooling high school program, at age 16.

Alice's grandfather, whom she calls the 'stem' who holds her up, had decided to abandon the trappings of middle-class life and lived as a recluse on a mountain in Arkansas. Having grown weary of dealing with people, 'he bought some land and moved back on a mountain in Arkansas. no electricity. no running water. no television. no phones, nothing.' For Alice, her grandfather's home was a refuge; a place of great natural beauty where she could enjoy stability, peace, and concentration. Although he did not actively encourage her to consider a college education, Alice's grandfather was nonetheless instrumental in her decision to go forward with this project, despite the fact that she had no financial means and little moral support from the rest of her family.

At 16, Alice enrolled in a regional college founded on a work study premise, where students financed their education in entirety through college-based employment. At this time, she began college-level language study, enrolling in two sequential introductory French courses. Within a year, her college education was interrupted for the first time because her initiative to pursue a degree had waned due to her relative youth and following a decision to set up housekeeping with her boyfriend. When this relationship failed shortly thereafter, Alice lost her social and material grounding. She experienced her life for the next two years as a downward spiral of transience, homelessness, and hardship. She worked at a series of service-oriented jobs in fast food restaurants and nightclubs. She was a cocktail waitress and an exotic dancer. She lived in improvised housing: a tent in an inexpensive campground, a car she bought for $50, and, for a time, a shelter for homeless and battered women. She became pregnant at 19, and decided to give the child up for adoption.

The birth and adoption of her child formed the turning point when Alice decided to make a definitive change in her lifestyle. Four weeks after the baby was born she returned to college to major in French. She studied French for three semesters, taking intermediate and conversation courses. One of these courses was a one-on-one conversation session each week with a teaching assistant from France. Throughout this period, her name was on the Dean's List, an honor roll of students earning excellent grades. Then she decided that she should upgrade her college education by leaving the work-study college for the regional state university, even though that move would require hard work and financial aid, including loans. For two semesters prior to enrolling at the university, she worked: she was a full-time nanny and housekeeper, a part-time front desk receptionist in a Howard Johnson's chain hotel, a server in a McDonald's restaurant, and a sales clerk at a kiosk in a shopping mall.

Prior to entering her study abroad program, Alice had reached and excelled in the third-year level of college instruction in French. When, in the first interview, I asked her how she was preparing for study abroad, she mentioned her use of French language chat rooms and e-mail, reading old textbooks, and listening to French music, but, above all, she was working:

> *everything is just working hard to save up the money and get good grades so I can go to France. that's the only thing that I'm working for. right now. and I and I know that I'm sacrificing some of the practicing I could be doing now. I know I'm sacrificing that by working so hard and not having enough time. but I'm going to be in France for a year. I'm gonna learn it. that's the only thing I think. I think right now I may not be learning a lot of French. I may not be as good as I wanna be in French, but I'm saving up money to go there. an' I **will** learn it. sooner or later.* (Interview March 1998)

Imagining France

Alice's motives are complex in that the themes she evokes relate both to her personal history, and to the broader themes of language ideology, in particular the ideologies of French that are prevalent in the discourses of American mass media and language teaching. These themes also relate to her desire to make French 'real' by learning with and from other people, and eventually to become a language educator. In this role Alice imagines herself as a dynamic, engaged teacher committed to the role of language learning in promoting intercultural awareness and social justice. Before Alice went to France, competence in French was both a 'dream' and a 'mission.'

Growing up in rural America, spending a lot of time on the road and, at 18, setting up housekeeping in the backseat of a car, Alice's access to foreign languages was limited. In evoking her history as a language learner, Alice remembers the significance she ascribed, as a small child, to the Spanish lessons on *Sesame Street* (Public Broadcasting's television program promoting basic literacy for pre-schoolers). She was thrilled to discover the parallel semantic universe of a language different from her own, and eager, even as a pre-school child, to share the excitement she experienced as she learned Spanish words.

Throughout Alice's study of French in college, she nurtured a romantic image of France. In describing the way she imagined France before her sojourn there, the picture she draws is of a mystical paradise:

> *before I went umm it's always been kinda like Oz, it was like the fairytale land like you know like Wonderland. I thought that the, that the atmos-, that the, even the sky was gonna be different cause you know when you dream about things they're kinda hazy and, and mystical and they, you know the colors seem different in your dreams. so when I got there I thought it was just gonna be this rolling, these rolling fields of green grass and clean everywhere and just fresh.* (Interview October 2000)

Alice's image of France recalls the many stereotypes of the French landscape within American cultural productions, such as French language textbooks, travel brochures, and television shows, where France is presented as a vast formal garden studded with works of monumental architecture. When Bart Simpson (of the popular animated television series *The Simpsons*) goes to France as an exchange student, for example, he finds a landscape entirely composed of Impressionist paintings. In this version of France there is of course no misery: no slums, no poverty, no anonymous low-income housing projects. Above all, there are no trailer parks.

Alice's dream is populated with refined, interesting, cultured people who are, in turn, interested in her. She sees herself as participating in a variety of communities of practice where access to knowledge of language and culture will be freely given as equal exchange within a context of higher cultural awareness:

> *I guess I expected some kind of cultural consciousness, I don't know like everyone, like everyone would be really cultural . . . I really thought that I was gonna meet a lot of friendly old people and even young people who would think that I was interesting and and umm that would invite me into their lives and you know tell me about themselves and teach me about being French, and and help me with the language and and would ask me questions about my country etc. etc.* (Interview October 2000)

In Alice's dream, the theme of higher cultural consciousness reflects, although perhaps distantly, ideologies of French language promulgated by representatives of the 'francophonie' movement. Here, the French language is not only linked to themes of equal rights and liberty, it is also framed as an ideal means by which abstract and universal ideas may be expressed (Ball, 1997). Perhaps more importantly, Alice's view of the French as a 'cultural' people may derive from American re-imagining of the French based on these ideologies. The essence of this image is that the French do in fact live in a highly 'cultural' world, but that this obsession with 'culture' leads inevitably to frivolity. In American animated films, for example, most French-accented characters are seen to live in constant, obsessive pursuit of refinement in matters of love (e.g. Pepe LePew) or of cuisine (e.g. the chef in *The Little Mermaid*) (Lippi-Green, 1997). Polly Platt's popular self-help book for expatriate executives in France, *French or Foe* (1994), derides the commonplace Anglo-Saxon image of the French as 'luxuriating lotus-eaters' (p. 16), but nevertheless maintains that 'culture in France is everything important – history, art, food, love, it's all part of culture' (p. 101).

It is cultural consciousness that Alice ultimately hopes to attain, but her aspirations have less to do with champagne and foie gras than with her nascent understanding of intercultural communicative competence and desire to become a language educator. Cultural consciousness is the link by which she connects participation in French-speaking settings to her broader professional goals, her 'dream' to her 'mission.' Alice settled on French as her language of choice because French will make her more 'cultural,' but she also sees the value of sharing her insights with others who, like her, did not enjoy them as children. In conversation with the French teaching assistant at her work-study college, Alice learned that

European children often begin their language study in elementary school. This discovery prompted her to imagine herself in a new light:

*I was like man I wish I had learned when I was nine. I'm like why can't we? why don't we? an' the more I got into the language the more I discovered the culture ... an' I was thinkin **man** if kids knew this stuff early there would never be any prejudice. if they had even a taste of culture of someone else's culture if they thought it was cool to be cultured. and to learn. instead of being so isolated from the rest of the world just because we have oceans on either side. y'know? then there wouldn't be- there would be such a higher level of tolerance. and interest. y'know? and there wouldn't just be America. they would go out and try to discover their planet. an' then I- that was what fired me. after that I was like I gonna do that. I'm gonna teach 'em. . . . once I had made the decision there was no stopping me. from there. it was just a mission. it was I am going to France. I am going to be competent in this language. an' I am going to teach it and I am going to make it fun. an' I'm going to make it interesting and I'm going to make it cool. and I'm going to make it in. it's gonna be in its not gonna be nerdy. to learn this stuff. its gonna be cool.* (Interview March 1998)

In Alice's life to date, moving around the country with her mother and living as a vagabond on her own, she had experienced mobility as impermanence and instability leading frequently to dire straits. Yet she was also frustrated by the limited way that cultural differences were perceived by her college friends, who 'lived in a box' and refused to venture outside the confines of their secure lives. In combination with her passion for a foreign language, she creatively reconstructed the impermanence of her life as flexibility and openness to difference, that is, her disadvantaged childhood became a distinct advantage in her search for a satisfying professional life.

Access to Language Learning at Home and Abroad

Like the learners described in Norton (2000), Alice frequently describes her experience as a struggle both with the language itself and for access to participation in social interaction. This theme runs through all of her accounts of learning, from the description of her earliest experiences to the present, and is often framed as withholding of knowledge by more powerful individuals.

Alice recounts an anecdote from her pre-teen years that illustrates her early discovery of the frustration she would feel when knowledge of language was unavailable to her in social interactions. This story is about an innocent crush on a man twice her age, that is, it is a story about a romantic partner who is unmistakably more powerful than she. The symbol of this power is the man's knowledge of French deliberately withheld from her:

> **A:**   *anyway um. then when I was twelve? I met this guy and I got this crazy crush on him. an' he was really immature. he was twenty-**five** but he was really immature an' he liked me back. an' he even asked my mom if he could marry me.*
>
> **CK:** *oh really?*
>
> **A:**   *yeah. back then it seemed really romantic now it seems kinda weird that he did that but- anyway um. he had taken French and he used to speak some French to me an' an' it would just be **agonizing** cause he wouldn't tell me what it meant. he wouldn't tell me what he- what he was saying. an **he** worked with us on our crew? an' it was kind of a migrant working situation. we all traveled around in a crew together an' we lived in our- in our automobiles and everything. well we he would **pay** me about once a month to clean out his car?*
>
> **CK:** *yeah,*
>
> **A:**   *an' I was cleanin' it out one time an' he had written me a note. on um a restaurant ticket. he wrote me a note in French. I think I still have it. an' um. it just just gnawed at me I'm like **what** does this mean what does it mean. I wanna find out what this means. an' um that was one of the motivators.* (Interview March, 1998)

In retrospect, of course, Alice recalls this event as 'kinda weird,' but many of Alice's accounts of learning environments are populated, as noted above, by persons in positions of relative power who deliberately marginalize her by withholding language. It is this withholding of language that stands in the way of her ability to reorient herself within the 'dream' of French language use. Alice accordingly reacts with frustration, and occasionally with anger. In an account of her subsequent experience of learning French at the work-study college, Alice describes her encounters with a domineering French teacher ('the tyrant') and the young woman, already competent in French, who was the teacher's pet. Here, in contrast to the case above, Alice constructs herself as a competitor (Bailey, 1983)

> *there was this **girl**. she was such a snob. I hated her. an' she worked in the language lab her name was Jenn and she had gone, to. Normandy? or something like that? and learned French fluently? and she was my age. and **she** was a bitch. an' I- part of wanting to learn French so bad there and part- part of the motivation ta- ta- to deal with the tyrant was to **spite** her ass.*

*I could **not** stand her. I was like um . . . I can do this. If she can do this. I
can do it. I'mean this- she thinks she's **better** than me. watch **this**.*
(Interview March 1998)

In the summer of 1998, Alice began the sojourn abroad that she hoped
would offer unlimited access to French language use. She prepared for
study in France with a five-week French language immersion course in
Quebec. In this program, she was placed into the highest level offered for
courses in phonetics, grammar, and oral expression, and she signed a
contract stating that she would speak only French during her stay.
Unfortunately, however, in the residence hall where she lived with 12
other Americans, this contract was not respected. As reflected in her
journal, the Quebec experience was mixed. Alice perceives her progress
as too slow and hampered by the social and linguistic constraint represented by the American group. At the beginning of her stay, Alice
cautions herself against the danger of spending too much time with the
other Americans:

> *mon niveau est 'avancé' et maintenant j'ai peur. C'est claire je j'aie beau-
> coup besoin de pratiquer et étudier. Et aussi, je ne peux pas sortir encore
> avec les autres étudiants dans le groupe. Ils parlent seulement en anglais –
> tous le temps – c'est si si si mauvais pour moi.* (Journal, Quebec, July 7,
> 1998)
> (My level is 'advanced' and now I am scared. It is clear that I need
> to practice and study. And also, I cannot go out again with the other
> students in the group. They speak only in English – all the time – it
> is so so so bad for me.)

By the midpoint, she has begun to distance herself from the group:

> *Je suis allée en ville avec quelques étudiants dans mon groupe . . . on est
> allée au zoo. C'était très bien pour moi. Les autres filles (femmes – qui sait?)
> ne parlaient pas français, donc je les ai quitté - puis j'ai entendu plusieurs
> conversations quebecois! C'est amusant.* (Journal, Quebec, July 19, 1998)
> (I went to town with some of the students in my group . . . we went
> to the zoo. It was very good for me. The other girls (women – who
> knows?) didn't speak French, so I left them – then I heard several
> Quebecois conversations! It is fun.)

On the day before her departure from Quebec, she expresses continued
ambivalence about the progress she has made:

> *J'ai peur de partir en France. Je ne pense pas que je suis prête. Quand j'ai
> décidé de venir ici, ma mission était de perfectionner mon français pour que*

*je puisse penser en français très vite. Je ne voulais pas de credits où des notes,
etc. Je voulait de me préparer pour mes études en France. J'admet que j'ai
appris beaucoup ici: ma classe de grammaire était bon parce que j'avais besoin
de répétition, et mon cours de 'textes oraux' etait très dûre donc ma
compréhension devenait meilleure, et mon cours d'expression orale était fun
et j'aime mon professeur . . . Mais je ne suis pas completement contente avec
le façon dont je parle. Je deteste ça. J'espère que je serai capable que je vais
en France.* (Journal, Quebec, August 8, 1998)

(I am afraid to go to France. I don't think that I am ready. When I
decided to come here, my mission was to perfect my French so that
I could think in French very fast. I didn't want credits or grades, etc.
I wanted to prepare myself for study in France. I admit that I learned
a lot here: my grammar class was good because I needed repetition,
and my *'textes oraux'* course was very hard so my comprehension was
getting better, and my course in oral expression was fun and I like
my professor. But I am not completely happy with the way I talk. I
hate that. I hope I will be capable when I go to France.)

That fall, on the evening before her departure for France, Alice
visited me at home. She had a little more than $100 in her pocket, a plane
ticket, and the journal she had bought to record her language learning
experience.

Altogether, Alice spent two years in France. During this time, her
images of France and of herself as a student and a speaker of French were
repeatedly challenged. For the first year she took part in the activities of
the study abroad program in Caen and Lille, and lived in university residence halls. In Caen, she was again placed in the highest level possible,
'avancé,' for a three-week language course. In Lille, the first three weeks
of the program involved (for Alice) a third intensive language course,
after which she was entitled to enroll in regular university courses.
During the second year she lived in Lyon and attempted to enter the
university there as an independent student. At no point during this time
did she achieve an understanding of the university system that would
permit her to become fully engaged and to view her studies as productive and useful.

Like other participants in study abroad programs, Alice had access to
a group of compatriots with whom she could construct a hybrid subcul-
ture to sustain her efforts (Kline, 1998). But Alice's position within the
group was unique: she was older than the others, with more experience
of personal hardship, an acute awareness of the privileges afforded to her
as a study abroad participant, and fewer material resources. She knew
that she would have to approach her language learning strategically.

Nevertheless, Alice's initial experiences both in school and out were so unproductive and frustrating, and her disappointment so palpable, that she became progressively depressed to the point of contemplating suicide.

Alice's position in the early weeks is summarized in the following entry from her journal, written in Caen during her initial language training. Here, she records the fact that she is both an insider and an outsider within the group of American students, notes her first impressions of her courses, and describes the strategy she adopts to gain contact with French-speaking people by letting 'old, French men' buy her drinks:

> *A little bored and a teeny tiny bit depressed. Everyone has gone off to Paris to have fun. I'm staying here because I don't have the money to fly off and vacation. I have to keep reminding myself that I'm not like the others. This is a real opportunity for me. I have to be careful and frugal in order just to survive. It's so important for me to concentrate on the reason I came here: to Study French. But I fall asleep in these classes. I mean, the first week is over and I have two more to go and I'm having a hard time deciding how I'm gonna pull it off w/o skipping classes. I try to pull away from the group whenever I can but they keep making such efforts to keep me in. (. . .) everyone went out last night to the discotheque, but I stayed at the campus bar and let old, drunk French men buy me drinks. At least I got to practice my French. (Journal, Caen, September 11, 1998)*

After she moved to Lille Alice realized that she would not be living in a rural Wonderland, but in a gritty, industrial, urban environment with a cold climate. She perceived everyone she met as 'closed,' 'rude,' and 'unhappy.' She made repeated attempts to gain access to social interaction using the strategies for demonstrating openness and friendliness that she had developed at home, but was constantly rebuffed:

> **A:** *I just feel like I'm a part of everything and I really need to you know scramble that up, go and experience that and nobody, I wasn't getting any output from anyone. and then I had this experience and I was already down, I was walking to the tobacco store and umm, and I passed this man on the street and I was like look I'm in France! I'm in France and so I smiled and I said bonjour- he crossed the street.*
>
> **CK:** *yeah.*
>
> **A:** *he freaked out and crossed the street so that just made it even worse.* (Interview October 2000)

Alice's recorded reactions to her experiences in school were similarly characterized by expressions of anger and frustration. Having been placed into the advanced level at the three institutions where she had taken placement tests, in Lille she enrolled in regular university courses. However, she received no guidance on strategies for registering and locating courses, and she was unprepared for the style of classroom conduct that she witnessed in her classes:

> *I'm in class right now, but it's the wrong class. I was looking for a fucking linguistics class and ended up in some stupid class about psychology. I fucking hate France!!! They fucking know absolutely nothing about assigning room #s. I'm so sad and frustrated right now, that I have to keep writing not to cry. . . . This is just shit! I fucking hate it here! I cannot believe that this is just culture shock! I have another class today @ four o'clock if this fucking piece of shit class ever gets over. . . . Here in France everyone just fucking talks during class and you can't even hear or understand the prof. I'm so sick of it already. How am I ever going to survive a fucking year here? It's a good thing that I don't have enough $ to go home for X-mas cause I wouldn't come back. Hate France, Hate French, Hate Life. I can't believe that this was my fucking life's dream!* (Journal, Lille, October 15, 1998)

It was at this point that Alice 'hit rock bottom' and became severely depressed. She was convinced that the competence in French that she had worked so hard to attain prior to her arrival in France was proving inadequate. In her courses, when she was able to find them in the first place, she was encountering a set of unfamiliar norms for interaction (Wylie & Brière, 1995). In the American classrooms she had frequented to date, students tended to compete with one another for personal attention from an instructor whose charge included remaining accessible to the students. By contrast, in Lille the professor was a distant figure with whom she had no personal contact. Her fellow students enacted a relationship of in-group solidarity, interacting extensively with each other in class, chatting and sharing information, but excluding Alice. Alice could not even hear what the professor had to say, because she was surrounded by the other students' conversations. Her interactions with French people outside of class were extremely limited. She saw no way to realize her 'dream':

> **A:** *I was suicidal. I mean and it wasn't even like a self-pity suicidal it was like just a decision. like I have been working for the past five years for something, I got there, I hated it and there was nothin' left to do. you know basically I had worked all this time for somethin' that turned out to be a sh- you know just shit and there was nothing left, there were no more steps, I had done what was left to be done and it was*

just too hard to get up in the morning. (. . .) the thing about this depression was it was so matter of fact. it seemed so logical to me that okay look I did, I held my end up you know of the bargain, I gave up my kid, I went back to school, you know I started to you know change my life and everything and, and I cleaned up and I worked and I got to France and then whoever was supposed to hold up their end of the bargain didn't.

CK: *yeah.*

A: *I was like okay so it's only fair that I can just you know duck out of this now. just let me go to sleep I'm just tired I don't wanna do this anymore (mmm, hmm), and it was **the** closest I think I've ever actually come to killing myself, but I made no attempt.* (Interview October 2000)

Alice traversed this crisis by joining the American group on a pleasure trip to the south of France during which she contemplated her situation and concluded that she would abandon her academic pursuits in favor of seeking out speaking practice in whatever informal contexts presented themselves. She stopped trying to find her classes. At the same time, she began to keep her journal in French rather than in English, recording in detail her social interactions in the residence hall and campus bars. She summarized her approach in a letter of December 17, 1998:

Et maintenant, mes études. . . . Je ne sais pas ce que tu ailles penser du paragraph suivant. Tu rapelles que j'étais au Québec cet été . . . J'ai pris des cours de grammaire, etc. là. Donc, quand je suis arrivée à Caen, des cours là sont les même (mais pas si bons) j'ai seché des cours et j'ai passé de temps au bar et en faisant le tourisme avec les français . . . Et puis, quand je suis arrivée ici à Lille, j'ai essayé pendant les premières trois semaines de suivre des cours ici, mais ils étaient complètement nulles! J'ai pris le cours intensif et après ça . . . j'ai seché encore des cours. Franchement j'ai mar des papiers et des expos et des classes plein d'étudiants qui chuchoataient derrière moi sans respect pour les profs!!!!

Et ensuite, il reste que 9 heures pour moi pour finir ma spécialité de français à l'université, et ma raison pour avoir venir ici c'est pour perfectionner la langue parlée. Donc, je fais le même que j'ai fait à Caen . . . Je passe le temps avec mes amis français. Je lis des livres . . . Livres que J'AI choisi. J'écris des amis français par courrier et par Internet. J'écris dans mon journal.

(And now, my studies. . . . I don't know what you are going to think about the next paragraph. You remember that I was in Quebec this summer . . . I took grammar courses, etc. there. Then, when I got to

Caen, the courses there are the same (but not as good) I skipped classes and I spent my time in the bar and touring with French people ... And then, when I arrived in Lille, I tried for three weeks to take classes here, but they were completely dumb! I took the intensive course and then I skipped even more classes. Frankly, I'm fed up with papers and exposés and classes full of students who whisper behind me without respect for the profs!!!!

And then, I only have nine more hours to finish my French major and my reason for coming here is to perfect my spoken language. So, I am doing the same thing I did in Caen ... I spend time with my French friends. I read books. Books that I have chosen. I write French friends by mail and Internet. I write in my journal.)

From this point forward Alice deliberately situated her learning experience in the social networks she developed by hanging out in local watering holes and making the rounds of rooms in the residence hall where students gathered to eat and drink. She worked to get introduced into student cliques and organized most of her time around these, hosting dinner parties in her room, going to where other parties were taking place, and having sophisticated conversations. During the second semester of the first year she found employment as an English language teaching assistant at a local high school, earning enough money to sustain her. By the end of the year, she was 'the Queen of France' (Interview September 2001):

> *I would sit around with all my fellow students and we would sit around with our coffee and our cigarettes and we'd have these **long** philosophical conversations using big long French words and I was so French.* (Interview October 2000)

Alice's quest for higher cultural consciousness was also ultimately satisfied, though this process took place entirely in informal settings and often against her will. An example of this process is provided in Alice's account of an argument with one of her companions over the significance of political events in the wider world. Alice had positioned herself as a non-participant in discussions about politics, and had in fact bracketed that entire domain as one in which she took no interest. When her companions not only refused to respect her decision to ignore politics, but also focused their own critique on the political actions of her home country, she expressed her extreme frustration in her journal:

> *On a commencé de parler des vacances mais Cedric a dit qqch de Bill Clinton ... Moi, je fais pas la politique, je m'en fous ... et je peux pas expliquer ce*

que est arrivé après ça sauf qu'il a mis toute d'erreurs de la terre entière sur Bill Clinton . . . On a disputé un peu et puis car je fais pas la politique, j'ai demandé si on pourrait changer le sujet . . . j'ai essayé au moins 3 fois de changer mais chaque fois il a continué. Enfin, il a dit 'Franchement, je n'aime pas les États-Unis . . .' Moi, j'ai pris ça un peu personelle. Il voulait pas parler d'autres choses, donc, j'ai arrêté de parler. Je voulais pleurer franche-ment! (. . .) Je fais pas la politique et en plus, je sais pas m'exprimer quand même – je connais pas la vocabulaire . . . et je m'EN FOUS.

Après quelques minutes pas du tout confortables, ils ont dit 'bonne nuit' et sont partis. J'étais cassée. Je me suis allongé sur mon lit et j'ai pleuré. Je voulais être toute seule . . . Je voulais rentrer aux États-Unis car si c'est 'Français' de faire la politique . . . si je dois parler de choses qui m'inter-essent pas, je devrais quitté ce pays maintenant parce que je ne suis pas ici pour ça. Je suis pas Française et je veux pas être Française . . . donc j'ai toujours le droit de refuser de parler de n'importe quoi. (Journal, Lille, January 4, 1999)

(We started talking about the vacation but Cedric said something about Bill Clinton . . . I don't do politics, I couldn't care less . . . and I can't explain what happened after that except that he put all the mistakes in the whole world on Bill Clinton . . . We argued a little and then since I don't do politics, I asked if we could change the subject . . . I tried at least 3 times to change but each time he continued. Then, he said 'Frankly, I don't like the United States . . .' I took that a little personal. He didn't want to talk about other things, so, I stopped talking. I wanted to cry frankly! (. . .) I don't do politics and plus, I don't even know how to express myself – I don't know the vocabulary . . . and I DON'T CARE.

After a few minutes that were not at all comfortable, they said 'good night' and left. I was broken. I stretched out on my bed and I cried. I wanted to be all alone . . . I wanted to go back to the United States because if its 'French' to do politics . . . if I have to talk about things that don't interest me, I should leave this country now because I'm not here for that. I am not French and I don't want to be French . . . that way I still have the right to refuse to talk about whatever I want.)

By the time of our interview in 2000, once she had returned to the regional state university to complete her college education in the United States, her interpretation of these events had changed radically. She had become critical of her own formerly complacent attitude, eager to learn about world news, and grateful to Cedric for 'forcing' her to develop political awareness:

A: *I had a huge fight with this guy named Cedric because he was like what do you think about this whole bombing thing? I'm like I don't care! I'm not there, I don't know what's going on, I don't care! He's like how can you say that that's so irresponsible! you know you're dropping bombs on people I'm like yeah I'm flying the plane that's right, you're, yeah you're right, push the button. and so then you know he actually did in a roundabout indirect way force me into having a political s-, you know hav- having a political awareness.*

CK: *and do you feel that that's continuing now? I mean*

A: *yes. as a matter of fact I'm extremely dissatisfied with the, with the, the media situation here (hmm), that the only world news that we get is anything having to do with the US, anywhere we're involved and that's considered world news but, but two countries that are having problems with each other that's not world news? (. . .) I feel so cocooned! (mmm, hmm) I'm sure that's a safe happy thing but I liked it better when I felt stuff, when I saw what was going on in Zimbabwe you know with the white farmers and when I saw what was happening with the oil spill on the coast of France and you know and just* **world world** *news and I* **saw** *graphic pictures of* **dead** *bodies being* **bull- dozed** *into* **holes***. that, that, I've never seen anything like that before (mmm, hmm), but I felt, and I felt in my gut and that felt so alive. as horrible as it was it still felt more alive than this ho hum nothing's wrong in the rest of the world thing.* (Interview October 2000)

Lessons in Persistence

In the process of becoming competent in French, Alice continuously reconstructs her motives for learning, as she is challenged by the real difficulties of developing advanced language proficiency, by the shock of the language immersion experience, and by the discovery of new social networks, their values along with their vocabulary. At the same time, however, there is a constant return to the theme of persistence and of the coherence language learning has added to Alice's life story. French is 'sticky': both because the challenges it presents consistently draw Alice's attention and because the language learning process itself has taught her 'to stick with things':

> *I never thought about what I was gonna do with French. I was like I don't care I just like the language I have this amazing passion for this language an' it's sticky. it was sticky back then it was* **so hard** *for me to learn. I couldn't understand. I couldn't comprehend? when people spoke to me? but*

I could write an' I could read it well. an' I just- the thing that kept me going was I just had a passion for it. I had to learn it. I had to stick to it an' I have to say French is probly- French has taught me to stick. with things. cuz its the first thing I really did stick with. so that's really good. that's good because its kept me in a couple of jobs. (Interview March 1998)

Two and a half years later, Alice characterizes her learning experience as upward mobility organized as series of 'planes' interspersed with 'stickiness':

I worked and I worked and I worked and then I, like, well it's like, can't even describe it, it's like actually getting your hands to like fit something? putting like putting your hand through something and you try and you try and you try and you can't get your hand through there, and finally it emerges on the other side. like a plastic bag or somethin', you stretch and stretch and stretch it and finally it breaks and your hand goes through. and that's how I felt, like I was being, I don't know, like I was trying to dig into a plastic bag and it wouldn't give, and then finally it would give and I would be on this plateau where I was like yeah okay so I'm alright. and I really wouldn't think about how good my French was because it was just a, a a practical thing, I mean I just used it. I had no choice. it was an everyday thing. and then I would come to a point where I was like, something else would challenge me, like somebody would say, Emilie would say something, (. . .) and I was like what the hell does that mean? what, what the hell does that mean? and then that just made me realize that there are lots of little expressions that I don't really know, so I learned some more expressions, and then I felt like I mastered those, and then I just kept doing this plateau-sticky thing, plateau-sticky thing all the way up. (Interview October 2000)

By the end of her sojourn in France, Alice had achieved awareness of the complexity of language learning and of the serious effort it requires. Moreover, for Alice language learning is a metaphor linking the efforts of everyday work to the attainment of a coherent, meaningful life. To reach this goal, she must maintain her focus. In deciding each day to continue reaching for her dream despite many obstacles, Alice has in fact learned how to overcome her previous general tendency to abandon difficult pursuits. When she returned to the regional state university to complete her degree, Alice had learned to maintain her efforts in school and has returned to academic work with a clear sense of purpose:

A: *I think the main thing that I'm discovering this semester is mainte- nance (. . .) now I have to maintain my reading, not only do I maintain my reading but I go and I type my own study guide (mmm,*

*hmm), like I pick out the important things of the, of the chapters and
I type them up and then I, I review 'em every day? instead of just the
night before the test?*

CK: *yeah?*

A: *and so that has really changed my study habits, but it's also changed
my motivation because I really appreciate education now.* (Interview
October 2000)

Alice is no longer a drifter, but a 'great student' working on a graduate
degree. She is currently focusing on her aspirations to become a language
educator and to help others as they struggle with a new language.

Conclusions

Alice's journey thus far has involved negotiation of many facets of her
identity: social and linguistic, but also gender and class identity, which
are tightly interconnected and have been challenged simultaneously in
complex ways over the course of her foreign language learning. Perhaps
the difficulty of teasing apart these aspects of identity negotiation stems
from the comprehensive nature of Alice's goal. For Alice, becoming a
speaker of French is a way of reorienting herself in the world – a 'mission'
wherein she summons her own strategic use of personal experience, talent
and resources to upgrade her access to cultural capital, become a cultured
person, and share her knowledge with others. In this sense, Alice's efforts
toward French language competence are just as much an 'investment' in
social identity as those of the immigrant women in Norton's (2000) study.
Alice's stake in language learning is also a bid to break free of the
confining circumstances of a peripatetic, working-class childhood and to
become a person she can admire. Her personal mission is explicitly linked
to professional aspirations. Alice insists that she feels no shame about her
background, but only frustration at the limited perspectives it offered,
and desire to move beyond them.

Alice's motives, her investment in language learning, and the meaning
she ascribes to foreign language competence can only be understood by
examining the sociocultural worlds from which they emerge, and their
dynamism over time. Initially, Alice was not drawn to French because of
its instrumental or utilitarian value, but precisely because of the prestige
of that language in the United States as a language of culture. In this way,
Alice's story problematizes foreign language as an object of desire in
ways that are obscured, within contemporary educational approaches, by
emphasis on functional language use. She was also motivated by her
desire to become a language educator, and because she saw in language

learning a way to profit directly from the impermanence in her life – to turn her painful experience of instability on its head and make of it a virtue. Her initial experiences as a study abroad participant in social settings both in and out of school were powerful demotivators (Dörnyei, 2001) leading her to the brink of despair in her conviction that her investments had proven worthless. Eventually – without the assistance of her academic program – she succeeded in gaining access to interaction with French-language speakers on an informal basis. In challenging her self-image along with her language skill, and teaching her 'maintenance,' these interactions became the context in which she recovered her motivation to upgrade her political awareness and to return to school.

Above all, in sketching Alice's history as a learner of French, this paper proposes that the categories emerging from research on language learning as social practice are relevant to the foreign language field. Foreign language learners are people too; people whose history, dispositions toward learning, access to sociocultural worlds, participation, and imagination together shape the qualities of their achievements.

Appendix

Key to transcription conventions

. . . Long pauses, of five seconds or more
oui? Rising intonation, as in a question
oui, Rising intonation, suggesting intention to continue speaking
oui! Strong emphasis with falling intonation
oui. Falling (utterance final) intonation
oui Marked prominence through pitch or amplitude
oui- An abrupt cut-off with level pitch
(. . .) A section cut from the transcript

References

Bailey, K. (1983) Competitiveness and anxiety in adult second language learning: Looking at and through the diary studies. In H. Seliger and M. Long (eds) *Classroom oriented research in second language acquisition* (pp. 67–102). Rowley, MA: Newbury House Publishers.

Bailey, K. (1991) Diary studies of classroom language learning: The doubting game and the believing game. In E. Sadtano (ed.) *Language acquisition and the second/foreign language classroom* (pp. 60–102). Singapore: SEAMEO Regional Language Centre.

Ball, R. (1997) *The French speaking world: A practical introduction to sociolinguistic issues*. New York: Routledge.

Dörnyei, Z. (2001) *Teaching and researching motivation*. London: Longman.

Fry, J. (1988) Diary studies in classroom SLA: Problems and prospects. *JALT Journal* 9, 158–167.

Harré, R. and Gillett, G. (1994) *The discursive mind*. Thousand Oaks, CA: Sage.

Judd, E. (1992) Language-in-education policy and planning. In R. Kaplan and W. Grabe (eds) *Introduction to applied linguistics* (pp. 169–188). Reading, MA: Addison-Wesley.

Kalaja, P. and Leppänen, S. (1998) Towards a discursive social psychology of second language learning: The case of motivation. *Studia Anglica Posnaniensia* 33, 165–180.

Kaplan, A. (1993) *French lessons: A memoir*. Chicago: University of Chicago Press.

Kasper, G. (1997) 'A' stands for acquisition. *The Modern Language Journal* 81 (3), 307–312.

Kline, R. (1993) *The social practice of literacy in a program of study abroad*. Unpublished Ph.D. dissertation, The Pennsylvania State University (Dissertation Abstracts International, A: The Humanities and Social Sciences, 1993, 54 (5), Nov., 1785–A).

Kline, R. (1998) Literacy and language learning in a study abroad context. *Frontiers: The Interdisciplinary Journal of Study Abroad* 4, 139–165.

Lantolf, J. and Pavlenko, A. (2001) (S)econd (L)anguage (A)ctivity Theory: Understanding second language learners as people. In M. Breen (ed.) *Learner contributions to language learning: New directions in research* (pp. 141–158) London: Longman.

Lippi-Green, R. (1997) *English with an accent: Language ideology and discrimination in the United States*. New York: Routledge.

Long, M. (1997) Construct validity in SLA research. *The Modern Language Journal* 81 (3), 318–323.

Moseley, M. (1996) *Bonita Faye*. New York: Harper Collins.

Norton, B. (2000) *Identity in language learning: Gender, ethnicity and educational change*. New York: Pearson.

Norton, B. (2001) Non-participation, imagined communities and the language classroom. In M. Breen (ed.) *Learner contributions to language learning: New directions in research* (pp. 159–171). London: Longman.

Padilla, R.V. (1999) HyperQual3, Version 1.1.

Platt, P. (1994) *French or foe?* Skokie, IL: Culture Crossings.

Polanyi, L. (1995) Language learning and living abroad: Stories from the field. In B. Freed (ed.) *Second language acquisition in a study abroad context* (pp. 271–291). Amsterdam/Philadelphia: John Benjamins.

Talburt, S. and Stuart, M. (1999) What's the subject of study abroad? Race, gender and 'living culture.' *The Modern Language Journal* 83 (2), 163–175.

Watson, R. (1995) *The Philosopher's Demise: Learning French*. Columbia, MO: University of Missouri Press.

Wilkinson, S. (1998) On the nature of immersion during study abroad: Some participants' perspectives. *Frontiers: The Interdisciplinary Journal of Study Abroad* 4, 121–138.

Wilkinson, S. (2001) Beyond classroom boundaries: The changing nature of study abroad. In R. Lavine (ed.) *Beyond the boundaries: Changing contexts in language learning* (pp. 81–105). New York: McGraw Hill.

Wylie, L. and Brière, J. (1995) *Les Français* (2nd edn). Englewood Cliffs, NJ: Prentice Hall.

Chapter 8
Intersections of Literacy and Construction of Social Identities

BENEDICTA EGBO

Introduction

The impact of literacy on learners remains a contentious issue in much of the literature. However, beyond the polemic, there is consensus that literacy leads to the acquisition of encoding and decoding skills, intersects with cognition, enhances linguistic and communicative competence and increases life chances. What is less known is how the acquisition of literacy affects individuals' perceptions of their selves and social positioning, particularly in contexts with asymmetrical power relations and social inequities. Drawing on evidence from research work among literate and non-literate rural women in Nigeria, this chapter is primarily intended to examine the interface between literacy and the construction of social, individual, and group identities in a postcolonial context. In particular, how does literacy affect ways in which these women (re)conceptualize themselves and their roles in society? How do literate individuals perceive themselves in relation to non-literates, particularly in contexts of overall low literacy rates such as sub-Saharan Africa? These questions constitute the main focus of the chapter. To provide a contextual framework within which to address issues of literacy and identity, I begin with a brief discussion of the origins of women's current literacy status in the region.

Gender and Literacy in Sub-Saharan Africa

Historically, the roots of women's limited access to literacy in sub-Saharan Africa can be traced to the discriminatory colonial education and language policies that excluded women from schooling and access to the discourses that were considered valuable capital and prerequisites, at that time, for full participation in national life. The salient role that was accorded to Western languages and ideologies taught in schools and the simultaneous devaluation of native languages and culture placed women at the fringes of important social institutions in their societies. It is safe to argue that the imposition of Western ideologies and discourses on African society by the colonialists was in itself unfortunate. However, denying women access to such discourses and subsequently preventing them from better negotiating and appropriating their identities in terms of their role and status in the emergent social order was, in my view, doubly oppressive. As Pavlenko and Blackledge argue in the introduction to this volume, identities are historically either valued or devalued depending on prevailing social ideologies. A colonial homogenizing view of the role of women in society as exclusively located within the domestic sphere – a role that the colonialists argued did not require formal education – was ideologically motivated and contributed significantly to the diminution of their status in their respective communities. Even in contemporary contexts, there is compelling research support for the view that gender inequity in access to literacy continues to be one of the major causes of women's marginal status in sub-Saharan Africa (Ballara, 1992; Chlebowska, 1990). While much of the resulting discourse centers around the more obvious and unfortunate socioeconomic consequences of persistently excluding women from access to literacy (Ballara, 1992; Stromquist, 1990; United Nations, 1991), it is also generally agreed that women's social distance from legislative, decision-making bodies, and other positions of power excludes them from influencing social policies, leading to the feminization of poverty in the region.

But, just as there is strong belief in the emancipatory power of literacy, there are equally strong reservations about its potential as an enabling tool for improving the life chances of, and reconstituting the social identities of, women in the region (Hollos, 1998; Odora, 1993). For questioners of the ameliorative potential of literacy, empowerment has not been the logical consequence of women's access to literacy so far, since male-oriented gender ideologies continue to thrive in the region. To support their position, critics are quick to point to the case of developed Western societies, where equal access to educational opportunities has not guaranteed women social equality. For these critics, engendering female praxis would require a shift from literacy and education more generally, to the broader task of dismantling existing patriarchal structures that reify subordination. There is indeed abundant evidence that, in advanced societies where women have achieved normative educational parity with men, gendered literacy practices in schools as evidenced in language construction, discourse norms, and texts, are implicated in women's limited access to positions of power and authority. Corson (1993) and Luke (1994) present persuasive arguments on how power relations and social identities are constructed through school texts, the media, and other educational materials, all of which convey to women their subordinate social status.

While both sides of the debate make a compelling case for their positions, the conceptual posture adopted in this chapter is that the exclusion of women from access to literacy involves questions of legitimacy, self-determination, self-identity, and, ultimately, social justice. As Rockhill succinctly puts it:

> The construction of literacy is embedded in the discursive practices and power relationships of every-day life: it is socially constructed, materially produced, morally regulated. . . . Literacy is caught up in the material, . . . and sexual oppression of women *and* it embodies their hope for escape. (1993: 171)

Although the present study specifically examined the impact of literacy as a social artifact on the lives and social identities of two groups of women, it should be noted that the discussions here are also predicated on postmodernist perspectives that see literacy as a fluid, context-bound phenomenon. Such views, e.g. Street's (1993) ideological model and Lankshear and McLaren's (1993) critical literacy paradigm, assume an interconnection between language/literacy practices and the reproduction of power structures in society much like other scholars' analysis of the interface between literacy/language practices and social reproduction, including Bernstein (1977), Bourdieu (1991), Bourdieu and Passeron (1977), Foucault (1980), and Freire (1970). Moreover, any potent analysis of literacy must of necessity take into account its dialectical nature as a simultaneously powerful tool for either empowerment or hegemony. Depending on the contextual variables, disempowerment may arise either from the nature and kind of literacy received by certain groups in society, in particular by women and ethnic and linguistic minorities (see Blackledge, 2000 and Corson, 1993 for detailed discussions of this issue) or through denial of access as in the case of women in sub-Saharan Africa.

Women, Literacy, and Hegemony

Hegemony has much to do with the maintenance of social control by dominant groups over less powerful groups through apparent consensus, state institutions, and discourses that prevent alternative world views from gaining any kind of legitimacy. But hegemonic power is never *une affaire classée*. As its best-known analyst Gramsci (1971) argues, individuals are not passive subjects and therefore have the potential of resisting their ideological colonization.

Michel Foucault, another theorist whose work has been very influential in poststructuralist critical theory, paints a similar picture of power to Gramsci. He extends his analysis of power beyond its nature and structure to an examination of how dominant powers control, and perhaps even eliminate, resistance and opposition by (re)presenting imposed ideology as a regime of truth and common sense (Foucault, 1980). Through this process of normalization, oppressed groups internalize and accept their subordinate conditions oblivious of the colonizing process that is actually at work. But, like Gramsci, Foucault theorizes that power is not static and domination is never total since the 'subject' is capable of resistance:

> The individual is an effect of power, and at the same time, or precisely to the extent to which it is that effect, it is the element of its articulation. The individual which power has constituted is at the same time its vehicle. (Foucault, 1980: 98)

The concept of hegemony is germane to a discussion of the identities of women in sub-Saharan Africa such as this in two important ways. First, women's identities are tied to the nature of the socialization they receive – typically unobtrusive control and indoctrination, which they themselves subconsciously reinforce. However, because hegemony in a Gramscian sense relates to the kind of power that survives to the extent that the subordinated contributes to its sustenance, the condition of the dominated is not immutable.

A second and perhaps more important reason why the idea of hegemony is pertinent here, is the notion of agency which is implicit in the concept as a dialectical construct. As I argue in more detail elsewhere (Egbo, 2000, where I discuss the present study in its entirety), critical action and hopes for social reconstruction in Africa depend on agency by women provided they have access to prerequisite tools such as literacy. We must, however, bear in mind that, as critical literacy theorists persistently argue (see Freire, 1970; Freire & Macedo, 1995; Lankshear & McLaren, 1993), becoming literate means or *should* mean more than the ability to encode and decode written material including textual conventions.

Making a similar point, Bee (1993) creates a link between literacy and the politics of gender. She argues that, while economic independence is key to women's emancipation, achieving it requires that women also understand the structural forces that sustain their exclusion and keep them at the periphery of their respective societies. According to Bee:

> Merely enabling women to read and write without reference to their social and political inequality and its origins contributes materially to maintaining their oppression. . . . Teaching women to read and write through critical analysis . . . will enable . . . [them] to travel with a different consciousness of their world, their place within it, and their personal and collective power to transform what is inhumane and unjust. . . . Any lesser view of the aims and purposes of literacy for women effectively promotes and prolongs their *domestication* – in Freire's sense of the word. (1993: 106, 107)

Thus, in her account, literacy should facilitate individual independence, economic emancipation, and full participation in society as well as the ability of oppressed groups, such as women, to critically assess and change their world.

Parajuli and Enslin (1990) provide an example of how women can acquire critical consciousness through popular literacy programs. They describe how a group of women in rural Nepal were able to assess their sociocultural condition and eventually transform their social condition through participation in a literacy program. Through the program, the women not only learned how to read and write, they also learned how to discuss and find solutions for the pressing problems they faced particularly with regard to power relations between men and women both within their households and within the larger community. Parajuli and Enslin (1990: 45) conclude that, while the women's initial reasons for demanding literacy instruction (reading and writing) were related to their need to fulfill some higher spiritual needs according to their religious beliefs:

> in their pursuit of learning, they discovered a shared sense of oppression with other women . . . [and] . . . moved beyond the pursuit of learning to demand legitimate spaces in which they could evolve programs for social reform. . . . While pedagogy began with a struggle for education, it evolved in sociocultural struggle. (1990: 45)

This example is significant in that it shows how literacy can be simultaneously functional (in terms of its practical and everyday uses) and consciousness-raising, leading people to challenge and change oppressive social structures. Indeed, the entire idea of literacy as a transformatory artifact hinges on the rationale that, through reading and writing and the concomitant expansion of language and knowledge base, people can begin to deconstruct and reconstruct their identities, and personal and collective histories, thus replacing hegemony with critical action. Put differently, depending on the degree of group subordination, in some social contexts, simply having access to literacy may be empowering in very important ways.

Literacy and Social Identity

In many parts of the world, access to literacy is often associated with increases in life chances that are a function of two elements – options and ligatures. *Options* are choices, while *ligatures* are bonds that individuals form through immersion in a given culture or by virtue of their social positions and roles in society (Dahrendorf, 1979). Options and ligatures are critical to the empowerment of any group, particularly those that have historically been at the sidelines of their societies. With regard to literacy and education, options increase opportunities, while ligatures are the ties people develop with others as a result of their shared experiences in education (Corson, 1993).

In his account of the enduring association that emerged among the alumni of a school in Sierra Leone, Corby (1990) provides a compelling example of how collective experience of literacy and education can create ligatures that facilitate access to powerful positions in society. According to Corby, Bo School, an all-male institution which was created by the colonialists with the intention of creating a literate, albeit inferior, working class, eventually developed into a powerful network that offered graduates advantages, when they sought access to jobs and other social rewards, as a result of the camaraderie that developed while they were in school and that continued throughout their lives. Also within the African context, a study of literacy learning in a work-related context (Marshall, 1993) reports how literacy was used to advance the cause of freedom, as well as to fight against Portuguese colonialism in Mozambique. In many instances then, the acquisition of literacy provides people with more than new communicative codes – it also becomes a powerful marker of group identity, a sense of 'us.' In the present study, while there was no organized attempt to forge an alliance by either group of women, clear patterns emerged vis à vis how each group perceived itself in relation to the other group and the broader social network of women in their communities. For example, there was evidence of an intra-group sense of affiliation; the literate women were more favorably disposed to others like themselves and, from my observations and their reports, had a mooted discriminatory attitude toward the non-literate women. They also held similar views about critical social issues that affect women's lives in their communities.

At the individual level, studies have shown that literacy has some implications for self-esteem. One study of semi-literate adult Hispanics in Canada (Klassen, 1987) suggests that, in addition to having its constitutive meaning in given contexts, literacy or lack of it can affect people's feelings of inclusion or exclusion. McCarthey's (2001) study of identity construction among elementary readers and writers provides more recent evidence of how literacy can affect individuals' sense of self. Other researchers identify higher self-esteem, self-confidence, and an overall sense of well-being (Ballara, 1992; Chlebowska, 1990; Stromquist, 1997) as some of the psychological benefits that accrue to beneficiaries of literacy, although such feelings are particularly manifest in adult neo-literates as Stromquist asserts:

> beyond a sense of comfort given by increased coding and decoding skills, literacy has been found to produce feelings of confidence when the former 'illiterates' now see themselves as regular and 'normal' adults, as individuals with a certain autonomy of judgment, mobility, and increased freedom to move and act. (1997: 138)

As will be seen later, the idea that non-literates see themselves as less than adequate, which is implicit in Stromquist's views above, was indeed evident in my discussions with some of the non-literate participants in the present study.

The Research Project

The study described here explored the living conditions and life chances of literate and non-literate rural women in Nigeria, based on their own accounts. The study focused on identifying factors that impeded or facilitated access to literacy in two groups of women within the same setting. It also explored the linkages between literacy and the empowerment of women, including how it affects recipients' sense of self and their perceptions of their 'place' in society. In essence, the study looked at how literacy, or lack of it, shapes identities.

Methodology

The study was informed by 'critical realism,' a philosophical perspective that views agents' accounts as warrantable knowledge since social structures do not exist independently of the activities they govern (Bhaskar, 1986, 1989; Corson, 1993). Critical realism was particularly relevant for this study because it assigns considerable importance to the power of human agency. Moreover, any inquiry that is underwritten by a critical realist philosophy must of necessity give voice to the voiceless. A major goal of this study was to find out what it is like to be literate or non-literate within a rural setting in sub-Saharan Africa, from the perspectives of those who actually live and experience it. In other words, by using the views of the participants as primary data, the study sought to give voice to the women. Finally, in my view, research done in contested sites where certain groups are marginalized ought to be a form of praxis-oriented explanatory critique, simultaneously exposing unwanted social realities and providing a framework for raising consciousness and implementing critical action both at the micro and macro levels of organized society. Corson summarizes the essence of research that is guided by the philosophical underpinnings of critical realism:

> A critical realist account is concerned with identifying the actual structures that constrain human action, structures whose modification and removal can prove emancipatory for human beings in general. . . . [It] takes into account the wider contexts of human social interaction and the power relations that both constrain and liberate that interaction. (1995: 8–9)

Because the study was grounded in critical realism and qualitative methods, it used a unique approach that is best described as philo-ethnographic, a terminology I use to capture the linkages between the deep philosophical grounding of the research, the participants' narratives, and the ethnographic methods that were used.

The participants

Two rural communities in south-western Nigeria were chosen for the study. The study sample consisted of 36 respondents between the ages of 23 and 52: 18 literate and 18 non-literate women, all of whom have lived in rural communities for most of their adult lives. Although the collection of data was based on purposive sampling, identifying the pool of potential informants involved generating a list of likely participants with the help of 'guides' in each community. These guides also accompanied me to the homes of the women during the initial visits. Although relying on locals in choosing the participants was potentially problematic because of the possibility of bias on the part of my guides, it was the logical option since there were no official records or statistics from which I could draw a list of participants. I however adopted several strategies to minimize the potential influence of my guides on the selection process.

With an average of 10.9 years of schooling, most of the literate participants (61%) were teachers, while the other half included nursing assistants, a seamstress, petty traders, and micro-entrepreneurs. A majority of the non-literate participants considered themselves full-time farmers (55%), while the others stated that they also engaged in petty trading in addition to their farming activities. Three of the non-literate participants also worked as manual laborers on a poultry farm. All the literate women were married to literate men who had similar or slightly higher levels of schooling, while 72% of the non-literate women were married to literate men. Despite the differences in occupations and educational status, all the participants share a similar sociocultural background – they come from the same communities and speak the same native language. However, while the literate participants were bilingual (English and the local language), the non-literate participants were monolingual (they had only spoken knowledge of the local language).

Data collection

Data for the study were collected through in-depth one-on-one interviews, focus group discussions, and participant observations. In addition to participating in focus group discussions, each participant was interviewed at least twice. The first session was designed for meeting with a potential participant as well as for arranging a formal interview. In many cases, the introductory session became a forum for establishing rapport and beginning a dialogue with the participant. This helped to put her at ease during the formal interview. For me, it was often an opportunity to enter into the 'world' of the participants, observing them within their own environment, and noting how they interacted with others.

An area of concern with regard to the collection of data which deserves mention here had to do with the fact that I could be considered an 'insider' (albeit one in diaspora) to the extent that my roots are in the communities in question, although for all intents and purposes I was an outsider. This ambivalent connection did raise for me questions about potential difficulties in remaining detached through the process. After all, as some researchers have argued, maintaining absolute objectivity during research is often problematic, since our paradigms or world views ultimately insinuate themselves into the process and possibly inform the research choices we make (Hughes, 1990; Kuhn, 1970; Merriam, 1988). In my own case, remaining relatively neutral was quite easy since in many ways I was an outsider as pointed out above. Moreover, outside of the researcher/interviewee relationship, I had no prior acquaintance with the participants.

The interviews were semi-structured to allow flexibility, although a previously selected set of questions provided the framework and served as the discursive compass that steered the interviews back on track whenever there appeared to be a significant digression. The interviews were conducted in three languages in which I am fluent: English (the official language and lingua franca of Nigeria), Igbo (the local language), and pidgin English (a non-standard variety of the English language).

Doing research in Nigeria, like most multilingual settings, requires a complex amalgam of working knowledge of local languages, customs, and semantic sensitivity, particularly during interviews and discussions with participants (Egbo, 1997). Because of the complex sociolinguistic landscape of Nigeria (an estimated 250 ethnic groups and as many as 400 indigenous languages), literacy teaching and educational instruction are given in the English language, although in principle the government advocates the use of local languages at the initial stage. Due to the reduced importance accorded to native languages in education in Nigeria, most of the participants, literate and non-literate alike, had only spoken knowledge of the local language. In effect, much of the discussion here refers to English literacy. It is worth emphasizing that, because of the importance assigned to English (as the official language) in Nigeria, English literacy is a prerequisite for access to critical social rewards, such as the labor market and positions of power, even within the postcolonial context. This is as true for men as it is for women.

Discussion of Findings

As will be demonstrated below, the findings of the study suggest that, while literate women have not become the official leaders of either researched community, they do enjoy a comparatively enhanced quality of life, and have increased life options as well as some social influence. Based on their accounts and personal observations, literacy also appears to have given the women a sense of personal uniqueness and self-efficacy, it is also an effective tool for negotiating their identities within their households and larger community by increasing their employment opportunities and access to the means of production. For example, all but one of the literate women were engaged in the formal wage sector. Evidence from the data also shows that access to formal labor translated into higher income and economic independence for the literate partici-pants. In contrast, the non-literate participants were predominantly engaged in labor-intensive subsistence farming and reported the sale of surplus farm produce as their major source of income.

According to the findings of the study, two major factors affected whether the women had access to literacy – availability of financial resources and parental perception of the value of educating girls. The latter attitude may be the result of patriarchal structures that place different values (often to the detriment of girls) on the male and female child. Overall, there was remarkable difference between the living condi-tions of both groups of women. For example, as Tables 8.1 and 8.2 show, even their daily routines are markedly different; the literate women

Table 8.1 Typical daily routine of non-literate rural women

Time	*Daily routine*
4:00–5:00 a.m.	Rises/continues food processing from previous day/prepares family breakfast
7:30 a.m.	Sends children off to school
8:00–9:00 a.m.	Prepares for/walks to the farm
9:00–3:00 p.m.	Works on the farm
3:00–4:00 p.m.	Returns from the farm/prepares for market
5:00–7:00 p.m.	At the market
7:30–9:00 p.m.	Prepares/has dinner
9:00–11:00 p.m.	Does food processing/household chores
11:00 p.m.	Goes to bed

Table 8.2 Typical daily routine of literate rural women

Time	*Daily routine*
6:00 a.m.	Rises/washes and dresses/prepares family breakfast
7:30 a.m.	Sends children off to school
8:00–1:45 p.m.	Works
2:00–4:00 p.m.	Lunch/siesta
4:00–6:00 p.m.	At the market/leisure
6:00–8:00 p.m.	Prepares/has dinner
8:00–9:00 p.m.	Miscellaneous (chores/leisure)
9:00 p.m.	Goes to bed

work considerably fewer hours than their non-literate peers, leaving them enough time for leisure, which is in itself an indicator of enhanced quality of life.

In what follows, I discuss the details of the major findings of the study. It should be noted that, because the interviews with the non-literate participants were conducted in the local language and pidgin English, the statements that are quoted here were translated from the vernacular, although in doing so I have tried to retain the nuances that were integral to the vernacular version. With only minor grammatical corrections, the statements of the literate participants are quoted in their English original.

Group and self-identity

There was a sharp contrast between the accounts of both groups of women with regard to how the women perceive themselves and their social location within their communities. A good number of the literate respondents reported feeling positive about themselves, particularly because of the relative financial independence and the 'elite' status they seemed to enjoy. The non-literate group, on the other hand, constantly referred to their lack of literacy as a state of 'blindness.' They seemed quite aware of the advantages of literacy, perhaps because most (72%) were married to literate men. Illiteracy, they reported, limited their potential, as two participants, one of them an adult literacy student, point out in the following:

If someone came in now and asked me to sign something, even my name, I can't because I do not know how to . . . that is very bad. Such a simple thing.

It has always upset me that I did not go to school, hence I enrolled in the adult education program; but the important reason that prompted me to enroll is so that I can read sign posts and to know where I am when I travel or visit other places.

The latter participant's attitude is supported by Stromquist's (1997) assertion (discussed earlier) that literacy increases an individual's sense of mobility and freedom. Conversely, lack of literacy can be quite limiting, particularly in contemporary contexts.

There was a perceived relationship between literacy and self-worth among virtually all the participants in the study. One non-literate participant reported that she deliberately avoids social events that involve the active participation of literate women because they tend to dominate such events:

> *It* [lack of literacy] *makes me to withdraw because there are things your mates will say and if you do not respond very sensibly, they will say that if you had gone to school, you would not have responded the way you did. They do not say it directly to you. They just whisper among themselves. That is very embarrassing. The only illiterate women they listen to are old women. I think they respect the age of the women.*

This attitude is reminiscent of the findings of Klassen's (1987) study, which implicates literacy in people's sense of inclusion and exclusion. Interestingly, despite the statement of this participant, many of the non-literate participants informed me that they often sought the advice of their literate peers on certain issues because they considered them to be much more knowledgeable in many aspects of life.

Early marriages

A common personal impact of illiteracy which has some bearing on the self-perceptions of the non-literate women is early marriage, although most conceded that they were too young to appreciate the implications at the time. What seemed obvious then, according to their account, was that they had no career to look forward to and so marriage appeared to be the logical and inevitable option. In their view, had they gone to school, the number of years required to complete even basic schooling would have meant getting married much later than they did.

While the non-literate group reported early marriages, many before the age of 20, the literate group reported getting married between the ages of 20 and 25. All cited schooling as the reason for the higher age at marriage. Indeed, at the time of the field work, several of the literate informants were well over the age of 25, but were still single. They reported being more concerned about furthering their education than about marriage. Perhaps because of their relative financial independence, they had more ways to seek their status and self-validation than just through family roles as wives and mothers. This kind of attitude toward marriage is particularly instructive if one considers the social stigma that is typically attached to women who remain single past their early twenties within the local culture.

Although attitudes are beginning to change (Egbo, 2000), a major problem affecting women's school attendance in Nigeria and elsewhere in sub-Saharan Africa is indeed the practice of early marriage. It is not unusual for girls to get married at the age of 12. In some communities, girls' education is considered a wasteful undertaking for parents because of the belief that the 'benefits' accruing from such an investment would be reaped by someone else after marriage (Etta, 1994). It is also believed

that women eventually settle down to raising children rather than participate in the formal wage sector where educational qualifications are
required (UNESCO, 1991; WIN, 1985). Such ideological views of the value
of women's education are, undoubtedly, residues of colonial discriminatory literacy and educational practices (Egbo, 2000).

Self-esteem

Perhaps as a direct consequence of the low valuation of their work, the
non-literate women tended to see themselves as dependent on their
husbands. For instance, despite the fact that they provide for a good part
of the essential survival needs of their families, most had difficulty admit-
ting this, opting rather to say that they played only 'supportive roles.'
According to them, the powerful position men occupy within their
households means that women can only play subordinate roles. Such
perceptions of their position at home and in the wider community are
indicative of hegemonic processes at work and appear to have become
part of their *habitus*, to borrow Bourdieu's (1991) terminology.

In contrast, the literate women reported feeling empowered enough to
control their own destinies within boundaries *they* set themselves, even
though such boundaries may coincide with prevailing societal norms.
Most considered themselves autonomous individuals and reported that
they often challenge male authority whenever they feel that there is a
need to do so. They had no difficulty reporting that they played equal
and, in some instances, greater financial roles than their husbands within
their households. This does not mean, however, that the literate participants of this study have achieved social parity with the men in their
communities. What my findings show is that, on a continuum, literate
women are able to negotiate power relations within their households
much more successfully than their non-literate peers. It would appear
that, when women are more economically independent (as the literate
participants in the study), there is a tendency toward greater autonomy
and power within their households regardless of the overall societal
perceptions of women.

Perceptions of women as a group

Much has been written about the marginal status of women in sub-
Saharan Africa. As a consequence, one of the goals of the study was to find
out women's views on the issue from their own perceptions. My findings
show that a distinct dichotomy exists between attitudes toward both
groups of women in both local communities. The general perception is

that literate women are much more knowledgeable even in mundane community matters. One literate participant describes why and how this happens:

> *being literate has given me some knowledge and wisdom. It has also exposed me to the community . . . There are some things that may be happening in the community. Being a literate person, they call on me to help explain and help them understand. . . . I enlighten them by telling them whether or not the thing is good or bad . . . that way they [the community members involved] learn from me.*

During my discussions with the women, there was some evidence of attitudinal biases from the kind of language each group used to describe the other. While my intention here is not to conduct a formal discourse analysis, the use of certain words, particularly by the literate women, did imply a subtle psychological and social distance between both groups of women. The phrase 'these women' was often used pejoratively by the literate women in reference to their non-literate peers. It was clear during the interviews that non-literate women are often considered 'backward.' This attitude is perhaps the result of the differential social spaces both groups of women occupy within their communities. From their own accounts, non-literate women are quite aware of this 'elitist' attitude by some literate women and feel stigmatized. The compounding effect is a further erosion of their self-esteem as they consider themselves inadequate even among other women.

To further explore how the women assess their own conditions, one strategy adopted in this study was to find out from each group of women their perceptions of the living conditions and status of women in general. This revealed not only additional information about participants' perceptions of their own individual situations and identities, but also their views on the social condition and quality of life of the other group. Most of the women stated that, in general, women are the subordinate gender in their communities, but that some fare better than others. Both groups of participants believe that the literate women have higher status because they constitute a visible 'elite' group, while non-literate women are less visible and more prone to being discriminated against in important community gatherings.

Non-literate women and literacy-related activities

Another area where lack of literacy appears to have had some bearing on the non-literate women's psychological well-being relates to reading and writing letters. Because they cannot read or write, it is not unusual for the women to go into the community looking for someone to read or write letters for them, either because their husbands are not willing to do so, or because they do not want their husbands to know the contents of the letter. The women consider this loss of privacy a constant reminder of the impact of illiteracy on their personal lives:

> *Whenever I receive a letter from one of my children, I look for someone to read it for me. Sometimes, I give it to a young child to read. I have to accept whatever the person tells me, because I cannot verify what is written in the letter. The same thing happens when I want to write a letter. I tell the person what I want to say in Igbo and they write it down in English. When the content of the letter is confidential, you have to be careful who you ask to read or write for you.*

This participant also stated that, while she has learned to cope with the situation, frustration sets in when she asks the 'scribe' (in the case of letter-writing) to recap the contents and finds that what she had dictated had been wrongly translated, thus giving an entirely different meaning from that which she intended.

(Re)negotiating Power Relations

An important goal of this study was to determine whether or not female literacy influences power relations within the household. The view that women's often peripheral position within the domestic sphere is at once the catalyst and reflection of their status in society is well established among feminist scholars. Glenn (1987) for instance, argues that:

> [Any] debate about women's place in the family is actually a debate about *women's place in society* [emphasis mine]. We cannot compre-hend women's subordination within the labor market [for instance] without taking into account the organization of household labor. . . . Nor can we understand the exclusion of women from centers of public political power without referring to their encapsulation within the family. (p. 348)

Arguing from Glenn's assertion, it seems logical to assume that the enhancement of women's status within the household would, in all like-lihood, ameliorate their marginal status in larger society.

The literature on family decision-making asserts that education has an impact on the balance of power in familial decision-making (see Kasarda *et al.*, 1986, for an excellent review of the literature). While it is not exactly clear how this happens, as views in academic literature are divergent, one particular version that offers a plausible explanation is the Theory of Resources in relation to marital power (Rodman, 1972). Briefly, Rodman's reconstitution of an original theory by Blood and Wolfe (1960) suggests that the more resources a partner brings into a marital union, the more likely the chance that the individual will have some power within the union. While I have presented a very truncated account of Rodman's theory, it is significant to our discussion here because Rodman includes education and income among the so-called empowering assets.

Thus, access to literacy and education offers a woman more options in life, including entry into the formal labor market. The resulting income, an important asset, provides her with more independence, leverage, and subsequently more power to influence decisions within the household (Kasarda *et al.*, 1986; Rodman, 1972). This ability to influence decisions tilts the balance of power closer to the center. Kasarda *et al.* summarize the argument in this way:

> A married woman's entry into the labor force does much to alter her position in the household. Gainful employment allows a woman to contribute financially to the operation of her household, thereby providing her with a sense of independence and more power than a non-working woman to influence family decisions. . . . Moreover, when women work, they are more likely to perceive themselves as better able to manage their own lives. (1986: 123)

The benefit of literacy in terms of increased participation in household decision-making was reported by the literate women in this study. Both groups of participants claimed that literate rural women have more decision-making power within their households because of the visible economic role they play. The non-literate women in the sample argued that such roles narrow the power gap in the union, enabling more collaborative decision-making between the spouses. Among the participants there was a perceived relationship between literacy, women's economic independence, and their degree of participation in household decision-making, much like Kasarda *et al.*'s (1986) analysis above. Ironically, most of the non-literate women in the study are not, in reality, economically dependent on their husbands since they contribute substantially to the sustenance of their families through their income-generating activities in the informal labor sector (predominantly farming-related). The difference between the non-literate women and their literate peers is that their struggles for the survival of their families yield less-tangible economic rewards because of their distance from formal means of production.

There are, however, some contradictory research findings with regard to the linkages between women's education and their status within the household. In a study conducted among urban and rural households in south-western Nigeria, for instance, Hollos (1998: 271) reports that some educated urban women were less empowered within the domestic sphere as a result of 'increasing submission to their husbands and a decline in their autonomy,' even though they were employed in the formal wage sector. Hollos (1998) attributes this limited status to the fact that the urban educated woman, although economically active, contributes fewer resources than her husband and therefore becomes subsumed as one of his dependents. However, like the present study, that study also shows that participation in household decision-making increased significantly with spousal economic contribution to the unit.

One interesting corroborating piece of evidence with regard to decision-making within the participants' households deserves mention here. With very few exceptions, the non-literate informants insisted that I ask for their husbands' permission before they could participate in the study. In some instances, I first had to explain the purpose of the study to their husbands. Curiously, once permission had been granted, the husbands seemed proud that their wives were part of such a project. I do not recall any of the literate women requiring their husbands' permission to participate in the study. In instances where I had pre-interview discussions with husbands, they were encouraging and generally interested in the study per se, rather than in the potential implications of their wives' participation, as was probably the concern of the husbands of the non-literate group. My conclusion, then, was that the husbands of the literate women believed in their wives' ability to make such judgments for themselves.

Group Consciousness and Social Political Action

As discussed at the beginning of the chapter, a vexing issue for feminists who query the enabling power of literacy is the chequered success it has had in engendering women-friendly social reconstruction in Africa. Indeed, some of the questions that framed this study included those that have to do with the participants' perceptions (as critical stakeholders) of the limits and possibilities of literacy. For example, to what extent did access to literacy raise the consciousness of the women to the point of changing unwanted social realities? My findings are quite revealing in this regard. From personal observations, interviews with the women and informal discussions with members of community, I found out that most of the women who were actively involved in causes that were geared toward the advancement of the status of women in both research communities were literate women. Many of them believe that their contributions to the socioeconomic development of their communities as well as their advocacy are only possible because they had gone to school. They maintained that literacy had given them 'license' to lead their peers, and to make demands from, and be heard by, male community leaders most of whom are themselves literate. As one participant, a teacher and community activist, puts it:

> *Being literate makes one powerful in the community . . . it has also helped me to earn my living. It gives me some status within the community and enables me to participate in the development of my community. It helps me to mobilize the women in so many areas. Without being literate, I wouldn't be able to do so.*

Almost without exception, the participants reported that literate women, many of them teachers, were leading the efforts to eradicate certain cultural practices, which in their view constitute gender-based oppression. The rite of widowhood, during which women are subjected to difficult traditional rituals, is a case in point. Some of the literate women in one community reported that, at one point, they had actually mobilized their peers to write petitions to community leaders about abolishing the practice. Such a move is no small feat considering the potential sanctions the women could have faced. While the likelihood of succeeding in their advocacy is debatable, the degree of conscientization among the women was quite apparent. I found that many of the literate women were questioning the realities of their existence and challenging the structural forces (including cultural practices) that they perceived as oppressive. Thus, while cultural and traditional dogmas may not often allow them to make needed changes as quickly as they would like to, they appear to know that choices exist and that, if they are so inclined, they can make those choices. This finding returns the discussion back to Bee's (1993) view, shared in the present paper, of an empowering literacy as that which serves simultaneously as a catalyst for women's economic independence and as a tool that provides them with a framework for deconstructing and challenging their social condition.

One unexpected and intriguing finding related to female advocacy in the local communities is the opposition from other women that female activists face. One activist reported that, while some of them were leading the move to abolish certain undesirable traditional practices, others, mostly non-literate elderly women, were thwarting their efforts.

She explains the difficulties she and other women encountered in their attempts to stop the rites of widowhood:

> *We have been trying to stop it, but the women have not agreed. There was a time we held a meeting in this community. We were all invited and the question was raised as to what should be done by us (women) to remove us from this bondage* [rites of widowhood]. *Some women said they would fight to abolish it, but some refused, saying that it was handed down to them by their mothers and that since their mothers had observed such rituals, they too are bound to do the same.*

This finding underscores the difficulties and contradictions that are inherent in the complex process of negotiating social identities as individuals struggle with the tension between their autonomous self, the extent of their identification with collectivities, e.g. solidarity among women (Papanek, 1994), and their appropriation of identity options that are available to them as social actors, i.e. the tension between 'me' and 'we' (Thoits & Virshup,1997; van Knippenberg, 1999).

Conclusions

A key stance adopted in this study is that, juxtaposed with critical social policies, literacy can empower women in Nigeria and sub-Saharan Africa more generally. Admittedly, it is not a panacea for all the social problems women and other marginalized groups in that part of the world face. Indeed, it is quite logical to argue that any view that sees literacy as the sole vehicle for transforming women's social condition in Africa and elsewhere in the world is rather myopic. At the same time, literacy appears to be a necessary prerequisite for enabling women, through increases in their knowledge base which allow them to better understand their social, political, and material world, with a possibility of reconstructing that world and their social identities. The account presented here shows that literacy can indeed enable women to (re)negotiate their individual and social identities in empowering ways. Although there was no evidence that access to literacy provided my literate informants with ligatures in any substantive way since there were no organized alliances, there was evidence that it increased their options. Even though, relatively speaking, women remain excluded from the official administration of their communities, literate women by virtue of the informal leadership role they play in their communities constitute a visible and forceful group. My findings suggest that, while access to literacy may not completely eliminate deep-rooted patriarchal ideologies and repressive and gendered cultural practices, it does neutralize or at least minimize the impact, thus bringing women closer to the center from the margins.

In contrast, lack of literacy seems to have contributed to the diminution of the self-image of the non-literate women. Phrases like 'I feel cheated,' 'I feel inferior,' and 'I feel as if I am blind' were commonly used in their personal descriptions of their condition and seemed to be an integral part of how they saw themselves. It is my view that, in most societies in sub-Saharan Africa, certainly in Nigeria, women have always contributed to the development of their communities; what they lack is the power to put them in a position to institutionalize and legitimize that role. A starting point for that process is a profound analysis of their social positioning as well as an understanding of the repressive structures that impinge on their lives. Access to literacy appears to be a powerful catalyst for such scrutiny.

References

Ballara, M. (1992) *Women and literacy*. New Jersey: Zed Books.

Bee, B. (1993) Critical literacy and the politics of gender. In C. Lankshear and P. McLaren (eds) *Critical literacy: Politics, praxis, and the postmodern* (pp. 105–131). Albany, NY: State University of New York Press.

Bernstein, B. (1977) *Class, codes and control, Vol. 3: Towards a theory of educational transmission* (2nd edn). London: Routledge and Kegan Paul.

Bhaskar, R. (1986) *Scientific realism and human emancipation*. London: Verso.

Bhaskar, R. (1989) *Reclaiming reality: A critical introduction to contemporary philosophy*. London: Verso.

Blackledge, A. (2000) *Literacy, power and social justice*. Stoke-on-Trent: Trentham Books.

Blood, R. and Wolfe, D. (1960) *Husbands and wives: The dynamics of married living*. New York: Free Press.

Bourdieu, P. (1991) *Language and symbolic power*. Cambridge: Polity Press.

Bourdieu, P. and Passeron, J. (1977) *Reproduction in education, society and culture*. London: Sage Publications.

Chlebowska, K. (1990) *Literacy for rural women in the Third World*. Belgium: UNESCO.

Corby, R. (1990) Educating Africans for inferiority under British rule: Bo school in Sierra Leone. *Comparative Education Review* 34 (3), 314–349.

Corson, D. (1993) *Language, minority education and gender: Linking social justice and power*. Clevedon: Multilingual Matters.

Corson, D. (1995) Discursive power in educational organizations: An introduction. In D. Corson (ed.) *Discourse and power in educational organizations* (pp. 3–15). Toronto: OISE Press.

Dahrendorf, R. (1979) *Life chances*. Chicago: University of Chicago Press.

Egbo, B. (1997) Female literacy and life chances in rural Nigeria. In V. Edwards (ed.) *Literacy* (pp. 215–223). Boston: Kluwer Academic Publishers.

Egbo, B. (2000) *Gender, literacy and life chances in Sub-Saharan Africa.* Clevedon: Multilingual Matters.

Etta, F. (1994) Gender issues in contemporary African education. *African Development* 19 (4), 57–84.

Foucault, M. (1980) *Power/knowledge: Selected interviews and other writings 1971–1977.* New York: Pantheon Books.

Freire, P. (1970) *Pedagogy of the oppressed.* New York: Herder and Herder.

Freire, P. and Macedo, D. (1995) A dialogue: Culture, language and race. *Harvard Educational Review* 65 (3), 377–402.

Glenn, E. (1987) Gender and family. In B. Hess and M. Ferree (eds) *Analyzing gender: A handbook of social science research* (pp. 348–380). Newbury Park: Sage Publications.

Gramsci, A. (1971) *Selections from the prison notebooks.* New York: International Publishers.

Hollos, M. (1998) The status of women in Southern Nigeria: Is education a help or a hindrance? In M. Bloch, J. Beoku-Betts, and R. Tabachnick (eds) *Women and education in Sub-Saharan Africa.* Boulder: Lynne Rienner Publishers.

Hughes, J. (1990) *The philosophy of social science research* (2nd edn). London: Longman.

Kasarda, J., Billy, J., and West, K. (1986) *Status enhancement and fertility: Reproductive responses to social mobility and educational opportunity.* Orlando: Academic Press Inc.

Klassen, C. (1987) *Language and literacy learning: The adult immigrant's account.* MA thesis, University of Toronto.

Kuhn, T. (1970) *The structure of scientific revolutions* (2nd edn). Chicago: University of Chicago Press.

Lankshear, C. and McLaren, P. (eds) (1993) *Critical literacy: Politics, praxis, and the postmodern.* Albany, NY: State University of New York Press.

Luke, A. (1994) On reading and the sexual division of literacy. *Journal of Curriculum Studies* 26 (4), 361–381.

Marshall, J. (1993) *Literacy, power and democracy in Mozambique.* Boulder, CO: Westview Press.

McCarthey, S. (2001) Identity construction in elementary readers and writers. *Reading Research Quarterly* 36 (2), 122–147.

Merriam, S. (1988) *Case study research in education: A qualitative approach.* San Francisco: Jossey-Bass Inc.

Odora, C. (1993) *Educating girls in a context of patriarchy and transformation: A theoretical and conceptual analysis.* Masters thesis, Institute of International Education, Stockholm University.

Papanek, H. (1994) The ideal woman and the ideal society: Control and autonomy in the construction of identity. In V. Moghadam (ed.) *Identity politics and women: Cultural reassertions and feminism in international perspectives* (pp. 42–75). Boulder, CO: Westview Press.

Parajuli, P. and Enslin, E. (1990) From learning literacy to regenerating women's space: A story of women's empowerment in Nepal. *Convergence* 23 (1), 44–47.

Rockhill, K. (1993) (Dis)connecting literacy and sexuality: Speaking the unspeakable in the classroom. In C. Lankshear and P. McLaren (eds) *Critical literacy:*

Politics, praxis, and the postmodern (pp. 335–366). Albany, NY: State University of New York Press.

Rodman, H. (1972) Marital power and the theory of resources in cultural context. *Journal of Comparative Family Studies* 3 (1), 50–69.

Street, B. (1993) (ed.) *Cross-cultural approaches to literacy.* Cambridge: Cambridge University Press.

Stromquist, N. (1990) Women and illiteracy: The interplay of gender, subordination and poverty. *Comparative Education Review* 34 (1), 95–111.

Stromquist, N. (1997) *Literacy for citizenship: Gender and grassroots dynamics in Brazil.* New York: State University of New York Press.

Thoits, P. and Virshup, L. (1997) Me's and we's: Forms and functions of social identities. In R. Ashmore and L. Jussim (eds) *Self and identity* (pp.106–133). New York: Oxford University Press.

UNESCO (1991) *World education report.* Paris: UNESCO.

United Nations (1991) *Women: Challenges to the year 2000.* New York: United Nations.

van Knippenberg, A. (1999) Social identity and persuasion: Reconsidering the role of group membership. In D. Abrams and M. Hogg (eds) *Social identity and social cognition: An introduction* (pp. 315–331). Malden: Blackwell Publishers.

Women in Nigeria (WIN) (1985) *Women in Nigeria today.* Zaria, Nigeria: Ahmadu Bello University.

Chapter 9
Multilingual Writers and the Struggle for Voice in Academic Discourse

SURESH CANAGARAJAH

Introduction

The philosophical rethinking and empirical efforts to understand the representations of self in social life have initiated much-needed changes in second language acquisition (SLA) and English as a second language (ESL) pedagogies. From focusing on the abstract grammar system and treating learners as a bundle of psychological reflexes, scholars have begun to consider how learners negotiate competing subject positions in conflicting discourse communities. As a former ESL student, I am personally encouraged by this 'social turn' in applied linguistics. After being treated as non-entities in SLA research and feeling silenced, we ESL students have now achieved complexity, with researchers straining their ears to catch every inflection and modulation in our 'voice.' After being theorized and objectified, imposed with flat stereotypical identities, we see ourselves celebrated as hybrid subjects who defy analysis.

This exhilarating time of fresh thinking and research has generated new paradigms for the study of subjectivity in our field. SLA has become very interdisciplinary, borrowing constructs from disciplines as diverse as philosophy, rhetoric, literary criticism, and the social sciences. We see different theoretical positions adopted by researchers studying identity these days – i.e. Foucauldian poststructuralism, Bakhtinian semiotics, feminist scholarship, and language socialization, to name just a few. As part of our disciplinary shift we have a confusing array of terms and tools for our analysis. In recent conferences and publications, I find scholars using constructs such as the following: identities (and their qualified variants, linguistic identity, cultural identity, national identity, the 'scientist researcher' identity, and ghetto identity – which are not all on a par), identity positioning, subjectivity, subject positions, ranks, roles, selves, and voice. Even the most theoretically sophisticated researchers would have problems navigating their way through the incommensurate constructs used to study identity or developing an integrated perspective out of the diverse movements contributing to this discourse. These problems would be even more keenly felt by practitioners who need clarity in the field to facilitate the linguistic negotiations of the students in their classrooms. Before comparing some of the strategies used by multilingual students to strive for voice in academic writing, I have to define my orientation to self.

Towards an Analytical Model

Though the field may appear confusing, we do share some basic assumptions about human subjects now. There is an evolving consensus in orientating to selfhood as multiple, conflictual, negotiated, and evolving. We have travelled far from the assumptions up to the 1980s, when the self was treated as static, unitary, discrete, and given. The following assumptions – deriving from schools like poststructuralism, postcolonialism, social constructionism, and feminism[1] – are now widely shared in the field of applied linguistics:

- that the self is shaped considerably by language and discourses;
- that the self is composed of multiple subjectivities, deriving from the heterogeneous codes, registers, and discourses that are found in society;
- that these subjectivities enjoy unequal status and power, deriving from differential positioning in socio-economic terms;
- that, because of these inequalities, there is conflict within and between subjects;
- that, in order to find coherence and empowerment, the subject has to negotiate these competing identities and subject positions in relation to the changing discursive and material contexts.

I define voice as a manifestation of one's agency in discourse through the means of language. This largely rhetorically constructed manifestation of selfhood has to be negotiated in relation to our historically defined *identities* (such as race, ethnicity, and nationality), institutional *roles* (like student, teacher, and administrator in the educational institution), and ideological *subjectivity* (i.e. our positioning according to discourses such as 'responsible citizen/lazy immigrant/dependent foreigner,' or 'authoritative native-speaker/blundering non-native speaker,' which embody values according to the dominant ideologies in the society). These three constructs – identity, role, and subjectivity – which are largely extra-linguistic (because they are relatively less linguistically constituted compared to voice) can be imposed on us or ascribed to us. But it is at the level of *voice* that we gain agency to negotiate these categories of the self, adopt a reflexive awareness of them, and find forms of coherence and power that suit our interests. Related to this exercise of agency is the fact that, while the other three constructs are largely macro-social (experi-enced at the level of history, society, and ideology respectively), voice manifests itself in micro-social contexts of personal communication. It is at the micro-social level of everyday life and linguistic interactions that one is able to resist, modify, or negotiate the larger social structures. Language is especially suited for this function as its heterogeneity, hybridity, and polyvalence provide the resources for subjects to resist impositions of any kind.

The struggle for voice in relation to the selfhood imposed by macro-social and extralinguistic constructs is explained by Foucault (1972) as the conflict that we always have between instinct and institution. 'Institution' represents established or preordained selves that are historically, socially, and ideologically established. Taking on these selves results, for Foucault, in a form of silencing. This is because the 'voices' represented are those of dominant institutions and discourses. The temptation, in this context, is to abandon all forms of ready-made discourses and speak with 'instinct' – i.e. one's true voice. But this pre-linguistic, extra-discursive, asocial construct (instinct) is a myth. We cannot speak outside discourses. The challenge therefore is this: although we cannot speak outside discourses and institutions, we should not conform to them wholesale. We have to negotiate a position in the interstices of discourses and institutions to find our own niche that represents our values and interests favorably. This is how we construct a voice for ourselves.

A pragmatic question that comes up in this kind of analysis is whether there is room for writers to negotiate an independent voice in academic discourse. We must acknowledge that academic writing has clearly defined and often rigidly imposed conventions. Writers who deviate from the established conventions find their articles rejected by journals. Students who deviate may receive a failing grade. But my position is that discourses and institutions cannot be totally deterministic. There is always room to negotiate, modify, and reconfigure – if not resist – dominant discourses (see Canagarajah, 1999a,c). However, negotiat-ing dominant discourses is a creative and constructive process. It cannot be done haphazardly. One cannot write without any relevance to the established discourses. The dominant conventions have to be taken seriously and reworked sensitively in order to find acceptance. If we remember that, even among rhetorically conservative teachers, it is not a slavish parroting of a discourse, but 'fresh' and 'original' writing, that is preferred, we can understand that there is space for one's voice in the dominant discourses.

Research Orientation

The objective of this paper is to examine the diverse strategies adopted by multilingual writers for voice in relation to the identities they bring with them and the roles and subjectivities established in mainstream educational institutions. I focus specifically on academic writing. My interest is in comparing the strategies emerging from academic essays of novice and established multilingual writers to develop a typology that may help teachers understand their potential for critical expression.[2] In a field that is becoming highly interpretive, we have many case studies that describe the strategies adopted by multilingual academic writers (see, for example, Belcher, 1997; Belcher & Connor, 2001; Kramsch, 2000; Li, 1999). But we need a comparative perspective that integrates such examples to develop an understanding of useful approaches.

The texts of novice writers that I analyze (those of Irina, Sri, and Viji below) come from classroom ethnographies I have conducted with ESL students in Sri Lanka and the United States. The texts of expert writers (those of Li, Connor, and Suseendirarajah) are those of well-acquainted multilingual colleagues who have discussed their writing strategies in conversations with me. In analyzing these texts I go beyond the usual structuralist analysis of such schools as Text Linguistics (see de Beaugrande & Dressler, 1981) or Genre Analysis (see Swales, 1990). I bring to bear the information I have of the social and cultural location of these writers to interpret their strategies. John Swales' (1998) neologism for a method he was using for his description of disciplinary literacies comes close to the methodology I have adopted. *Textography* is an interpretation of texts in the light of ethnographic information: 'something more than a disembodied textual or discoursal analysis, but something less than a full ethnographic account' (Swales, 1998: 1).

Another method that influences my analysis is Dwight Atkinson's (1999) *rhetorical analysis*, which situates texts in sociohistorical context and uses interpretive frameworks from different disciplines. Atkinson elaborates that this mode of analysis is eclectic, multidisciplinary, contextual, bottom-up, and genre-sensitive. Focusing on texts and literacy practices,

I marshal social and cultural information to complement my analysis. Reading these essays closely in the context of the genre conventions for academic writing, similar to those described by Swales (1990) for research articles, I attempt to identify the strategies manifested by the writers. Analytical orientations from literary criticism are useful as much as genre analysis, in keeping with the eclectic, multidisciplinary orientation encouraged by Atkinson's rhetorical analysis model. There is a frank acceptance in this kind of research that rhetorical analysis is a highly interpretive activity. The focus of my interpretation is on how writers adopt a position between the established academic conventions and the non-academic discourses they bring with them (from their homes, communities, nationality, or race).

Writing and Identity

The interplay between different dimensions of our self has considerable implications for writing. Rather than thinking of texts as simply reflecting a pre-linguistic and pre-defined subjectivity, we must consider how selfhood is constructed in the process of writing. Writing itself is a linguistic activity that shapes the self in complicated ways. We textually construct images of the self that appeal to us and display to our readers the types of identity that are to our advantage in specific communicative situations. In fact, writing has special resources that are suitable for negotiating identities effectively. Considering the texts of expert multilingual writers, Kramsch and Lam discern the power these authors experience in creating alternate textual identities to resolve the conflicts they face in the competing languages:

> Written texts offer non-native speakers opportunities for finding textual homes outside the boundaries of local or national communities. . . . Indeed they make non-nativeness in the sense of 'outsideness' one of the most important criteria for creativity and innovation'. (1999: 71)

It is easy to understand how writing can create a safe haven from the identity conflicts one experiences in society in everyday life. Not engaged in face-to-face communication, non-native students have the detachment and relative freedom to construct (sometimes playfully) alternate identities to transcend the conflicts they experience in social life.

Asking my ESL students about their attitudes to writing compared to speaking in English, I was surprised to find that they all preferred writing (see Canagarajah, 1999b). Among the reasons they gave were the following:

- speech accent (which draws attention to their non-nativeness) is not foregrounded in their writing;
- lacking the necessity to be spontaneous, they had the freedom to plan and craft the text in the ways they desired;
- writing gave them more scope for control in communication (i.e. they can choose to submit or destroy the text they had produced);
- as the principal is somewhat detached from the text (unlike in face-to-face oral communication), one could animate alternate identities (sometimes playfully) without the need to tie oneself rigidly to one's ascribed ethnic/race/national identities;
- writing gave more scope for collaboration and help in text construction, unlike speech which is more individual.

Multilingual students thus recognize that writing provides some interesting avenues and resources for the construction of a more empowering sense of self.[3]

Avoidance

This doesn't mean that all writers will realize texts that represent their identities in empowering forms. Much depends on their specific motivation in writing and having the linguistic resources to realize their interests. To appreciate the conflicts and negotiations taking place in the writing self, consider the following essay by Irina, an ESL student from Ukraine in my class in New York, that provided the above interview data. This is an end-of-term reflective essay titled by her as 'My experience with ESL at X college':

> When I first faced the WAT [writing assessment test] in August I spoke English good enough to communicate in. But I did not know how to write a good essay. That is not that I could not write or I did not know the letters, that is just I did not know much about the structure and developing of the American essay. So, I decided: 'I should take the ESL class.' Obviously, I did not pass my first WAT.
>
> On the first day in my ESL class I understood that I was in a right place. In a first time I got to know that each essay is suppose to have thesis statement, which consist the main idea of the essay. To my surprise, I've got to know that thesis statement is not the last thing that we have in the essay. Also, there are a few paragraphs accompanied by topic sentences. And I have to tell those knowledge were amazing and useful to achieve. It may sound silly that someone who is an adult doesn't know simple things about writing. But I really did

not know, just because in Ukraine we do not write in same way as we do here.

After I started write essays as I was taught in America I found that writing was not simple. I had to keep things relevant to each other, prove my thesis statement and given reasons. Thus, the second thing what I understood that I had to read a lot in order to gain a lot of information, examples, ideas (about different topics) which would help me to write my essays. I started paying more attention to what I was listening in the news, reading in newspapers and watching in T.V. In a few weeks later I knew pretty much about private life of selebraties, ruling of American governmen, rate of abortions in U.S., percentage of divorces in NY, level of medical treatment of eldery people and a lot more.

My next and important step was to utilize gathered information in my essays. Successfully or not, it is up to the teacher to grade my work, but I really tryed to do my best.

Moreover, a group work, which was provided by the teacher, helped me to understand meaning of the given passages, which some-times were very confusing. Also, from group work I obtained a lot of different ideas and opinions.

Besides, I've made so many friends in my ESL class that I do not have in any other classes. I care about everybody in my ESL group as they are my own sisters and brothers.

I would say that everybody who feels like to get some knowledge in writing should attend ESL classes. This is the only class where you can get an answer on any questions that you have about writing, also, individual help from a teacher, which you can hardly expect in regular English classes. I was fully satisfied with my ESL class.

We see in the writer a conflict between past and present identities. From her past experiences of schooling and life in Ukraine, there is a progression in acquiring a new identity as a person who is knowledge-able about American culture and lifestyle. There is also the assumption that the American style of writing should be known by everyone. Hence her apology for not knowing these constructs even though she is 'an adult.' Many factors in her background could explain Irina's adoption of this discourse. Even though she had to write essays in Russian and Ukrainian literature classes in her schools in Ukraine, she has not been formally taught expository writing (as is true of many other countries outside the United States where 'composition' is not an institutionalized or professionalized activity). At the same time, her bilingual education exposed her to both Ukrainian and Russian expository discourse. Also, as a member of the local Ukrainian community, she would have shared its oral discourse values.[4] What is interesting is that these other discourses from her background don't actively/consciously inform her use of American academic conventions.

In representing this progression from her past to the present, Irina adopts the 'good student' role. She represents herself as a student who is highly motivated to learn English and writing – someone who is prepared to do hard work, appreciates the course, and benefits from the instructor and her fellow students. In a course that is graded, where the teacher is the primary audience for one's writing, it is to be expected that Irina will find this role advantageous to her. In deploying these roles and identities somewhat consciously, Irina unwittingly takes on other subjectivities valued in this community. For example, she takes on the ethos of a person who succeeds through hard work. Of course, this is the dominant liberal democratic ideology of individualism – so different from the traditional Marxist ideology of collective empowerment that has been (stereotypically) associated with the former Soviet system that Irina comes from. She also seems to invoke the 'multiculturalist discourse' that is popular in American academia (and to some extent in the former Soviet Union, which attempted to incorporate many different nationalities). She is happy to have interacted with culturally diverse students, whom she considers 'my own sisters and brothers.'

What is more important is the way Irina negotiates these roles, identities, and subjectivities to construct a voice for herself in the essay. Irina chooses to accommodate to the dominant discourses and institutions in order to get approval and respect from the instructor. It is understandable that, since this course is graded, Irina is under compulsion to satisfy the dominant discourses and institutions. In the process, she fails to resolve some of the tensions in her text. Though she adopts the multiculturalism discourse in showing respect for students from other cultures, she doesn't seem to develop a respect for her native Ukrainian and Russian discursive backgrounds. She is also diffident about claiming success in her education, as she hedges tentatively: 'Successfully or not, it is up to the teacher to grade my work, but I really tryed to do my best.' Despite the grammar problems, she constructs a decent set of paragraphs to claim a voice for herself. One can only imagine how a more creative and independent voice could have been constructed if she had wrestled with the competing discourses more directly. It would have made a difference to the essay if she had attempted to bring more actively her Ukrainian identity and negotiated her English writing with her native discourses (from diverse sources, including Russian and Ukrainian prose tradition, and local oral traditions). After all, instructors are more impressed with writing that comes out of a more rigorous and frank engagement with one's conflicting selves. Though Irina knows this (having associated with me for a whole semester), the product oriented final examination system in this institution (graded by unknown instructors) perhaps pressures her to adopt the safe approach of representing the dominant notions of the self in the academic context. Also, the excitement of learning expository writing formally for the first time would have blunted the strength of the alternate discourses she brings with her from her home. I call this strategy 'avoidance' as this is a somewhat one-sided move to the dominant discourses without sufficient negotiation with the other discourses one uses. Also, the move to the academic discourse is done as a default position, in situations where the writer doesn't wish to wrestle critically with competing discourses.

Transposition

To illustrate more effective ways of negotiating discursive tensions, we have to go to the professional writing of multilingual scholars who are under less institutional pressure to conform than students categorized as remedial. Xiao-Ming Li (1999) narrates how she has struggled with her non-nativeness in English all her educational life. Though she has reached the position of being published in academic and journalistic circles in English, she still considers herself 'non-native' in English academic literacy. But she has now matured to the position of looking at this tension as an advantage. She considers her non-nativeness as providing her with a critical vantage position, just as her English educational background provides her with unique insights into her native Chinese language and culture. She states:

> To honor one's own voice is both liberating and challenging. Each writing becomes an exploration of the world and self, and a constant wrestling with words to go beyond the ready and given. Yet the process is complicated by the fact that I am still a language learner and imitation is part of learning a new language. . . . But being a non-native speaker, I have learned, does give me the license to march to a different drum, to some extent. (Li, 1999: 50)

One might interpret the negotiation of her selves in the following way: though she has conflicting identities (Chinese and English), the roles she has had to play in American educational institutions as a successful and persevering student have motivated her to develop an alternate voice. In the process, she has also developed a critically informed subjectivity – one that is mutually detached from both Chinese ideologies and American discourses. Unlike Irina, who avoids these tensions, Li confronts them frankly and constructs a voice that benefits from her disadvantage, lack of proficiency, and alienation in the English-speaking academic context.

In a sense, the position articulated above by Li is what is theorized by Kramsch and Lam (1999: 70–71) as the 'third positions' of textual identities: 'the potential of written text to help non-native speakers define their relation toward the native speakers whose language they are using and to offer them what we [call] "textual identities of the third kind."' A case study I conducted on the writing of a scholar in Sri Lanka shows even more complex negotiation of discourses in the Research Article (RA) genre. I present below excerpts from two essays by a Tamil professor, both written in English, but for different academic communities. The first paper was presented in a local academic forum, while the other appeared in an international scholarly journal (published in the US). Suseendirarajah constructs a voice that is different from the preferred discourses of both communities, although it is clear that it is his competence in both discourses that gives him the resources to develop this critical voice.

The opening of the first paper, 'English in our Tamil society: A sociolinguistic appraisal' (Suseendirarajah, 1992), is somewhat narrative and informal. The author sets the scene well before beginning his sociolinguistic analysis. Though this opening resembles many of the academic papers written in Tamil (see Canagarajah, 2002a), his tone is a bit more objective in this paper. The paper begins with an announcement of his research objective:

> An attempt is made in this paper to present briefly the status and functions of English in the modern Sri Lankan Tamil society and to discuss the attitudes of different categories of people in the society towards English. As a preamble, a brief historical view of the position occupied by English during the past, especially before the independence of Sri Lanka is presented. Generally, the status and functions of English in the Sri Lankan society have been and are governed by the language policy of the government. The societal attitudes too have been responsible for the position of English todate.

The subsequent paragraphs in the introduction go on to distinguish sociolinguistic tendencies of different Sri Lankan communities. Though the paper adopts a narrative flow throughout, and develops views on bilingualism without empirical data, the author adopts a formal researcher-like prose in the conclusion:

> A separate detailed study of the status and functions of English in our universities both in academic as well as administrative sections will be a desideratum. A comparison of language use among universities may be useful to understand language trends and problems in our universities.

Though the body of the paper conforms to the largely narrative structure preferred in the local community (thus signalling the author's ethnic identity and conforming to the preferred roles in the local academy), it is not wholly so. The greater level of formalism in this paper (compared to the more narrative and impressionistic papers generally submitted in this forum in Tamil) is motivated by a need to instil a more disciplined and objective stance in local academic discourse. The author has written elsewhere of the need to adopt an empirical approach in local research activities, especially in those close to the interests of local culture, as monolingual Tamil scholars tend to be too emotionally involved and tradition-affirming in their scholarly work (see Suseendirarajah, 1991). The writer is therefore constructing a somewhat hybrid text for the local academic context. The more objective and analytical sections insert a new subjectivity into local discourse that challenges traditional ways of constructing knowledge. Thanks to his proficiency in English and research training in the West, the author is able to negotiate an independent footing and voice in the local academic discourse. The paper therefore makes a critical contribution in attempting to shift local conventions of knowledge-making in new directions. The critical new conventions he infuses into this discourse generate respect from the local community as Suseendirarajah is able to address the community as an insider who is proficient in the local discourses.

But consider a paper written for the western academic community. The paper titled 'Caste and language in Jaffna society' was published in the mainstream journal *Anthropological Linguistics* (Suseendirarajah, 1978). The introductory paragraph is uncharacteristically brief:

> The purpose of this paper is to correlate caste and language in the Jaffna Hindu Tamil society. This study is mainly based on data collected from a few sample villages in the Jaffna peninsula where the political and economic ascendancy of the VeLLaaLas (landlords) was very dominant in the recent past.

Unlike in his previous paper, where the introductory section runs to about five paragraphs, in this paper there are only two sentences for introduction. Recognizing that the relaxed and personal tone of local academic discourse may not be appreciated by the more focused western academic audience, he orchestrates the preferred roles and identities of the western research article.[5] But he still does this with a difference. The other obligatory features of introductions in RAs (see Swales, 1990) are not adopted. The need to create a niche for one's study after a thorough literature review of related studies and the announcement of one's main findings or thesis are not included by Suseendirarajah. Local academics feel that such an opening is too individualistic and aggressive, pitting the author's study against those of previous scholars. They also dislike the explicit and 'front-weighted' strategy of declaring one's thesis ahead of time (similar to the Finnish academic community described by Mauranen, 1993), preferring rather to respect the intelligence of the reader to work out the argument for themselves through the more implicit development of the paper (see Canagarajah, 2002a).

While the introductory section of the paper seems to accommodate somewhat the western conventions of RAs in its matter-of-factness, objectivity, and restraint, the body of *this* paper is a very detached citation of data. All this shows some deference to the preferred roles of the western academy. In the final paragraph, however, some aspects of the writer's discourse seem peculiar:

> In concluding, it may be said that man has awakened. He has a sense of human equality and humanity. He is for better change. Sooner or later we may miss most if not all of the sociolinguistic correlates recorded herein. They are on the verge of dying out.

The writer indulges here in a moralizing/moralistic discourse. Statements of this nature are often freely interspersed in the local academic writing. It is possible therefore that the writer is reacting here against an excessively depersonalized discourse that suppresses his identity. Though indulging in this discourse in other high-visibility sections of the paper, like the introduction or methodology, may prejudice the referees against publishing the paper, the writer strategically makes a space for it in the innocuous section of conclusion. Perhaps he is assuming that the editor/referees may be less critical of this discourse when it appears in this context. There are other minor ways in which the writer diverges from western RAs. Western scholars may have chosen to have a greater sense of closure in the final paragraph by summarizing the paper or identifying future areas of research (in fact, the writer does precisely this in his earlier paper to the local audience). Belanger (1982) prescribes such moves, following an empirical study of conclusions in RAs. But in this paper, preferring the more implicit development of his argument, the author expects the readers to infer his thesis with minimum authorial control.

The way to explain these divergences is that the writer is making critical adjustments as he writes for different communities. 'Critical,' because he wants to infuse his desired oppositional discourse into the established conventions of both communities. In fact, by using the discourse of the alternate communities he enjoys membership in, he is able to challenge each community strategically. This is precisely the advantage of our multiple memberships in discourse communities. We might say that his common institutional role as a researcher and academic influences him to take some conventions of academic discourse seriously (such as the objectivity and detachment in the introductory moves in the RA) in both his essays. But he uses his Sri Lankan identity to construct a resistant voice that builds some differences into the established discourse in the West. Similarly, he uses his bilingual identity to construct a voice that is different for the local community, encouraging a more empirical orientation to knowledge construction.

Accommodation

We mustn't forget that the outcome of discursive negotiation depends on the motivations and interests of each writer. Therefore, not everyone resolves the conflict in the way Li and Suseendirarajah do, even if they have the linguistic competence to do so. Ulla Connor (1999), reflecting on her bilingual writing experience, finds how she has quite deliberately moved from her Finnish identity to a distinctly American identity. Finnish identity is associated with restraint and reserve, while she experiences American writing as more aggressive and individualistic. After struggling to gain the latter discourse, aided by editorial help from her American husband and colleagues, she discovers during a furlough in her native Finland that she has indeed become very Americanized. Her Finnish colleagues discern the distance she has travelled during her writing experience away from home. Her comments on a Finnish colleague's work reveal her changed subjectivity:

> It's all fine text, but I find it incoherent in places. I expect the main point at the beginning of the paragraph. I expect a paragraph to contain examples about the main point – no jumping between several points. (Connor, 1999: 35)

Connor recognizes that these are the expectations of American academic rhetoric, different from the more relaxed and implicit style of the Finnish (and Sri Lankan) scholars. She decides soon after that experience to get American citizenship. What her experience exemplifies is the reverse situation of the examples discussed above. Rather than national identity shaping one's voice, the newly acquired voice imputes a nationality. That is, her realization that her voice has become Americanized leads her to claim American citizenship. This is a testament to the power of discourses in shaping social identities. Connor's experience is important for another reason. We see an ESL writer accommodating the 'non-native' identity quite willingly, without displaying much tension or conflict.

The difference is clear in her successive texts. Though she initially adopts a discourse of indirection, suppression of personal reference, understatement of the thesis, and 'end-weighted' development of the argument that she associates with the Finnish identity, she goes on to adopt a more explicit and authoritative style. Consider the voice in the opening of her dissertation:

> By means of statistical analysis I attempt to trace the gradual change in position of adjectives in Milton's poetry. I have tried to utilize my data, avoiding as much as possible a merely mechanical approach. I have tried to cite the forms illustrating each practice in sufficient context to show unmistakably their grammatical functions. I have used Helen Darbishere's careful edition of *The Poetical Works of John Milton*. (Connor, 1971: 8)

The personal referents and explicit claims characterize her new role as an insider in the American academy. Though Connor acknowledges that, at this stage, the voice here is that of her thesis advisor, transferred to her text through multiple rounds of revision, she considers her writing career as one of trying to make this voice her own. Her professional publications show that she has indeed been successful in adapting to this voice.

What makes Connor different from Li and Suseendirarajah has to be explained in terms of sociohistorical differences. Coming from a European nation that shares other cultural/historical connections with the United States, her transition is relatively smooth. But Li and Suseendirarajah are physiognomically different, and they cannot escape their ethnic/race identity easily. The far greater cultural differences between Asian and American communities would also create deeper conflicts for shifting to an American identity. Furthermore, the Asian communities have had an unequal relationship with the West historically that would make Li and

Suseendirarajah adopt a more critical attitude toward its discourse compared to Connor. Therefore, Li and Suseendirarajah negotiate a voice that strategically resolves their discursive conflicts in a way that is advantageous to them.

Opposition

We must add to this list a few other ways of negotiating identity conflicts that may fall between the above extremes. Some may directly resist the established discourses in order to adopt a clearly vernacular (or L1-based) voice in academic writing. In a case study on theses written by Sri Lankan graduate students, I found Sri's writing exemplifying this strategy. Sri shared the Hindu religious background of a traditionally monolingual family. In a community that was going through a national-istic struggle for self-determination, Sri valued the Tamil ethnic identity. Ideologically, he was at home in a subjectivity influenced by discourses of linguistic and cultural purism popular in this community at this time (see Canagarajah, 1995). Sri therefore adopted the role of a 'radical student' – a person who questions the institution and defines himself as different. He considered a voice shaped by the vernacular discourses as appropriate for this purpose. In a case study on the writing pedagogy in his school, Sri writes:

> Whenever I ask to write a composition on one of the given topics, only the very same students write, but even then, they too never speak or utter sentences in English. From my observations they feel shy, hesitation in pronouncing words in English. [They feel] others might laugh at me, etc. This creates problem in the language class-rooms. Only some students volunteer to read a passage or answers written by them. There are some students who perform well, who have a good family background ... Making meaning in the actual context is also a problem to many students. At least I could conclude, from the interviews, questionnaires, and observations most of the students (I am not ashamed to say even the teachers, including myself) need much attention not only in the field of writing English but also in the fields of listening, speaking and reading, in order to acquire or learn and master the language. (pp. 38–39)

There is a relaxed conversational tone as he narrates his classroom experi-ence. We see little attempt to document his observations or to authenticate their veracity (in keeping with the conventions of research reporting). In the final sentence there is a surprising personal interjection which is honest in its appraisal. Also, the reference to other skills ('listening, speaking and reading') in research focused on writing seems to be a deviation. But such is his discursive background that the writer feels comfortable about commenting on many things in his teaching experience as he goes along with his narration. These rhetorical features are acceptable in the vernacular academic discourse. Sri is also frank in using a creolized form of local English with its own grammar (e.g. 'Whenever I ask to write a composition on one of the given topics, only the very same students write').

To sum up, though there is some negotiation in textualizing the strengths of vernacular discourses in an alien language, and claiming a role that goes against the dominant discourses in this genre of academic writing, the voice lacks complexity. Sri adopts the vernacular discourse one-sidedly, without creatively constructing a place for this voice in this specialized genre. I label this strategy *opposition*, to distinguish it from *appropriation* (a more synthetic and dialogical strategy of negotiating a space for one's vernacular-based voice in the established mainstream discourses).[6]

Appropriation

bell hooks (1989) demonstrates how a more dialogical voice of appropriation would sound. Her book, appropriately titled *Talking Back*, employs street speech, vernacular idioms, narratives, anecdotes, and verbal play in an argumentation that is addressed to the mainstream scholarly community. Of course, she is informed by the constructs and discourses generated in academic contexts. But she pushes the conventions of citations and documentation to the endnote, so that the vernacular identity will receive greater prominence. What hooks does is to appropriate the academic discourses for her purposes. Motivated by the desire to present an African-American ethnic identity and oppositional ideological subjectivity, and inspired by the need to expand the academic discourse and ensure a democratic inclusion of other knowledge-making practices, she adopts a critical voice. While being distinctively Black and working class, the voice shows modifications deriving from a negotiation of the established discourses for this academic genre. hooks talks as a person knowledgeable about the academic discourses, but one who strategically resists them and infuses them with her vernacular rhetorical values. We may call this strategy of taking over dominant discourses and using them for one's own agendas *appropriation*. This strategy is different from *transposition*, in which both discourses are taken to a different level, to the extent that the achieved voice differs from that typically associated with either. In appropriation, the writer is infusing the established conventions with one's own discourses in a direct act of resistance. The dominant discourses are shaped to reflect the values and interests of the writer.

Among my Sri Lankan students, I find Viji adopting such a strategy for producing a hybrid text as her thesis. As a committed Christian and a female scholar, Viji was dissatisfied with what she perceived as the rigidities and detachment of academic prose. As a woman, she expressed preference for a discourse that is involved and personal. Her Pentecostal Christian background also predisposed her toward a more passionate and direct expression of her views. To make matters more complicated, her argument that the pedagogies and curriculum of past missionary ESL teachers were quite successful is unpopular in the contemporary context of Hindu chauvinism and linguistic nationalism. Her resolution of her discursive problems was wise: she produced a text that follows the usual conventions of cause/effect organization, occupation of a niche, rigorous archival research, and meticulous documentation, while still employing a narrative flow to subtly embed her argument. As she interjects her religious ethos in a relevant way into the academic discourse, her text gains a creative and critical edge. Viji thus attempts to find a space and voice for herself in the range of available discourses to encode the messages she desires. Taking seriously the academic discourses, she brings in her preferred values to construct an independent voice.

In the following excerpt from Viji's first chapter, where she establishes the background to missionary education, consider her use of the standard practices of quotations and citations:

> 'Ye shall be witnesses unto me unto the utmost part of the earth' (Holy Bible Acts 1:8) – the final command of the Master to the disciples of Jesus Christ has been fulfilled through the centuries ultimately paving the way for a band of missionaries from the American Board to reach the shores of Jaffna in 1813. Though the supreme goal of the missionaries was to evangelize, they found themselves being compelled 'to seek the aids of learning' (Plan: 1823) in order to prepare the ground for sowing the seed of the Gospel. (p. 1)

It is interesting that the quotation from the Bible which was cited in her initial drafts as a proud announcement of the educational endeavors of the missionaries is cited here dispassionately to indicate the rationale for their educational activities. The citation that follows is from the proposal by a school board for starting one of the first missionary educational institutions. The Biblical quotation is subtly juxtaposed with the bureaucratic text, finding an appropriate space in the dissertation.

As the first chapter continues, we find that Viji adopts both a narrative and polemical structuring. After orientating readers to the colonial period, she introduces the main terms of the debate regarding the missionary educational enterprise in the introductory chapter. She uses this chapter effectively to create a niche for her work in the scholarly conversation: she cites a variety of local educationists, linguists, and social theorists of the postcolonial period who have criticized the missionary educational enterprise to show why a re-examination is necessary in order to arrive at a more balanced assessment. She also argues that, since the missionaries didn't leave adequate records of their teaching mission (as they were preoccupied with evangelization), there is a need to reconstruct this dimension of their work. The political and academic significance of her thesis are made to stand out as the text is situated in the relevant discursive contexts. Viji then uses her insider status in church circles to obtain rare documents and interview accounts to present the missionaries as having practiced a pedagogy resembling communicative language teaching far ahead of their times. She adopts a chronological structure to narrate (with striking vignettes) the scenes of missionary language teaching in Sri Lankan villages. Viji thus appropriates the dominant academic conventions of research reporting for her own purposes. She infuses academic discourses with oppositional ideologies for a critical voice.

Similarly, in an illuminating case study of a Chinese and a Japanese female graduate student, Diane Belcher (1997) shows how they produced embedded forms of argumentation in otherwise narrative texts in order to gently and tactfully challenge the biases of their faculty advisors (and, in effect, the dominant discourses in their field). This writing strategy derives from a community-based and gender-influenced desire to show respect, understanding, and cooperative engagement in dialogue, different from the antagonistic forms of academic knowledge construction. (As we know, the typical strategy in new knowledge creation is to set oneself against the research that has come before, identify a gap in existing knowledge, and show how one's own findings answer the dominant problems in the field.) These writers infuse the academic text with a more relaxed, empathetic, involved prose that introduces a critical voice into the academic discourse. Despite the risks involved in antagonizing their thesis committee and losing their degrees, the students managed to evoke respect for their argument. Belcher goes on to make a case for such non-adversarial forms of argumentation, in terms of the discourses preferred by certain feminist and minority scholars. Belcher, in fact, takes this example a step further to argue that these alternate modes of argumentation and reasoning are a healthy corrective to the established identities in academic discourse. She relates how mainstream scholars are themselves reconsidering the place of adversarial modes of argumentation and identities which are not conducive to generating meaningful dialogue and cultivating ethical relations in intellectual engagement. The value of the critical voice emerging through strategies of textual appropriation is that it creatively challenges the established ideologies and subjectivities in the academic community.

Assessing Strategies

In order to develop a taxonomy of strategies multilingual writers may employ to negotiate the conflicts they face in writing, we may define the strategies discussed above as follows:

(1) Avoidance: e.g. adopted by Irina as she chooses not to engage with the conflicting identities from the Ukrainian and American communities, or to foreground them in her writing. Though we cannot say anything decisively about the intention of the writer, what we know from the text is that there are no signs of a productive tension between the diverse discourses one confronts. Though it may be liberating for the writer to adopt this position, the text fails to develop a creative or critical discourse that arises out of a negotiation of conflicting discourse traditions.

(2) Accommodation: e.g. exemplified by Connor as she resolves her conflicts in favor of adopting a voice and identity influenced by American discourses, and restrains her native Finnish. Accommodation shows a more conscious internalization of the dominant discourses that differs from the somewhat hesitant and surface-level adoption displayed by avoidance. It is therefore a more cultivated adoption of the dominant discourses.

(3) Opposition: e.g. illustrated by Sri's writing as he represents himself primarily through the vernacular discourse. Though this is in opposition to the dominant academic discourse influenced by western/English thought conventions of objectivity and rationality, there is no negotiation evident in the text. Like the previous two strategies, this too displays a 'univocal' discourse that adopts one strand of the conflicting discourses without negotiating an independent voice.

(4) Appropriation: e.g. demonstrated by Viji who takes over the dominant academic discourses to infuse them with strengths from her preferred personal discourses. This is a strategy of finding a favorable space for one's own voice in the established discourses.

(5) Transposition: e.g. developed by Li and Suseendirarajah as the 'third voice' that defines itself dialectically by working against the conflicting discourses and forming a new discourse that transcends the earlier dichotomies.

It is important to realize that each of these strategies may have different outcomes in terms of stylistic effectiveness and critical communication. It is clear that some strategies have possibilities of challenging the dominant discourses and textual conventions to democratize knowledge and communication. Others strengthen the established discourses. Among the strategies we have observed, accommodation affirms the established discourses. The writer's voice may succeed in being coherent and homogeneous, while somewhat lacking in ideological complexity. The potential for critiquing and expanding academic discourses may be limited. In avoidance conflicting discourses are left unresolved. The writer may unwittingly generate unfavorable identities and roles, ironically, while deferring to the dominant discourses. What is valued in the academy is a critical and creative engagement with the existing conventions. One-sidedly adopting the dominant discourse may indicate a lack of originality and independence in the student. In Foucault's terms, such one-sided leaning toward the dominant discourses (as displayed by both accommodation and avoidance) may lead to a form of silencing.

The other three strategies (transposition, opposition, and appropriation) construct independent voices by positing a counter-discourse to that of the established writing practices. The strategy of opposition, however, is not sufficiently dialogical or negotiatory in promoting the vernacular discourses in the new communicative situation. Although this strategy has critical potential, there is the danger that the text may not communicate to the target audience that comes with different genre and discourse expectations. Seeing little connection to the present rhetorical situation, the audience may rule the text as irrelevant, ascribing pejorative roles and identities to the writer. The writer may be denied entry into that communicative circle and the voice silenced. The final two strategies, transposition and appropriation, have more critical and communicative potential. Although they set up a counter-discourse to that of the dominant conventions, they still create a point of connection with the established genre conventions. Therefore, the audience for that genre of writing may find some bridges in their effort to understand and appreciate the new oppositional discourse. Writers using these strategies are negotiating with the established rhetoric to thus construct a more positive voice for themselves. These strategies have greater chances of challenging the dominant discourses and inserting the alternate values and ideologies represented by the writers. The writers themselves are empowered as they work out an independent voice for themselves, rather than being silenced, compromised, or rejected by the dominant discourses.

In terms of the comparison between writers from different proficiency levels, it is interesting that these orientations to voice are not affected by one's novice status. As we see above, the graduate students of Belcher (1997) and Viji in my study adopt a critical orientation to the competing discourses. They are able to thus shape a new discourse that suits their purposes and preferred voice. This finding helps us realize that critical modes of negotiating discourses don't have to be taught. Writers may develop these discourse strategies if they come to the communicative context with the frank and bold attitude of engaging with their conflicting discourse backgrounds to find a niche favorable to their purposes. Their social positioning as members of communities with a history of contesting colonization also helps to some extent.

Note that the assessment of these strategies is not reductive. A single strategy is not held up as leading to the preferred mode of critical writing. Both transposition and appropriation have different ways of constructing a critical voice. Also, the assessment attempts to address multiple claims on effective writing – especially ideological and rhetorical claims. So an approach that may not be ideologically oppositional can still display rhetorical coherence (i.e. accommodation as practiced by Connor). On the other hand, a 'politically correct' strategy of ideological opposition may still be rhetorically/linguistically ineffective (as we saw in the case of Sri). Similarly, though Irina may have good reasons for adopting the dominant American academic discourse, she misses an opportunity to negotiate a rhetorically more complex text arising from the multiple discourses she brings with her. Voice therefore has to be truly 'negotiated' in relation to the ideological, institutional, linguistic, and rhetorical contexts of communication as Foucault articulates. At any rate, this list of strategies is only a beginning; we have to refine it as more studies emerge. The intention here is not to seek acceptance of this typology; it is rather to construct a heuristic that will help us to develop an integrated perspective by comparing the different studies emerging on writing and identity.

Conclusions

To develop more complex orientations to voice in the writing of multilingual students, teachers and researchers must acknowledge the following principles that emerge from the preceding discussion:[7]

- that it is not by avoiding, but by acknowledging and confronting the conflicts in discourses and identities that students can find their voice;
- that there is no voice outside discourses and, for that reason, the dominant discourses in each communicative context or community have to be taken seriously, even for purposes of resistance;
- that it is not by conforming uncritically, but by working against the dominant discourses, that one constructs an independent voice;
- that multilingualism is a resource, not a hindrance, for the achievement of a critical voice.

Notes

1 For a review of the literature that develops such a perspective on self, we need to understand developments in postmodernism (Foucault, 1990), poststructuralism (Spivak, 1990), postcolonialism (Hall, 1990), and feminism (Butler, 1990). A simpler – i.e. more readable – introduction to some of these movements are Belsey (1983) or Coward and Ellis (1977). A more critical review of theories on identity is Smith (1989).

2 By 'established' I refer to those who have published in respected scholarly or public circles. By 'novice' I mean largely students at various proficiency levels who seek more practice and instruction to become confident writers.

3 For a similar argument with regard to bilingual writers, see Pavlenko (2001).

4 I thank Aneta Pavlenko (personal communication) for a more complex understanding of Irina's discursive background.

5 This discourse is of course mediated by the comments of referees and the journal editor. The author himself acknowledges the help of an American scholar who was in Sri Lanka as a visiting scholar at that time. But the fact that the author chooses to incorporate some of these suggestions to write this paper indicates his desired discourse here. It is appropriate therefore to credit him for the construction of this discourse.

6 I borrow this distinction from Giroux (1983: 109), who warns that 'the concept of resistance must not be allowed to become a category indiscriminately hung over every expression of "oppositional behavior."' Giroux distinguishes between *resistance*, which he sees as displaying ideological clarity and commitment to collective action for social transformation, and mere *opposition*, which is unclear, ambivalent, and largely passive.

7 The pedagogical implications of this orientation to voice are discussed more completely in Canagarajah (2002b).

References

Atkinson, D. (1999) *Scientific discourse in sociohistorical context*. Mahwah, NJ: Lawrence Erlbaum Associates.

Belanger, M. (1982) A preliminary analysis of the structure of the discussion sections in ten neuroscience journal articles (mimeo). In J. Swales *Genre analysis*. Cambridge: Cambridge University Press.

Belcher, D. (1997) An argument for nonadversarial argumentation: On the relevance of the feminist critique of academic discourse to L2 writing pedagogy. *Journal of Second Language Writing* 6 (1), 1–21.

Belcher, D. and Connor, U. (eds) (2001) *Reflections on multiliterate lives*. Clevedon: Multilingual Matters.

Belsey, C. (1983) *Critical practice*. London: Methuen.

Butler, J. (1990) *Gender trouble: Feminism and the subversion of identity*. New York: Routledge.

Canagarajah, S. (1995) The political-economy of code choice in a revolutionary society: Tamil/English bilingualism in Jaffna. *Language in Society* 24 (2), 187–212.

Canagarajah, S. (1999a) *Resisting linguistic imperialism in English teaching*. Oxford: Oxford University Press.

Canagarajah, S. (1999b) *Comparing teacher-facilitated and student-constructed safe houses: The coping strategies of bilingual students in academic literacy*. Report submitted for NCTE grant in aid Baruch College (mimeo).

Canagarajah, S. (1999c) On EFL teachers, awareness, and agency. *ELT Journal* 53 (3), 207–214.

Canagarajah, S. (2002a) *A geopolitics of academic writing*. Pittsburgh: University of Pittsburgh Press.

Canagarajah, S. (2002b) *Critical academic writing and multilingual students*. Ann Arbor, MI: University of Michigan Press.

Connor, U. (1971) *The use of adjectives in Milton's earlier and later poetry*. Unpublished Master's thesis, University of Florida, Gainesville.

Connor, U. (1999) Learning to write academic prose in a second language: A literacy autobiography. In G. Braine (ed.) *Non-native educators in English language teaching* (pp. 29–42). Mahwah, NJ: Lawrence Erlbaum Associates.

Coward, R. and Ellis, J. (1977) *Language and materialism: Developments in semiology and the theory of the subject*. London: Routledge.

de Beaugrande, R. and Dressler, W. (1981) *Introduction to text linguistics*. London: Longman.

Foucault, M. (1972) The discourse on language. In M. Foucault *The archeology of knowledge* (pp. 215–237). New York: Pantheon.

Foucault, M. (1990) *The history of sexuality* (Vol. 1). New York: Random House (original work published 1980).

Giroux, H. (1983) *Theory and resistance in education: A pedagogy for the opposition*. South Hadley: Bergin.

Hall, S. (1990) Cultural identity and diaspora. In J. Rutherford (ed.) *Identity, community, culture, difference* (pp. 222–237). London: Lawrence and Wishart.

hooks, bell (1989) *Talking back: Thinking feminist, thinking Black*. Boston: South End Press.

Kramsch, C. (2000) *Linguistic identities at the boundaries.* Paper presented at the annual convention of the American Association of Applied Linguistics (AAAL), Vancouver, Canada, 12–14 March.

Kramsch, C. and Lam, W. (1999) Textual identities: The importance of being non-native. In: G. Braine (ed.) *Non-native educators in English language teaching* (pp. 57–72). Mahwah, NJ: Lawrence Erlbaum Associates.

Li, X. (1999) Writing from the vantage point of an outsider/insider. In G. Braine (ed.) *Non-native educators in English language teaching* (pp. 43–56). Mahwah, NJ: Lawrence Erlbaum Associates.

Mauranen, A. (1993) *Cultural differences in academic rhetoric.* Frankfurt am Main: Peter Lang.

Pavlenko, A. (2001) 'In the world of the tradition, I was unimagined': Negotiation of identities in cross-cultural autobiographies. *The International Journal of Bilingualism* 5 (3), 317–344.

Smith, P. (1989) *Discerning the subject.* Minneapolis, MN: University of Minnesota Press.

Spivak, G. (1990) *The post-colonial critic.* New York: Routledge.

Suseendirarajah, S. (1978) Caste and language in Jaffna Society. *Anthropological Linguistics* 20, 312–319.

Suseendirarajah, S. (1991) *PantiTamaNiyin peerum pukaLum vanTa vaaRu* [*Accounting for the name and prestige of Panditamani*]. Paper presented at the Academic Forum, University of Jaffna, Sri Lanka (mimeo).

Suseendirarajah, S. (1992) *English in our Tamil society: A sociolinguistic appraisal.* Academic Forum, University of Jaffna, Sri Lanka (mimeo).

Swales, J. (1990) *Genre analysis: English in academic and research settings.* Cambridge: Cambridge University Press.

Swales, J. (1998). *Other floors, other voices: A textography of a small university building.* Mahwah, NJ: Lawrence Erlbaum.

Chapter 10

Identity and Language Use: The Politics of Speaking ESL in Schools

JENNIFER MILLER

Introduction

In globalized societies, multilingual contexts are a fact of life, which has stimulated an increasing academic interest in identity and its relationship to language use. Multilingual contexts in education mean that, at any time, many students are acquiring and performing in new languages, and that, in a range of contexts, many students are linguistic minority speakers. Over 25% of children in Australia are from non-English-speaking backgrounds (Glew, 2001), with percentages over 90% in some schools. Recent studies have shown that students using English as a second language have lower literacy levels than English-speaking students (McKay, 1999) and also that many immigrant students encounter racism and social isolation in schools (Matthews, 1997).

The emergence of sociocultural perspectives on language, typified by the understanding that meanings are negotiated within diverse social contexts, indicates an important new direction for theorists and practitioners in the field of second language use. The underlying theoretical position of this volume is that identities are discursively constructed, and are also embedded within social practices and broader ideological frameworks. The understanding that identities are invoked, constructed, and negotiated through discourse is therefore central to this chapter, which focuses primarily on educational contexts. However, to understand the lived experiences of linguistic minority speakers in schools, key theoretical strands need to be clearly articulated. This chapter uses theory from Bourdieu, Gee, and others, along with data from an empirical study of migrant students in school in Queensland, Australia, to develop the notion that there is a politics of speaking which implicates speaker and hearer in ways that are ideologically loaded, and which may be the basis of empowerment or discrimination. To explain how speakers are positioned or may position themselves through the use of a second or third language, I will appeal to the notion of *audibility* (see also Miller, 1999a,b, 2000). In simple terms, audibility is the degree to which speakers sound like, and are legitimated by, users of the dominant discourse. It therefore requires the collaboration of speaker and listener.

Reframing Language as Discourse

Within the fields of sociolinguistics, discourse analysis, ethnography of communication, and pragmatics, there is an increasing awareness that language use is a form of self-representation, which implicates social identities, the values attached to particular written and spoken texts, and, therefore, the links between discourse and power in any social context. Linguistic minority students must achieve self-representation in the dominant discourse, if they are to participate in mainstream social and academic contexts, renegotiate their identities in new places, and accrue the necessary symbolic capital (Bourdieu, 1991) to successfully integrate into school and the wider society.

A number of significant recent works on language in use have conceived of language practice as socially constituted (Bourdieu, 1991; Gee, 1996; Heller, 1994; Hymes, 1996; Norton, 2000; Rampton, 1995). Embedded in these works is the assumption that discourse cannot be viewed in isolation from its cultural and social context. This shift means that using language involves contextually situated discursive practices and that we are shaped by and through our language use. In theoretical terms this has led to a developing hybridization in research, incorporating a range of fields, including second language acquisition (SLA), discourse analysis, sociolinguistics, cultural studies, and conversation analysis. Examples of this hybridization may be found in a number of recent works on language use (see Gee, 1996; Lippi-Green, 1997; van Dijk, 1997), which demonstrate that linguistic relations are social relations, but also power relations, and the power of language to legitimate and maintain ideologies is a recurring theme in the literature. However, in educational contexts, one often reads or hears of learning a language, as if there were only one, or one with finite content. In fact, learning a language entails mastering complex sets of discursive practices for use in a range of social contexts. The complex and dynamic processes involving language, social membership, culture, and identity are central to the position advocated by Gee (1996), who places discourses at the heart of the matter. He defines Discourses, with the characteristic capital D, in the following way:

> Discourses are ways of being in the world, or forms of life which integrate words, acts, values, beliefs, attitudes, and social identities, as well as gestures, glances, body positions, and clothes. A Discourse is a kind of identity kit which comes complete with the appropriate costume and instructions on how to act, talk, and often write, so as to take on a particular social role that others will recognize. (Gee, 1996: 127)

Using myself as an example, on any one day I may move through the discourses of, for example, censorious parent, ESL teacher, sympathetic colleague, university lecturer, dissatisfied shopper, intimate friend, e-mailing lobbyist, and so on. Through these discourses I construct a range of identities to serve specific purposes, memberships, and contexts. Such identity kits, linguistic repertoires, and routines are designed to make us recognizable to others, and effective in our communicative practices. They are integral to the process of positioning outlined by Pavlenko and Blackledge in this volume. Our knowledge of language is therefore far more than a knowledge of words and how to combine them to form grammatical sentences. This is in contrast to the language learner in much of SLA theory, who has been constructed as a kind of ahistorical stick figure, appearing without a past, existing outside of any social context (see also a similar critique in Kinginger's chapter). The learner's relation to the social order *outside* the classroom seldom enters into the picture (Auerbach, 1995). Gee's definition of Discourses implies viewing the linguistic minority student not as a learner of any particular language, but as someone who needs to acquire a range of discursive practices in addition to those already possessed.

A number of researchers have suggested that moving toward a more discourse-based perspective will open up new ways of looking at how language is socioculturally constituted (Firth & Wagner, 1997; Miller, 1997). Wagner (1993) also suggests that the input from other disciplines generates a new set of questions and represents a powerful innovation to researchers in the relevant fields. To view language as discourse, we need to incorporate a number of perspectives sometimes missing from traditional SLA research. These include the view of any communicative performance as socially contextualized and mediated, the questioning of 'standard language' (see Davies, 1991; Lippi-Green, 1997), the understanding that competence is realized by *all* speakers to varying degrees in different settings, the understanding that local contexts are contingent and ideologically laden, the reconceptualization of motivation as investment in learning (Norton Peirce, 1995), and, finally, the importance of access to linguistic resources (Pavlenko, 2000), with the focus on the impact of social hierarchies and the possibilities of the collaboration of native and non-native speakers. In its search for general truths about how languages are learned, SLA research has relied predominantly on cognitively-oriented methodologies and theories applied to formal or experimental learning environments (Firth & Wagner, 1997). The perspective of language as discourse moves us beyond the notion of non-native speakers as deficient, and throws into question traditional SLA principles, such as age-on-arrival and length of residence, interlanguage, the 'good language learner,' and communicative competence. Restoring some of the sociocultural complexities and unique contextual circumstances of the interactions of second language users has become a priority in a number of recent works on language use (e.g. Lippi-Green, 1997; Norton, 1997; Norton Peirce, 1995; Rampton, 1995) and on ESL education (Mohan *et al.*, 2001). These complexities and contexts highlight the need for serious consideration of the ways in which language use is linked to the negotiation of identity.

Identity and Audibility

For many theorists, particularly those working within the field of cultural studies, the notion of representation is often tied to a metaphorical use of the term *voice*. Giroux's (1992) concern is with the politics of voice and difference, that is, the wider issues of how students function as agents, and how they are rendered voiceless in certain contexts, or silence themselves as a result of intimidation, real or imagined. Giroux (1992: 203) labels the silencing of the 'voices of subordinate groups whose primary language is not English and whose cultural capital is either marginalized or denigrated by the dominant culture of schooling' as a racializing practice which occurs in schools. This is a slant on racism qualitatively different from that manifested by overt violence, or racial slurs. There is no direct attack implied here – just a denial of the right to speak and be heard, and the non-hearing of first languages other than English. In my view, the term *voice* undergoes here a qualitative shift, from its metaphorical sense of an authorized claim, to a more literal yet highly symbolic sense – spoken voices. Students from subordinate groups are silenced because they are unable to represent themselves or to negotiate their identities through their first languages at school. Some are both seen and heard as different.

Speaking is itself a critical tool of representation, a way of representing the self and others. It is the means through which identity is constituted, and agency or self-advocacy is made manifest. In other words, we represent and negotiate identity, and construct that of others, through speaking and hearing. Speakers may be marked as belonging to specific groupings by their use of spoken language, which provides for hearers an index to gender, age, ethnicity, geography, and education (Lippi-Green, 1997). According to Lippi-Green (1997), the dominant group speaks the dominant variety of English, the so-called unmarked or unaccented form. Children who lose their native accents are thus judged to have no accent. And there are social, personal, and academic rewards for those who sound similar to the dominant majority. Linguistic skills in English are therefore symbolic resources not equally available to all persons, and are heavily endowed with social currencies.

Bourdieu (1977: 648) has referred to speaking as 'the power to impose reception,' which cannot sensibly be divorced from listening, and which involves the conditions of reception. Furthermore, when students speak another language, or English with an accent, or in ways that are heard as non-standard, there are often consequences for the speaker. Normally, in spoken interactions the responsibility for keeping the communication alive is shared. In the case of linguistic minority students, speakers and listeners have to work hard sometimes to 'foster mutual intelligibility,' which requires both an effort of will and a degree of social acceptance (Lippi-Green, 1997: 70). However, Lippi-Green points out that, at times, the dominant speaker may refuse to carry any responsibility for the communicative act. What she calls 'language ideology filters' come into play whenever an accent or a hesitant 'non-standard' voice is heard, causing the listener to reject 'the communicative burden' (1997: 70). In some instances, there may be a negative evaluation not just of the accent, but of the social identity of the speaker. Being audible to others, and being heard and acknowledged as a speaker of English, determines the extent to which a student may participate in social interactions, negotiation, and practices within the educational institution and in the wider society. Being audible also provides the means of self-representation, as well as the essential underlying condition for the ongoing acquisition of English and continuing identity work in a range of contexts. For newly arrived students from non-English-speaking backgrounds, schools provide critical contexts where they must find a voice, through which new identities may be negotiated or indeed resisted.

Discourse and Identity in Schools

Schools comprise particular sites of representation where linguistic minority students often struggle to be authorized as members of the mainstream, and to be heard as legitimate speakers of English. The notion of sites of representation is a useful one which throws into relief the textualized and contextualized nature of the discourses of identity. As we move from one site to another, encountering different partners in interaction, we invoke different representations of our identity, and draw on different linguistic resources. Within school there are, for example, many sites one could observe – visualize the ESL classroom, the mainstream English classroom, the school assembly, the handball court, the canteen queue, a corridor, the administration lobby, the manual arts center, the music block, the place near B block where the in-crowd sits, the home economics staffroom, of the bus stop outside the school. As the eye roams like some wild hand-held camera, we hear the different discourses, and take note of their dissonances. Each of these sites affords linguistic minority students different opportunities, constraints, and conditions to speak and to represent themselves through language use. Beyond the school, other sites present other possibilities, constraints, and conditions.

In regard to such sites of representation for minority students, it is impossible to avoid the question of *which* language is in use. For ESL students there are sites of first language use, sites of second and third language use, and sites where these overlap and intersect. How we speak and are heard within sites is critical to social identity work. Furthermore, the sites are themselves value-laden, as are the discourses within them. Local sites of representation can therefore be compared to Bourdieu's *fields*, defined as 'semi-autonomous, structured social spaces characterized by discourse and social activity' (Carrington & Luke, 1997: 100). As indicated throughout this section, these sites provide places in which identity is enacted, where social interactions, cultures, languages, and identities are made manifest, where the 'insidering' and 'outsidering' is done, where spoken discourse is heard or not heard, is validated or remains unacknowledged, and where membership is made available or denied. In terms of the negotiation of identities, these sites are embedded with social and institutional practices which position minority speakers in particular ways. Some students, it will be seen, are complicit in, or may resist, such positioning.

Speaking out at school

In education contexts, speaking audibly and without anxiety in another language is an enormous challenge for all but the most extrovert and intrepid students, if they are recently arrived. Reticence in speaking, particularly in the early stages, is a natural and very common phenomenon and may manifest itself as silence, minimal responses or extreme soft-spokenness (Tsui, 1996). Mainstream interactions may also be inhibited by sociopsychological and in-group factors (Davison & Williams, 2001). In many mainstream classes, I have witnessed frequent admonitions from teachers for ESL students to speak up or speak louder. I heard mainstream students call out 'Can't hear!' when ESL students spoke, and I had transcripts with many turns marked 'inaudible.' As indicated above, schools provide a series of microcontexts for students, 'borderlands crisscrossed with a variety of languages, experiences and voices' (Giroux, 1990: 109), in which the social relations and identities are in a constant state of flux. This is even more marked where there are more than two languages within the student community. One school in the study used here proclaimed itself to be the school of '55 nations,' in which over 30 languages were used. Students may therefore function in two or three language domains at school, as well as in a multiplicity of contexts. The language domains are not symmetrical in terms of fluency, proficiency, or confidence in performance, nor are they equally valued by the school. In what follows, I look at a range of school contexts, which include initial arrival for ESL students, the playground and social interaction, classwork, and oral presentations.

Methodology

If we broaden the language focus of the research to include an understanding of social contexts, representation, and discourse, we can infer a methodology which has four critical characteristics or criteria. First, it will look at language in a sociocultural matrix, which shows sensibility not just to proficiency in a second language, but to the social and cultural salience of language use. Second, it must reveal contextual features in local settings. Third, it must incorporate an *emic* perspective, the voice and subjectivities of both participant and researcher present in the writing. Finally, it must allow for ongoing flexibility in the data collection and analysis, drawing on whatever fields prove productive for the project (Nelson *et al.*, 1992). Case study and ethnographic approaches have the potential to satisfy all four criteria, but can also accommodate a focus on issues of language, representation, and social organization.

Hornberger (1995) has outlined the importance of linguistically informed approaches, particularly discourse analysis, to ethnographic research. She writes: 'notions of situated discourse and multiple and alternative social roles and identities ... are fundamental to all of the sociolinguistically informed approaches to ethnography' (Hornberger,

1995: 244). However, studies concerned with social identities have often been resistant to incorporating methods such as discourse analysis, and reluctant to theorize how social members position themselves and are positioned by discourse (Antaki, 1996).

Data used in this chapter are selected from a recent three-year study of 10 high school students from non-English-speaking backgrounds (Miller, 1999b). These students were tracked over a period of 16 months from their stay in an on-arrival intensive ESL program at Newnham High School (pseudonym) through to integration in their local or chosen high schools. Participating students had only been in Australia from two to ten months when data collection began, so that the study represents the very early phases of their arrival and integration into Australian schools. I have kept in touch with several of the students, and have therefore followed their progress five years along the track. Data sources in this study included the following:

- semi-structured interviews in both English and the L1 for some students;
- student diaries;
- focus groups;
- classroom observation in ESL and mainstream contexts;
- observation of playgrounds and other microcontexts of the school;
- attendance at key school events and ceremonies (multicultural concert, student symposium on multiculturalism, Anzac day);
- talks with mainstream and ESL teachers;
- talks with school administrators;
- the collection of work samples and school documents;
- phone conversations with students;
- attendance at ESL staff meetings and morning teas;
- the collection of media articles on ethnic minorities, migration, and multiculturalism;
- informal encounters with the students and their teachers.

Each data set corresponded to a different site of representation. All interviews, the videotaped focus groups, talks with administrators, one staff meeting, and some phone conversations were recorded and transcribed. Detailed field notes were made during and immediately after observations, participation in school events, and informal talks with staff and students. The primary or core data sets included audiotaped interviews, student diaries, and observation in a range of contexts within the schools.

The interviews in English were viewed as instances of contextualized communicative competence in spoken English, but also as accounts of the students' positionings and insights into the social order of the school. I had often worked as an ESL teacher in the intensive reception center, and felt a strong degree of familiarity and identification with the students and staff. I was able to generate lots of data with the two Bosnian students, who spoke quite fluently, in spite of having arrived only weeks before I met them (for transcription conventions, see Appendix on p. 313). The Chinese-speaking students, who spoke Mandarin, Cantonese or both, had far more limited English, and so interviews in their languages were conducted by native-speaking research assistants, who then also translated the transcripts. These were then cross-checked with other native speakers. The transcription conventions were not used in the translations of these interviews as I was unable to verify these elements in the talk. Another data source comprised student diaries, written in English with myself as the intended reader. Several students from China and Taiwan wrote prolifically in these diaries, which contained reflections on their learning and social experiences. It seemed that these students were able to represent themselves far better in writing than in speaking English, for a number of reasons.

Diaries constitute a form of communication which takes the heat off the speaker. There is no wait time for responses, no awkward long pauses, no pressure to respond, no agonizing search for an unknown or forgotten word. Students can formulate in their own time what they want to say, and the discourse is not overtly shaped by the researcher. As the researcher and as a former ESL teacher, I had observed how students may be made voiceless. I was also aware that some students have a greater facility in writing than in speaking English, partly due to the nature of their prior language learning. The use of diaries also opened the way for students to use narrative accounts, a form that, while not particularly valued as a school genre, allows the student creative freedom in the discourse. As Drake and Ryan (1994: 49) point out, 'a narrative format allows students to present views of the world that are not necessarily filtered through a perspective that assumes uniformity of experience.' I was also interested in the ability of narrative, in which experience and responses are constructed and located in text, to provide a resource for the display of identity (see Schiffrin, 1996).

A range of discourse analytic methods was used in the analysis. Luke (1998: 55) stresses that interdisciplinary techniques of analysis may involve 'a series of text analyzes that use different analytic tools, but which are nested within an overall set of social theoretic frameworks and sociological questions.' The tools I selected included, but were not limited to, the five interrelated systems of discourse (prosody, cohesion, discourse organization, contextualization signals, and thematic organization) outlined by Gee (1996) and aspects of critical discourse analysis (Caldas-Coulthard & Coulthard, 1996; Luke, 1998).

Arriving in High School

Having experienced a very supportive environment in the intensive ESL school in which their nascent English language skills and identities were valued (see Miller, 1999b), the ESL students in this study were shocked that this was not always the case at high school. Aged 13 to 15 years, they had left the ESL school with hopes of finding new English-speaking friends and eagerly anticipated going to what several described as 'real school.' Here are comments by some students on settling in at high school (Newnham is the pseudonym used for the ESL school; R stands for the researcher):

> In a high school, it's like (.), like you have to catch up with **the others** so you have to work harder. Well, in Newnham you just, you know, just learn not very hard. Not really really really hard but, you just **learn**. In here, we have to like, catch up, like that.

> I didn't have many friends, or most of the time I just stayed up here, up in ESL, because there was no people who spoke my language then. It was only me. So all these Australian people, they are nice (.) but like, now they really won't, you know talk to you.

> At Newnham, we just, like, play games, not really learn.

> **R:** Does it depend on whether you speak English?

> **N:** Yes, it does. That's the only reason. Because if you don't, you just don't feel confident, like to talk to them, to be with them, you know you think they don't like you, or something like that. When you know English, it's that you really feel confident.

> (on what happens when you speak your first language)
> If you say in your language, nobody can hear anything, because they just say: What? What?

There is almost a sense that the students felt they had been misled at Newnham into believing that their English was adequate for high school, whereas it was not heard that way in high school. By way of contrast, the intensive reception program had offered a particular environment where all students were from another place, all were learning English, and multilingualism was heard as the norm. The critical difference in the move to high school entailed the presence of large numbers of mono-lingual speakers of Australian English. And according to the students in this study, native English-speaking students were often unwilling to provide the attentive and sympathetic listening that their ESL teachers and many of their peers had done.

This was particularly a problem for the Mandarin speakers, who often found many other Mandarin speakers in their schools, and for whom opportunities to use English outside of class were thus even further reduced. They had a strong sense of identity as Taiwanese. When asked why this was the case, one student named Tina said, 'Because everyone around me is still Taiwanese, no matter where I go, still Taiwanese. What I feel here is the same as what I feel in Taiwan.' The Mandarin speaking interviewer (F) elicited the following:

F: You once said to Ms Miller that at this school you didn't need to speak English. What is it like now?
T: The same.
F: Why?
T: Because friends of mine speak the same language, the same, they are all from the same place, all come from Taiwan, China or Hong Kong. So it is not necessary to use English.

It is worth noting that the student's identity here hinges on language rather than place. Tina hears her friends as from the same place, while specifying three different source countries for the group. Tina also stated that, whereas she spoke English with her fellow migrant and refugee students at Newnham, her chances to use English at high school were reduced:

T: After I came to this school, I seldom talk (1.0) speak English. Before, when in Newnham, there were some friends from, not Australian – there was a chance, sometimes to speak English, but now, here, no.
F: Is that because there are so many Taiwanese students or
T: Yeah, and the Australian classmates won't actively talk to me, so I won't go to talk to them.

It was ironic that, in a high school population of 650, where over 550 spoke English as a first language, she felt more constrained in using English than on arrival in the country. By her own admission, she did not take risks, or reach out to the 'Australian classmates,' but she was also very anxious about her English. A similar situation existed for one Vietnamese student, Tien:

R: I noticed at lunch time you sit mostly with your Vietnamese girl-friends. Do you also mix with the other students? Is that easy?

T: Um, only in class time, we mix everywhere, but in lunch time or something, or morning tea, we just go to our friends, our Vietnamese friends because sometimes we just practice to speak Vietnamese, or English as well. Sometimes we just miss, you know, each other, so we just talk.

The most significant social interaction between students in schools takes place in the breaks, at recess, and at lunch. Tien's idea that 'only in class time, we mix everywhere' was more a description of the class composition than of the social interaction possible in such settings. The key interaction times were eating times and these she spent with her Vietnamese friends, using her first language. I have heard Australian teachers and students argue that groups like Tien's were marginalizing themselves, failing to mix. Yet, with limited English, the temptation to withdraw to the safety of one's language group must be great. As one Bosnian student said:

I don't know, sometimes depends on personality, like, if you are outgoing and you're friendly and want to talk to people, everyone's gonna accept you but if you're not, no-one's really gonna . . . but English yeah, it is a big advantage for, if you know English.

It seemed to me that 'knowing English' and 'being outgoing' were related in identity work at school. It is also worth recalling Savignon's (1991) claim that language learning results from participation in communicative events. This is indeed hard to contest. The problem is that learners cannot choose the social conditions surrounding their language acquisition and production, nor the responses of the target language community. In terms of identity, the gap between the Chinese speakers' need to speak English and their opportunities to do so was noticeable in this school. How did classrooms help students from non-English-speaking backgrounds to bridge the gap?

Using English in the Classroom

Ostensibly, ESL students in Australian high schools are in what Spolsky (1989) terms 'natural acquisition contexts,' which include learning for communication, unmodified language input, being surrounded by native speakers, a real-world social context for learning, along with a primary focus on meaning. These students are partially integrated into a mainstream curriculum and are receiving ESL instruction which is contextualized through mainstream subject areas, such as science and geography. They also travel on buses and trains, go shopping, see movies, talk to other students, use the Internet, send e-mails, field phone calls – all in English. There is, one would suppose, ample opportunity for multiple interactions and opportunities to practice English, which Spolsky stresses is essential for acquisition. However, there was much evidence from this study that these conditions did not, of themselves, facilitate English language use and acquisition. For some students, English was only encountered in formal class environments, as shown in this exchange during an interview, conducted in Cantonese and then translated into English:

D: Then, is there any time that you speak English in school?
J: When I talk to teachers.
D: That means you will only speak English in the classroom and speak no English outside the classroom.
J: No, I will not.
D: Do you have any Australian or English-speaking friends?
J: (Pause) Greeting only. There is little communication between us.

When another student was asked if she got to talk with Australian students, she said, 'Yeah, at mainstream, they are all foreigners, so I speak English to them.' The *foreigners* were of course the English-speaking Australian students. This view was reinforced by other students, who maintained that using English in class only occurred if there was group work (and their group had English speakers in it) or if a 'foreign kid' sat beside them by chance. My own observation was that ESL students very often sat alone, or together. Once again, the conditions were often not favorable for opportunities to use English and to be heard as a speaker of English. In their case study of ESL in the Australian mainstream, Davison and Williams (2001) suggest that the mainstream curriculum offers ESL students insufficient opportunities to develop social language. They also question the assumption made by the ESL community that Cummins' (1980) representation of BICS (basic interpersonal communication skills) and CALP (cognitive academic language proficiency) meant that the BICS was more basic and less problematic for learners. One could argue that the grammar of speaking and the rules of spoken discourse are just as complex as the rules governing academic output.

Sometimes the absence of any comprehensible interaction with English-speaking peers leads linguistic minority students to assume the worst, namely, that they are neither liked nor accepted. Tina, for example, maintained that Australian students were unwilling to talk to her and, in the following interview excerpt, she offers an account of this.

> **T:** Seems that they don't like the 'black hairs.' Because I have a classmate from Bosnia now in my class. If we go to (a mainstream) class together, they, they know that she is not Australian, don't speak much English, but go to talk to her not me.
>
> **F:** Why?
>
> **T:** Don't know.
>
> **F:** Where is she from?
>
> **T:** Bosnia. Blondy hair.

In each case, 'they' refers to the Australian students. By 'black hairs' she was referring to Asian students. She makes the point here that the act of speaking to one student and not another in fact constitutes a racializing practice on the part of Australian students, a differentiation made on the basis of whether someone looks Anglo or Asian. I had asked where the student was from, to which she answered not just the country, Bosnia, but what was for her a critically defining physical characteristic, 'blondy hair.' She had used the expression 'black hairs' and made a similar point to me at other times. Some months later Tina also recounted to me the first time she worked in groups with Anglo-Australian students. In Geography, the teacher had randomly selected groups of three to do research on Africa and present the findings orally. She wrote in her journal:

> *My group decided to do the Zulus of Africa. And I am doing the 'Art' of Zulus. This is my first time doing something with Australians. I hope I could do as well as them.*

Although the Australians are still 'them,' the ones she wants to do as well as, it is *her* group, and she has a specific role in it. Tina had arrived in Australia 13 months earlier, and been at Taylor High for seven months. Her account of this oral project as the first time she had done something with Australians is even more significant in this light. To her, it was worthy of noting in her diary, and it signalled a new range of practices, both socially and linguistically. Later in the diary, she writes of the project's outcome:

> *Today is the due day of our geography assinment and oral. I was the second speaker of our group. I was so nervous and my voice was shaking. My group used fourteen minutes to discribed the culture of Zulus. When we finished*

the class, we went to ask Mr L what result did we get. It's a A–. We thought it's a pretty good result.

In this excerpt, there is no mention of 'they' or 'them.' The cohesion of the group is expressed by the use of first person pronouns. Tina represents herself not as a 'black hair' or as different in any way from the other students. Within the mainstream context, she had begun slowly to shift from the positioning of herself as an ESL student, and as different.

On some occasions, it is teachers rather than students who construct ESL students as incompetent, or who deny their participation in class activities. Nora, one of the Chinese participants in this study, recently recounted to me an incident in which a teacher said loudly in class to her Chinese friend, Alicia, 'You don't listen to what I say. You don't even understand English!' Nora claimed that later, during recess, Australian students in the class branded the teacher's remarks as racist. Even they recognized that here was a public, 'authorized,' and totally misleading representation of Alicia, a mainland Chinese student, as someone who didn't speak or understand English. The incident also revealed the importance of English in representation for linguistic minority students, and the power attached to English. Nora spoke Shanghainese and Mandarin, while Alicia spoke Cantonese and Mandarin. Both girls had been in Australia for over a year and spoke good functional, although accented, English. The public put-down was both inaccurate and inappropriate.

In contrast to the haphazard way in which students were able to use English in the classroom, on certain occasions they had no choice but to speak English, and in a very visible and public way. I am referring to oral presentations, which are standard in school subjects such as English, Geography, Science, and Social Science. 'Orals,' as students call them, are contexts where students must speak up, speak English, and speak in front of the whole class. They are hard enough for many native-born Australian students and can be extremely difficult for students of other language backgrounds.

Oral Presentations in Class

Delivering oral presentations in front of the class is an integral part of the curriculum in many subjects, and ESL teachers try to forearm their students with some experience of what is for many students an unfamiliar genre at school. There is a marked difference between answering a question or speaking informally in class, and the stress of speaking in front of a group in the sustained and structured way implied by the oral presentation genre. The latter is nerve-racking for most students, but especially for linguistic minority speakers. Nora wrote in her Newnham class diary:

> *Today we had lecture about 'book talk.' I very worried. In front of the students and teachers I very nervous. Before I stayed home recite from memory to my father. That's very fluent. But at critical moment I all the forget. So I got C+. I very feel unwell.*

What makes her nervous is in part the thought of being physically in front of the students and teachers, who are watching and listening. Nora's practice run, recited by heart to her father, was 'very fluent,' but how well she describes the real thing, albeit with Chinese syntax – 'at critical moment I all the forget.' And once again, a judgment is made in the most concrete, confining, and defining way. Her talk got a C+. She took this personally. That is, *she*, not her talk, got C+, and she felt ill.

After six months in the Newnham reception program, Nora completed six months in the ESL unit, along with partial mainstream integration. Along with her friend Alicia, she moved to another high school, where there were only a handful of Chinese students. Nora had once commented to me that 'writing orals' was one of the most difficult types of assignments. Just as she had written her book report oral at Newnham and memorized it, this was also the accepted strategy for orals at high school. This, I came to understand, was standard practice among *all* students, except many students did not learn their presentations by heart, but simply read them out aloud. Later in the year, I observed both Nora and Alicia doing oral presentations in their Year 9 English class. For the English oral in question, they had to invent a product and devise the marketing strategy for it. Nora had invented a chair which performed magical transformations, such as putting hair on bald people, and making students more intelligent. Alicia had also worked on a chair idea, basically a 'water-bed chair.' They had written their scripts in full and shown these to the ESL teacher. Here is what the teacher said to me about Nora's:

> When she showed me her script I thought oh my god where do I start? If I fix it and make it perfect it's no longer theirs, but we took the most glaringly obvious expressions, we talked about how to express various bits. Even though their language was, you know, what are they trying to say here? (.) they had all the right features of adverts. They understand what they're supposed to do, and some of the subtleties of what they're trying to produce and it's the language that's their biggest problem.

Although the task is basically an oral, students are expected to draft a complete written version. This creates anomalies for all students in regard to the nature of spoken discourse as opposed to, say, an essay, but places particular pressure on ESL students, who must show mastery of standard grammatical forms in the written draft. The oral is in essence another written task, an uncomfortable fusion of oral and literate practice. There was no concession to the fact that developing the marketing strategy for an imaginary product, complete with visual aids, was quite a demanding task. Nor was there any acknowledgment that these girls were operating in their third language. In fact, while the teacher stated that the girls understood the generic features of advertisements, their use of language (English) was constructed as 'their biggest problem.' The teacher's impulse was to take their idiosyncratic discourse and to 'fix it and make it perfect.'

In the lesson at which the oral presentations were made, two Anglo-Australian boys volunteered to do theirs first. Each came to stand at the front of the class and each read, with an unwavering flat delivery, the entire talk from palm cards. There was desultory applause at the end of each talk. The teacher then asked Alicia, but Nora said she'd go first. Her voice was soft but she could be heard with effort. She had memorized most of her script, and Alicia stood beside her with Nora's 'visual aid' completely covering her (Alicia's) face. It was a drawing of the miraculous chair, which Nora called a 'sofa.' Nora giggled at times, but got through it quite confidently. The students were listening, and it occurred to me it was possibly the first time they had heard her voice, although she had been in the class for two months. Overall, it was not audible enough for students to actively participate as listeners, but the class was attentive and applauded at the end. Alicia was next. She read her script in a tiny voice. The teacher asked her within 30 seconds to speak louder, but the volume didn't really change. The students were basically quiet, but unable to hear. One boy near me called out, 'Can't hear.' Alicia continued reading, her lips moving, almost soundlessly . Students knew it was over when she moved to sit down, and there was brief applause. The doing of 'orals' raised several issues for Nora and Alicia. They were, as Nora described, 'critical moments' in a number of senses. They entailed the stress of standing very visibly in front of the class, being observed and listened to in a way that was unfamiliar, by class members who, due to limited interaction within and outside the class, were also unfamiliar. There were judgments made on what was heard, and presumably on what was inaudible, informally by students, and formally by the teacher. Finally, the accepted practice of doing orals incorporated a full written script, and, often, when students used palm cards, the cards basically contained every word of the talk. To illustrate this point further, here is a typical example of a Year 11 oral task:

> You have been working undercover as a private investigator on the scene of the Shakespearean play you have studied. You have been commissioned to examine incidents of deception and their consequences. You are not to read your talk, however it is *compulsory* for all students to submit a transcript of their oral to the teacher before they present their address. In order to speak for 3–4 minutes your transcript will need to be 500–600 words.

As mentioned above, this makes the oral an intrinsically written exercise, subject to the same stringent grammatical criteria as formal written text, not to mention a highly complex, linguistically demanding, and sophisticated artifice. And, although Nora had memorized her talk, she was penalized for being soft-spoken.

To transform learning activities, such as oral presentations, into experiences which take into account these students' identities, a number of shifts would need to occur. It is not hard to imagine how oral presentations could be made easier for linguistic minority students. Performing in front of smaller groups would help, as would the use of small microphones, chances to rehearse to a sympathetic listener, and rethinking the oral presentation as a contextualized spoken performance, rather than a formal speech which had to be drafted in entirety, and from which the features of conventional spoken discourse were absent. If the written form remains as standard, genres which reflect the identities of the writer, such as personal journals, could be used occasionally. For example, a task could be to write the voice-over for a particular character, to be used as a link between two scenes in a movie. Such a task has more authenticity as a pre-written, but orally delivered text. In the interests of fairness, it also seems that students who bother to rehearse and learn their talks should be rewarded for doing so.

Audibility

The data I have used in this chapter were selected from various Chinese-speaking students in the study. I also have data from Bosnian students which show a somewhat different picture of identity negotiation through English language use. One of these students, Milena, was a powerful agent for her own interests within a few months of arriving in Australia, and through the medium of her third language, English. When

Milena exited the intensive ESL school and entered high school, she was placed in Year 10, on the advice of her former ESL teachers, and after an interview with the high school ESL staff. I interviewed Milena two weeks after she had started high school, and she was in Year 11. Here is what she said:

> Um, I should actually be in (.) Year 10. But because of my age, er, I asked Mrs Parditch (*the ESL coordinator*) if I may, er (.) move to Year 11. Because I really think (1.0) this Year 10 is easy for me. And er many of my friends are Year 11, many Bosnians (*inaudible*). So it's like, easier to be with them (.) they can help me finding something, an', I just, and my parents think that, er, it's, 11, grade 11, no that grade 10 is too easy for me, so, I'm (.) I'm (.) I choose English, Maths B, Theatre Arts, Drama, Music and Biology. And (.) it's not **hard**, at all. Just sometimes in Music (.) I find a bit difficult because I don't know, do all, all the words, but I know them in Bosnian, so they just bit different.

In this excerpt, Milena reveals an analytic standpoint, enunciating five grounds which constituted her case for a change of year level, presumably all of which she used with Mrs Parditch. These included her age (objectively a very minor one-year difference), the 'easiness' of the work in Year 10, the presence of her friends in Year 11 (former Newnham students), the fact that her Bosnian friends could help her with the work, and parental support for the move. Mrs Parditch commented briefly on the change when I raised it with her later, saying she was not entirely happy with it, that she didn't think Milena was ready, and that a lot of Bosnian students think they are better than they actually are. She gave me that resigned 'when-students-get-their-own-way' look. What can you do? A new NESB student had tackled the ESL coordinator in her new high school on a previously taken decision, and prevailed. I asked Milena later if she had a sense of belonging in the mainstream classes:

R: Do you, do you feel as if you **belong** (.) to the mainstream bunch of kids or do you feel different?

M: Erm, I feel as if I belong, but when I was in grade **ten**, first week, oh all the **kids**, they were only kids. I came first day into my **form meeting**, and some small guys and girls, and I, and I said to myself 'I'm out of here. I can't be in grade 10.' **Then** I went to Mrs Parditch and said 'Please please please please' and she talked to my **Mum** 'please please please' (1.0) and I moved (laughs).

R: Lucky it worked.

This is an account about Milena's identity work, but, at the same time, it is identity work in action, as she constructs for me the process of getting your own way with teachers, and displays her own competence. It was as if she had recreated the ruse, inviting my complicity. I did not disappoint, rounding off her anecdote with 'Lucky it worked.' In fact, I felt that luck was not really a factor. In this account, she had spent one week in Year 10, greeting with disdain and virtual disbelief the notion that she could ever belong to this group of 'small guys and girls' who were 'only kids.' Her response was summed up in her use of the youth vernacular 'I'm out of here.' Renegotiating her identity from a Year 10 student to a Year 11 one was, in my view, a significant achievement, which Milena could only have realized through the medium of English, used fluently and without an interpreter. Hers was an audible performance, and it got results.

However, it should be added that Milena had also accrued substantial linguistic and symbolic capital prior to arriving in Australia, which underpinned her agency. She had lived in Denmark for three years, where she had learned Danish. Thus, she spoke two languages, Bosnian and Danish, which shared many cognates with English, and developed a stock of language learning strategies which had worked for her in Denmark. She also had multilingual and college-educated parents, as well as a network of friends *in situ*, some of whom spoke English. Finally, and perhaps significantly, she was physically beautiful, not to mention white. It is important to note here that, even within the framing of audibility and audible difference I have suggested, it would be an analytical error to overlook the very real possibility that, for all students in this study, visible difference or ethnicity was highly salient to their language learning and use, and to their negotiation of identity. In my mind, it was unthinkable that any of the Chinese-speaking students in the study could have achieved the level of agency described above after two weeks at high school. Why was this so stark a contrast?

It is quite possible that the Chinese students were subject to discrimination and difficulties based on their Asian appearance, rather than what they sounded like. Tina expressed this perception quite overtly. Recent scholarship also stresses the importance of access to interactions in English for linguistic minority students (Norton & Toohey, 2001; Sharkey & Layzer, 2000), and the Asian students had few such interactions. Whether the Asian students were marginalized by mainstream students, or marginalized themselves or a combination, they had little access to the opportunities needed to develop confidence and competence in English.

Tina claimed she had been discriminated against or at least positioned on the basis of her being a 'black hair.' Categorization and representation of the Other are subtly shaped by implicit everyday practices, as well as by others' representations. Tina's view was heartfelt – it was what she experienced in a very real sense. On the other hand, there is still a case to be made for the importance of audibility. I have observed cases in many Australian classrooms over two decades where Australian-born Chinese students who spoke with broad Australian accents were *heard* (and I suspect seen by their friends) as 'Australian.' They were as loud and boisterous as any other student on occasion and were socially integrated into groups of their Anglo-Australian peers, both in class and out. Furthermore, students who use Australian-sounding discourses are generally observed by recently arrived migrant and refugee students as 'mainstream,' regardless of appearance. As one Taiwanese student in Year 11 confided:

> If your English is as fluent as Australian students', the Australian students do not really see you that much differently. I saw them talking to those Asian students whose English is good in the same way as they would to other Australian students.

What this suggests is that, in the negotiation of identity in multilingual contexts, if you *sound* alike within the Discourse, you are not *seen* as different. It is important, as Gee (1996) suggests, to *sound right*. An example of this is offered in a recent letter to the editor in a national newspaper which described a raucous bunch of Asian students on a Melbourne tram. The writer commented: 'Although judging by their faces, they were all of southeast Asian heritage, a smile came to my face when I heard the distinctive Aussie twang of their accents' (*The Weekend Australian*, May 19–20, 2002: 20). It was unspecified, but probable, that many of these students were Australian born, or had arrived here at a young age. What is clear from the letter is that the observer revised an initial assessment based on appearance to a more favorable, accepting, and amused representation based on audible similarity to the dominant discourse.

However, for more recently arrived immigrant students, the situation is far more complex and difficult. Expecting such students to sound like mainstream students, to do mainstream identities, and to negotiate their identities in school contexts defies what we know about how long it takes to acquire and use languages effectively (Collier, 1989). I have observed some students, like Milena, make dramatic and extraordinary progress in acquiring a range of Discourses in English, some within 12 months. But they are in a minority, and understanding how such lightning acquisition and school integration occurs would require another ethnographic study. All of the six Asian students in this study had difficulty being heard and understood, even two to three years on, as Collier suggested. Furthermore, Nora, Tina, and Alicia had difficulty finding contexts in which they could negotiate their identities through the use of English, socially and in the classroom. When I first met these three, they were in Newnham Intensive Centre and then moved to Year 8 in a nearby high school. At the time of writing they are in Year 12, the last year of high school. They are friendly with other students at school, but, after five years in Australia, not one of them has a native English-speaking friend whom they see outside of school. It would appear they are still heard as Chinese, although their English is fluent, but strongly accented and very soft.

Clearly there is much empirical research which documents discrimination based on visible difference. In Australia, following the September 11 terrorist attacks in the United States, and in the recent controversy over Afghani and Iraqi asylum seekers arriving in Australia via Indonesia, Islamic citizens in traditional dress or of Middle Eastern appearance have been the targets of racist attacks, both in society at large and occasionally in schools. This is all about how you look, and not about how you sound. My point is that, in most cases, these were random acts of racism, attacks committed in the absence of meaningful interaction, and mostly against 'strangers.' In multilingual school contexts, the negotiation of identity is far more complex. There may indeed be an interplay of audibility and visible difference for some students. Certainly Tina perceived that the 'black hairs' and 'blondy hairs' were positioned differently in her school. Yet, after four years at high school, and partly through her own choice not to negotiate her identity in English, Tina's school social group was 100% Mandarin-speaking, and her English was still a barrier to success in some academic subjects. Over these years she had fewer chances to negotiate her identity in English than, say, Milena, which suggests to me a link between audibility and negotiability.

Conclusions

Speaking constructs aspects of our identities, but requires the collaboration of the listener, who must not only hear, but, as Bourdieu (1991) points out, must also believe. Bourdieu (1991) suggests that authority and power derive from the differential uptake of the linguistic habitus in different social fields or sites of exchange where the *conditions of reception* are critical. It seems clear that we cannot view the competence of the speaker in isolation from the linguistic market, language in isolation from social practices, or speaking in isolation from hearing. Mey (1985: 240) once suggested that 'one's highest priority in speaking a foreign language should be to make oneself understood; sounding right is definitely a subordinate goal.' If he was referring only to speaking a foreign language on holidays, he may well have been right. However, for migrant students struggling to speak English in Australian schools, *sounding right* is important. Audibility means speaking loudly enough, and in a variety of the discourse that can be readily understood and acknowledged by other speakers, although it does not presume native-like, cultivated Australian or some chimerical 'accentless' dialect. Furthermore, the notion of *conditions* signals that negotiation does not take place within a social vacuum. Conditions at school, including social and institutional practices, may or may not provide an environment which favors the development of second language competence in a range of discourses. The question of who is heard, who is acknowledged and thereby legitimated as a speaker of English is an important one for all ESL students. The practical activity of speaking English is a move toward recognition in mainstream contexts, but, if students are to negotiate their identities through language in school settings, they need access to spoken interactions with English speakers in which their voices are heard, and their identities seen as usable capital in the first place. If this happens, some of the weight of communicative performance can be redistributed from the shoulders of the language minority student to other participants in communication.

Such a shift involves institutional practices, curriculum, and pedagogy. Institutional practices need to reinscribe linguistic minority students as linguistically and socially competent, but also maximize their chances to use the target language and thus to renegotiate their identities. The power of Discourses to privilege or subordinate minorities also needs to be better understood within institutional contexts. The curriculum should reflect the social lives of the students, embedding tasks within activities which connect students to their own linguistic and cultural backgrounds, and using their identities and first languages as resources for learning and teaching others. Students' personal narratives and visual texts should also be valued parts of the curriculum. Finally, pedagogical practices and preservice teacher education must enable the conditions for minority language students to speak and to be heard. Pedagogy should also incorporate a broader sociocultural framing of language use which values and develops the diverse social languages present in classrooms.

The research which forms the basis of this chapter indicates that there is a politics of speaking English as a second language in schools. Voices are differentially valued, differentially audible. Audibility means that there is an economy of reception, which allows or constrains both language development and the negotiation of students' identities. Giroux has suggested that

> it is important that educators possess a theoretical grasp of the ways in which difference is constructed through various representations and practices that name, legitimate, marginalize and exclude the cultural capital and voices of subordinate groups in society. (1990: 43)

As a teacher and researcher, I believe that institutions and those within them (including students) need to understand the sociological theory involved, but also must acknowledge the practical consequences for those marginalized groups or individuals who are denied a voice.

Appendix

Key to transcription conventions (based on Psathas, 1995)

(.)	untimed micro-interval
(2.0)	2 second pause
good	bold indicates emphasis
(*italics*)	transcriber's description
[	overlapping talk

References

Antaki, C. (1996) Social identities in talk: Speaker's own orientations. *British Journal of Social Psychology* 35, 473–492.

Auerbach, E. (1995) The politics of the ESL classroom: Issues of power in pedagogical choices. In J.W. Tollefson (ed.) *Power and inequality in language education* (pp. 9–33). Cambridge: Cambridge University Press.

Bourdieu, P. (1977) The economics of linguistic exchanges. *Social Science Information* 16, 645–668.

Bourdieu, P. (1991) *Language and symbolic power.* Oxford: Polity Press.

Caldas-Coulthard, C.R., and Coulthard, M. (eds) (1996) *Texts and practices: Readings in Critical Discourse Analysis.* London: Routledge.

Carrington, V. and Luke, A. (1997) Literacy and Bourdieu's sociological theory: A reframing. *Language and Education* 11 (2), 96–112.

Collier, V. (1989) How long? A synthesis of research on academic achievement in a second language. *TESOL Quarterly* 23, 509–531.

Cummins, J. (1980) The cross-lingual dimensions of language proficiency: Implications for bilingual education and the optimal age issue. *TESOL Quarterly* 14 (1), 175–187.

Davies, A. (1991) *The native speaker in applied linguistics.* Edinburgh: Edinburgh University Press.

Davison, C. and Williams, A. (2001) Integrating language and content: Unresolved issues. In B. Mohan, C. Leung, and C. Davison (eds) *English as a second language in the mainstream: Teaching, learning and identity* (pp. 51–70). London: Longman.

Drake, S. and Ryan, J. (1994) Narrative and knowing: Inclusive pedagogy in contemporary times. *Curriculum and Teaching* 9 (1), 45–56.

Firth, A. and Wagner, J. (1997) On discourse, communication, and (some) fundamental concepts in SLA research. *The Modern Language Journal* 81, 285–300.

Gee, J.P. (1996) *Social linguistics and literacies: Ideologies in discourses* (2nd edn). London: Taylor and Francis.

Giroux, H. (1990) *Curriculum discourse and postmodernist critical practice.* Geelong: Deakin University Press.

Giroux, H. (1992) Resisting difference: Cultural studies and the discourse of critical pedagogy. In L. Grossberg, C. Nelson, and P. Treichler (eds) *Cultural studies* (pp. 199–212). New York: Routledge.

Glew, P. (2001) Staking out the territory for intensive English programs in secondary school contexts. *TESOL in Context* 11 (1), 15–20.

Heller, M. (1994) *Crosswords: Language, education and ethnicity in French Ontario.* Berlin/ New York: Mouton de Gruyter.

Hornberger, N. (1995). Ethnography in linguistic perspective: Understanding school processes. *Language and Education* 9, 233–248.

Hymes, D. (1996) *Ethnography, linguistics, narrative inequality: Toward an understanding of voice.* London: Taylor and Francis.

Lippi-Green, R. (1997) *English with an accent: Language, ideology and discrimination in the United States.* London: Routledge.

Luke, A. (1998) Critical Discourse Analysis. In L. Saha (ed.) *International encyclopedia of the sociology of education* (pp. 50–57). New York: Elsevier Science Ltd.

Matthews, J.A. (1997) A Vietnamese flag and a bowl of Australian flowers: Recomposing racism and sexism. *Gender, Place and Culture* 4 (1), 5–18.

McKay, P. (1999) The bilingual interface project: The relationship between first language development and second language acquisition as students begin learning English in the context of schooling. *Queensland Journal of Educational Research* 15 (1), 123–132.

Mey, J. (1985) *Whose language? A study in linguistic pragmatics.* Amsterdam/ Philadelphia: John Benjamins.

Miller, J. (1997) Reframing methodology in second language research: From language to discourse. *Australian Educational Researcher* 24 (3), 43–56.

Miller, J. (1999a) Becoming audible: Social identity and second language use. *Journal of Intercultural Studies* 20 (2), 149–165.

Miller, J. (1999b) *Speaking English and social identity: Migrant students in Queensland high schools.* Unpublished Ph.D. dissertation, University of Queensland. Brisbane.

Miller, J. (2000) Language use, identity and social interaction: Migrant students in Australia. *Research on Language and Social Interaction* 33 (1), 69–100.

Mohan, B., Leung, C., and Davison, C. (eds) (2001) *English as a second language in the mainstream: Teaching, learning and identity.* London: Longman.

Nelson, C., Treichler, P., and Grossberg, L. (1992) Cultural studies: An introduction. In L. Grossberg, C. Nelson, and P. Treichler (eds) *Cultural studies* (pp. 1–16). New York: Routledge.

Norton, B. (1997) Language, identity and the ownership of English. *TESOL Quarterly* 31, 409–429.

Norton, B. (2000). *Identity and language learning: Gender, ethnicity, and educational change.* London: Longman.

Norton, B. and Toohey, K. (2001) Changing perspectives on good language learners. *TESOL Quarterly* 35 (2), 307–322.

Norton Peirce, B. (1995) Social identity, investment, and language learning. *TESOL Quarterly* 29, 9–32.

Pavlenko, A. (2000) Access to linguistic resources: Key variable in second language learning. *Estudios de Sociolinguistica* 1 (2), 85–105.

Psathas, G. (1995) *Conversation analysis: The study of talk in interaction.* Thousand Oaks, CA: Sage.

Rampton, B. (1995) *Crossing: Language and ethnicity among adolescents.* London: Longman.

Savignon, S. (1991) Communicative language teaching: State of the art. *TESOL Quarterly* 25, 261–277.

Schiffrin, D. (1996). Narrative as self-portrait: Sociolinguistic constructions of identity. *Language in Society* 25, 167–203.

Sharkey, J. and Layzer, C. (2000) Whose definition of success? Identifying factors that affect English language learners' access to academic success and resources. *TESOL in Context* 34 (2), 352–368.

Spolsky, B. (1989) *Conditions for second language learning.* Oxford: Oxford University Press.

Tsui, A. (1996) Reticence and anxiety in second language learning. In K. Bailey and D. Nunan (eds) *Voices from the language classroom* (pp. 145–167). Cambridge: Cambridge University Press.

van Dijk, T. (ed.) (1997) *Discourse as social interaction.* London: Sage.

Wagner, J. (1993) Ignorance in educational research or, how can you not know that? *Educational Researcher* 22 (5), 15–23.

Chapter 11

Sending Mixed Messages: Language Minority Education at a Japanese Public Elementary School

YASUKO KANNO

Introduction

Language minority education in Japanese public schools has a short history. Until the early 1990s, public schools in Japan operated with the assumption that all the students they must educate were native speakers of Japanese. It is only within the last decade that the rapid increase in the number of foreign-born children has forced Japanese schools to deal with those children for whom Japanese is not the first language (L1). The number of language minority students in public elementary and junior high schools that are identified as needing special instruction in Japanese as a second language (JSL) more than tripled over the last decade, from 5463 in 1991 to 18,432 in 2000 (Monbukagakusho, 2001).

A number of reasons exist for the sudden increase of foreign residents in Japan. Of particular importance is the 1990 revision of the Immigration Control and Refugee Recognition Law, which eased restrictions on the kinds of jobs ethnic Japanese of other nationalities and their families can legally engage in (Sato, 1995; Vaipae, 2001). The revision has led to an influx of South Americans of Japanese descent. Also important in the context of this study are Chinese 'war orphans' and refugees from Southeast Asia. The former are Japanese children who were abandoned in China during the chaos of the Second World War and subsequently adopted by Chinese parents (Tomozawa, 2001). Their repatriation started in 1982, and a bill in 1994 increased the government's responsibility in sponsoring the return and settlement of the orphans and their families. The number of refugees from Vietnam, Laos, and Cambodia that Japan has received is small compared with other developed countries; nonethe-

less, 10,666 refugees have been officially recognized and have permanently settled in Japan (Gaimusho, 2001). Since most of these newcomers
are unskilled laborers in the context of the Japanese market economy, by
default they send their children to public schools, where the tuition is
free, hence the sudden influx of language minority children in Japanese
public schools.

At this stage, programs catering to the needs of these students in public
schools are far from adequate. The task of supporting JSL students falls
mostly on the good will of individual teachers, teachers who may not
have had any special training in second language (L2) teaching or multicultural education. However, some schools, especially in areas where
foreign residents are concentrated, are more active in exploring effective
ways to educate culturally and linguistically diverse children. This study
examines the policies and practices of one such school, which I will call
Sugino Elementary School.

The purpose of this chapter is twofold. First of all, since few scholars
outside of Japan are aware of the multicultural tide that is sweeping
Japan, my broader aim is to help make this recent development more
visible internationally. My second goal is more specific. I aim to investigate how the identities of language minority students are represented,
nurtured, and oppressed by the policies and practices of the school.
Researchers studying the state of language minority education in Japan
tend to portray Japanese schools as an oppressive environment for language minority students. An ethnographic investigation of educational
policies and practices at Sugino suggests that a more nuanced understanding of the complex and contradictory nature of school practices is
necessary. A school is rarely all oppressive or all enabling to language
minority students. Teachers send conflicting messages about the virtues
of multilingualism and multiculturalism; language minority students, too,
stress their special identities in one context, and yet demonstrate their
eagerness to assimilate in another. In this chapter, I argue that schools
constitute a socially, culturally, and politically complex milieu in which
both teachers and students hold contradictory orientations to language
and identity, without necessarily being aware of these contradictions.

Language Minority Education in Japan

Growing research on language minority education in Japan paints a
grim picture. It highlights the lack of systematic JSL instruction, indifference toward the children's first language and culture, and the homogenizing effects of Japanese schooling. Vaipae and associates (Vaipae, 2001)

conducted a multi-method project on the state of language minority education in Japanese public schools. Based on a country-wide survey of teachers and parents, several case studies, and interviews with parents, teachers, administrators, and policy makers, Vaipae identifies a number of serious problems in the current system. A vast majority of language minority students, scattered as they are throughout the country, receive no JSL instruction; where JSL classes are available, they focus on basic conversation skills in Japanese rather than on academic literacy; few JSL teachers receive professional training in language pedagogy; principals and teachers exhibit no awareness of the special needs of language minority students; and parents do not have a full grasp of the difficulties their children are experiencing. Pointing out these and many other problems, Vaipae (2001: 199) argues: 'The only language education model apparent in our observation was submersion with the goal of assimilation.'

Ota (2000) conducted an ethnographic study of the education of Nikkei South American children in a city in the Tokai region, west of Tokyo. In addition to arriving at many of the same conclusions as Vaipae (2001), especially about Japanese schools' emphasis on sameness and lack of support for the development of academic language skills, Ota offers insights deriving from his ethnographic observations. He notes, for instance, that the JSL classroom is often located in an isolated corner of the school and that activities that take place there are hidden from Japanese students. Ota also points out that Japanese schools on the whole offer extremely limited opportunities for language minority students to use their L1. Virtually no JSL teachers at the schools he studied spoke Portuguese or Spanish beyond some basic vocabulary. The only place where the students could use their L1 comfortably was in the JSL class. Ota (2000: 176) observes that the students 'come to the Japanese Language classroom not so much to learn Japanese as to regain their sense of self' (original in Japanese, my translation). However, as their length of residence extended, even the conversation in the JSL classroom shifted to Japanese because of the rapid L1 attrition. While they had not yet acquired grade-level Japanese language proficiency, the language minority students rapidly lost their L1, resulting in quintessential subtractive bilingualism (Lambert, 1975).

Other researchers note that the 1990s brought in some progress. Noyama (2000) reports various forms of JSL support that are being implemented across the country, such as pull-out JSL classes, the Center School system (where JSL students from nearby schools are gathered in one school to receive JSL instruction on a regular basis), and team-teaching between homeroom and JSL teachers. For many of these classes, bilingual instructional aides who speak the students' L1 have been hired on a part-time basis (Enoi, 2000). Meanwhile, community-based efforts for L1 maintenance are also taking root. The L1 maintenance classes typically take place outside of the regular schools and are run by parents, volunteer groups, and churches (Noyama, 2000). According to Ishikawa (1999, cited in Noyama, 2000: 205), in Kanagawa Prefecture alone there are 40 such mother tongue classes (*bogo kyoshitsu*).

On the whole, however, the picture of language minority education in Japan that these studies paint suggests that language minority students are being forced to assimilate into the education system which hardly recognizes their different identities and needs, and that support for L1 maintenance, if it exists at all, comes from sources outside of the school.

Theoretical Framework

For the theoretical framework of this study, I adopt Cummins's (2000a,b) theory of identity negotiation. Cummins is interested in how different orientations to cultural and linguistic diversity are reflected in the policies and practices of schools, and particularly in the process of identity negotiation between students and teachers. Noting that micro-level interactions between individual educators and students reflect the macro-level relations of power in the broader society, he points out that teachers may be unwittingly engaged in what he calls 'coercive relations of power' (2000a: 44) by failing to question social inequality and preparing their students to accept the status quo. Education operating on the principles of coercive relations of power is very effective in suppressing language minority students' linguistic and cultural identities because it makes students internalize the message that the values and rules imposed by the dominant group are 'natural, normal, universal, and objective, and that it is in everyone's interest to accept those rules' (Heller & Martin-Jones, 2001: 6). If language minority students do not fit, that is because there is something wrong with *them*, not with the school.

Schools or teachers engaged in coercive relations of power are not necessarily blatantly racist or oppressive. Cummins (2000a: 249–251) provides a much more subtle example of coercive relations of power. B. Dudley Brett, a science teacher in a Canadian school, sent a letter to a national newspaper expressing his frustration with the limited English skills of ESL students, who constituted about half of his class. Brett is aware that these students 'have a superior prior education in their own language.' He writes: 'They are well-mannered, hard-working and respectful of others. I enjoy having a multiracial society in my classroom'

320 *Identities in Multilingual Contexts*

(Brett, 1994, cited in Cummins, 2000a: 250). However, Brett is frustrated with communication barriers between himself and his ESL students and with the fact that he has to give them a failing mark because they cannot demonstrate their comprehension.

This is a common story many teachers facing language minority students in their classroom can identify with. In his letter, Brett comes across as a committed and caring teacher. However, as Cummins (2000a: 251) argues, 'Nowhere in his letter is there a sense of the need to address his own acknowledged "incompetence"':

> It is the ELL student who requires 'fixing' through more intensive and extensive ESL instruction rather than Brett's own teaching abilities and strategies. Brett does not problematize his own identity as a competent science teacher despite the fact that he is unable to teach science to almost half of the students in his science class. (2000a: 251)

Thus, even committed and well-intentioned teachers can be involved in the perpetuation of the coercive relations of power if they fail to question the fundamental power structure of their schools that works to marginalize minority students.

While acknowledging schools' role in social reproduction, Cummins (2000a,b) also recognizes the possibility that schools can become agents in reversing social inequality. He advocates a shift from 'coercive relations of power' to 'collaborative relations of power' (Cummins, 2000a: 44). In the latter orientation, power is not seen as pieces of a pie – one's gain is another's loss. Rather, 'the more empowered one individual or group becomes, the more is generated for others to share, as is the case when two people love each other or when we really connect with children we are teaching' (Cummins, 2000a: 44). At the heart of the collaborative relations of power is an affirming relationship between teacher and student. A student Nieto (1994) interviewed captures the essence of this teacher–student relationship. According to this student:

> If you don't know a student there's no way to influence him. If you don't know his background, there's no way you are going to get in touch with him. There's no way you're going to influence him if you don't know where he's been. (Nieto, 1994: 418)

A teacher who cares to get to know each student as a whole person and genuinely respects what each student brings to the classroom is likely to make a more tangible difference than any instructional techniques or innovative measures (Cummins, 2000b).

At the same time, collaborative relations of power are not the same as the warm, fuzzy 'we accept all of you' approach to education. Full participation in the school community should constitute a step toward learning to participate fully in a truly democratic society. Concrete steps to take include efforts to encourage language minority students to develop literacy skills in their L1 and building classroom instruction on their prior knowledge. Teachers may also choose to teach their students the rules of the dominant culture so that the students can appropriate them in order to voice their opinions and be taken seriously (Delpit, 1988; Nieto, 2000). In addition, education based on collaborative relations of power needs to incorporate the learning of critical literacy 'where [students] become capable not only of decoding the words, but also reading between the lines in order to understand how power is exercised through various forms of discourse' (Cummins, 2000a: 46). In short, schools need to help students acquire awareness and skills to challenge disabling identities that may be imposed upon them and to negotiate more dignified identities for themselves.

In this study, I adopt Cummins's frameworks to examine what kinds of language ideologies and relations of power operate in the policies and practices of one public elementary school in Japan, and how these ideologies and power relations influence students' identities. Ultimately, what I want to show is that contradictory orientations to language and identity coexist in the school, which sends students mixed messages about what identities are available for appropriation and which are particularly desirable. The children are highly sensitive to these conflicting messages: While young ones show considerable pride in their linguistic and cultural heritage, older students seem increasingly drawn to identities that are in line with the dominant values of the society that emphasizes homogeneity and the primacy of Japanese.

Methodology

This study is part of a larger project that examines education of bilingual students in Japan. Sugino Elementary School was one of the five schools where I conducted fieldwork. I visited the school nine times between October and December 2000. Taking detailed field notes, I observed classes in each grade as well as monolingual and bilingual JSL classes. I also interviewed teachers, administrators, and bilingual instructional aides.[1] I made some attempts to interview students formally; however, given their young age, they were not able to abstract information from their daily experience very well to answer specific questions about language, culture, and identity. Much more informative were informal conversations I had with them during lunch, the recess, and in the hallways. Because these conversations were situated in particular contexts and in what they were doing at that time, what the students told me spontaneously in those moments was more illuminating.

The staff was extremely open and warm; anyone I approached was willing to sit down and talk to me, and to let me into their classroom. Generally speaking, I observed the same class for the whole day, and at the end of the day interviewed the teacher who taught that class. In the JSL classes I participated in class activities. Since JSL teachers wanted to give as much attention as possible to individual students, anyone coming into their classes instantly became an informal teaching assistant. In the homeroom classes, I was largely a non-participant observer, staying at the back of the classroom. Only when the activities were more individual- or group-based (which happened often in this school), did I help out by circulating around the room and working with individual students or groups. In Japanese public schools, homeroom teachers eat lunch in their classroom together with their students; likewise, during lunch I sat among the students and ate the lunch the school provided.

Public elementary schools are part of the larger educational system and are strongly influenced by the municipal and prefectural boards of education and neighborhood public junior high schools. For this reason, in addition to conducting fieldwork at Sugino Elementary School, I also interviewed a teacher's consultant at the municipal board of education in charge of multicultural education and a veteran JSL teacher at the neighborhood junior high school, which almost all Sugino students attend after graduation.

Sugino Elementary School

Sugino Elementary School is located in a city neighboring Tokyo. The school is located in a large subsidized housing project and has an unusually high proportion of foreign-national students. At the time of my fieldwork there were 226 students, 99 (or 43%) of whom were language minority students (66 of them were of foreign nationalities and 33 naturalized Japanese). Of the foreign-national students 53% were Chinese, and the others were mostly the children of war refugees from Vietnam, Cambodia, and Laos. The majority of them came to Japan at a young age or were born in Japan. Many of Sugino's children come from single-parent homes and families on welfare. Many of the parents are blue-collar workers, and in today's recessionary Japan they are facing constant fear of being laid off.

Although the surrounding high-rise apartment buildings are by no means luxurious, they are clean and well maintained, as is the school itself. At its peak, it used to accommodate 2000 students and, now that the student population has decreased to a tenth of that size, the school enjoys the abundance of space unusual in an urban school in this country. Many of the original classrooms have been collapsed into larger rooms for special purposes, such as a computer lab and meeting spaces. The major bulk of the south wing, where all the homeroom classrooms are located, has been renovated, and with wide windows facing south the place feels airy and bright. Fresh flowers are placed in the hallways and in the classrooms. Each homeroom class is assigned two classrooms, one for regular instruction and another for storage and group work. Because of the abundant space, amid the usual noises of elementary school one can find moments of serenity.

Most of the language minority students at Sugino intend to live permanently in Japan; many hope to obtain Japanese citizenship as soon as possible. The challenge of Sugino School then is how to help these immigrant children become members of Japanese society, a point Ms Takano, the principal, emphasizes:

> People who live here are permanent residents; they are going to live permanently in Japan. So we have to help [the children] gain enough power to be able to survive in Japan. We want to guarantee academic abilities that become the foundation of that power. So our role as an elementary school is to make them learn basic academic skills. (IN November 24, 2000)[2]

A veteran and committed educator, Ms Takano notes that her philosophy as principal is to think of the large number of foreign students as an asset that enriches the school rather than as a problem.

JSL Instruction

Thirty-two percent of the language minority students receive pull-out instruction in the JSL classroom. JSL students from the same homeroom class, usually four or five students, are pulled out together, three or four times a week. Two JSL teachers, Ms Ayabe and Mr Nakamura, are in charge of the JSL classes. Although both teachers used to be regular homeroom teachers, by now they are seasoned JSL specialists. Ms Ayabe was a JSL teacher in her previous post; Mr Nakamura had lived in Taiwan

and speaks Chinese. Both of them receive in-service training in JSL education on a regular basis from the city and prefectural boards of education.

Most JSL classes I observed involved reading aloud or copying down
passages from the grade-level language arts textbook, practicing Grades
1–3 *kanji* (Chinese characters), and playing games with *hiragana* and
katakana (basic scripts) cards. I helped Kim, a Grade 5 Vietnamese boy,
read aloud a passage in the textbook. The passage was about the history
of the earth and when the human species came about. Although Kim was
able to read aloud the text, in which he had spelled out the reading of the
Chinese characters in *hiragana*, it was clear that he was not paying any
attention to the content. When I asked him whether he understood what
he was reading, he said, 'Oh, I don't know. I'm not good at *Kokugo*
(Japanese language arts).' I called out to Ms Ayabe and asked whether
we were just supposed to read aloud the text. She answered that at this
stage that was all that was expected.

To an outsider like myself, it appeared that the activities in the pull-out
classes could have been made more intellectually stimulating. However,
both JSL teachers said that they wanted to make the JSL classroom a
safe haven where JSL students could be themselves. Mr Nakamura said:

> We do not have an overly-demanding curriculum in JSL, and it could
> be said that it is intentional. The students are stressed out in the
> regular classroom and, if the JSL class added more stress, then they
> would have nowhere to go. (IN November 21, 2000)

Indeed, Kim told me that he prefers working in the JSL class because, he
said, 'Here I can understand everything.'

Recent arrivals who are not yet conversational in Japanese are pulled
out to attend bilingual JSL classes with instructional aides who are native
speakers of their L1s. Unlike the monolingual JSL classroom, which is a
recently renovated, bright room in the south wing of the school building,
bilingual JSL classes are held in an old art studio in the north wing. It is
dark and cold and feels removed from homeroom classrooms. When I
observed a class, Ms Sugi, a former Cambodian refugee who has been
living in Japan for 15 years, was working one-on-one with Tak, a Grade
2 Cambodian boy who had arrived in Japan two months before. Ms Sugi
used Japanese most of the time, but when giving instruction and
explaining the meaning of a word, she sometimes switched very briefly
to Cambodian. It was odd to see two native speakers of Cambodian
conversing in Japanese, which one of them hardly speaks. As in the monolingual JSL class, decontextualized, drill-type exercises were common in
this class.

The existence of the two types of JSL classes and their respective locations suggest a complex identity management pattern in this school. Both classes focus exclusively on the development of Japanese, and both employ a decontextualized drill-type method of teaching Japanese. However, the monolingual JSL class, taught entirely in Japanese by licensed teachers and thereby seen as promoting a 'mainstream' Japanese identity, enjoys a more legitimate status than the bilingual class. As far as the monolingual JSL class is concerned, I did not sense any of the secretive or shameful connotations associated with JSL classes that Ota (2000) pointed out in his study. In contrast, many homeroom teachers seem ambivalent about the use of students' L1 in the bilingual JSL class, and that ambivalence is reflected in the isolated location of the classroom. It is as if the use of minority languages needed to be contained, and hidden from regular (i.e. legitimate) activities of the school. Going into the bilingual JSL classroom in the north wing, through a hallway, does feel like you are stepping out of the regular part of the school.

At the same time, the very distance of the bilingual JSL class, and of the monolingual JSL class to a lesser extent, from homeroom classrooms serves to create a sanctuary for language minority students. In a way, the students are appropriating the isolation of the JSL classes as a way to give themselves space to express identities that are hard to express in the regular classroom. Many of the language minority students, even ones who are no longer taking JSL classes, simply 'hang out' in both JSL classrooms. By coming to JSL classes, they are taking 'time out' from the pressure of the homeroom activities. Also, during one JSL class, I heard two fourth graders talking enthusiastically to Mr Nakamura about their experience in Vietnam. When I moved to their table, the two boys pulled out a picture book on Vietnam from the shelf and started to explain the photos to us. When they found a photo of Ho Chi Minh City in the book, one of them exclaimed, 'I know where it is! I've been there!,' followed by the other boy's 'Me too!' I did not witness such an open display of enthusiasm about their native countries outside of the JSL classrooms.

Student-centered Activities

Homeroom teachers, who teach most of the classes, varied in their attention to language development across the curriculum. Mr Saito, a Grade 2 homeroom teacher, stood out in this regard. He was extremely skilled at making students aware of their own language use. For example, Grades 1 and 2 classes were planning to cook sweet potatoes they had harvested as a science project. The students split into four groups, each making a different dish. Saito was in charge of the group making *daigakuimo* (candied potatoes):

> After discussing how many potatoes they need for their part, they realize that they need to know how many the other groups are going to need – after all there are only so many potatoes. So Saito-sensei dispatches several kids to the other three groups to find out. But before he sends them away, he gets the students to practice how they might go about asking the question. Shota [a Chinese boy] offers, 'How many potatoes do you need?', but the teacher points out that people would be taken aback if he just turns up in their classroom and asks the question out of the blue. Other children suggest that he should start with 'I am Shota from the *daigakuimo* group.' The teacher is happy with this introduction and gets each member to rehearse the entire sequence of questions before letting them go. (FN November 21, 2000)

This way, the first and second graders learned how to ask a question in an appropriate manner in the context of a science project. Although this mini-lesson was improvised chiefly for Shota's benefit, other children also participated in the learning by offering their ideas of socially acceptable ways of asking a question and going over the flow of the discourse they were supposed to follow.

In the same session, something else happened. The potato-cooking project was a joint project among four classes, and Motoe, a Chinese girl in one class, discovered that Shota, who belonged to another class, was also Chinese. She said to him, in Japanese, 'Oh, you are Chinese too?' Mr Saito took advantage of the situation and asked the whole class a series of questions: 'Who among you are Chinese?', 'Who speaks Chinese at home?', 'Who can understand videos in Chinese?', and 'Who can understand Chinese and Sign Language?'. The last question was for Shota, whose parents are both deaf. Every time Saito asked a question, many hands shot up in the air. He greeted the enthusiastic responses with the equally energetic 'That's great!' and 'Wonderful!' He sounded so genuinely excited about having Chinese speakers and users of Sign Language in his class that even those children who did not qualify raised their hands to be included.

As the potato harvesting and the subsequent cooking project indicate, the curriculum at Sugino is rich in hands-on, student-centered activities. Among various activities I observed, particularly notable were sixth graders' projects on wars. Mr Mikami, Grade 6 homeroom teacher, pointed out to me that war is the underlying cause for virtually all of Sugino's language minority students' residence in Japan: the Chinese students are grandchildren and relatives of 'war orphans' and the children from Southeast Asia are refugees who escaped civil wars in their countries. Grade 6 students investigated those wars that were most relevant to them and interviewed family members and people in the local community about their war experiences. Projects such as this can be seen as the beginning of an effort to promote critical literacy. All students were encouraged to reflect on their socio-political environments, and language minority students, who knew more than majority students about a topic that was deemed important in the academic curriculum, were able to assume authoritative identities. Similarly, community members were for once also construed as experts whose knowledge and experience had much to offer to all students. This project shows that, even in the context of the mainstream curriculum, teachers' creative efforts can accord more recognition to language minority students' knowledge.

L1 Attrition

In contrast to their respect for *cultural* diversity and efforts to incorporate it into the curriculum, teachers and administrators at Sugino were less willing to embrace *linguistic* diversity. In the Sugino community, language minority students' L1s play an insignificant role. The only place where their L1s are given an official function in academic instruction is in the bilingual JSL classes. Ms Ayabe, a JSL teacher, told me that even this level of L1 use was difficult to introduce initially: homeroom teachers did not understand the point of incorporating the students' L1s into the school curriculum.

With respect to the students' bilingualism, most teachers seem to prefer the 'division of labor' principle: that is, the school supports students' L2 development while the home can help maintain their L1. Ms Takano, the principal, stated clearly:

> In a public school I don't think it is necessary to look after [language minority students'] mother tongue, not unless you can afford to. So if the parents think that mother tongue education is necessary, they can teach it at home or make use of classes run by volunteer groups, of which there are many. (IN January 24, 2001)

This division of labor principle sounds reasonable in theory, but may prove problematic for many students. The principal referred to the existence of heritage language classes in the neighborhood. It is true that such classes exist. But Mai, a Vietnamese fifth grader I interviewed, said that she used to attend a Vietnamese class but had stopped going because she needed to take a bus and a train to get to the class. Her parents considered such a trip too dangerous for an 11-year-old. A heritage language class appropriate for each student may not be in the vicinity of the housing project, and, given the young age of these students, their parents may be reluctant to send their children to a class far away. In such a case, the task of L1 maintenance falls entirely on the shoulders of the parents, who may be out of the home most of the day in an effort to make ends meet.

Even when it is possible for the home to foster L1 maintenance, it may not be wholly approved of by the teachers. Contradictory ideologies surround language minority students' use of L1 in the home. Officially, it is considered desirable for parents to speak to their children in their L1 and encourage L1 maintenance/development in the home. Less officially, some teachers believe that language minority students' use of L1 hinders their Japanese development. One teacher said: 'Their vocabulary is inevitably small because they are not exposed to Japanese in the home.' This was not an isolated remark in this school. No teachers ventured to argue that the students ought to be speaking Japanese at home. But it was evident that many of them subscribed to the maximum exposure hypothesis of L2 acquisition – the idea that 'success in learning [an L2] is more likely to be assured if instructional time through [the L2] is maximized' (Cummins, 2000a: 241) – and viewed the students' limited exposure to Japanese in the home as a problem.

With little systematic support for L1 maintenance, many language minority students are rapidly losing their L1, while at the same time not acquiring the grade-level Japanese language proficiency. Ms Ayabe was worried about the negative effects of L1 attrition on the students' cognitive development. Being in close touch with the JSL students, she was acutely aware of the difficulties they were experiencing in academic learning:

> Nothing sticks. They can't remember things. It's not that they are not making an effort. When I came to this school, I talked to the previous JSL teacher. We initially said that maybe these kids have fewer drawers [in their head]. But gradually, we started to say, maybe it's not the drawers but they don't even have a place to put the closet. (IN October 16, 2000)

She noted that bilingual students generally have difficulty moving beyond Grade 2-level Japanese literacy, a tendency also observed by Ota (2000). Ayabe suspects that between the Grade 2 and 3 materials lies a sudden cognitive leap: concepts to be learned become more abstract and complex. Those students who are losing their L1 may not have enough cognitive maturity to handle the age-appropriate curriculum in Japanese, she said.

Academic Underachievement

Stepping out of the JSL classroom, it does not take long for a visitor to realize that underachievement is not limited to language minority students, but is a school-wide phenomenon at Sugino. The academic level of the school, as judged by the standardized tests the city administers every year, is considerably lower than the city's average. The seriousness of the students' underachievement becomes more apparent in upper grades. I observed a Grade 6 math class in which students were writing an end-of-unit test:

> Some are making incredibly simple mistakes. For instance, in solving a problem that asks the surface area of the side of a cylinder, a boy simply multiplies the diameter of the cylinder by its height. Some are having difficulty coming up with an answer for 4 times 9. Mr Mikami [the homeroom teacher] estimates that probably a fifth of the students can't recite the multiplication table correctly. He also says that when he asked the class the formula for calculating the area of a triangle, only a third of the students got it right. (FN August 12, 2000)

When I hear the word 'test,' I tend to think of students answering questions unassisted. However, Mr Mikami provided a considerable amount of help. The review of the section they had done on the board just before the test was not erased: there was a large poster on the wall with a list of various formulae for calculating areas and volumes; and Mikami told the students to circle the word *volume* and *area* in the word problems, so that they would not get the two confused. Even with all this support, Mikami predicted that on average the class would get half the answers wrong. Speaking of the gap between the demands of the Grade 6 curriculum and the students' abilities, he said: 'It's like going to a store to buy a fur coat with 10 yen in hand.'

The teachers blamed poverty, parental neglect, and lack of discipline in the home as the causes of students' underachievement. Some teachers talked in a sympathetic manner about the difficult situations many families were in, noting that many Sugino children come from single-parent homes on welfare. Other teachers were more critical of parents' neglect of their children. One teacher said: 'These kids don't go to *juku* [cram school] after school, and it's not as if their parents are in when the kids come home either. So many of them are just left by themselves.' The principal had an interesting twist to add to the 'blame the family' discourse. She told me that language minority children lead more regulated lives than their Japanese counterparts and that their parents have higher academic expectations of them. Once bilingual students overcome the linguistic hurdles, she said, they tend to outstrip Japanese peers academically and start taking leadership roles in the class:

> Those Vietnamese students who are doing well come from homes where the amount of TV watching is strictly limited. I wonder if the Japanese families are doing the same. Likewise, I hear that Chinese families – I suppose this would be the ones that are not doing part-time work – eat dinner together. Many foreign families remind me of the older days in Japan – call it 'dignified poverty' (*seihin*) – where people were poor but led a disciplined, beautiful life. (IN November 24, 2000)

Ms Takano's comment is interesting because she is effectively making a claim that middle-class values that some students bring to the school are in the end a stronger determinant of their academic success than native/non-native proficiency in Japanese. Parents of language minority students may be placed at the bottom rung of the socioeconomic hierarchy in Japan, but back in their native countries many of them were professionals. It is a very well-documented phenomenon that middle-class students are more advantaged in school performance than working-class students because the culture of the school reflects middle-class values (e.g. Feldman, 2001; Heath, 1983; McCallum & Demie, 2001; Sacks, 2000; Shannon, 1996; White, 1982). The class factor is often difficult to distinguish from ethnic and linguistic factors since more often than not language minority children belong to the working class. However, Ms Takano is suggesting that school success is ultimately a class issue, rather than a linguistic or ethnic one. Those students who can access middle-class identities either from their past or present are more likely to achieve school 'success,' so that language minority students who come from a former middle-class background may in the end be at a greater advantage than working-class native Japanese-speaking students.

Student Identities

Most teachers I talked to said that students in this school take multi-culturalism for granted and that being different is part of their everyday life. Because many of them grew up in the housing complex where the community is so culturally diverse, diversity is what is 'normal' for these children. It is the adults who are overly sensitive about ethnic issues, they said. Indeed, although bullying the weak does happen in this school, as in any other school, children at Sugino do not seem to be bullied because of their foreignness, which has been reported in other public schools (Vaipae, 2001). In Grades 5 and 6, especially, the more socially powerful members of the classes are bilingual students, and anyone who dared to utter racist remarks would quickly be sanctioned. Further, ethnicity or language background does not seem to play a major role in the children's socialization patterns. A student's best friend may well be someone from the same ethnic background, but I did not observe a noticeable Japanese/ non-Japanese fault line among the students.[3]

Indeed, the official discourse of the school celebrating diversity was to a certain extent internalized and utilized by students. Students' backgrounds were openly talked about, both by teachers and students. In this school, 'Where are you from?' is a form of greeting and was asked of me often when I moved to a new class. When I said that I was Japanese, but had lived in Canada for a long time, the student often responded by saying where he or she came from. In the Grade 5 class, one girl told me with obvious pride: 'In this class 13 [out of 35] are foreigners (*gaikokujin*); I'm half-Chinese, and another one is quarter-Chinese.'

Coexisting with this openness to and acceptance of diversity, however, are forces of assimilation. Physically few students stand out. Because most students are Asian, in any homeroom class I found it extremely difficult to tell who was Japanese and who was not unless the teacher specifically pointed them out to me. Some faces might strike me as somewhat darker or deeper-featured, but so are many Japanese faces. In many ways, their physiognomic similarity makes the 'mainstream' Japanese identity more accessible to many language minority students at Sugino. Recent studies in the Western context (Kanno, 2003; Miller, 2000; Tse, 2000) suggest that physiognomic differences – that is, being a visible minority – limit minority students' ability to assimilate: no matter how much they wish to be the same as the dominant group, their physical features mark them as different. But, at Sugino, many language minority students can 'pass' (Furnham & Bochner, 1986) as Japanese if they want to.

In addition to the physical homogeneity, what is striking about this school is its linguistic homogeneity. Throughout my fieldwork I never heard bilingual students speak their L1, except on a few occasions when the teachers solicited it. Even children of the same language background converse with one another in Japanese. As a result, sometimes students from the same country do not realize their shared background, as the earlier example of Motoe and Shota suggests. Even so, younger children like it when they can display their L1 competence. In an International Understanding (*kokusai rikai*) class, which is a mixture of conversational English and introduction to various cultures, the instructor, Ms Cho, is Chinese. Although in principle she is supposed to teach the class in English, she sometimes incorporates some basic Chinese expressions to good effect. One day she taught a short Chinese song to second graders. The Chinese students in the class were obviously able to sing it better than the others. Billy, an Indonesian boy, said exasperatedly to a nearby Chinese girl: 'Rika, it's normal you can do this because you're Chinese!' Rika bobbed her head with a smug grin on her face.

As they get older, however, students become more reluctant to display their L1. The Grade 5 homeroom teacher, Ms Imanishi, said that the bilingual students in her class do not like it when she singles them out and asks them, for instance, 'What do you call this in Vietnamese?' It is hard to know whether they do not like being singled out this way because they do not know the appropriate words in their L1 or because they do not want to be identified as speakers of a minority language. My suspicion is that it is both. In an environment with little support for their L1, many students are going through L1 attrition. It is also likely that, by the time they reach the upper grades, they have assimilated the society's message that their L1 has little value as cultural capital (Bourdieu, 1991) in Japan.

Discussion

The above brief portrait of the policies and practices of the Sugino community suggests that several orientations to linguistic and cultural diversity and multiple relations of power are operating in the school. Given the prominence of problems and criticisms toward language minority education in Japan in the existing literature, it is important to acknowledge the concerted efforts that the Sugino staff are making to respect students' diverse backgrounds. The principal's policy to view cultural and linguistic diversity as an asset sets the overall tone of the school's approach to language minority education. Rather than focusing on language minority students' assimilation into the Japanese school, the JSL teachers are concerned about the emotional and psychological well-being of the students. The homeroom teachers are incorporating into the curriculum a number of activities and projects which either directly address multiculturalism or can effectively utilize multicultural resources in the class. Many of them also try to send messages to the students about the value of being able to speak another language.

It is in the micro-level interactions between teacher and student where students' identities are affirmed or denied (Cummins, 2000a,b). And it is in the micro-level interactions with the students where many Sugino teachers showed their strengths. During my fieldwork I witnessed many beautiful moments where the teachers spontaneously created opportunities for language minority students to shine. When Mr Saito had Chinese speakers and users of Sign Language raise their hands, everyone in the room understood his message that proficiency in those languages was an ability one should be proud of. Similarly, when Mr Mikami proposed a project on wars, he gave bilingual students in his Grade 6 class an opportunity not only to reflect on their reasons for coming to Japan, but also to see themselves as knowledgeable about issues with which mainstream Japanese students had little experience. These examples demonstrate that, given the right framework, language minority students can take on identities of competence within the public school setting. In such instances the teachers created collaborative relations of power that affirmed the strengths that bilingual students bring to the classroom and that are rarely valued in the broader society.

Alongside those practices that demonstrate collaborative relations of power exist other practices that suggest coercive relations of power. The formal structure and curriculum of the school accord a very small role to bilingual students' L1s. While *cultural* diversity has been extensively and ingeniously incorporated into the curriculum in every grade, the references to bilingual students' L1s were limited to the teachers' spontaneous comments during the class, such as 'How do you recite the multiplication table in Vietnamese?' and 'Oh, you sing this song in China, too?' Although such remarks help communicate to the students that their L1s are not irrelevant, they do very little for actual L1 maintenance.

In the absence of any recognition of the role that students' L1 can play in academic learning, it is deemed absolutely necessary for non-Japanese-speaking students to acquire Japanese as fast as possible so that they can start learning content. The homeroom teachers send language minority students to JSL classes in the hope of having them learn Japanese quickly; however, in JSL classes the students are often engaged in cognitively undemanding, content-less language exercises. The result is that some JSL students continue to advance through the grades and exit elementary school without having learned the grade-level curriculum. A veteran JSL teacher at the junior high school pointed out:

> For those who arrive in Japan in the middle of elementary school, Japanese language instruction takes the priority, which means that

subject matter learning is put on hold. And the students arrive in junior high school without having filled in the missing parts. When they arrive in junior high and come face to face with even more difficult instruction, they are totally lost. (IN February 8, 2001)

Thus, alongside efforts to nurture an identity of competence (especially on the part of individual teachers), there is also a mechanism in place that forces language minority students to take on an identity of incompetence. The way the system works is reminiscent of the situation Toohey (2000) describes with regard to ESL students in a Canadian public elementary school:

> The specific practices of their classrooms 'produced' the focal children as specific kinds of students, with the identity 'ESL learners' as a more or less important marker. They held the positions, not the internal essence, of being 'ESL' and 'quiet' or 'clever' or 'not so clever' and so on; these identities made sense only within the context of these particular practices. ... As central practices, schools evaluate and rank children and thus manufacture identities for them. (Toohey, 2000: 125)

There is no question that, while protecting and empowering language minority students, schools such as Sugino are also contributing to social reproduction of coercive relations of power.

As the adult members of the Sugino community send the younger members highly mixed messages about linguistic and cultural diversity, the students also exhibit mixed attitudes toward each other's differences. On the one hand, the students take for granted different skin colors, non-Japanese-sounding names, and the fact that some of their classmates are pulled out to JSL classes every so often. Power among the children is sufficiently evenly distributed to enable language minority members of the community to play leadership roles. Whereas adults tend to be far more conscious of linguistic and cultural diversity and tiptoe around issues of difference, for the kids it is a fact of life. On the other hand, to become powerful members of the school community requires a certain degree of linguistic and cultural assimilation. Younger children respond enthusiastically to opportunities to showcase their multilingual and multicultural identities. By contrast, older students show more reluctance to speak their L1 in front of others, suggesting that they have internalized the dominant values of the society and covet an identity that has more currency value in Japan.

Conclusions

A school constitutes a complex organism in which multiple overlapping sub-communities are interacting with one another (Wenger, 1998). Just like a person (McKay & Wong, 1996; Norton, 2000; Norton Peirce, 1995), it has multifaceted, contradictory, and dynamic identities. The policies and practices that aim to nurture cultural and linguistic diversity can coexist with discourses that imply that such diversity is a problem. At Sugino, both teachers and students held contradictory orientations toward multilingual and multicultural identities. The same teachers who claim that cultural and linguistic diversity is a treasure of the school may just as sincerely worry about the negative impact of language minority students' use of L1 in the home on their Japanese development. Students, too, may appropriate the discourse that celebrates multiculturalism and proudly announce to the visitor which student came from which country. But they rarely use their L1 in the school.

At Sugino, there was a clear limit up to which staff members were willing to make accommodations and beyond which they would not go. They were quite willing to help language minority students adjust to the existing structure and culture of the school. They did not leave the students to their own devices to sink or swim. Individual teachers tried their best to help language minority children take pride in their linguistic and cultural heritage. But they did not examine whether the existing policies and practices should continue in the face of increasing diversity. Their limitations have to do with the lack of awareness rather than any ill intention. It would be a misrepresentation on my part to claim that the Sugino teachers and administrators deliberately avoided discussing sociopolitical factors which contribute to student underachievement because they were uncomfortable acknowledging their own role in perpetuating coercive relations of power. Rather, it is my belief that the notion of education as politics (Shor & Pari, 1999) has not yet permeated Japanese public schools. But no educational practices are politically neutral (Wiley, 1996), and that includes the practice of remaining blind to the process of 'how power relations in the broader society get translated into educational failures within the schools' (Cummins, 2000a: 43). For, in the absence of the awareness of power relations in society and within the school as causal factors in underachievement, teachers and administrators at Sugino were apt to blame the bilingual students' L1 or low-income-family students' life style at home for their underachievement.

When Ms Ayabe says that some bilingual students may not have enough space in their heads to put a closet, she is implicitly attributing the cause of the problem to the students. It does not seem to occur to the teachers to examine the adequacy of the current instructional practices. Further, when the principal remarks that some non-Japanese students are better prepared for schooling than Japanese students, she is suggesting that the families are responsible for aligning their home cultures to the culture of the school. But the dominant, middle-class values and behaviors promoted in the school may not be so readily available to low-income families as she assumes. It is not seen as the school's responsibility to change *its* policies and practices so that the children from foreign and/or non-middle-class backgrounds can learn.

More than 40% of Sugino students are language minority students. This means that educational policies and practices that were originally developed for 'mainstream,' native Japanese-speaking children may not be appropriate for nearly half of the student population in this school. Nonetheless, just like Cummins's (2000a) example of the Canadian teacher, the staff at Sugino did not problematize their identities as competent teachers. Rather, the problem was construed as one of students' identities not fitting comfortably into the existing structure.

Notes

1 At this school I was not able to interview the parents since, during the period of my fieldwork, there were no particular events such as teacher–parent conferences and class observations that would bring them to the school.
2 Excerpts from interview transcripts are identified by IN, followed by the date of the interview. All the interview quotations are my translations from the original Japanese. Field notes are indicated by FN.
3 Peer groups divided according to ethnicity or L1 were more noticeable in some of the other schools I observed.

References

Bourdieu, P. (1991) *Language and symbolic power.* Oxford: Polity Press.
Cummins, J. (2000a) *Language, power and pedagogy.* Clevedon: Multilingual Matters.
Cummins, J. (2000b) Negotiating intercultural identities in the multilingual classroom. *The CATESOL Journal* 12 (1), 163–178.
Delpit, L. (1988) The silenced dialogue: Power and pedagogy in educating other people's children. *Harvard Educational Review* 58 (3), 280–298.
Enoi, Y. (2000) Atarashii gaikokujin/newcomer no kodomo no nihongo/bogo shido ni tsuite (On the newcomer children's Japanese language development and mother tongue maintenance). In M. Yamamoto (ed.) *Nihon no bilingual kyoiku (Bilingual education in Japan)* (pp. 125–164). Tokyo: Akashi Shoten.
Feldman, S. (2001) Closing the achievement gap. *American Educator* 25 (3), 7–9.

Furnham, A. and Bochner, S. (1986) *Culture shock: Psychological reactions to unfamiliar environments*. London: Routledge.

Gaimusho (Ministry of Foreign Affairs) (2001) *Nanminmondai to nihon* (*The refugee problem and Japan*). On WWW at http://www.mofa.go.jp/mofai/gaiko/nanmin/main3/htm. Accessed March 13, 2002.

Heath, S.B. (1983) *Ways with words: Language, life, and work in communities and classrooms*. Cambridge: Cambridge University Press.

Heller, M. and Martin-Jones, M. (2001) Introduction: Symbolic domination, education, and linguistic difference. In M. Heller and M. Martin-Jones (eds) *Voices of authority: Education and linguistic difference* (pp. 1–28). Westport, CT: Ablex.

Kanno, Y. (2003) *Negotiating bilingual and bicultural identities: Japanese returnees betwixt two worlds*. Mahwah, NJ: Lawrence Erlbaum.

Lambert, W.E. (1975). Culture and language as factors in learning and education. In A. Wolfgang (ed.) *Education of immigrant students: Issues and answers* (pp. 55–83). Toronto: Ontario Institute for Studies in Education.

McCallum, I. and Demie, F. (2001) Social class, ethnicity and educational performance. *Educational Research* 43 (2), 147–159.

McKay, S.L. and Wong, S.-L. C. (1996) Multiple discourses, multiple identities: Investment and agency in second-language learning among Chinese adolescent immigrant students. *Harvard Educational Review* 66 (3), 577–608.

Miller, J. (2000) Language use, identity, and social interaction: Migrant students in Australia. *Research on Language and Social Interaction* 33 (3), 69–100.

Monbukagakusho (Ministry of Education and Science) (2001) *Heisei 12nendo nihongoshidou ga hitsuyou na gaikokujin jidou-seito no ukeire joukyoutou ni kansuru chousa no kekka* (*Results of the 2000 survey on the acceptance and instruction of foreign children and students needing Japanese language education*). On WWW at http://www.mext.go.jp/a_menu/shotou/clarinet/data4.html. Accessed March 15, 2002.

Nieto, S. (1994) Lessons from students on creating a chance to dream. *Harvard Educational Review* 64 (4), 392–426.

Nieto, S. (2000) *Affirming diversity: The sociopolitical context of multicultural education* (3rd edn). New York: Addison Wesley Longman.

Norton, B. (2000) *Identity and language learning: Gender, ethnicity and educational change*. London: Longman.

Norton Peirce, B. (1995) Social identity, investment, and language learning. *TESOL Quarterly* 29 (1), 9–29.

Noyama, H. (2000) Chiiki-shakai ni okeru nensho-sha eno nihongo-kyoiku no genjo to kadai (Issues and state of Japanese language education for minors in local communities). In M. Yamamoto (ed.) *Nihon no bilingual kyoiku* (*Bilingual education in Japan*) (pp. 163–212). Tokyo: Akashi Shoten.

Ota, H. (2000) *Newcomer no kodomo to nihon no gakkou* (*Newcomer children in Japanese public schools*). Tokyo: Kokusai Shoin.

Sacks, P. (2000) Predictable losers in testing schemes. *School Administrator* 57 (11), 6, 8–9.

Sato, G. (1995) *Susumu gakkou no kokusaika* (*The growing globalization in schools*). In A. Nakanishi and G. Sato (eds) *Gaikokujin jido-seito kyouiku e no torikumi* (*The education of foreign students*) (pp. 1–11). Tokyo: Kyouiku Shuppan.

Shannon, P. (1996) Poverty, literacy, and politics: Living in the USA. *Journal of Literacy Research* 28 (3), 429–449.

Shor, I. and Pari, C. (eds) (1999) *Education is politics: Critical teaching across differences, K-12*. Portsmouth, NH: Boynton/Cook.

Tomozawa, A. (2001) Japan's hidden bilinguals: The languages of 'war orphans' and their families after repatriation from China. In M. Noguchi and S. Fotos (eds) *Studies in Japanese bilingualism* (pp. 133–163). Clevedon: Multilingual Matters.

Toohey, K. (2000) *Learning English at school: Identity, social relations and classroom practices*. Clevedon: Multilingual Matters.

Tse, L. (2000) The effects of ethnic identity formation on bilingual maintenance and development: An analysis of Asian American narratives. *International Journal of Bilingual Education and Bilingualism* 3 (3), 185–200.

Vaipae, S. (2001) Language minority students in Japanese public schools. In M. Noguchi and S. Fotos (eds) *Studies in Japanese bilingualism* (pp. 184–233). Clevedon: Multilingual Matters.

Wenger, E. (1998) *Communities of practice: Learning, meaning, and identity*. Cambridge: Cambridge University Press.

White, K. (1982) The relation between socioeconomic status and academic achievement. *Psychological Bulletin* 91, 461–481.

Wiley, T.G. (1996) *Literacy and language diversity in the United States*. Washington, DC: Center for Applied Linguistics and Delta System.

Index

Names

Adamic, L. 39, 41-42, 49, 51-52, 56
Ager, D. 94-95, 109
Agnihotri, R. 4
Aguillou, P. 94, 97, 99-100
Ahmad, W. 158
Albert, S. 120
Alvarez, J. 55, 62
Alvarez-Caccamo, C. 9
Anderson, B. 17, 24, 35-36, 41, 71-72, 93
Andreini, L. 94
Antaki, C. 297
Antin, M. 37, 41-45, 48-51, 53, 59-60, 62
Aramburo, A. 127
Ardener, S. 189
Armour, W. 7
Atkinson, D. 269-270
Auer, P. 9-10, 20, 22
Auerbach, E. 292
Azra, J.-L. 94, 97, 120

Bach, E. 42
Bachmann, C. 99-100
Bailey, B. 22
Bailey, K. 220, 230
Baker, C. 163, 174
Bakhtin, M. 21, 26, 68, 78, 80, 168, 196, 266
Baldassar, L. 204
Baldassare, A. 198
Ball, R. 228
Ballara, M. 244, 249
Bammer, A. 13-14, 18
Bannerman, C. 140
Barnett, S. 158
Bartholdt, R. 38-39, 45-49, 59-61
Basier, L. 99-100
Bee, B. 246-247, 261
Beglinger, N. 45
Belanger, M. 278
Belcher, D. 269, 283-284, 286
Belsey, C. 287
Bernstein, B. 245
Berry, J. 4-5
Bézard, C. 94, 97

Bhabha, H. 13, 17, 95-96, 106
Bhaskar, R. 250
Bhavnani, K. 170
Billy, J. 264
Birman, D. 7
Blackledge, A. 2, 13, 15, 17, 19, 21-22, 25-26, 28, 95, 172, 244-245, 292
Blanc, M. 5
Blommaert, J. 68-69, 71, 74, 93-94, 114
Blood, R. 259
Bochner, S. 331
Boelhower, W. 40-41, 44-45,
Bok, E. 37-38, 41, 45-49, 51, 56, 59
Bokhorst-Heng, W. 71
Bourdieu, P. 3, 10-11, 13, 15, 35-36, 47-48, 68-69, 72, 88-89, 93, 198, 245, 256, 290-291, 294, 311, 332
Boyer, H. 94, 99, 120
Boyer, J.-C. 121
Brah, A. 13, 18
Brandeis, L. 48
Breitborde, L. 6
Brière, J. 234
Brown, C. 139
Brumberg, S. 59
Bucholtz, M. 20, 95, 106
Bujaki, M. 29
Bullock, B. 94
Burnett, A. 5
Burton, P. 164-166
Burton, S. 190
Butler, J. 287
Byrne, J. 4, 6-7

Cahan, A. 38, 46, 49, 51, 57, 60
Caldas-Coulthard, C. 299
Calvet, L.-J. 99-100, 120
Cameron, D. 9
Canagarajah, S. 16, 22-23, 25-26, 28, 268, 270, 275, 277, 280, 287
Carrington, B. 138
Carrington, V. 295
Cerulo, K. 13

Chamba, R. 142
Cheneau, V. 94, 97,120
Chianello, J. 199
Chinchaladze, N. 165
Chlebowska, K. 244, 249
Chouliaraki, L. 192
Cillia, de, R. 92
Clément, R. 5-6, 32
Collier, V. 310-311
Collins, J. 11
Connor, U. 269, 278-280, 284, 286
Constantinidou, E. 164-166
Corby, R. 248
Corker, M. 134, 146
Corson, D. 245, 248, 250
Coulthard, M. 299
Coward, R. 287
Crichton, J. 47
Cross, W. 126, 140
Cummins, J. 16, 194, 302, 319-321, 328, 333, 335-336
Cutler, C. 9
Czarniawska, B. 17-18

Dahrendorf, R. 248
Danesi, M. 194, 199
Danquah, M.N. 54, 62
Davies, A. 292
Davies, B. 3, 13-14, 20, 96
Davies, L. 167
Davis, A. 126
Davison, C. 296, 302, 314
De Beaugrande, R. 269
Decker, J. 44
Delpit, L. 321
DeMaria Harney, N. 198-199
Demie, F. 330
Demougeot, M. 97
Denzin, N. 39
Dively, V. 142
Doran, M. 17, 21-26, 28, 121
Dorfman, A. 54, 62
Dörnyei, Z. 241
Doucet, R. 73
Dragadze, T. 166
Drake, S. 298
Dressler, W. 269
Dubet, F. 120-121
Dulong, R. 121
Durand, J. 94
Duvillard, J. 122
Dyson, K. 166, 189

Eastman, C. 22

Eckert, P. 95, 102, 111
Edwards, J. 13-14
Egbo, B. 16, 21-23, 25-26, 28, 246, 252, 255-256
Ellis, J. 287
Enoi, Y. 319
Enslin, E. 247
Erikson, E. 126
Etta, F. 255

Fabrice, A. 94
Fairclough, N. 68, 71, 78-79, 81, 88, 170, 192
Feldman, S. 330
Firth, A. 292-293
Fischer, M. 62
Fishman, J. 8, 175
Foucault, M. 184, 245-246, 266, 268, 285-287
Fowler, R. 68
Freire, P. 245-247
Fry, J. 220
Furnham, A. 331

Gadet, F. 102
Gal, S. 10-11, 13, 15, 27, 68-72, 79-80, 84-85, 87, 164
Gardner-Chloros, P. 74
Garnier, J. 121
Gee, J. 290-292, 299, 310
George, K. 99
Gergen. K. 13-14
Giampapa, F. 14, 17, 21-22, 25-26, 28, 194-195, 199, 207, 214, 216
Giddens, A. 192-193
Giles, H. 4, 6-7
Gillett, G. 222
Giroux, H. 287, 293, 296, 313
Gitlin, A. 195
Giudicelli, A. 121
Glenn, E. 258
Glew, P. 290
Goffman, E. 126
Goudailler, J.-P. 94, 97, 99-100, 120
Gramsci, A. 71, 246
Green, M. 35, 41
Grillo, R. 4, 72-73, 94
Grimard, M. 192-193
Grossberg, L. 314
Guiraud, P. 100
Gumperz, J. 7-8

Hairston, E. 127
Hall, S. 3, 13, 17-19, 126, 170, 193, 287

Hamers, J. 5
Handlin, O. 37, 48
Hargreaves, A. 95
Harré, R. 3, 13-14, 20, 96, 222
Hartmann, E. 41, 58
Harvey, P. 164-165
Heath, S. 330
Heller, M. 3, 8-13, 22, 27, 73, 291, 319
Higgins, P. 125-126
Hill, J. 95, 104
Hill, K. 104
Hoffman, D. 5-6
Hoffman, E. 54, 62-63
Hokenson, J. 35, 40, 44, 62
Hollos, M. 244, 260
Holmes, J. 111
Holt, H. 36, 39, 41, 44, 52-53, 56, 60
Holte, J. 37-38
Honeyford, R. 81
Hong, L. 164
hooks, b. 126, 281
Hornberger, N. 296
Hughes, J. 251
Humphrey, C. 165
Humphries, T. 125
Husband, C. 5-6
Hutner, G. 37-38, 43, 48
Hymes, D. 73, 291

Iacovetta, F. 199, 205
Ingram, N. 159
Irvine, J. 15, 68-72, 79-80, 84-85, 87

Jacobson, R. 6, 8-9
Jacques, M. 193
James, H. 59
James, M. 16-17, 21-23, 25-26, 28, 126
Jayaratne, T. 167
Jazouli, A. 121
Johnson, M. 162
Johnstone, B. 9
Jones, L. 158
Josselson, R. 168
Judd, E. 221-222

Kalaja, P. 223
Kanno, Y. 15, 22, 24-26, 28, 331
Kaplan, A. 224
Kasarda, J. 258-259
Kasper, G. 220
Keith, M. 193
Kelly, L. 167
Khanna, A. 29
Kim, E. 48

Kim, U. 29
Kim, Y. 4
Kinginger, C. 17-18, 21-23, 25, 28, 34, 292
Kingston, M. H. 61-62
Klassen, C. 249, 255
Kline, R. 222, 232
Kloss, H. 60
Koven, M. 170
Kramsch, C. 34, 269-270, 275
Kroskrity, P. 69
Kuhn, T. 251

Labrie, N. 192-193, 211
Ladd, P. 125
Lakoff, G. 162
Lam, W. Sh. E. 34, 270, 275
Lambert, W. 318
Lane, H. 125
Lankshear, C. 245-246
Lantolf, J. 34, 55, 220, 223
Lapeyronnie, D. 120-121
Laurioz, H. 122
Lawson, L. 125
Layzer, C. 309
Lee, G. 139
Lefkowitz, N. 94, 97, 99-100, 120
Le Page, R. 8, 106
Lepoutre, D. 99-100, 120-121
Leppänen, S. 223
Leung, C. 314
Li Wei 5, 9-10
Li, X. 269, 274-275, 278-280, 285
Liang, A.C. 30
Liebhart, K. 92
Lippi-Green, R. 228, 291-294
Lo, A. 9, 95, 196
Long, M. 220
Love, D. 127
Lucas, C. 159
Luebke, F. 49
Luke, A. 245, 295, 298-299
Lvovich, N. 54, 62

Macedo, D. 246
Macias, R. 58
Mackey, W. 166, 174
Mamoud, M. 124
Mangez, C. 121
Marconot, J.-M. 93, 100
Marcowicz, H. 125
Marcoz, L. 122
Marshall, J. 248
Martin-Jones, M. 319
Matthews, J. 290

Mauranen, A. 277
Maximé, J. 145
May, S. 2, 4
McCallum, I. 330
McCarthey, S. 249
McConnell-Ginet, S. 95, 111
McDonald, M. 164-166
McKay, P. 290
McKay, S. 6, 335
McLaren, P. 245-246
McNamara, T. 7
Meherali, R. 127
Meir, G. 1-2
Méla, V. 94, 97, 99-100,120
Merle, P. 94
Merriam, S. 251
Mey, J. 312
Meyerhoff, M. 111
Miller, Jennifer 15, 21-22, 24-26, 28, 291-292,
    297, 299, 331
Miller, J. 158
Mills, J. 14, 21-22, 25-26, 28, 161, 167
Minces, J. 120
Mohan, B. 293
Montgomery, G. 158
Moraes, M. 168
Mori, K. 54, 62
Moseley, M. 219
Myers-Scotton, C. (*see also* Scotton, C.) 8-9

Nelson, C. 296
Nielsen, T. 39, 43, 45, 49-51, 53-54, 56-57,
    60-61
Nieto, S. 320-321
Noels, K. 4-5
Norton (Peirce), B. 6, 221, 223, 229, 240, 291,
    293, 309, 335
Noyama, H. 318-319

Odora, C. 244
Ogulnick, K. 54, 62
Olneck, M. 53
Ota, H. 318, 325, 328
Ouseley, H. 81, 87

Padden, C. 125, 146, 223
Padilla, R. 223
Panunzio, C. 38, 41-46, 49, 51-53, 56
Papanek, H. 262
Paperman, P. 121
Parajuli, P. 247
Pari, C. 335
Passeron, J. 245
Paul, E. 100

Pavlenko, A. 5-7, 13, 17-19, 21-26, 28, 34, 40,
    49, 54-55, 58, 60, 62, 73, 95, 205, 220-221,
    223, 244, 287, 292-293
Payne, C. 94
Petitpas, T. 94
Philips, S. 71
Phillipson, R. 2, 162
Phoenix, A. 170
Pierre-Adolphe, P. 94, 97
Pile, S. 193
Piller, I. 2, 74-75
Platt, P. 228
Plénat, M. 94
Polanyi, L. 220, 222
Pon, G. 32,
Power, S. 29
Prys Jones, S. 174
Psathas, G. 313

Quell, C. 192

Rampton, A. 138
Rampton, B. 9, 22, 96, 102, 112, 213, 291,
    293
Rapanà, A. 196, 200
Rassool, N. 172
Ravage, M. 37, 42-47, 49-52, 56-57, 59-60
Reed, R. 159
Regan, L. 190
Reisigl, M. 92
Ricoeur, P. 19
Riis, J. 36-37, 41, 45, 47-50, 52, 56, 59
Roberts, P. 42
Rockhill, K. 245
Rodman, H. 259
Rodriguez, R. 54, 61-63
Romaine, S. 162, 165
Rooker, Lord 85-89
Roosevelt, T. 47
Russell, R. 195
Ryan, J. 298

Sachdev, I. 29
Sacks, P. 330
Saifullah Khan, V. 5-6
Saïki, N. 94, 97, 99-100
Sato, G. 316
Savignon, S. 301
Schieffelin, B. 73
Schiffrin, D. 298
Schmidt, Richard 6
Schmidt, Ronald 61, 73, 84
Schnapper, D. 121
Schumann, J. 6, 34

Scotton, C. (*see also* Myers-Scotton) 8, 22
Seguin, B. 121
Sewell, P. 94
Shannon, P. 330
Sharkey, J. 309
Sharma, A. 127
Sherzer, J. 163
Shor, I. 335
Silverstein, M. 72
Skutnabb-Kangas, T. 2, 162-163
Smith, D. 139
Smith, L. 127
Smith, P. 287
Smolicz, J. 177
Sollors, W. 34, 41, 44, 47, 56
Souilamas, N. 95, 109
Spivak, G. 287
Spolsky, B. 301-302
Stavans, I. 54, 62
Stein, R. 22
Steiner, E. 37, 43, 45, 49-51, 56
Stewart, A. 167
Street, B. 245
Stromquist, N. 244, 249, 254
Stroud, C. 6
Stuart, M. 222
Suseendirarajah, S. 269, 275-280, 285
Sutton, L. 30
Swales, J. 269-270, 277
Swann, M. 138
Syed, Z. 5

Tabouret-Keller, A. 8, 14, 106, 174
Tajfel, H. 4
Talburt, S. 222
Tannen, D. 9
Taubenfeld, A. 40
Taylor, G. 127
Teillard, F. 121
Thoits, P. 262
Tifrit, A. 98
Ting-Toomey, S. 4
Tomozawa, A. 316
Toohey, K. 309, 333
Torres, L. 102
Treichler, P. 314
Treffers-Daller, J. 9
Trickett, E. 7
Troyna, B. 138

Tse, L. 34, 331
Tsui, A. 296
Tzanos, G.-O. 124

Vaipae, S. 316-318, 331
Valdman, A. 94
Valli, C. 127-128, 157
van Dijk, T. 291
van Knippenberg, A. 262
van Langenhove, L. 13-14, 20
Verschueren, J. 68-69, 71, 75, 93-94, 114
Vieillard-Baron, H. 121
Virshup, L. 262
Voloshinov, V. 68

Wagner, J. 292-293
Watson, R. 224
Weber, E. 94
Weedon, C. 13, 35, 170, 185
Weinberger, S. 94
Weiss, B. 41
Wenger, E. 111, 335
West, C. 126
West, K. 264
White, K. 330
Wiley, T. 49, 60, 335
Wilkinson, S. 222
Williams, A. 296, 302
Williams, G. 5
Williams, R. 71
Wing, Y. 48
Winncott, D. 126
Wodak, R. 68-69
Wolfe, D. 259
Woll, B. 16-17, 21-23, 25-26, 28, 125
Wong, S.-L. C. 6, 40, 335
Woodward, J. 125, 127
Woolard, K. 3, 10-11, 13, 27, 69, 104, 115
Wrench, J. 139, 158
Wright, C. 138
Wylie, L. 234
Wyman, M. 58

Yezierska, A. 38, 41, 43, 48-51
Yin, X. 40
Young, M. 29

Zaborowska, M. 63
Zentella, A. 102, 104

Subjects

Abruzzese 197, 206
academic writing 266-287
accent 294
access to
– cultural capital 240
– interactional opportunities 229-238, 241, 309, 312
– linguistic resources 6, 221, 229-238, 293
– literacy 243-244, 248, 253, 259-263
– social networks 220-223, 229-238
– symbolic and material resources 72, 193
accommodation 278-280, 284-285
acculturation 5-7
acts of identity 106
affect 170
affiliation 177, 180, 248
Africa 28, 94, 99, 128, 135, 139, 142-143, 150, 243-263
Africaans 165
African-American 222, 281
agency 20, 83, 86, 172, 180, 193, 220-222, 246, 250, 267-268, 293, 307, 309, 320
Algeria 102
allegiance 174
Americanization, 34-63, 73, 221-222
Anglo-Saxon, 45-46, 53, 59
appropriation 281-285
Arabic 23, 94, 97, 103, 111, 167, 176
argot 100
Asia 28, 94
assimilation 1, 34-63, 73, 109-110, 202-203, 222, 318-319, 331-334
assimilationism 137
attrition (*see* language attrition)
audibility 24-25, 291, 293-294, 307-313
Australia 15, 24, 28, 75, 290-313
autobiography 34-63, 187, 224
avoidance 271-274, 284-285

Bangla 77, 79, 82
basic interpersonal communication skills (BICS) 302
Belgium 8-9, 74
Bengali 166
Berber 111
bilingual
– classes 324
– conversation 10
– education 59-60
– writers 34-63, 266-287
Black
– feminist theory 126
– Sign Language 28, 148-150

borrowing 97-98
Bosnian 24, 298, 307-311
Breton 164-166
Britain 14-15, 18-19, 26, 68-89, 125-158, 161-187
British Sign Language 17, 23, 125-158

Calabrese 196
Cambodia 316, 322
Cambodian 324
Canada (*see also* Quebec) 14, 75, 192-217, 249
Cantonese 298, 300-311
Caribbean, the 94, 128, 135, 137, 142-143, 150
Catholic (*see* religion)
center, 192-217
China 298, 300, 316
Chinese 5, 24, 274-275, 283, 298, 300-311, 316, 322, 324-327, 330-333
Christian (*see* religion)
Christianity 37, 43, 194
citizenship 21, 68-89, 192, 200-206, 279, 323
class 21, 62, 114-116, 330
code-switching 7-9, 22-23, 103, 200, 202, 204
cognitive academic language proficiency (CALP) 302
communicative competence 228, 234, 290-313
communities of practice 111, 223, 228
conditions of reception 311
consciousness-raising 247
content analysis 26
critical
– action 246, 248
– analysis 247
– consciousness 247
– discourse analysis 26, 68, 299
– ethnography 26, 195
– expression 269
– literacy 245-246, 321, 327
– realism 249-250
– theory 10-20, 35, 246
– writing 286
crossing 22, 96, 112
cultural
– awareness 228
– capital 202, 240, 293, 313, 332
– consciousness 228, 236

Danish 39, 50, 53, 60-61, 309
Deaf community 16-17, 23, 125-158
Denmark 39, 49, 309

desire 219, 228, 240
dialogism 168-169
diary 298
disability 126
discourse, definition of 292
discourse analysis 26, 291, 296-299
discrimination
– ethnic 56
– linguistic 53-55
– racial 56, 136-142
domestication 247
Dominican-American 55
dual-language instruction 59
Dutch 9

emotional
– development 163
– well-being 332
emotions 162, 165
English
– as a second language (ESL) 266-287,
    290-313, 319-320
– as a supranational language 2
– domination 11
– language 1, 5, 8, 11-12, 23, 94, 97, 111,
    161-187, 201, 207-208, 252
– learning and use of 34-63, 68-89
– literacy (see literacy, English)
erasure 70-71
Estonian 2
ethnicity (see also ethnic identity) 12, 21, 24,
    42, 61-62, 106-109, 128, 150, 162, 166,
    192-217
exclusion 177, 249, 255, 258

feminism 267, 287
feminist
– approaches 167
– perspective 220
– scholarship 266
feminization of poverty 244
field 68-69, 295, 311
Finnish 278-280, 284
Flemish 74
foreign language learning 219-241
fractal recursivity 70, 80
France 18, 23, 93-120, 219-241
–francophonie, la 228
French 5, 9, 12, 17, 23, 38, 53, 60, 93-120, 164,
    166, 219-241

Gaelic 88-89, 165-166
gender (see also stereotyping, gender) 20-21,
    43, 62, 154, 161-187, 194, 207, 243-263, 283

Georgian 165
German 37-38, 60, 74-75
German-American 39, 49, 59
Germany 21, 38, 74-75
globalization 192, 290
Great Migration 36, 40, 61
Greek 52-53, 60

habitus 68-69, 256, 311
Hebrew 1, 37, 43, 60
hegemony 71, 194, 245-248, 256
heteroglossia 26, 111
heterosexuality 205, 216
Hong Kong 2, 300
hybridity (see also identity, hybrid) 17, 268

iconization 70
identity
– American 34-63
– assigned 109
– assumed 21
– authoritative 327
– bicultural 133
– Black 16-17
– Black Deaf 16-17, 125-158
– class 62, 240
– collective 126, 128
– conflicting 274
– construction 35
– consumer 2
– Deaf 16-17, 125-158
– Deaf Black 16-17, 125-158
– definition of 19, 35, 170
– development 126-127, 154-155, 172
– English-speaking 54
– ethnic (see also ethnicity) 2, 4-5, 11, 42, 62,
    106-109, 142, 150, 192-217
– ethnolinguistic 4-5
– function 100
– gender 43, 62, 240
– group 243, 248
– hybrid 5, 13, 17, 54, 62, 96, 104
– hyphenated 54, 58, 203-204, 216
– and imagination 17-18
– imposed 21, 215
– linguistic 54, 57, 61-62, 240
– mainstream 310, 325, 331
– management of 172, 325
– manufacturing of 334
– markers 176
– middle-class 330
– mixed 95
– multicultural 109-112, 334
– multiple 170-171

– narratives 18-19, 35, 48, 192, 195-196, 200, 298
– national 2, 40-41, 44-49, 71-73, 93, 279
– negative 106
– negotiation of 1, 3-4, 8, 12, 20-24, 48-49, 57, 63, 96, 106-119, 128, 154-155, 170, 200-216, 220, 240, 258-262, 268, 270, 274, 291, 293-294, 307, 309-311, 319
– non-native 279
– non-standard 95
– of competence 333-334
– of incompetence 334
– options 1-2, 10, 12-14, 17, 21, 25, 35, 96, 262
– performance 3, 20
– personal 53, 126
– politics of 49, 73, 192-193
– positive 106, 125
– professional 53-54
– public 54
– racial 62, 128, 142-144, 150
– religious 43, 194, 203-204, 210, 216
– self-defined 109
– sexual 14
– social 4, 8, 42, 96, 100, 165, 170, 222, 240, 245, 279, 291, 295
– textual 266-287
– theories 126, 287
– transnational 2, 54
– vernacular 281
– work 295, 301, 309
– working-class 95
– and writing 266-287
Igbo 252
imagination 17-18, 62, 193, 219, 227-229, 241
imagined communities 17, 24, 36, 72, 75, 93, 95, 104, 106-107, 120, 223
immigrant(s)
– African 93-120
– Asian 22, 48, 61, 63, 68-89
– autobiographies (memoirs) 34-63
– children 51-53, 56, 58, 77-85, 316-336
– European 22, 34-63
– first generation 42, 48
– Latin American 61
– middle-class 56
– 'new' 40, 47, 57, 59
– 'old' 40, 47, 59
– Russian 6
– second generation 48, 107
– Slavic 42
– working-class 24, 36, 52
immigration 34-63
inclusion 177, 249, 255
indexicality 8-9, 70

indexing 111
Indonesian 332
insider status 165, 205, 251, 279, 283, 295
interactional sociolinguistics 7
intercultural competence 228
inter-group approaches 4-7
interpreters 131-132, 149-150, 164
interview 25, 132, 167-169, 187, 195, 251-252, 297
investment 23, 240-241, 255, 292
Iran 5
Islam (*see* religion)
Islamophobia 78
Israel 1
Italian 14, 38, 45, 49, 192-217
Italian Canadian 14, 17, 192-217
italianità 14, 194, 196-200, 204, 211, 213-217
Italiese 197, 216
Italy 38

Japan 15, 25, 316-336
Japanese 25, 283, 316-336
Japanese as a second language (JSL) 316-336
Judaism (*see also* religion) 37, 43

language
– attitudes 161-187
– attrition 176-177, 318, 327-329, 332
– choice 7, 9, 12, 22, 164-166, 186, 215
– death 166
– ideologies 2, 11-12, 14, 57-61, 68-89, 93-94, 161, 204, 221-222, 224, 227-229, 294, 321, 328
– immersion 231, 238
– maintenance 60, 161-187, 204, 319, 328, 333
– mixing 111
– norms 11-12
– play 213
– policy 243
– proficiency 74, 162, 174, 238
– socialization 62, 183, 266
– testing 21, 73-75
Laos 316, 322
Latin 60
Latvian 2
ligatures 248, 262
lingua franca 1, 5, 252
linguistic
– achievement 63
– assimilation 55
– capital 309
– competence 6, 9, 12, 14, 22-23, 278

– discrimination 53-57
– diversity 2, 327-336
– heterogeneity 72-74
– homogeneity 72
– hybridity 63, 111
– identity 54, 57, 61, 63
– innovation 23
– intolerance 63
– majority 4, 68, 194
– marketplace 11
– membership 126
– minority 4-5, 68, 120, 125, 143, 161-187, 194, 198
– minority education 316-336
– minority students 290-313, 316-336
– poverty 81, 84
– practices 9-12, 161-162, 291
– repertoire 5, 8, 17, 96, 103, 194
– resources 6, 9, 14, 271, 295
– rights 63
– stratification 10, 13
– tolerance 60, 62-63
– trajectory 62
– varieties 11
literacy
– English 16, 243-263, 266-287
– French 222
– Japanese 324, 328
– Urdu 183
Lithuanian 2, 52, 60

Macedonia 70
Mandarin 298, 300-311
markedness model 8
memoirs 34-63
metaphor 162, 166, 175, 193, 239
Mexican-American 8
Mirpuri 162, 167, 175-176, 178
misrecognition 10, 15, 69-70
monolingual bias 5-6
Morocco 102
motivation 238-241, 271, 278, 292
mother tongue 12, 14, 63, 161-187, 327
Mozambique 248

narratives 18-19, 34-63
– of identity 18-19, 192, 195, 200, 298
– immigrant 34-63
– language learning 34
– personal 39-40, 298, 312
native-speaker/non-native speaker status 54, 270, 274, 293, 330
naturalization testing (*see also* language testing) 71, 74-75, 84-89

negotiation of identities (*see* identity, negotiation of)
Nepal 247
Netherlands 37, 49
Nigeria 16, 243-263
North Africa 94, 99, 102

official English debates 73
opposition 280-281, 284-285, 287
Other, the 112-113, 168, 205, 207, 310
output 233
outsider status 168, 205, 251-252, 270, 295, 324

Pakistan 99, 104, 161-187
periphery, 192-217
pluralism 137
plurality 170, 186
Poland 38, 99
Polish 52, 60
Polish-American 62
polyvalence 268
Portugal 94, 99
Portuguese 5, 97, 318
positioning 20-21, 69, 127, 157, 161, 193, 197, 201-202, 209, 211, 215, 243, 263, 267, 286, 292, 295, 297, 304, 310
postcolonialism 243, 267, 283, 287
postmodernism 245, 287
poststructuralism 3, 10-20, 35, 95-96, 246, 266, 267, 287
power relations 10-13, 15-16, 69, 169, 193, 207, 222, 230, 243, 245-247, 256, 258-260, 291, 319-321, 332-335
Punjabi 77, 79, 82, 162, 167, 175-176, 178-179, 183

Quebec 9, 11-12, 223-224, 231-232
Quechua 164-165
questionnaires 7

race 24, 61-62, 73, 89, 106-109, 125-158, 210, 222
racial (*see also* stereotyping, racial)
– inequities 49
– minorities 22, 49, 63, 73-74
racism 78, 137-139, 293, 303-304, 311, 331
religion
– Catholic 43, 194, 197, 210-211
– Christian 43, 194, 197, 210, 282
– Hindu 280, 282
– Islam 161-187, 311
– Jewish 37, 43
– Lutheran 39, 43

– Methodist 38-39
– Pentecostal Christian 282
– Protestant 43-44
resistance 171, 195, 209, 246, 268, 278, 282, 287
rhetorical analysis 269-270
right to speak 81, 85, 293
Romani 94, 97, 111
Romanian 37, 56-57, 60
Russia 38
Russian 1-2, 6, 37, 60, 271-274

schools
– Deaf 136-139
– elementary 15, 316-336
– evening 51, 58
– high 15, 290-313
– homeschooling 225
– mainstream 136
– public 51, 56, 58, 316-336
second language
– acquisition 6, 34, 50, 221, 266, 291
– learning 23, 50-55, 61-63, 219-241
– use 290-313
self 162, 168, 170-171, 174, 193, 243, 249,
     266-287, 293, 318
self-
– actualization
– advocacy 293
– awareness 205
– censoring 207
– confidence 249
– consciousness 174
– construction 161, 172
– definition 161-162, 164, 172, 174
– determination 245
– efficacy 252
– esteem 178, 249, 256-257
– identification 126, 172, 178, 192-217
– image 241, 263
– positioning 209
– representation 192-217, 266-287, 291, 294
– translation 55, 73
– validation 255
– worth 178, 254
semiotics 266
sexism 141
sexual
– harassment 222
– orientation 192, 194, 204, 210
sexuality 21, 192, 196, 205-206, 211, 216, 222
Shanghainese 304
Sierra Leone 248
Sign Language (*see also* British Sign
     Language) 326

silencing 266, 268, 293
Slovakia 37
Slovenia 39
Slovenian 39, 42, 49
'snowballing' 129
social
– constructionism 13, 266
– control 245
– differentiation 199, 202
– disorder 68, 79, 89
– frontiers 69, 88
– inequality (inequity) 15, 243, 319-320
– justice 4, 245
– reproduction 320
– turn 266
sociopsychological approaches 4
South Africa 165
South America 316, 318
Soviet Union 2, 165, 273
space 192-217
Spain 99, 222
Spanish 8, 103, 165, 227, 318
Sri Lanka 269, 275-278, 282
standard assessment 220
standardization 72
stereotyping
– age 208
– ethnic 198-199, 208
– gender 208
– racial 138
study abroad, 219-241
subjectivity 168, 170, 266, 267-268, 275, 278,
     280-281, 296
subject position 180, 266, 267
submersion 318
Sub-Saharan Africa 243-263
subtractive bilingualism 318
Swedish 52
symbolic
– capital 10, 193-194, 215, 223, 240, 291, 309
– domination 10-11, 15, 71-72
– power 15, 28
– resources 72, 294
– violence 69, 71, 88

taboo topics 100
Taiwan 298, 300, 323
Taiwanese 300-311
Tamil 275-278
textography 269
third space 95-96, 106, 193
transfer 56
translation (*see also* interpreters) 180, 213, 298
transposition 274-278, 281-282, 285

Ukraine 271-274
Ukrainian 271-274, 284
United Kingdom (UK) (*see* Britain)
United States (US) 18-19, 21, 34-63, 73-75,
    221-224, 269
Urdu 103, 167, 175-176, 178-179, 183

Verlan 17, 28, 93-120
Vietnam 316, 322
Vietnamese 300-311, 324-325, 327-328, 330-333
visibility 24

voice 22, 196, 250, 266-287, 293, 312-313

Welsh 88-89
West Africa 94, 99
Wolof 23, 97
workplace 22, 195, 207-213
writing 266-287

Yiddish 1-2, 37-38, 43, 56-57, 60

Zulu 165